Festschrift Günter Wagner

International Theological Studies: Contributions of Baptist Scholars

General Editor

Thorwald Lorenzen

Advisory Editorial Board

Bruce Rumbold
Glenn Hinson
Günter Wagner

Vol. 1

PETER LANG

Bern · Berlin · Frankfurt a.M. · New York · Paris · Wien

Festschrift
Günter Wagner

Edited by
Faculty of Baptist Theological Seminary
Rüschlikon/Switzerland

PETER LANG

Bern · Berlin · Frankfurt a.M. · New York · Paris · Wien

Die Deutsche Bibliothek – CIP-Einheitsaufnahme

Festschrift Günter Wagner / ed. by Faculty of Baptist
Theological Seminary, Rüschlikon/Switzerland. - Bern ;
Berlin ; Frankfurt a.M. ; New York ; Paris ; Wien :
Lang, 1994
(International theological studies ; Vol. 1)
ISBN 3-906752-07-0
NE: Baptist Theological Seminary <Rüschlikon>; Wagner, Günter:
Festschrift; GT

Foto von Günter Wagner © Pleyer Photo

© Peter Lang, Inc., European Academic Publishers, Berne 1994

FOREWORD

With respect and affection, the faculty of Baptist Theological Seminary Rüschlikon honours with this Festschrift an outstanding colleague and friend, Günter Wagner. Contributions are included from his teacher and students as well as from his colleagues and dialogue partners in ecumenical committees. Günter Wagner joined Rüschlikon Seminary as a student in 1949 - the first semester of its existence. Apart from two years employment as Research Assistant and representative of the German Free Churches at the Ecumenical Centre of the "Arbeitsgemeinschaft Christlicher Kirchen" in Frankfurt (1954-1956) and occasional sabbatical leaves, he has faithfully served this institution from his youth to retirement, working as teaching fellow (1954-1956), instructor (1958-1961), associate professor (1961-1965) and full professor (1965-1993) for New Testament. Refusing to leave Rüschlikon despite numerous offers, Günter Wagner has inspired generations of students and colleagues with his profound insights especially in the areas of New Testament studies and ecumenical dialogue. His personal friendships with professional colleagues and church leaders around the world have enabled students and faculty to multiply their partners in dialogue. His ability and willingness to share problems and interests of other persons to whom he related in the classroom, the church, and ecumenical committees have encouraged many to find new hope and to search for creative solutions to problems, whether personal, ecclesiastical or societal.

For all of this and for much more, the faculty of Rüschlikon Seminary thanks Günter Wagner and expresses its appreciation for an exceptional person, scholar and friend, who has greatly enriched the lives of his colleagues. We look forward to many more years of continuing friendship.

Heidrun Bärenfänger
Kent Blevins
Keith Dyer
John David Hopper
Thorwald Lorenzen
Hans Mallau
Phyllis Rodgerson Pleasants

TABLE OF CONTENTS

CONTRIBUTORS

Prof. Dr. G.R. Beasley-Murray, 4 Holland Road, GB-Hove, E. Sussex BN3 1JJ, England

Bishop Dr. Pierre Duprey, Pontifical Council for Promoting Christian Unity, I-00120 Vatican City, Vatican

Prof. Dr. Günther Gassman, World Council of Churches, 150 Route de Ferney, P.O. Box 2100, CH-1211 Geneva 2

Prof. Dr. Erich Geldbach, Eifelstrasse 35, D-64625, Bensheim, Germany

Prof. Dr. David Hellholm, University of Oslo, Faculty of Theology, P.O. Box 1023, Blindern, N-0315 Oslo, Norway

Prof. Dr. Thorwald Lorenzen, Baptist Theological Seminary, Gheistrasse 31, CH-8803 Rüschlikon, Switzerland

Prof. Dr. John Mbiti, Einschlagweg 11, CH-3400 Burgdorf, Switzerland

Prof. Dr. Damaskinos Papandreou, Metropolit der Schweiz, Fondation du Centre Orthodoxe du Patriarcat Oecuménique, 27, Chemin de Chambésy, 1292 Chambésy, Geneva, Switzerland

Dr. Wiard Popkes, Theologisches Seminar, Rennbahnstrasse 115, D-22111 Hamburg 74, Germany

Prof. Dr. Jannes Reiling, 5 Merellaan, NL-3722 AK Bilthoven, Netherlands

Prof. Dr. Eduard Schweizer, Emeritus Professor of Zürich University, Restelbergstrasse 71, CH-8044 Zürich, Switzerland

Prof. Dr. Martin Scott, 8 Wellacre Avenue, GB-Flixton, Manchester M31 3WA, England

Prof. Dr. Jean Marcel Vincent, Hustadring 20, D-44801 Bochum, Germany

Prof. Dr. Lukas Vischer, 29 ch. Grange-Canal, CH-1208 Geneva, Switzerland

Prof. Dr. Gerhard Voss, Abtei Niederaltaich, D-94557, Niederaltaich, Germany

Prof. Dr. Günter Wagner, Emeritus Professor for New Testament, Baptist Theological Seminary, Gheistrasse 31, CH-8803 Rüschlikon, Switzerland

Tabula Gratulatoria

Pierre Duprey
  Vatican City

Keith Dyer
  Rüschlikon

John H. Edgington
  Doncaster

Jaap Euwema
  Tiel

Manfred Ewaldt
  Hagen

Facoltà Valdese di Teologia
  Roma

Faculté de théologie de l'Université
  Neuchâtel

The Faculty of the Baptist Theological
College of Western Australia
  Bentley

Fédération des Eglises Evangéliques
Baptistes de France
  Paris

Max Frey
  Einsiedeln

Walter Füllbrandt
  Ellerbek

Günther Gassmann
  Geneva

Simon Gebs
  Rüschlikon

Erich Geldbach
  Bensheim

Marcia K. Glenn
  Albuquerque

Mr. & Mrs. Ralph Glenn
  Colorado City

Franz & Dagmar Gollatz
  Rüschlikon

Norbert Groß
  Hamburg

P.-M. Guillaume
  Épinal

Franz-Werner Hacker
  München

Ron Ham
  Melbourne

David Hellholm
  Oslo

Kurt & Claudia Herren
  Amriswil

James D. Hester
  Redlands

I. Howard Marshall
  Aberdeen

John Mbiti
  Burgdorf

James Wm. McClendon, Jr.
  Altadena

Edgar V. McKnight
  Greenville

Ellen & Wolfgang Meckbach
  Stadthagen

Theophil Meister
  Zollikerberg

Fernando Méndez
  Elda

Mennonite Brethren Biblical Seminary
  Fresno

Bernhard & Yvonne Meyer
  Basel

Morling College
  Eastwood

David L. Mueller
  Louisville

Wolfgang Müller
  Siegen

Neutestamentliches Seminar der
Universität
  Hamburg

Horst Niesen
  Sindelfingen

Markku Niskanen
  Helsinki

Per Nørgaard
  Tølløse

Peder Nørgaard-Højen
  Nivaa

Örebro Theological Seminary
  Örebro

R. Eugene Owens
  Charlotte

Damaskinos Papandreou
  Geneva

Phyllis Rodgerson Pleasants
  Rüschlikon

Wiard Popkes
  Hamburg

Blasco Ramirez
  Rome

Salvatore Rapisarda
  Rome

Theologisches Seminar des Bundes
Evangelisch-Freikirchlicher
Gemeinden in Deutschland
  Hamburg

Bob & Shirley Thompson
  Auckland

Etienne Trocmé
  Strasbourg

Universität Tübingen Kath.-Theol.
Seminar
  Tübingen

Jean Vincent
  Bochum

Lukas Vischer
  Geneva

Gerhard Voss
  Niederaltaich

Dan Warria
  Sissach

A. J. M. Wedderburn
  München

Markus Wehrstedt
  Rüschlikon

Christoph & Sonja Weichert
  Bielefeld

Ilse & Friedrich Emanuel Wieser
  Graz

Carol Woodfin
  West Palm Beach

Robert Owusu Yaw
  Rüschlikon

THE PROBLEM OF INFANT BAPTISM:
AN EXERCISE IN POSSIBILITIES

G. R. BEASLEY-MURRAY

The title of this essay could be viewed as typically Baptist: most Baptists would affirm that they have no "problem of infant baptist" for they do not practise it - it's the Paedobaptists who have that burden! Contrarywise another reaction is possible: taking into account the traditions of the Churches through the ages and throughout the world it is evident that most Christians see no problem in infant baptist; they are happy with it, and regard the Baptists, who reject it, as the people with the problem!

In reality there is a variety of problems connected with infant baptism, and they are acknowledged by theologians, ministers and clergy of all denominations. They are thrust upon them partly through the endeavour to understand the Bible objectively and to submit the traditions of the churches to the judgment of the Word of God; partly through the disintegration of the State Church system, and a recognition that all the churches are in a situation of mission; and partly through ecumenical pressures on the churches to reach a common understanding of baptism, which is generally viewed as the door into the Church. These issues weigh upon us all, including Baptists.

Of the questions raised by infant baptism the following are particularly pressing:

i. Was infant baptism practised in the New Testament Church?

ii. Is infant baptism compatible with the apostolic theology of baptism?

iii. Does infant baptism entail a modification of the New Testament instruction on baptism, and if it does, what kind of modification is proposed?

iv. Does infant baptism preserve the essential significance of the one baptism of the New Testament and the Creeds?

It is evident that these questions are closely related, and their answers inevitably impinge on each other. The critical issue of the validity of infant baptism, with its corollary of so-called "rebaptism" of Christians baptized as infants, can be satisfactorily discussed only in the light of the conclusions which we reach regarding the prior issues. Accordingly we shall do our utmost to throw light upon them in the following pages.

i. The most charitable answer to the question, "Was infant baptism practised in the churches of the New Testament period?" (and in the view of many the answer most congruent with the evidence) is *non licet*, "not proven". We are aware that notable Protestant writers, like Cullmann, Jeremias, Marcel, Stauffer have laboured to demonstrate that infant baptism was practised in the apostolic age. Nevertheless many Paedobaptist scholars have felt compelled to reject the arguments adduced by such writers. The Jesuit theologian Joseph Eagan, who has made a prolonged study of baptism, particularly as featured in the conversations about baptism promoted by the World Council of Churches, stated in the Louisville Consultation on Baptism in 1979 that (a) the New Testament focuses exclusively on the baptism of adults, and the various theologies of baptism arising out of such baptism, and (b) there is no conclusive evidence that Christians baptized their babies in the New Testament period (nor indeed in the second century of our era). Nevertheless in his view the reasons for adhering to infant baptism are independent of this issue. [1]

Baptists, for their part, should be ready to acknowledge that there are some historical issues in this area over which certainty cannot be attained. This applies to the question whether any very young children were included in the household baptisms mentioned in the New Testament. Admittedly no mention is made of such infants, and no hint is provided as to what their baptism could have meant in the primitive Church, but "not proven" must stand over the problem.

ii. Like Joseph Eagan, many theologians regard as irrelevant the date of the emergence of infant baptism. The question at issue is whether the Church was justified in applying baptism to infants, at whatever date it first happened. Catholics maintain that the Church has ever been subject to the guidance of the Spirit-Paraclete, in accordance with the promises affirmed in the Upper Room discourses of John 14-16; the conviction that infant baptism came to be established in the Church under his guidance is for them sufficient reason for believing it to be the will of God, and so self-evidently in harmony with apostolic baptism. T. W. Manson, a Presbyterian, put that in an undogmatic way: "It is inevitable that the Church should learn by experience what Christ means her to do, and how to do it

---

[1]"The Authority and Justification of Infant Baptism", *Review and Expositor* 77 (1980) 47-61. The significance of this consultation, organized by the Faith and Order department of the W.C.C., is that it brought together for the first time in W.C.C. discussions on baptism an equal number of representatives of Paedobaptist and Believer Baptist traditions. See further the significant admission in Baptism, Eucharist and Ministry, Faith and Order Paper no. 111, paragraph 11,(W.C.C. Geneva 1982.)

most effectively"[2].   That was said explicitly in relation to infant baptism, and in that respect Manson believed that the Church had "learned".

Orthodoxy would not dissent from that viewpoint, but it maintains a simpler conviction: there is no principle difference between the baptism of infants and that of believers, since in baptism babies *are* believers.

Luther came to accept a similar view, and many of his followers are prepared to maintain it today, buttressed by psychological considerations of the impressionable nature of infants. Chiefly, however, Luther clung to the conviction that baptism is the command of God, which the Church must obey, and since faith is the gift of God at all times, it cannot be made a condition of baptism.

Anglicans through the years have, with Catholics and the Orthodox, acknowledged the importance of tradition together with the Scriptures, and this applies to the authority for infant baptism. Modern Anglicanism recognizes the baptism of believers as the norm by which baptism should be understood, but affirms that infant baptism is a legitimate adaptation of it, the sponsors supplying the answers to questions of faith and intention within the community of faith, and the parents pledging their resolve to provide Christian nurture for their child.

The Reformed tradition has the distinctive view of baptism as relating to the one covenant of grace that has continued through the ages. The unity of the old and new covenants, with their accompaniments, is stressed, so that for them there has ever been only one gospel of God, one plan of salvation, one promise concerning it, and one condition of receiving it - faith; the Church of God is one through the ages, and possesses essentially the same sacraments - circumcision and baptism, passover and Lord's Supper being closely related, and all possessing the significance as "seals" by which the promises of God are sealed to his people. The solidarity of the people of God is stressed: that God has promised to be their God to the thousandth generation is held to demand the application of baptism to their offspring (Exod 20:5f etc.).

Free Churches tend to emphasize the symbolic nature of baptism and its function as introducing a child to the community of grace. Donald Baillie, although a member of the Church of Scotland, spoke for many Free Church men in affirming:

If a baby must have love, it is also true that a baby must have the grace of God in

---

[2]"Baptism in the Church", *SJT* 2 (1949) 403.

order that it may grow as a truly Christian child. And it is through the faith and love of the Church and its parents, directed upon the children through physical channels and using the effective symbolism of baptism, that the grace of God reaches the scarcely conscious child.[3]

Others stress the future prospect in infant baptism; to H. R. Mackintosh it is "a promise clothed in sense",[4] to P. T. Forsyth "the sacrament of the future".[5] F. J. Leenhardt more cautiously spoke of it as "a promise with a condition", namely that the response of faith will later be made by the baptized child.[6]

It would take longer time than we can give to recount the variations and expansions of these themes in various church traditions, but it is unnecessary for us to do more than offer a few comments on those we have mentioned.

The Roman Catholic assumption that tradition always expresses the inspiration of the Spirit is unacceptable to most Protestants in view of the actual developments of faith and practice within that church, some of which appear to them highly questionable. The Orthodox notion that in baptism babies are actually believers appears to us an extraordinary notion, despite the weighty support of Augustine.[7] Luther's insistence that baptism is the command of God is acknowledged in all the Christian traditions, but his mode of applying the Great Commission to infants is the very point at issue. The Reformed view of baptism as relating to the covenant of grace is sound, but the virtual equation of the new covenant with the old, and stress on the continuity of the old and new, diminishes the radical discontinuity which the eschatological kingdom of promise, inaugurated by Jesus, inevitably brought about. The new covenant belongs to the new age - the new creation

---

[3]*The Theology of the Sacraments and Other Papers*, (London:, 1957) pp. 80-87.

[4]"Thoughts on Infant Baptism", *The Expositor*, 8th Series vol. 13 (1917) 202.

[5]*The Church and the Sacraments*, (London: Hodder and Stoughton 1917), p. 168.

[6]*Le Baptême Chrétien, son origine, sa signification*, Cahiers Théologiques de l'Actualité Protestante, no. 4, (Neuchâtel:Delachaux et Niestlé), 1946, pp. 71-72.

[7]In a letter to Boniface, Augustine affirmed that an infant becomes a believer through receiving "the sacrament of faith", i.e. baptism (Ep.98,9,10). J. G. Davies cited Augustine with approval (*The Spirit, the Church and the Sacraments*, (London:Faith Press, 1954), p.151). Colin Buchanan, Evangelical Anglican, similarly asserted, "There is faith in a newborn infant" (*One Baptism Once*, (Grove Books Ltd. no.61, Nottingham 1978), p.17), and expounded the view in *A Case for Infant Baptism*, (Grove Books no.20, 1973), p.27, n.1.

introduced through the ministry, death and resurrection of Jesus and sending of the Spirit, whereby redemption from this present evil age is accomplished (Gal 1:4) and life in the new creation in Christ is bestowed (2 Cor 5:17). The ordinances of the new age are conditioned and governed by the redemption which initiated it, and should not be conformed to the age which at best anticipated it.

To Baptists, however, who have generally stood in the theological tradition of Calvin, this apologetic is not integral to Reformed theology (witness the Baptist adoption in 1678 of the Westminster Confession, with slight revisions, as their own understanding of the Faith). It is no accident that the belief that infant baptism so drastically changes the context of Biblical baptism as to demand a modification of the apostolic theology of baptism in its interpretation is not uncommon among Reformed theologians,[8] and that conviction is increasingly voiced in other traditions. [9]

iii. The burning issue which concerns Baptists is whether baptism can be so interpreted that, while its scriptural norm and most powerful expression is exhibited in the baptism of believers, room can be found for infant baptism as a valid accommodation of the norm. For years I have maintained that this cannot be done, not least because I have not read any attempt to justify this position that has compelled my assent. I confess, however, to have less assurance about this matter now. Tentatively I present some consideration which could conceivably lead to a *modus vivendi* between Baptists and their fellow Christians on the administration and interpretation of baptism. I venture to hope that some at least of our Paedobaptist friends may also freshly consider their own position regarding this perpetually contentious issue.

---

[8]Karl Barth, with his emphasis on the declarative function of baptism, rejected infant baptism as irreconcilable with the apostolic theology of baptism, and therefore did not even discuss this issue in his lengthy critique of infant baptism, *Church Dogmatics vol. 4, The Doctrine of Reconciliation, Part 4, Baptism as the Foundation of the Christian Life*, (Edinburgh:T & T Clark), 1969, 135-95. Emil Brunner, however, despite his strong criticism of the way infant baptism was often administered, conceded that infant baptism "rightly administered" may be viewed as "the sign that points to him (Christ), his grace which precedes all preaching and all faith", *The Christian Doctrine of the Church, Faith and the Consummation*, (London:Lutterworth), 1962 p. 57.

[9]See especially W. F. Flemington, *The New Testament Doctrine of Baptism*, (London:SPCK 1948), p. 82; also *The Theology of Christian Initiation* (The Report of a Theological Commission appointed by the Archbishops of Canterbury and York to advise on the relations between Baptism, Confirmation and Holy Communion), London:SPCK 1948, pp. 12 and 14.

a. We speak within the fellowship of faith, of those whose trust is in the God revealed supremely in Jesus Christ, our Lord, and who are united to him and to all God's people by the Holy Spirit.

The difficulty of attaining unanimity in matters of Christian doctrine is evident to all. Unfortunately this is not confined to peripheral matters. The doctrines of Incarnation, Trinity, Atonement, Kingdom of God and Judgment are of incalculable importance; but while affirming unreservedly the realities which these terms represent, Christians experience difficulty to interpret them in such a manner as to secure unanimity among all. We have to accord freedom to one another in our endeavours to explain the cardinal Christian doctrines.

The varieties of understanding of the Church, Ministry and Lord's Supper are especially pertinent here. The classic doctrine of the historic episcopate has been expounded in such a manner as to call into question the validity of all non-episcopal ministries, the ecclesiastical standing of communities served by them, and the validity of celebrations of the Eucharist that take place in them. This has appeared to many Christians besides Baptists as repugnant to the Word of God and unjust to Christian history, and many within the episcopal traditions have long repudiated these notions. Most Christians are moving to affirm the Churchly reality of all communities that own Christ in the Trinity according to the scriptures, and the validity of ministries in such Churches and celebrations of the Eucharist, without insisting on precise definitions concerning Church, ministry and worship.[10]

b. There are limits to which we can demand agreement on the administration and interpretation of believer's baptism among the Churches. All Paedobaptist denominations baptize converts to Christ who have not received baptism as infants. Roman Catholics in North America are taking this very seriously, and have reinstated the catechumenate both for adult converts and for children who request baptism. Naturally their instruction as to its meaning does not coincide with that given in Protestant, and in particular Free Churches. But do Baptists have to insist on a Baptist interpretation of believer's baptism in order to recognize

---

[10]That sentence was written immediately before the decision of the Synod of the Church of England in November 1992 to admit women to the priesthood; the reaction of about a thousand priests to consider defecting from the Anglican Church on the ground that women bishops and priests cannot represent the male Christ, hence that they would render the ministry and the eucharist invalid and turn the Anglican Church into a sect, represents a reversal to earlier inadequate views on apostolic succession, to say nothing of the nature of "man".

its authenticity when administered in other denominations? While many Baptists in the U.S.A. answer in the affirmative, most Baptists in the rest of the world deny any such notion. In reality there is no such thing as a Baptist theology of baptism, accepted by all Baptists; what they do not themselves possess they should not demand of others.

c. Infant baptism itself is, as we noticed above, variously interpreted in denominations that administer it. This has created problems for Baptists in their endeavours to come to grips with infant baptism, since the ground of argument changes so very frequently. But, as we have seen, the like applies to interpretations of believer's baptism. Accordingly differences in interpreting infant baptism do not foreclose the question whether there may exist a ground of acceptance of infant baptism, irrespective of the views of particular denominations.

d. A major obstacle to Baptists taking infant baptism seriously has been indiscriminate baptism, common among virtually all State Churches. Baptists, it should be recalled, began in countries where baptism was applied to entire populations. There is, however, widespread protest about this practice among Paedobaptist Churches throughout the world,[11] even though progress in implementing reform in this respect is slow in many countries. Nevertheless serious endeavour is being made to restrict infant baptism to Christian families, and to make provision for those baptized in infancy to receive instruction with a view to their confessing Christ on attaining an age of responsible decision.

e. Christian theologians increasingly acknowledge that the fundamental significance of baptism is that to which its symbolism points, namely the redemptive event of God in Christ for humankind and the inclusion of the baptized in that event. On this basis baptism may be said to presuppose and exhibit the following elements:

---

[11]Cf. Colin Buchanan: "The only case made above is for the baptism of a child of a believer or believers. To go on from this to the baptism of every newborn Englishman or Englishwoman is...to make it incredible", *A Case for Infant Baptism*, p. 30. To counter the effects of indiscriminate baptism Michael Green even expressed his willingness to give up infant baptism for one generation, if that were possible! "It would clear the ground, and enable us to have a fresh start, with the sign of the covenant marking out believers and their children. For this is the only sort of infant baptism which can be justified from Scripture, or, for that matter, from the formularies of the Church of England", *Baptism, Its Purpose, Practice and Power*, (London, Hodder & Stoughton, 1987), pp. 98-99.

1. The death and resurrection of the incarnate Lord for the establishing of the saving sovereignty (i.e. the kingdom) of God and the inclusion of a restored and renewed humanity in it.

2. The baptized as one for whom Christ achieved redemption.

3. God's readiness to make that redemption effective for the baptized as he/she in faith responds to the call of God in the gospel.

4. The hope and prayer of the Church for that redemption to be appropriated by the baptized. (Note: baptism is performed within and by the Church through its representatives).

5. The gift of Christ's salvation, which extends beyond the beginning of God's work in the baptized through all life to the resurrection for the final kingdom of God.

These elements of faith are cherished alike by churches which practice infant baptism and those which practice believer's baptism only. The moot point is precisely how baptism functions when applied to an infant. To the majority of Christians that must appear a curious assertion. In their view baptism is baptism, and there is no essential difference in its function whether applied to a mature believer or an infant. Such is clearly assumed in the 1982 Lima statement about Baptism, the fruit of years of labour in the Faith and Order Commission of the W.C.C. There baptism is affirmed to be "incorporation into Christ...entry into the New Covenant...participation in the life, death and resurrection of Jesus Christ...God's bestowal of the anointing and the promise of the Holy Spirit, who marks the baptized with a seal and implants in their hearts the first instalment of their inheritance as sons and daughters of God. Baptism initiates the reality of the new life given in the midst of the present world".[12] The only difference between infant baptism and believer's baptism stated in the text is that of the time of exercise of faith. A commentary on this adds that infant baptism emphasizes the corporate faith and the faith which the child shares with its parents: "Through baptism the promise and claim of the Gospel are laid upon the child. The personal faith of the recipient of baptism and faithful participation in the life of the Church are essential for the full fruit of baptism".[13] How the last sentence is meant to

---

[12]*Baptism, Eucharist and Ministry*, Faith and Order Paper no. 111, (WCC, Geneva 1982), pp. 2-3.

[13]*B.E.M.* p. 5.

qualify the features of baptism cited above (namely "incorporation into Christ...entry into the New Covenant..." etc.) is not explained. The classic theology of baptism expounded in the report is not essentially modified by that consideration. Pleas made within the Free Churches, and at times from within the Catholic, Lutheran, Reformed and Anglican traditions, that when baptism is applied to infants it cannot embody the full significance of the Biblical theology of baptism, have apparently fallen on deaf ears. In my experience of ecumenical conversations the typical representatives of the older churches have not modified their interpretations of infant baptism one whit and do not permit deviation from them.

There is nevertheless one approach to infant baptism more widespread than is commonly acknowledged by both Paedobaptists and believer-baptists which deserves careful consideration. This sees infant baptism as attesting the commencement of the work of grace within the baptized with a view to its blossoming into fulness of life in Christ and his Body the Church as the individual's life progressively opens to Christ.[14]

Here we face a question which has been too much neglected in theological and exegetical discussions, namely the relation of little children to the redemptive work of Christ. There's remarkably little said about this issue in the New Testament, and what is there is often ambiguous. Early Baptists in Britain thought much about this question, perhaps spurred on by the fact that theirs were virtually the only children in the country not baptized.[15] They took with seriousness Paul's exposition of the universal relevance of Christ's redemption over against the consequences of Adam's sin. In Romans 5:12-21 Paul affirmed that the solidarity of humankind with the first Adam was more than matched by its solidarity with the last Adam, since God's grace is greater than the corrupting power of Adam's sin. This naturally includes the children of the human race - a deeply significant factor when it is remembered that the majority of human beings have not outlived childhood. The Baptist pioneers probably did not ponder that last comment of mine, but, unlike most later Baptists, they were impressed with the significance of 1 Corinthians 7:14: "Your children...are holy". Nowadays,

[14]See especially the discussion in O. C. Quick, *The Christian Sacraments*, (London:Nisbet, 2nd.ed.1932), 168-74.

[15]Morris West pointed out to me that the Anabaptists in Zürich in 1524, even before they became "Ana"-baptists, were rejecting infant baptism and were discussing the consequent implications for their theology of the child. See the letter from Grebel and his friends to Thomas Muntzer 5.9.1524, published in *Spiritual and Anabaptist Writers*, ed. G. H. Williams and A. M. Mergal, (SCM Library of Christian Classics XXV, 1957) p. 81.

perhaps, we realize to a greater extent than they that in that statement Paul utilizes a concept of holiness derived from Jewish ceremonial terminology: over against the unclean world of nations the people of God are "holy", i.e. belonging to God. Paul affirms, for the encouragement of a Christian parent whose spouse is an unbeliever, that the unbelieving spouse is "sanctified" ("regarded as holy", Greek *hegiastai*) on account of the believing partner, as is evident from the fact that the children are not unclean but "holy" (*hagioi* -"regarded as belonging to God", the adjective having a similar meaning as *hagiazo*). By this terminology Paul sets forth the conviction that God has a special relation to the children of believers, short indeed of their being viewed as members of the Body of Christ (the unbelieving spouse is also "hagios"!), but which implies that they are linked in an undefined manner with God and his people. In this context Henry Lawrence, an early Baptist, wrote:

"We have Christ among us for our seeds, as well as for ourselves. And consider this that by all that is said, we reject no promises made to children in consideration of God's love, or affection to their parents, but we embrace them and expect and pray for the fulfilling of them".[16]

Lawrence spoke as a Calvinist, and unlike those Reformers who looked on infant baptism as an instrument of election, he regarded baptism as rightly applied when election is confessed. He further performed a service for Baptists in drawing attention to Tertullian's expression, describing the unbelieving spouses of believers (1 Corinthians 7:14) as *candidati timoris* ("probationers for fear") and the children of marriages where at least one parent is a Christian as *candidati fidei* ("probationers for faith"). The latter expression is especially appropriate for those enrolled in the catechumenate for instruction in the Christian faith with a view to baptism. Modern Baptists who advocate this view of the status of Christian children are clearly late in the day in catching on to that idea![17]

In the light of these ideas and of the increasingly widespread custom of Baptists providing a service for the blessing of infants (commonly called "dedication service"), we have here a situation to be pondered. Christians confess their faith

---

[16]*Of Baptisme*, 1646, cited by M. Walker, *Early Baptist Thought on the Child in the Church*, (unpublished M.Th. dissertation, King's College, University of London, 1963), pp. 255-56.

[17]See G. W. Rusling, "The Status of Children", *Baptist Quarterly* 18 (1960) 245ff; and G. R. Beasley-Murray, "The Child in the Church", in *Children and Conversion*, ed. Clifford Ingle, (Nashville: Broadman, 1970), 133-41.

in the God who in Christ has revealed his gracious attitude to all humankind and wills their salvation, hence Christians are commanded to take the good news to all. The Church is the community called into being by the Gospel, the fellowship of the life-giving Spirit and Christ's instrument in the world. Its members rejoice in the knowledge that the redemptive deeds of the Saviour included their children in the divine intention, and that such are objects of the divine love in the present, even though they cannot know it in their earliest days. How then should this faith be expressed?

Paedobaptists, viewing baptism as the sacrament of the Gospel, believe it right within the fellowship of the Gospel to apply the rite to their children, since it expresses the redemptive will of God in Christ for them and his claim on them as their Creator and Redeemer. After baptism they have the duty to help their children to respond to the grace of God manifest in the death and resurrection of Christ, in the Church, and in the Christian home, and so lead them to confess Jesus as Saviour and Lord that they may enter in to the full privileges and responsibilities of membership in the Church.

How do Baptists express this faith? Unfortunately, all too often uncertainly. Typically we are so concerned to affirm the love of God for all children, we hesitate to affirm that there is any difference between the position of children in Christian families in the Church and those born and reared in non-Christian families, whether in London or Beijing or Tokyo or Bombay or Moscow or New York. Similarly we are so convinced that we cannot make an undertaking before God on behalf of our newborn offspring, we bring them to Church for a so-called "dedication service", wherein emphasis is laid on the dedication of *parents and congregation* to bring up the child in the Christian way. This surely reflects the nontheological thinking that has afflicted Baptists during the past century or more. We, along with other Christians, are freshly realizing how blessed Christians and their families are, and we should gladly acknowledge that fact from life's beginning. It is our privilege to bring our children to a service of thanksgiving and prayer for *them* - thanksgiving not simply for their safe entry into this creation, but for the provision that has been made for their entry into the new creation; for the love of the Father towards them *now*; for the redemption of Christ that has been achieved for *them*; for the presence of the Spirit that surrounds them in a Christian home and in a Christian church; for the prospect of their experiencing the grace of God in home and in church through their years of growing; hence the entire appropriateness of prayer *for them*, that they may so unfold to those influences of grace and instruction in the gospel that at length they may freely confess Christ in baptism and become responsible members of the Body of Christ.[18]

In communities where infant baptism is interpreted as above, and those where a service for thanksgiving and blessing of children is so understood, the differences of procedure, process and goal are distinctly less significant than their commonality. Indeed, the process and goal, viewed in terms of growth towards confession of Christ, the experience of salvation and full membership of the Church, are little distinguishable. The beginning and the end of the process are certainly very differently expressed, the one starting with baptism with a view to full membership of the Church, the other *ending* with baptism with a view to full membership of the Church. The two administrations of baptism reflect different understandings of the rite, but where the interpretations here expounded are adopted, the theology expressed in the two administrations is very close. This is all the clearer when we recognize that both infant baptism and the service for the blessing of children are performed in hope of the grace of God in the life of the little one, and that both infant baptism and believer's baptism are beginnings in hope of final salvation by the grace of God.

I do not wish to press these similarities beyond reality, as though the differences were of little account, or to suggest that both forms of baptism equally well express all that baptism in the New Testament signifies. On the contrary, the above argument proceeds from the conviction that the theology of baptism in the New Testament cannot be applied without modification to infant baptism. Baptists have good reason to believe that the baptism of confessors of Christ more adequately corresponds to the apostolic practice and theology of baptism than any form of infant baptism. They cherish the hope that the Churches throughout the world may yet reform their baptismal practices and theologies to conform more closely to the apostolic pattern, and when the Churches do that, we shall all learn better together.

---

[18]The brief but penetrating article by Morris West, "Infant Presentation: an affirmation of God's love", *Baptist Times* (July 18, 1991), sets forth a closely similar view as that expounded above. The universal relation of Christ's redemption to humanity naturally extends to all children, and challenges our understanding of all initiatory rites and missionary commitment; see the Report of the Louisville Consultation on Believer's Baptism, *Review and Expositor* LXXVII (1980) 101-08, and my article "The Theology of the Child", *American Baptist Quarterly* 1 (1982) 197-202, together with the Lutheran and Baptist responses to the issues raised. (This issue of the *American Baptist Quarterly* presents articles and reports of conversations held between Lutherans and Baptists of North America 1979-81).

That, however, is not the point. The question is whether Baptists can acknowledge infant baptism, performed within the fellowship of faith for members of households of faith, as a form of the one baptism of the Bible, with emphasis on its prospective aspect, and believer's baptism as emphasizing the experience of grace and confession of the believer's faith, both forms of baptism looking to the completion of salvation in the final kingdom of God. I have already stated that for long I gave the answer "No" to the question implied in the last sentence. This was due to my conviction that Paedobaptist apologetic for infant baptism depended too much on traditional interpretations, which appeared to me neither to face the realities of history (Europe's millions of baptized pagans, for example), nor to relate adequately to the New Testament theology of baptism. I have, however, been impressed with the theologians in the historic Churches whose endeavours to order the life of the churches in the light of the maxim *semper reformandum* (i.e. ever to be subject to reform) have led them to conclusions consonant with those I have above outlined, as also with the likeness of Christian experience in Paedobaptist and Baptist churches which share the kind of attitude here described.

As to churches which hold a more sacramental view of infant baptism, the comments made in the early part of this article are to be borne in mind. Such churches have an equally sacramental interpretation of the baptism of *believers*; those of us who find such views unacceptable should not reject the validity of baptisms of believers performed within them. Similarly the rejection of the sacramental interpretation of infant baptism should not carry with it the dismissal of the rite itself. In this connection Joseph Eagan, Jesuit theologian, made two suggestions. First, the universal recovery of the ancient catechumenate would aid enormously. For Paedobaptists it could be applied in two ways, either continuance of infant baptism followed by an extended catechumenate leading to confirmation and adult entrance into the Christian community, *or* a religious ceremony for infants at birth and an extended catechumenate leading to baptism-confirmation-eucharist; the latter procedure would naturally be adopted in believer baptist congregations. Secondly, it would help greatly if instead of concentrating on infant baptism and believer baptism the churches adopted the term "initiation", recognizing that the latter includes the whole process of leading individuals to Christ and into the Church.[19]

These suggestions are closely akin to the position advocated in this article. I make the plea that churches which practise believer's baptism should consider acknowledging the legitimacy of infant baptism, and allow members in

[19]"The Authority and Justification for Infant Baptism", *Review and Expositor* LXXVII pp. 60-61.

Paedobaptist churches the right to interpret it according to their consciences. This would carry with it the practical consequence of believer-baptist churches refraining from baptizing on confession of faith those who have been baptized in infancy.

I am not sanguine enough to believe that members of believer-baptist churches will be convinced by the arguments presented within this essay. I would, however, remind my colleagues that many groups of churches, including the oldest Protestant denomination, the Waldensians of Italy, have for centuries proceeded on the basis of this position, and recent local ecumenical projects are doing likewise. I would further draw attention to the second phrase in the title of this essay: "An Exercise in *Possibilities*". It is at least in harmony with variations in the experience of baptism among the earliest believers recorded in the New Testament (cf. Acts 2:37-38, 8:14-17, 10:44-48, 11:1-18, 18:24-19:6). The great lesson of those variations is the freedom of God in bestowing his gifts. That freedom has been evident from the first generation of the Church's life to the present. What God has been doing through the centuries has been a means of instruction of his people, and of that no generation of Christians has been so conscious as ours.

In the Book of Revelation an appeal occurs as a climax to each of the seven letters to the churches:

> "You have ears,
> so *hear what the Spirit says to the churches!*"
> (Rev 2:7 etc. REB).

I leave it to my fellow believer-baptists to ponder whether the "possibilities" expounded in this article in any sense coincide with what the Spirit is saying to the churches today.

LA BIBLE, LIEU DE RENCONTRE ENTRE LES EGLISES ET LES CHRETIENS

Pierre Duprey

La parole, par laquelle Dieu interpelle, en dévoilant son dessein de salut, en appelant à y adhérer dans la foi et la fidélité, est toujours au centre de la réunion des siens. Elle convoque (ek-kaleô) son peuple pour réaffirmer ou renouveler l'alliance qui le constitue.

Pour mieux saisir le rôle de la parole de Dieu dans le rassemblement de son peuple, il serait peut-être bon de considérer deux événements que la Bible nous décrit: la lecture publique de la loi par Esdras (Néhémie 8-9) et la première description que nous ayons de l'eucharistie, par Paul en 1 Corinthiens 11,23-26. Dans les deux cas, nous avons un renouvellement de l'alliance et donc un rassemblement du peuple dans un élan renouvelé vers le terme auquel il est appelé.

1. La lecture publique de la loi par Esdras (Néhémie 8-9)

La destruction du royaume du nord, la manière dont Judas avait continué à vivoter jusqu'à la prise de Jérusalem et la déportation, toute cette période avait marqué l'écroulement progressif des espoirs qu'Israël avait mis dans son alliance avec le Seigneur. Malgré les appels des prophètes, ces catastrophes successives n'avaient pas approfondi suffisamment la conscience de son infidélité comme cause de ses malheurs. Josias avait bien tenté une réforme religieuse mais il avait été battu et tué par ses ennemis. Cet événement ne semblait-il pas donner raison aux politiciens contre les partisans intransigeants de l'alliance avec le Seigneur? Le temple et la ville étaient détruits. Le peuple était déporté. Non seulement tous les espoirs s'étaient écroulés, mais c'est l'espérance elle-même qui subissait une crise profonde. Nous sommes habitués, trop facilement, à considérer le retour d'exil comme une épopée triomphale. Le lyrisme des prophètes ont formé notre conscience à ce sujet. Mais il faut y regarder de plus près pour saisir réellement la situation et comment les caravanes successives ont trouvé au retour une situation qui était loin d'être idéale et qui n'a fait souvent qu'approfondir la crise de l'espérance.

La troisième partie du livre d'Isaïe, les prophètes Aggée et Zacharie nous aident à réaliser quelle était la situation réelle à l'époque du retour. L'introduction au livre d'Isaïe dans la TOB donne de cette situation une excellente synthèse. Les juifs revenus d'exil éprouvent de grandes difficultés à se réinstaller dans les domaines abandonnés et spoliés. Parmi eux il y a beaucoup de prêtres qui souffrent particulièrement de la cessation du culte.

Parmi les juifs restés dans le pays, il y a certes encore des fidèles, mais beaucoup sont devenus idolâtres et ne comprennent pas le zèle religieux de ceux qui rentrent. De plus, ils ont dû s'installer au détriment des exilés et ne voient pas leur retour et leurs revendications d'un bon oeil. Cela entraîne une double division, religieuse et sociale.

Pendant l'exil des étrangers ont pu s'établir en Judée à différents titres. D'autres accompagnent les caravanes du retour. Comment ces étrangers vont-ils être intégrés au peuple de Dieu?

Des juifs nombreux sont restés dans la diaspora. Les fidèles zélés veulent préparer leur retour. Voudront-ils revenir? Et, s'ils reviennent, le retour n'augmentera-t-il pas les difficultés provoquées par les précédentes caravanes. On est loin du rêve du retour longuement caressé dans l'exil. Devant l'inaction apparente de Dieu, l'espérance est durement mise en question. Cependant c'est dans ces circonstances que les prophètes et les leaders religieux tentent de reconstruire un peuple uni et saint, débarrassé du culte des idoles, solidaire et non plus animé de la haine entre frères; au mépris des étrangers il faut substituer la volonté de les convertir au vrai Dieu. C'est l'infidélité à l'alliance avec Dieu qui est la cause de la division et de la haine entre les frères. Il faut reconstruire le temple pour que le culte puisse être restauré et célébré. Il faut reconstruire Jérusalem, la ville sainte, mais l'un et l'autre n'ont de sens que par le peuple qui doit vivre en ces lieux et être la communauté que Dieu a choisie et a appelée pour lui rendre gloire, le louer par sa fidélité et son obéissance.

Même dans la meilleurs hypothèse le peuple juif a perdu son indépendance nationale et ses structures sociales. Il ne trouvera sa raison d'être et son unité qu'en insistant sur sa spécificité religieuse, sur son culte, sur sa loi et ses exigences. La parole du Dieu vivant qui parle et agit et vers lequel le peuple peut se tourner est le vrai, le seul point de restauration et de renouveau.

C'est dans ce contexte qu'il faut situer la lecture publique de la loi au chapitre 8 du livre de Néhémie. Ce récit est certainement assez idéalisé. Il décrit cependant un événement marquant de l'époque du retour: le renouvellement de l'alliance.

"Tout le peuple comme un seul homme se rassembla" pour écouter la lecture de la loi par le prêtre Esdras. Il s'agit d'une lecture liturgique durant laquelle le peuple exprime sa foi, son adoration, sa prière. Esdras et plusieurs de ses compagnons "lisaient dans le livre de la loi de Dieu, de manière distincte, en en donnant le sens et ils faisaient comprendre au peuple ce qui était lu" (8,8).

Le résultat de cette lecture commentée, priée, fut une prise de conscience par le peuple de son infidélité, de ses péchés qu'il reconnût et en même temps la proclamation renouvelée de sa fidélité en Yahvé son seul Seigneur: "C'est toi qui est le Seigneur, toi seul! C'est toi qui a fait les cieux des cieux et toute leur armée, la terre et tout ce qui s'y trouve, les mers et tout ce qu'elles contiennent, c'est toi qui leur donne la vie à tous, et l'armée des cieux se prosterne devant toi" (9,6). Cette profession de foi est suivie de la description des actes merveilleux par lesquels Dieu a mené son peuple depuis Abraham et, en contrepartie, la reconnaissance des révoltes et des infidélités au cours des générations. Et, "aujourd'hui, voici que nous sommes des esclaves dans le pays que tu as donné à nos pères afin d'en manger les fruits et les biens, voici que nous sommes des esclaves! Ces produits abondants sont pour les rois que tu établis sur nous à cause de nos péchés; ils dominent sur nos corps et sur notre bétail, selon leur bon plaisir; et nous, nous sommes dans une grande détresse" (9:36-37).

Cette fin abrupte, sans aucune demande, ou engagement, pourrait signifier la profondeur de la crise de l'espérance. Mais elle ne doit pas être séparée des versets qui concluaient le premier jour de la lecture de la loi: "Ne soyez pas dans la peine car la joie du Seigneur, voilà votre force... Tout le peuple s'en alla manifester une grand joie, car ils avaient compris les paroles qu'on leur avait fait connaître" (8:10,12). On peut aussi le rapprocher de la fin de la prière d'Esdras: "Seigneur, Dieu d'Israël, tu es juste: en ce jour même nous subsistons en effet comme un reste de réchappés. Nous voici devant toi avec nos offenses, alors que, dans ces conditions, nul ne peut se tenir devant ta face" (9:15). Nous pouvons aussi élargir la confession et l'engagement pris à propos d'un aspect particulier de l'infidélité et voir l'attitude générale engendrée par cette lecture de la loi: "Vous avez été infidèles... maintenant confessez-vous au Seigneur le Dieu de vos pères et faites sa volonté... C'est vrai! A nous d'agir suivant ta parole!" (10:10-12).

Ce renouvellement solennel de l'alliance est fondé sur la profession de la foi en Dieu qui, lui, est resté fidèle, et est toujours fidèle. La reconnaissance par le peuple de son infidélité s'accompagne de la décision d'être fidèle à la parole, d'observer les exigences de l'alliance. Le peuple est ainsi réconcilié avec son Seigneur et les membres du peuple redeviennent solidaires dans le bien cette fois-ci. Nous n'avons pas beaucoup d'informations sur la solidité de ces résolutions. Cependant, quelque 250 ans après, la persécution des Séleucides semble avoir rencontré une assez large connivence parmi le peuple en même temps qu'elle suscitait la révolte des israélites fidèles. Infidélité continue, repentance renouvelée, du côté du peuple, fidélité et providence continuelles de la part de Dieu, pardon toujours présent et accordé, ne sommes-nous pas en face de constante de l'histoire du salut?

2. La première description de la célébration eucharistique (1 Cor 11: 23-26)

Quelque trente ans après la dernière cène, Paul rappelle aux Corinthiens ce qu'il avait lui-même reçu d'une tradition remontant au Seigneur et qu'il leur avait déjà transmis à propos de "la nouvelle alliance" (11:25). Il le fait aussi dans le contexte d'une situation de la communauté de Corinthe qui est loin d'être idéalement chrétienne; il y a des divisions et des scissions dans cette communauté (11:18-19). Il est urgent de mettre fin aux abus dont est entouré le repas eucharistique. St Paul, dans sa description, se limite à l'essentiel de cette tradition. Il est cependant hors de doute que le repas était accompagné de la lecture de l'Ecriture par laquelle on rendait grâce (cf. 11:24). Un siècle plus tard, St Justin nous en fait une description beaucoup plus détaillée:

"Personne ne doit prendre part à l'eucharistie, sinon celui qui croit à la vérité de notre doctrine, qui a été baptisé pour obtenir le pardon des péchés et la nouvelle naissance, et qui vit selon l'enseignement que le Christ nous a transmis.

"Car nous ne prenons pas l'eucharistie comme un pain ordinaire ou une boisson ordinaire. De même que Jésus Christ, notre Sauveur, en s'incarnant par la parole de Dieu, a pris chair et sang pour notre salut; ainsi l'aliment devenu eucharistie par la prière contenant sa parole, et qui nourrit notre sang et notre chair, en les transformant, cet aliment est la chair et le sang de ce Jésus qui s'est incarné. Voilà ce qui nous est enseigné.

"En effet, les apôtres dans leur mémoire qu'on appelle évangile nous ont ainsi transmis l'ordre de Jésus: 'Il prit du pain, il rendit grâce et il dit: faites cela en mémoire de moi. Ceci est mon corps. Il prit la coupe de la même façon, il rendit grâce et il dit: ceci est mon sang. Et c'est à eux seuls qu'il les distribua'. Depuis ce temps, nous n'avons jamais cessé d'en renouveler la mémoire entre nous. Parmi nous, ceux qui ont de quoi viennent en aide à tous ceux qui sont dans le besoin, et nous sommes toujours unis entre nous. Dans toutes nos offrandes, nous bénissons le créateur de l'univers par son fils Jésus-Christ et par l'Esprit-Saint.

"Le jour appelé jour du soleil, tous, qu'ils habitent la ville ou la campagne, ont leur réunion dans un même lieu, et on lit les mémoires des apôtres et les écrits des prophètes aussi longtemps qu'il est possible. Quand le lecteur a fini, celui qui préside fait un discours pour nous avertir et pour nous exhorter à mettre en pratique ces beaux enseignements.

"Ensuite nous nous levons tous et nous faisons ensemble des prières. Puis, lorsque nous avons fini de prier, ainsi que je l'ai déjà dit, on apporte le pain avec le vin et l'eau. Celui qui préside fait monter au ciel des prières et des actions de grâce autant qu'il en est capable, et le peuple acclame en disant: Amen. Puis on distribue et on partage à chacun les dons sur lesquels avait été prononcée l'action de grâce; ces dons sont envoyés aux absents par le ministère des diacres" (Apologie pour les chrétiens, 1, 66-67).

Pour l'Eglise de Rome, vers 150, comme pour celle de Corinthe, vers l'année 55, l'écoute de la parole de Dieu dans l'action de grâce et l'annonce de la mort du Seigneur dans l'espérance de son retour (cf. 1 Cor 11:26) sont au coeur de la vie de la communauté. C'est là que la foi dans la vérité de la doctrine professée est solennellement proclamée. C'est là que scission et division doivent prendre fin. C'est là où la cohérence entre la vie concrète et la doctrine à laquelle on adhère trouvent leur origine et leur force. C'est là que la communauté construit et renforce sa solidarité. C'est là quelle renouvelle son espérance et son dynamisme apostolique. Dans l'humilité, la repentance et l'espérances, les membres du peuple de Dieu ont à renouveler continuellement et à approfondir leur engagement dans cette alliance "nouvelle et éternelle" que Dieu a scellée une fois pour toutes, lorsque, par le Christ, il nous a réconciliés avec lui (cf. 2 Cor 15:18). C'est dans cet engagement qu'ils trouvent leur unité.

La fidélité à l'alliance est nourrie, développée et approfondie par l'écoute et la méditation de la parole de Dieu. La description de ce que doit être la communauté chrétienne dans les Actes des apôtres est très claire sur ce point: "Ils étaient assidus à l'enseignement des apôtres et à la communion fraternelle, à la fraction du pain et aux prières" (Ac 2:42).

3. Dans l'Eglise d'aujourd'hui

Qu'il me soit permis ici de me référer à un événement de première importance pour l'Eglise catholique: le deuxième concile du Vatican. Chaque jour, la réunion conciliaire commençait par la célébration de l'eucharistie dans laquelle était entendue la parole de Dieu et annoncée la mort du Seigneur dans l'espérance de son retour. Puis, le livre des évangiles était solennellement intronisé au milieu de l'assemblée, au-dessus des pères. Ce geste symbolique indiquait clairement l'attitude fondamentale de l'assemblée conciliaire, telle que les pères devaient l'exprimer dans le préambule de la constitution sur la révélation divine: "Ecouter religieusement la parole de Dieu pour pouvoir la proclamer avec assurance". Les évêques étaient réunis en concile pour examiner, à la lumière de la parole de Dieu, la fidélité de l'Eglise catholique au dessein divin, à la mission reçue du Seigneur. Par une écoute religieuse renouvelée de la parole de Dieu ils devaient, pour reprendre une parole de Jean XXIII, enlever de la face de l'Eglise la poussière que les siècles y avaient accumulée, approfondir sa fidélité dans les circonstances nouvelles du monde d'aujourd'hui, proclamer cette parole avec assurance dans une espérance s'appuyant sur celui qui est toujours fidèle à son alliance et dont la parole est toujours efficace. L'Eglise catholique a approfondi sa conscience d'elle-même en méditant l'Ecriture. Ce faisant, elle a jeté un nouveau regard sur ses autres frères chrétiens qui n'ont plus été vus comme des "non-catholiques", mais comme des frères, avec lesquels elle était dans une communion réelle, même si incomplète.

Voulant s'engager décidément avec eux dans la recherche de l'unité, elle soulignait comme condition fondamentale de cet engagement le renouveau de l'Eglise: "Attendu que toute rénovation de l'Eglise consiste essentiellement dans une fidélité grandissante à sa vocation, c'est là certainement le sens et le ressort du mouvement vers l'unité. L'Eglise, au cours de son pèlerinage, est appelée par le Christ à cette réforme permanente dont elle a perpétuellement besoin en tant qu'institution humaine et terrestre" (Unitatis Redintegratio, 6). Aussitôt d'ailleurs les pères affirmaient comme autre condition fondamentale de l'engagement oecuménique la conversion du coeur: "Il n'y a pas de véritable oecuménisme sans conversion intérieure. En effet, c'est du renouvellement de l'esprit, du renoncement à soi-même et d'une libre effusion de charité que partent et mûrissent les désirs de l'unité" (U.R. 7).

Conversion du coeur, renouveau de l'Eglise, c'est ce recentrement continuel dont la personne et la communauté ont besoin pour répondre à l'appel de leur Seigneur. En vue de cette conversion et de ce renouveau, le concile donnait à la parole de Dieu une place unique dans sa constitution dogmatique sur la révélation divine. Je ne m'y arrêterai pas, nous avons eu l'occasion déjà de nous entretenir de ce que cette constitution voulait promouvoir dans l'Eglise. Je voudrais seulement signaler ici la très intéressante et importante conférence que le cardinal Martini, archevêque de Milan, faisait à Rome le 13 décembre 1990 sur l'usage pastorale de la lectio divina. Cette conférence a été publiée en français et en anglais dans notre Service d'information, mais aussi en italien dans son texte original. Elle montre tout l'effort qui doit être fait et l'effort qui se fait pour que cette lectio divina devienne vraiment le coeur de la vie spirituelle de tous les catholiques.

Plus récemment, la session spéciale du synode des évêques consacré à l'Europe affirmait au n 7 de ses conclusions: "Pour promouvoir l'oecuménisme, l'apostolat biblique venant d'un respect commun pour la sainte Ecriture, est d'une grande importance". L'effort que l'Alliance Biblique Universelle et la Fédération Biblique Catholique menent ensemble au service de la traduction et de la diffusion de la parole de Dieu a une importance oecuménique de premier ordre. Les chrétiens se rencontrent dans l'écoute religieuse de la parole de Dieu en vue d'une assurance renouvelée dans sa proclamation.

Rencontrant récemment à Rome des représentants des Sociétés Bibliques, j'avais esquissé une réflexion sur différents thèmes qui sont actuellement au centre du dialogue oecuménique et que cette nouvelle familiarité avec la Bible permet d'approfondir ensemble. La notion de communion (koinonia) qui a permis l'approfondissement de la conscience ecclésiologique de l'Eglise catholique dans la Lumen Gentium, son ouverture oecuménique dans Unitatis Redintegratio, est maintenant au coeur de la plupart des dialogues.

Ce qui avait été l'occasion ou la cause des séparations de la réforme, la question de la justification par la foi seule, est maintenant surmontée. Je crois que l'on peut dire qu'entre catholiques et luthériens, qu'entre catholiques et réformés, ce n'est plus un sujet de division. Tous nous sommes d'accord sur l'absolue gratuité de la justification et sur la réalité du changement qu'elle opère dans le justifié, du commencement en lui de la nouvelle création. Certes, des différences d'accent restent encore si l'on veut préciser le lien entre justification et sanctification, mais ces différences n'existent pas seulement entre protestants et catholiques, mais aussi entre différentes familles protestantes et elles ne sont plus des différences qui puissent diviser. Il faut maintenant tirer les conséquences ecclésiologiques de cette commune et intégrale notion de justification. C'est le travail depuis des années de la commission catholique-luthérienne, travail qui vient de s'achever et sera publié prochainement.

Au sujet de l'eucharistie, tant dans les dialogues bilatéraux que dans le dialogue multilatéral qui se fait au sein de "Foi et Constitution", la redécouverte de toutes les dimensions de la notion biblique de mémorial a permis de progresser considérablement vers un accord sur notre foi dans cette réalité centrale de la vie de l'Eglise. Une meilleure connaissance de la formation de l'Ecriture dans la communauté, de la formation du canon de l'ancien et du nouveau testament, nous permet de progresser dans l'effort pour surmonter l'opposition superficielle et artificielle entre Ecriture et Tradition.

Je ne signale ces exemples que pour montrer comment, aujourd'hui comme toujours, l'Ecriture est le point de rencontre entre les chrétiens et les Eglises encore divisées. C'est par une fidélité toujours renouvelée et approfondie à l'Ecriture dans toutes ses dimensions, ses exigences et ses implications que ces divisions pourront être surmontées et que tous ensemble nous pourrons alors renouveler notre fidélité à l'alliance, nouvelle et éternelle, en célébrant son mémorial, jusqu'à ce qu'il vienne.

THE UNITY WE SEEK

A Review at the End of an Ecumenical Century

Günther Gassmann

1. An Old Theme, Question and Goal

The unity of Christians or the unity of the churches was the goal which gave rise to the early ecumenical movement and converted the hearts and minds of our ecumenical forbears into a committed yearning, reflection and action. This goal of unity was plausible enough at a time when an emerging world-wide Christianity offered a scandalous, depressing spectacle of division, enmity and strife.

The unity of the churches was re-discovered in this situation as the goal of a movement from sinful disobedience towards faithfulness to God's gift and calling in Jesus Christ. Yes, it was seen as a movement of repentance and renewal, guided and inspired by the Holy Spirit. It was a movement which inaugurated not only a new phase in church history, but which was also clearly a part of world history.

This wider horizon of the early ecumenical movement seems to be as relevant today as it was seventy, eighty years ago. Yet within this historical perspective the more specific question concerning the goal was soon asked: **What kind of unity** are we actually seeking in this new ecumenical movement? What do we mean by "unity"? There were those with a more pietistic or evangelical background who were convinced that the divisions among Christians were the result of an over-emphasis on theological controversies among debate-loving theologians. When the resulting theological/doctrinal differences are given their proper place, usually a secondary one, then the true and persisting unity of Christians would shine forth again: the unity of hearts and souls grounded in the experience of God's love in Jesus Christ and expressed in common prayer and mutual respect and love. Others, with a more liberal outlook, aimed primarily at friendship and cooperation on social, political and missionary tasks. They regarded forms of a federation between churches which enabled such activities as a sufficient - or at best a preliminary - expression of Christian unity. And there were those who aimed at and hoped for more: a full communion - altar and pulpit fellowship - between churches based on agreement in faith and sacraments (many Lutherans) or an organic union of hitherto divided churches in a united church (many Anglicans) on the basis of the common confession of faith, mutual recognition of sacraments and ministries, communion in the historic episcopate.

A spiritual unity among believing Christians, a federation between churches for better understanding and cooperation, a full communion between churches which nevertheless preserve their denominational and organisational identities, and an organic union between churches which form a united church in each place (country or region) - these were thus the concepts of the "unity we seek" which emerged in the first phase of the ecumenical movement before 1948. This was a period when the Orthodox churches were only partially involved in the ecumenical movement, the Roman Catholic Church was definitely refusing any participation, and the churches in the missionary continents of Africa and Asia had not yet been given independence and their own voice. And still, though with modifications, these earlier concepts of Christian or Church unity have continued to be present in reflections on the goal of the ecumenical movement up to this day.

But this question about the "unity we seek" is posed today in a new, significantly changed context compared to that earlier period. We have taken a glimpse at that earlier period in the hope that this may make us aware that we are part of a movement in history which began at the dawn of this century, the close of which we will be witnessing rather soon. With this awareness we should now look at the changed context in which our ecumenical faithfulness is to be implemented and our commitment to the goal of unity is to be renewed.

2. The Ecumenical Century: Achievements and Uncertainties

What I have experienced in my limited personal ecumenical involvement during my lifetime gives me the assurance to speak, first of all, of the immense achievements of the movement towards the "unity we seek" in this century and especially in this second part of it. Looking beyond my own sphere of experience, we can quite generally say that all the historic Christian confessions and traditions have entered a radically changed relationship. They have moved away from - in several cases centuries-long - mutual isolation, misunderstanding, misinterpretation, enmity and competition. They have developed relationships of mutual respect, better understanding, multiple contacts and forms of cooperation and association, common prayer and worship, theological dialogue and common witness and action in society. Through their active involvement in the ecumenical movement, many churches have learned to look beyond their own borders and internal affairs. They have thus been given a glimpse of a fuller awareness of the universal and catholic character of Christ's Church as a living reality in all conditions and contexts of this world. They have expressed this universality through solidarity with those who suffer in distant countries; they have experienced this catholicity by being enriched with the spiritual gifts of other traditions.

A number of churches have gone one step further by entering into a union with each other, forming a united church. Others have established full communion while remaining separate organisations. With the exception of the Orthodox Churches, practically all member churches of the WCC practise eucharistic hospitality. Christian World Communions - the confessional families - are playing an active ecumenical role, especially since they initiated the growing number of bilateral dialogues more than twenty years ago. These dialogues have led to remarkable convergences in formerly dividing issues such as baptism, eucharist, ministry, nature and mission of the Church, justification and sanctification, Scripture and Tradition, marriage, and other issues. Regional and National Councils of Churches have in many places grown in importance and have been able to become more representative in membership than the WCC, especially by including local Roman Catholic Churches.

Of special significance for the movement towards "the unity we seek" has been the document on *Baptism, Eucharist and Ministry* (BEM), adopted by the WCC Faith and Order Commission at Lima, Peru, in 1982. Within the last ten years BEM has become the most widely translated (34 languages), distributed (ca. 450,000 copies) and discussed (thousands of groups, seminars, lectures, hundreds of publications) document in the history of the ecumenical movement. More than 180 churches have elaborated an official response to BEM - again an unprecedented event. For the first time the Roman Catholic Church has officially responded (in 1987) to an ecumenical document. In our evaluation of this broad process of discussion and of the responses of the churches (cf. *Baptism, Eucharist and Ministry 1982-1990*. Report on the Process and Responses, Geneva, WCC, 1991), we have described the general acclamation of the significance of this document, the great measure of agreement with its content (especially regarding baptism and eucharist), and the more critical comments which require further work on (a) the fundamental criteria or norms of the Christian faith - Scripture and Tradition; (b) the different interpretations of the notion of "sacrament" and "sacramentality" and (c) the understanding of the nature and mission of the Church in an ecumenical perspective.

The impact of the BEM text and the discussion about it is considerable. The text has helped to change and broaden the theological perceptions of many people and has contributed to the renewal of worship life and spirituality. The text has served to build bridges between churches with a strong liturgical and sacramental tradition and churches of a more Protestant tradition. BEM is now used in bilateral dialogues and in inter-church agreements as an expression of ecumenical convergence on which further steps towards unity can be based. The discussion on BEM continues. It has, finally, underlined the need to undergird all our necessary concerns for the future of humanity by a deepened understanding and practice of our Christian faith. Our task is now not to lose the ecumenical advance achieved by the BEM process but to make use of it in furthering ecumenical relations and steps ahead.

In general, there is much reason to be thankful for the ecumenical advances and achievements which have marked this century as an "ecumenical century". However, at the same time we should be aware of new problems and difficulties on our ecumenical pilgrimage. The "success" of the ecumenical movement has in many circles led to a certain satisfaction with the degree of friendly relations and forms of cooperation so far achieved. We experience at larger ecumenical gatherings a growing preponderance of narrowly particularistic concerns (of churches or regions) over common ecumenical visions and tasks. This tendency becomes even more serious where it is linked to a resurgence of nationalistic or ethno-centric claims. In many places there is still a reluctance to do together what is ecumenically possible, and also to receive into the life of the churches the theological advances achieved in ecumenical dialogues. Churches which have developed close relationships in the recent past see these now endangered by new problems, like the "Uniate" problem in Eastern Europe, differences on social ethical issues, on the relationship between gospel and culture, or the ordination of women to the priesthood and episcopate.

One response of the ecumenical movement to these and other new problems would be to highlight and reformulate our ecumenical goal in such a way that churches are encouraged and challenged to recommit themselves to the goal of visible unity and thereby become true instruments of God's reconciling and renewing purpose for all humanity and creation.

3. Re-stating the Goal: Canberra

After more than 15 years - since Nairobi 1975 - an Assembly of the WCC has made a new attempt to state and circumscribe the goal of our ecumenical journey. Drafted by the Faith and Order Commission and revised at the Assembly, the Canberra Assembly adopted the statement on **The Unity of the Church as Koinonia: Gift and Calling**[1] It may be one of the few documents of this Assembly which will be of significance for some time, and a number of churches and national councils have already taken it up. The Joint Working Group between

---

[1]Printed in the Canberra Report *Signs of the Spirit*, ed. Michael Kinnamon, Geneva, WCC, and Grand Rapids, Wm. B. Eerdmans, 1991, pp. 172-174.

the Roman Catholic Church and the WCC is to prepare an ecumenical interpretation of this statement. Behind these efforts lies the expectation that this statement may enable us to recover a sense of direction and focus for our ecumenical efforts during the coming years.

Let us look now at some of the aspects of the Canberra statement which may help us to clarify our question about the kind of "unity we seek". First of all, the statement clearly continues the line of earlier Assembly statements, especially those of New Delhi 1961 and Nairobi 1975, when it states the basic conditions of Christian unity in para. 2, namely: "The common confession of the apostolic faith; a common sacramental life entered by the one baptism and celebrated together in one eucharist; a common life in which members and ministries are mutually recognised and reconciled; and a common mission witnessing to all people to the gospel of God's grace and serving the whole of creation... This full communion will be expressed on the local and the universal levels through conciliar forms of life and action." All our ecumenical dialogues must struggle with these basic conditions and expressions of unity - and we have, indeed, come a long way towards their implementation and acceptance.

But there are also quite a number of new elements or emphases in the Canberra statement compared with New Delhi 1961 and Nairobi 1975. These are a reflection of ecumenical developments during the last decades.

Firstly: The term "unity" or "visible unity" has been substituted in most cases by the term and concept of *koinonia*, i.e. by "communion", which refers in the New Testament to participation, partaking, sharing, community, communion, fellowship. Compared with the term "unity", the concept of *koinonia*, communion, is in its essence more dynamic and open to diversity. But above all it is able to indicate the inter-relation between different levels of communion like (1) the communion within the Trinitarian God - Father, Son and Holy Spirit; (2) the communion between this God and the Church through Christ's sustaining and renewing presence in the Holy Spirit within the life of the Christian community; (3) the communion among the members of the Christian community thus established and nourished, a communion transcending all human barriers, inclusive of all; and, finally (4) the communion of God with all humanity and creation according to God's ultimate design and purpose, for which the Church already now should be a foretaste, sign and instrument.

Secondly: It is therefore within this comprehensive vision of *koinonia*, communion, that the Canberra statement does not start with the Church, but with the purpose of God - para. 1.1 - "to gather the whole of creation under the

Lordship of Christ in whom, by the power of the Holy Spirit, all are brought into communion with God (Eph 1)". It is within this all-encompassing horizon that the Church finds its place and calling - para. 2.1 -"to proclaim reconciliation and to provide healing, to overcome divisions based on race, gender, age, culture, colour, and to bring all people into communion with God." Where this happens, the Church is enabled - para. 1.1 - "to live as sign of the reign of God and servant of the reconciliation with God, promised and provided for the whole creation."

Thirdly: This wide horizon of God's design and the place and role of the Church within it is contrasted with historical reality in the form of the divisions among the churches. Para.1.2: "Their scandalous divisions damage the credibility of their witness to the world in worship and service... they contradict not only the Church's witness but also its very nature." But the movement away from division towards unity is also affirmed, a movement which has led to "a certain degree of communion already existing between the churches", as para. 1.3 formulates rather cautiously, probably because it seeks to characterise the situation within Christianity in general, including the Roman Catholic and Orthodox Churches. However, even to this positive statement is added the critical challenge that the "churches have failed to draw the consequences for their life from the degree of communion they have already experienced and the agreements already achieved."

Fourthly: This challenge is more directly and explicitly addressed in para. 3.2 to "all churches" (not only the WCC member churches) by calling them to implement the basic conditions of *koinonia*, communion, mentioned before, by:

(1) recognising each other's baptism (the foundation of communion with Christ and with one another;

(2) recognising the apostolic faith as expressed through the Nicene Creed in the life and witness of one another (the common apostolic faith is to be recognised, not the Nicene Creed as such or by itself);

(3) considering forms of eucharistic hospitality wherever appropriate (i.e. possible);

(4) moving towards mutual recognition of ministries (where the greatest barriers still seem to exist);

(5) giving common witness to the gospel as a whole (i.e. the gospel in relation to the faith of the individual and of the community and in relation to the world);

(6) re-committing themselves to work for justice, peace and the integrity of creation, linking more closely the search for the sacramental communion of the church with the struggles for justice and peace; and

(7) helping congregations and communities to express in appropriate ways locally the degree of communion that already exists.

This is a fairly clear and straightforward list of reflection and action, a kind of check-list for each church or group of churches in order to test how far they have come and what still needs to be done if they are faithful to their ecumenical calling.

Fifthly: Among the new elements in the Canberra statement is, finally, a particular emphasis on diversity. Here, the open, dynamic character of the concept of *koinonia*, communion, again proves to be helpful, and the statement declares in para. 2.2: "Diversities which are rooted in theological traditions, various cultural, ethnic or historical contexts, are integral to the nature of communion." They can contribute "to the richness and fullness of the Church of God". They are part, one could add, of the catholicity of the Church.

But the statement immediately proceeds also to the delicate issue of limits to diversity - delicate, because it raises the question who decides about such limits and on what grounds? The drafters of the statement were aware of this question, and by choosing only one example for indicating a limit to diversity the statement refers indirectly to the "Basis" of the WCC to which the member churches have already committed themselves: "Diversity is illegitimate", says the text, "when, for instance, it makes impossible the common confession of Jesus Christ as God and Saviour, the same yesterday, today and for ever (Hebrews 13:8)." This issue of diversity within a communion and its limits, which is also closely related to the debate on gospel and culture, certainly must receive more attention in our ecumenical dialogue. But it will be only in the framework of a communion of churches that common criteria - the problem of Scripture, Tradition, the Church and the different contexts - for circumscribing diversity can be agreed on.

4. A Journey into a Known Future

Contrary to the earlier statements of New Delhi and Nairobi which advocated an organic union, i.e. a merger, of churches within a country or part of a country as the adequate organisational expression of unity, the Canberra statement leaves the question of the form or model of church unity open. I believe that this was wise, since it also reflects developments in recent decades on considerations about the forms of unity. There should also be diversity in the forms of implementing *koinonia* structurally according to diverse conditions, possibilities and needs. There will be situations in which churches are able to agree on all conditions of communion as outlined in the Canberra statement, yet decide to preserve their confessional identity and organisational independence. But even in such a relationship of full communion, they cannot remain unchanged. In order to reach such agreements, they have to move towards each other by renewing and modifying their doctrinal positions and their lives.

The conditions and the goal of "the unity we seek" have been clearly expressed by the Canberra statement, but the forms and structure of *koinonia* have been left open for diverse implementations. But what has *not* been left open is for me personally the most fascinating and encouraging - and sometimes still very much unfulfilled - element of our movement towards "the unity we seek": we are not, in the final instance, under a heavy obligation to seek unity by giving up something which has been dear to our respective traditions or by adding something to them which is strange and unfamiliar. Rather, what an immense liberation would it be for all of us to move beyond our provincial limitations into the wealth of insights and experiences of the wider, comprehensive Christian tradition! What immense enrichment, encouragement and consolation do we in fact experience when we discover in other Christian traditions forms of Christian thinking and life which we often miss in our own churches! What immense joy we experience when we discover that there is in the Christian community, across denominational boundaries, a great potential of Christian commitment and action on social issues which no other group in society, either national or world-wide, can mobilise!

This liberating, enriching and committing process towards *koinonia*, and as an expression of already existing *koinonia*, should not be misunderstood as a process towards a friendly but finally superficial pro-existence among Christians, in which everything is accepted and swallowed. In the ecumenical movement I have become more consciously a Lutheran than I was before, because I believe that our communion with each other will only be enriched if there are distinct theological profiles, forms of piety and spirituality, clear positions on social issues. What superficial communion would it be if we were so similar or, even worse, so undiscerningly open to every possible theological opinion and expression of Christian worship and life that nothing would be distinct, provoking or challenging any more! What saltless communion would it be if we were to reflect in an ill-conceived openness all the developments and tendencies in society!

Discussion and conflict will be unavoidable, but within a growing *koinonia* this should become an occasion for dialogue, not for exclusion. It should lead to dialogue with the conviction that God's truth for us is more comprehensive than can be captured in our own particular discernment, and that there might also be truth in the position of those with whom we disagree. *Koinonia* is not an ideal garden of like-minded people, clapping each other on the back. Rather, *koinonia* is created by the living Christ among us, who was open to all, accepted all and said to all: repent and follow me as a multitude of diverse people and diverse traditions, enriching and enabling each other, carrying each others' burdens and sharing each others' gifts and joys, bound together not by their like-mindedness but by the Holy Spirit through God's word and sacrament.

And for such a journey a historical pilgrimage city like Santiago de Compostela in Spain is perhaps an appropriate place to rest for a moment on that journey and reflect on the question: What have we achieved, what barriers have still to be faced, what will be our next steps in our pilgrimage towards "the unity we seek"? This will be the task of the Fifth World Conference on Faith and Order in August 1993 in Santiago de Compostela. The Conference will take up, broaden and deepen the Canberra perspective by reflecting on the different aspects of its theme "Towards Koinonia/Communion in Faith, Life and Witness". It will, by God's grace, provide encouragement and new impulses and directions for continuing a journey that seeks to be obedient to God's will and gift.

Taufe und Wiedertaufe. Einige historische Anmerkungen zu einem ökumenischen Problem.

Erich Geldbach

1. Das Verbrechen der Schwärmer: Wiedertaufe

Ganz gleich, an welcher Stelle man die Täuferakten aufschlägt, immer wieder stößt man auf eine religiöse Polemik, die betroffen macht. Die Wahl der Worte zeugt von einer solchen Abscheu gegen die "Wiedertäufer", daß sich spätestens nach dem Lesen eines zweiten Beispiels der Verdacht aufdrängen muß, es bei den beschriebenen Personen mit Wegelagerern, Räubern und Mördern zu tun zu haben, deren letztes Ziel es ist, sich zu einer großen Verschwörung gegen die legitime Obrigkeit zusammenzurotten. Die Reformatoren griffen auf die Imkersprache zurück, wenn sie die Täufer als "Schwärmer" bezeichneten. Dies bedeutete zweierlei: So wie ein Bienenvolk, wenn es ausgeschwärmt ist, zu nichts mehr nütze ist, weil es dem Imker keinen Honig mehr zuträgt, so waren die Täufer für die Gesellschaft nutzlos geworden. Das zweite folgt unmittelbar daraus: Nutzlose konnte man leicht hinrichten, ohne daß sich Gewissensbisse einstellen mußten.[1] So geschah es denn auch landauf, landab, daß scharenweise Frauen und Männer den Tod für ihr Verbrechen erleiden mußten. Doch worin bestand ihr Verbrechen?

"Dan es wandern heimlich durch ganz Theutschland hin und wider etliche umbleufer, phantasten und betrieger, wilche furnemlich die widertauf heimlich in besondern heusern oder welden, wo sie sich verpergen mogen, leren, verdammen den kindertauf, als solt der von got nicht eingesatzt sein, und teufen einander zum andermal zu einem zeichen solicher secten; haben auch neben diesem irtumb viel andere irtumb und torheit, und dweil sie wissen, das nichts creftigers sei, der mentschen gemut zu betriegen, dan ein gestalt grosser demut und gedult, so leren sie di guter in gemein zu bringen, und wollen, das ein christenman von gepurt oder erbschaft wegen nicht moge oberkeit haben, gericht und recht haben, und nemen im grund hinweck alle burgerliche ordnung, wilche got eingesatzt hat und becreftiget."[2] Mit diesem einen Beispiel soll es sein Bewenden haben, weil sich

---

[1] Kurfürst Johann Friedrich schrieb am 25. Mai 1533 an den hessischen Landgrafen Philipp, daß sein Vater nach Anhören der Theologen und Juristen in Übereinstimmung mit den kaiserlichen Mandaten mehrere Wiedertäufer habe richten lassen, und er daher ebensowenig wie dieser Gewissensbedenken habe. Günther Franz (Hg.), Urkundliche Quellen zur hessischen Reformationsgeschichte, IV. Band, Wiedertäuferakten 1527-1626, Marburg 1951, S. 60.

[2] Ebd., S. 163. Hinzuweisen ist, daß trotz der heftigen Sprache der hessische Landgraf außerordentlich nachsichtig mit den Täufern umging. "Und konnen noch zur zeit in

hier einige wichtige Hinweise ergeben. Die Passage stammt aus dem Entwurf eines Briefes, den der hessische Kanzler Johann Feige für seinen Landesherrn, Philipp von Hessen, zu Papier brachte. Der Landgraf seinerseits schickte den Brief am 9. September 1538 an den Kurfürsten Johann Friedrich, der ihn durch Melanchthon ins Lateinische übersetzen ließ. Diese Fassung ging dann zurück an Philipp, der das Schreiben an König Heinrich VIII. von England schickte. Die Obrigkeit zweier deutscher Länder will also den englischen König darüber aufklären, wer die Wiedertäufer sind; denn inzwischen sind sie auch auf die Insel vorgedrungen.

Worin besteht das Verbrechen der Leute? Hervorgehoben ist, daß sie heimlich ihr Wesen treiben. Sie wandern bzw. laufen verdeckt umher durch das ganze deutsche Land, ziehen sich aber auch in bestimmte Häuser oder Wälder zurück, um ihre Phantastereien und Betrügereien im Verborgenen ausrichten zu können. Ihr heimliches Verbrechen besteht nun aber in nichts anderem als daß sie die Wiedertaufe lehren, die Kindertaufe verdammen und einander die Wiedertaufe spenden, was als Zeichen ihres sektenhaften Treibens angesehen wird. Vage wird dann davon gesprochen, daß sie noch andere Torheiten vertreten, die indes nicht detailliert aufgeführt werden. Lediglich zwei andere Irrtümer werden aufgeführt: Sie vertreten das Gemeineigentum und wollen eigentlich keine obrigkeitliche Ordnung, weil ein Christ weder ein Regierungsamt noch das Amt eines Richters einnehmen darf. Beide Punkte sind indes nicht für die Täufer insgesamt, sondern für bestimmte Gruppen typisch, wobei die Polemik gegen Obrigkeit- und Richteramt sicherlich weiter verbreitet ist als die Propagierung des Gemeineigentums, was ganz besonders für die in Mähren ansässigen Hutterischen Brüder galt, in Hessen aber nur durch den Besuch Peter Riedemanns nachweisbar ist, der indes keine tiefen Spuren hinterließ.

2. Exkurs: Gütergemeinschaft und Obrigkeit

In den hessischen Täuferakten finden sich Passagen, die beide Vorwürfe zurückweisen. Ein Christ darf durchaus ein obrigkeitliches Amt innehaben, schreibt Georg Schnabel in einer Widerlegung der Vorwürfe und zieht 1 Kor 1:26 heran: "Nit vil gewaltigen seind berufen", was er dann so erklärt: "da laut der text, das etlich, aber doch weinig, berufen sein." Wenn auch die Zahl der Christen in obrigkeitlicher Position klein ist, so muß man dennoch aufgrund der angeführten

unserem gewissen nit finden, imandts des glaubens halben, wo wir nit sonst gnugsam ursache der verwirkung haben mogen, mit dem schwert richten zu lassen. Dan so es di meinung haben solt, musten wir keinen judden noch papisten, die Christum am hochsten blasphemiren, bei uns dulden und sie dergestalt richten lassen." Ebd., S. 38.

Bibelstelle davon ausgehen, daß es sie geben kann. Auch beruft er sich auf Röm. 13:1-3 und 1 Petr 2: 13-16 und erklärt: "So nu ein christ van der oberkeit gefordert die bösen strafen hilft, hat er nit zu einem bosen, sonder zu einem guten werk geholfen und sein glidmaiss zum waffen der gerechtigkeit begeben." Man will laut Schnabel mit Leib und Gut dafür einstehen, daß gerechte Ordnung und nicht Chaos im Gemeinwesen entsteht. Freilich soll die Ordnung "gerecht" sein, denn Schnabel sagt auch, daß man böse Werke der Obrigkeit, insbesondere ungerechte Kriege, nicht unterstützen kann: "Wo aber die oberkeit wolt kreigen [= Kriege führen] prachts oder hoffarts halber und unter dem deckel der fromheit witwen und weisen ohn ursach machen und unschuldig blut vergeissen, wilches got durch alle propheten teuer und hoch verboten hat...; da sehe dan ein jder, das er seine glidmass nit zu waffen der ungerechtigkeit gebe, Ro 6 [v.13], auch nit gemeinschaft habe mit den unfruchtbarn werk der finsternus.... Dan was bose ist, das sollen wir nit taun."[3]

Zum Vorwurf der Gütergemeinschaft sagt er: "Diser artikel wirt uns auch gleich wie anderen meher felslich und lugenhaftig nachgesagt...". Denn die Schrift zeige durchaus, daß Christen eigene Güter besessen und gläubige Knechte gehabt hätten. Christen seien jedoch angehalten, bei Notdurft des Bruders aus ihrem Überfluß Handreichung zu tun. Dabei beruft er sich auf Röm 15: 26f., 2 Kor 9 und 1 Joh 3: 17f. Schnabel benutzt die Gelegenheit, den Spieß umzudrehen und eine heftige Attacke gegen den "neuen Papst" Luther zu reiten. Denn unter dem alten Papst hat man von zwanzig Gulden jährlich einen als Steuer genommen, "dargegen muß man jitzunder ein malter korns geben, wilches zwen gulden" oder mehr ausmacht. Das aber, so habe der Marburger Professor Johannes Eisermann in seinem Büchlein "Vom gemeinen nutz" (1533) geschrieben, sei "böser dan heidenisch unde under frommen heiden dergleichen nie gehoret". Weil man den guten Baum an seinen Früchten erkennen könne, so sei hier der Beweis, daß sie "neit ein christliche, sonder ein heidenische gemein haben", was noch zusätzlich dadurch unterstrichen wird, daß die Obrigkeit mit Rat und Einwilligung Luthers und der Seinen "uns aus haus und hobe, van weib und kinden treiben und mit torn und stock peinlich martiren!" Dennoch seien die Täufer verpflichtet, Gott für sie zu bitten, "ob sei der mal eing [= dermaleinst] wolten nuchtren werden, sich zu bekeren van des teufels strick, darinne sei gefangen liegen etc."[4]

Schnabel reklamiert für seine Haltung, daß sie "nüchtern" sei, wohin Gott Luther und die Reformatoren zurückbringen möge; denn die Gemeinden der

[3]Ebd., S. 170.

[4]Ebd., S. 174 f.

"kindsgeteufen" ist voll von den Lastern, die sie den Täufern unterstellen, so daß die lutherische Seite keine christliche Gemeinde hervorgebracht hat. Dies wird nicht zuletzt am Beispiel der Steuer vorgeführt. Sie sollte eigentlich moderat sein und dem allgemeinen Wohl dienen. Kein Täufer, sondern ein Parteigänger Luthers, der Marburger Professor Eisermann, zeige jedoch, daß die Steuerpolitik der christlichen Obrigkeit schlimmer sei als bei den Heiden. Als "unnüchtern"[5] und gemeinschaftsvernichtend wird die Handhabung der Eigentumsfrage durch den "neuen Papst" und die von ihm hervorgebrachte Obrigkeit eingestuft. Diese herbe Kritik basiert jedoch nicht zuerst auf der Untersuchung Eisermanns; sie ist vielmehr an der Heiligen Schrift orientiert. Mit großer Akribie lesen die Täufer die Schrift und kommen zu Ergebnissen, die ansonsten in der Reformationszeit in der Gefahr standen, unterdrückt zu werden. Gerade das Beispiel der Eigentumsfrage zeigt, daß Schnabel das Eigentum als eine Verpflichtung zum gemeinen Wohl über eine angemessene Steuer und als Verpflichtung zum Wohl des in Not geratenen christlichen Bruders über eine freiwillige Hilfeleistung einstufte.

Der lange Exkurs zu den beiden Problembereichen Obrigkeit und Eigentum hatte den Sinn, die Unhaltbarkeit der Vorwürfe in der allgemeinen Art, wie sie von Kanzler Feige vorgebracht wurden, aufzuzeigen und zu unterstreichen, daß die Täufer durchaus ihre Bibel zu lesen fähig waren. Sie wollten diesem Maßstab und keinem anderen folgen.

3. Wiedertaufe: Verbrechen oder apostolische Taufe?

So bleibt also der von Kanzler Feige gemachte Hauptvorwurf, der ja auch betont zu Eingang genannt ist, nämlich die Verwerfung der Kindertaufe und die Propagierung und Praktizierung der Wiedertaufe. Das war das eigentliche Verbrechen der Schwärmer und Rottengeister. Die von ihnen betriebene "Wieder"taufe zeigte eindeutig an, daß man in der von allen Gliedern der damaligen Gesellschaft empfangenen ersten Taufe, der Säuglingstaufe, die christliche Taufe nicht erkennen konnte. Als Säugling war man nicht nach der Ordnung Christi getauft, sondern nach einer Menschenpflanzung, die in der Heiligen Schrift nicht enthalten und weder von Christus noch den Aposteln gelehrt oder praktiziert wurde. Die Säuglingstaufe war weder eine christliche noch eine apostolische Einrichtung. Daher war die nach der Schrift vorgenommene Taufe der Gläubigen auch keine "Wieder"taufe, sondern die rechte, in der Schrift gebotene, apostolische Taufform. Mit dem Schritt zur Gläubigentaufe trennte man sich von der bestehenden Kirche und dem corpus christianum "auf eine Weise, die

[5] D.h. eigentlich "schwärmerisch"; Schnabel dreht auch hier den Spieß um.

das Gefühl der Zeitgenossen für Norm und Konvention nicht empfindlicher hätte
verletzen können".[6]

Aber die Täufer wollten nicht am fremden Joch mit den Ungläubigen ziehen,
sondern sich absondern und dem einfältigen Wort Christi nachfolgen. Was aber
ist dieses "einfältige" Wort der ewigen Weisheit Gottes? "Dan der befelch vam
tauf stehet also: *Wer da glauben wirt und getufet wirt etc. So komt nu der glaube
aus dem gehoere der predige (das predigen durch das wort gottes)* etc. Solch
gehör ist je bei den kindern nicht, dan sei wussen weder guts noch boeses Deu 1
[v.39] auch ist der anfang christlicher leer und lebens und buss der toten und
bösen werk, so wussen noch erkennen die kinder kein böses, vil weniger haben sei
es getan."[7] Es gibt eine bestimmte Abfolge, die von der Schrift vorgegeben ist:
Zuerst kommt das Predigen des Wortes Gottes. Daraus folgt der Glaube; denn der
Glaube setzt das gepredigte Wort Gottes voraus. Solches aber kann bei Säuglingen
nicht geschehen, weil sie nicht hören können und weil sie auch inhaltlich mit dem
Gehörten nichts anfangen könnten. Vorausgesetzt ist doch, daß es bei der Predigt
des Evangeliums um eine Darlegung geht, die mit "Gut" und "Böse" zu tun hat,
was aber Säuglinge nicht unterscheiden können, und die mit Buße und Abstehen
von bösen Werken zu tun hat, was wiederum auf Kinder nicht zutrifft.

Interessanterweise setzt Schnabel bei der positiven Beschreibung dessen, was die
Taufe ist, bei der Reinigung an. Dies sei den Juden damals weder bei der
Johannestaufe noch bei der von Christus befohlenen Taufe als seltsam, fremd oder
wunderlich vorgekommen, weil das Judentum viele rituelle Waschungen gekannt
habe. Diese vielfältigen Waschungen seien aber nun alle in der einen Taufe
vereint, so wie auch alle Opfer in dem einen Opfer Jesu Christi gebündelt seien.
Deshalb kann Paulus sagen: *"es ist ein got, ein glaub, ein tauf"*, und weiter erklärt
Schnabel: "Diser tauf, der einich ist, heischet oder *ist ein bad der widergeburt*
Titum 3, [v.5], die uns behelt und uns selig macht, und *ein bund eines guten
gewissens ist mit got durch die aufersteung Jesu Christi* 1. Pet 3 [v.21] *ein
abweschung und vergebung der sunden* Act 2 [v.38]; 22 [v.16] Item er ist ein
begrebnus mit Christo, Ro 6 [v.4]; Co 2 [v.12], in seinen tod, das der gestorbene
mensch sich damit ader dadurch begraben lasse und absunderen van der
gemeinschaft der lebendigen in diser welt. Item, er ist ein inleibung in den leib
Jesu Christi, das ist in die gemeinschaft der heiligen, das der geteufte mit denen
allein ein leib ist. Er ist ein ingank in die wustenei oder in den forhof des dinsts

---

[6]Hans-Jürgen Goertz, Die Täufer. Geschichte und Deutung, München 1980, S. 77.

[7]Wie Anm. 1, S. 168 aus der "Verantwortung und Widerlegung" von Jörg (oder Georg)
Schnabel.

gottes 1 Co 10. Item der tauf ist ein anzeiung Jesu Christi, das der geteufte hinfort in Christo inhergange, seine unschult und fasstapfen nochfolge, der sunde lust und ungerechtigkeit gestorben und glaissen sich halte, Ro 6 [v.2]. Er ist ein reinigung der sunden durch das wort, ja durch des worts kraft.

Aus dem allen, ir allerliebsten, ir dan leichtlich sehend die planzung, brauch, ordenung und handelung Jesu Christi und seines geists im anfenklichen wolstand der heiligen kirchen uber solchen tauf, wilchen, so wir einfeltig sollen nachfolgen, seiner stim gehorchen und als treue schaflein van den frembden flehen, Joha 10 [v.25,27], und des wusten greuls, Ma 24 [v.15], an heiliger statt sollen warnemen und [von] dannen weichen ader machen mit schneller eil und keins unreins anruren wirt, 2 Co 6 [v.19], uns aus dem obgemelten bild genoch gesagt sein zur warnung und entscheidung, dass wir nemenlich an dem frembden joch mit den unglaubigen nit sollen zehen...".[8]

Das "Einfältige", um das es Jörg Schnabel ging, entpuppt sich bei genauem Hinsehen als Präsentation des ganzen Reichtums der neutestamentlichen Anschauung von der Taufe: Taufe ist ein Akt der Reinigung; sie ist das Bad der Wiedergeburt, der Bund eines guten Gewissens mit Gott, Vergebung der Sünden, Begräbnis mit Christus und in den Tod Christi, wodurch der Getaufte sich von der menschlichen Gemeinschaft absondert. Zugleich aber ist die Taufe die Einverleibung in den Leib Christi, so daß die Absonderung von der menschlichen Gemeinschaft nicht in eine Vereinzelung führt, sondern in eine neue Gemeinschaft, nämlich die der Heiligen: Die Getauften bilden den einen Leib. Weil diese neue Gemeinschaft in der Absonderung von der Welt lebt, ist die Taufe zugleich als Eingang in eine Wüste beschrieben, aber auch als Vorhof des wahren Gottesdienstes. Die Taufe ist weiterhin das Überkleidetwerden mit Jesus Christus, so daß der Getaufte in der Nachfolge steht und so der Sünde, der Ungerechtigkeit und dem heuchlerischen Wesen stirbt. Daher faßt Schnabel alles noch einmal dahingehend zusammen, daß die Taufe eine Reinigung durch das Wort, ja durch die Kraft des Wortes ist. Taufe und Wortverkündigung werden ineinander gesehen und bedingen einander.

Dieser ganze Reichtum der Taufe, die wirkt, was sie bezeichnet, knüpft an den anfänglichen Zustand der Kirche an. Die Täuferkirche ist somit apostolische Kirche. Dies erkennt man nicht nur daran, daß sie den Reichtum der Taufe auch tatsächlich entfaltet, sondern auch daran, daß sie als die treuen Schafe Christi den Greuel der Verwüstung an heiliger Stätte flieht. Der Vorwurf heißt mithin, daß die kirchlichen Gegner abgefallen sind, sich aber mit dem Schein der Wahrheit

[8]Ebd., S. 168 f.

umgeben. In Wirklichkeit aber können sie keinen Anspruch auf Apostolizität erheben. An der Taufe merkt man entweder das Ausmaß des Abfalls oder die Bereitschaft, dem einfältigen und dennoch reichen Wort Christi nachzufolgen.

Es ist auch deutlich, daß Schnabel keiner menschlichen Werkgerechtigkeit das Wort redet oder daß er etwa den Glauben des Menschen als eine menschliche Vorbedingung für die Taufe ansehen würde. Mit Bedacht wird alles, was zum Heil des Menschen dient, auf Gottes Wirken in Christus und durch den Heiligen Geist zurückgeführt: "Wie er dan und sein geist angefangen hat an der buss, bekerung der menschen durch verkundigung gottliches gerichts und zorns, demnach dem bekummerten gemut den glauben, erkentnus und genad Jesu Christi hat angezeigt und, so sei dem glaubten und gern gehorsam waren, si im tauf hat angenomen, ingeleibt und abgewaschen und Christo verbonden und mit im begraben und geplanzt zu gleichen der sund -- also sol es uns wolgefallen und sollen uns van herzen gern Christo ebengemess machen zur erfullung aller gerechtigkeit...".[9] Die Wiedertaufe, die für die einen ein Verbrechen darstellte, das nur mit der Todesstrafe geahndet werden konnte, war für die anderen keine zweite, "Wieder"taufe, sondern die wahre, apostolische Taufe, die auch über die wahre, heilige Kirche entscheidet.

4. Martin Bucer und Georg Schnabel

Georg Schnabel gehörte zu den Täufern, die gefangen genommen worden waren und sich auf Geheiß des hessischen Landgrafen Philipp einer Disputation mit dem aus Straßburg herbeigerufenen Martin Bucer stellen mußten. Die Disputation fand vom 30. Oktober bis 3. November 1538 in Marburg statt. Bucer fragt Schnabel, was er meine, wenn er seine kirchlichen Gegner des Mißbrauchs der Taufe beschuldigt. Die Antwort lautet: "Ir misprauchet den tauf, dweil die lere des evangelii ist, das man die mentschen erstlich uberzeuge ires bosen, darnach, das sie in die gemeinschaft der heiligen kirchen ingeleibt werden, wilchs ir underlasset, so ir die kinder teufet."[10] Bucer hatte es sichtlich schwer, sich mit diesen Argumenten auseinanderzusetzen. Er gesteht ein, daß es sich bei der von Schnabel dargestellten Ordnung um eine solche handelt, die für Erwachsene zutrifft: "aber mit den kindern hab es ein ander ordnung." Diese ist vorgebildet im Siegel des Abrahambundes, der Beschneidung. "Nu hab Christus uns heiden, die an in gleuben, solchen bund auch erworben und wil auch got unser kinder got sein

---

[9]Ebd., S. 169.
[10]Ebd., S. 224.

und dasselbig mit dem sacrament der widergeburt, wilche bei uns der tauf ist, wie bei den alten die beschneidung war, in seiner kirchen bezeugt haben."[11]

Bucer muß weit ausholen, um die Säuglingstaufe zu rechtfertigen. Gott mache auch die Kinder selig, denn er sei auch der Kinder Gott und nimmt sie in seinen Gnadenbund auf. Wenn die Alten angenommen sind, trifft dies auch für die Kinder zu. Die Frauen seien auch nicht deshalb vom Abendmahl ausgeschlossen, weil "kein weib darbei gewesen, da es der herre erstlich gehalten hat". Man muß die Art der Schrift ansehen; wer dies tut, "der wirt die kinder nit usschliessen", obwohl "wir sonst auch keinen usgedrugkten bevelh haben: Taufet kinder!"[12] Wenn man die Frauen nicht vom Sakrament des Mahls ausschließt und wenn man den Sonntag feiert, dann darf man auch "die sach mit dem kindertaufen nicht verdamen", nur weil man keinen ausdrücklichen Befehl in der Schrift findet. Die Jünger haben, trotz eines ausdrücklichen Gebots, am Sabbat Ähren gerauft und dennoch nicht gesündigt. Wenn im "Matthei ultimo" [26:18-20] der Befehl gegeben wird, alle Völker zu taufen und sie zu lehren, dann bedeutet dies, daß auch die Kinder beim "Volk" eingeschlossen sind und daß man sie nach der Taufe lehren kann, alles zu halten, was Christus befohlen hat.[13] Auch der von Schnabel gerügte "viele Mißbrauch" bei der Kindertaufe mit den Fragen an die Taufpaten und dem anschließenden "fressen und saufen" findet bei Bucer Gegenargumente: auch Abraham habe nach der Beschneidung seines Sohnes ein Fest gefeiert. Wenn er auch die Exzesse bei den Tauffeiern verdammt, so findet Bucer in der Schrift, daß bei Hochzeiten oder bei Geburt des Johannes "gessen und getrunken" wurde. Was die Gevatterschaft angehe, so ginge sie auf die Zeit Augustins zurück und "kome us der liebe".[14]

5. Zwei Ordnungen der Taufe

An zwei Stellen führt das Protokoll eine Zusammenfassung der Darlegungen Bucers an: "Die ordenung der aposteln ist gewesen, die alten zu taufen der ordenung, wie sie Jorg angezogen, die kinder aber nach ordenung der beschneidung, und sol man die kinder, wan sie erwachsen, treuelich catagisieren und leren halten alles, was der herr bevolhen hat."[15] Die zweite Stelle lautet:

[11]Ebd., S. 224 f.

[12]Ebd., S. 225.

[13]Ebd., S. 226.

[14]Ebd., S. 227.

[15]Ebd., S. 226.

Taufe und Wiedertaufe. Einige historische Ammerkungen zu einem ökumenischen Problem.

"Und ist das unser grund: wie die juden angenomen, also seind wir und unser kinder mit dem sacrament der widergeburt auch angenomen." Für Schnabel waren alle diese Argumente nicht überzeugend: Er wolle bei seiner Meinung bleiben, "und hab die schrift keinen besseren grund dan seinen."[16]

Wenn man sich die Argumente Bucers vor Augen führt, fällt auf, wie künstlich seine Begründungen ausfallen. Der neutestamentliche Reichtum, den Schnabel anführt, wird auf ein zweifelhaftes Analogiedenken reduziert: Wie die Frauen nicht vom Abendmahl ausgeschlossen werden, bloß weil es im Neuen Testament keinen ausdrücklichen Befehl gebe, und wie die Kinder zum Volk Israel durch das Bundeszeichen der Beschneidung gezählt werden, so werden auch die Kinder nicht vom Sakrament der Wiedergeburt ausgeschlossen, sondern dadurch zum Volk Gottes gezählt. Keines der Argumente Bucers ist tatsächlich im Neuen Testament zu finden. Die Methode der Analogie führt ihn dazu, das zu rechtfertigen, was bestehende Gepflogenheit ist. Freilich hat er sich einem Argument der Täufer nicht verschlossen, wenn er zugibt, daß die Kinder, wenn sie erwachsen geworden sind, katechisiert werden müssen. Die Idee eines nachgeholten Taufunterrichts führte als Ergebnis der Marburger Disputation schließlich zur Einführung des Konfirmandenunterrichts und der Konfirmation.[17]

Dennoch bleibt festzuhalten, daß es Bucer war, der die eine christliche Taufe in zwei Taufen aufgeteilt hat. Er gesteht Schnabel zu, daß dessen "Ordnung" die apostolische sei und auf die Erwachsenen zutreffe. Seine dagegen ist die Ordnung der Kinder, die er indes nicht als "apostolisch" erweisen kann. Für Bucer ist offenbar nur zu Beginn der Kirche die apostolische Taufe der Gläubigen durchführbar gewesen. Sobald aber die Alten durch die Taufe der Kirche einverleibt sind, gehören auch die Kinder durch das Sakrament der Wiedergeburt dazu. So will es das Analogiedenken. Heißt bei dem einen die Ordnung: Predigen, Buße, Glaube, Unterweisung, Erwachsenentaufe, Absonderung von der Welt, Gliedschaft am Leib Christi, wobei diese Aufzählung nicht im Sinne einzelner Schritte aufzufassen ist, weil vieles ineinander fließt, so heißt für den anderen die Ordnung: Säuglingstaufe als Wiedergeburt und damit Gliedschaft am Leib Christi, was identisch ist mit Gliedschaft im gesamten, getauften Volk, Unterweisung und Konfirmation als Taufvollendung. Hier sind es klar zu unterscheidende Schritte.

[16]Ebd., S. 227.

[17]Vgl. meinen Aufsatz "Taufe und Mitgliedschaft im Protestantismus. Konfessionskundliche und geschichtliche Anmerkungen", in: Una Sancta 48, 1993, 54-66, hier: 58 f.

Die zwei Ordnungen zeigen jedenfalls deutlich, daß Bucer nicht von einer Taufe ausging, sondern von zwei unterschiedlichen Taufen, wobei es ihm darum ging, die Säuglingstaufe als die in seiner jetzigen geschichtlichen Situation einzige und allein gültige Taufform zu erweisen. Das war er der Tradition und seinem Auftraggeber schuldig. Das Volk war "christlich", und so kann hier wie im alten Israel nur das Bundeszeichen für Kinder zur Anwendung kommen. Mit dem starren Festhalten an dieser einen Taufe provozierte man aber im Zeitalter der Reformation geradezu die "Wieder"taufe. Denn gründlichen Bibellesern mußte über kurz oder lang auffallen, daß das Neue Testament weder die Voraussetzung eines "christlichen" Volkes teilt, noch eine Analogie zur Beschneidung in Form der Säuglingstaufe kennt. Die im Neuen Testament bezeugte "Erwachsenentaufe" unterschied sich in ihrer Begründung und Auswirkung klar von der "Beschneidungs- und Wiedergeburtstaufe der Säuglinge", wie sie Bucer verteidigte.

6. Der Ort der Kinder

Die Frage, wie man mit Kindern verfährt, erhält in den Täuferakten eine durchgehend einleuchtende Antwort. Zunächst wird das Dogma der Erbsünde, das ja in der Tat in den biblischen Schriften schwer nachweisbar ist, zurückgewiesen. Die Säuglinge wissen noch nichts von Sünde. Infolgedessen fällt das in der Tradition seit Augustin gebrauchte Argument weg, die Säuglingstaufe wasche von der Erbsünde ab, so daß sich der Getaufte hinfort nur noch mit den Tatsünden konfrontiert sieht, wozu aber das Sakrament der Buße eingerichtet ist. Als zweites wird argumentiert, daß die Kinder von keiner Sünde wissen, sie willigten denn in die Sünde ein. Das aber setzt ein gewisses Alter voraus. Weiter fügt man an, daß die Säuglinge keinen Glauben haben, weil der Glaube aus dem Gehör folgt. Infolgedessen darf man sie aufgrund der Reihenfolge: zuerst Glaube, dann Taufe, nicht taufen. Die Kinder sollen aber unterrichtet werden: "Item ein kind sei kein Christ", sagt der Vachaer Bürger Hans Werner [oder Wagner] bei seiner Vernehmung im November 1531 und fügt hinzu: "sol aber zu einem gezogen werden etc., und sollen, wie [die] alten, zuvor durch das wort gelart werden; daraus volg glaub, darnach tauf etc."[18] Der Ort der Kinder ist daher nicht in der Gemeinde der Getauften, sondern in der Katechumenenschar vor den Toren der Gemeinde. Die Kinder sind der Verantwortung der Gemeinde anvertraut. Die Kirche hat eine pädagogische Pflicht gegenüber den Kindern, sie in den christlichen Glauben einzuführen.

---

[18]Wie Anm 1, S. 46.

Taufe und Wiedertaufe. Einige historische Ammerkungen zu einem ökumenischen Problem.

Hier wiederum berühren sich die Gedanken der Täufer mit denen Bucers. In beiden Fällen geht es um Katechismusunterricht. Dennoch besteht ein großer Unterschied. Bei Bucer ist der Unterricht ein nachgeholter Taufunterricht: Die Kinder werden auf ihre Taufe angesprochen und im Glauben unterrichtet, der ihnen bei ihrer Taufe fehlte; statt ihrer waren die Paten eingesprungen und hatten stellvertretend für die Kinder geantwortet. Bei den Täufern ist der Unterricht dagegen ein auf die eigenverantwortete Taufe hinführender Unterricht. Die Katechese knüpft nicht an die schon vollzogene Taufe an, sondern führt auf sie zu und beinhaltet so das Risiko, daß die Unterrichteten trotz der pädagogischen Bemühungen die Taufe nicht begehren oder sie ablehnen. Das Wort Gottes läßt sich pädagogisch nicht zwingen, und es bleibt ein Geheimnis, wer vom Wort getroffen wird und wer nicht: *ubi et quando visum est Deo*, sagte es die Confessio Augustana der Lutheraner.

7. Die Wiedertaufe in der Bibel

Die bibelfesten Täufer haben noch etwas ins Spiel gebracht, was offensichtlich die sie verhörende Obrigkeiten und die Pfarrer - oft war beides identisch - in große Verwirrung stürzte. Auf das Argument hin, daß in der Bibel von keiner Wiedertaufe die Rede sei, verwiesen einfache Leute wie die Hausfrau Grete Werner auf Apostelgeschichte 19.[19] Die Apostelgeschichte berichtet, daß Paulus nach Ephesus kommt, dort einige Jünger vorfindet und sie fragt, ob sie den heiligen Geist empfangen hätten. Sie hatten jedoch noch nie gehört, daß es einen heiligen Geist gibt. Paulus fragt sie sichtlich erstaunt, worauf sie denn getauft seien und erhält zur Antwort: auf die Taufe des Johannes. Paulus zeigt die Unzulänglichkeit der Johannestaufe, worauf sich die Jünger auf den Namen des Herrn Jesus taufen ließen.

Die Täufer sahen hier einen Vorfall von Wiedertaufe und verglichen dies mit ihrer eigenen Situation. Dies ist aber theologisch hochbedeutsam. Denn es bedeutet nichts anderes, als daß die traditionelle Säuglingstaufe als eine Taufe des Johannes eingestuft wird. Mit dieser Taufe ist die Gabe des Heiligen Geistes nicht verknüpft. Sie ist auf der Stufe des Gesetzes, nicht aber auf der des Evangeliums. Die Säuglingstaufe kann zur Erkenntnis der Sünde führen, weil sie eine Gesetzespredigt ist. Sie verweist als Vorläufer auf den, der nach Johannes kommt, nämlich Jesus. Die Gläubigentaufe dagegen ist in der Kraft des Wortes Gottes eine Evangeliumspredigt, weil sie von Jesus herkommt und in seinem Namen vollzogen wird. Sie ist keine "Vorläufertaufe", sondern eine Taufe die aus der

---

[19]Ebd., S.47, wo zwar die Bibelstelle falsch angegeben, aber eindeutig Apg 19 gemeint ist.

Erfüllung aller Verheißungen in Christus schöpft. Die Säuglingstaufe ist die Taufe des Gesetzes, während die Gläubigentaufe die Taufe des Evangeliums ist. Darum ist die Wiedertaufe gerechtfertigt, weil nur so eine Person in den Wirkbereich des Heiligen Geistes gelangt.

Mit dem Heiligen Geist ist zugleich die "Besserung des Lebens" verknüpft.[20] Der Schmied Adam Angersbach aus Niederhaun bringt den Zusammenhang zum Ausdruck: "So habe er bis daher wenig guts gesehen, das von der Lutherische pfaffen predigen komme, dan alle ergernus, freiheit, buberei, und sei boser und erger dan underm bapstum; und woe gotes wort, die warheit und der heilig geist rechtschaffen gelert, da breng es frucht, stehen die leut von sunde ab, bessern sich. Darumb konne er nit erkennen, das gotes wort warhaftig durch sie gelert, dan sie, die prediger, selbst furen offentlich ein sundlichs, ergerlichs leben. So sage Christus: *An fruchten soll man sie erkennen die falschen lerer, dan ein schleen dorn brenge kein weindreubel etc.* [Mt 7, v. 16]. Darumb glaub er nit, das sie den heiligen geist haben, dan der heilige geist wank nit wie sie, sei auch nit geizig etc., wie itzt unter den Lutherischen befunden als wol, als underm bapstum gewesen etc. Und woe nun der heilige geist nit warne und leer, do moge auch nit die warheit gelert und erkent werden."[21]

Der Antiklerikalismus, auf den Goertz immer wieder nachdrücklich als Bestandteil des Täufertums hingewiesen hat, ist auch hier erkennbar. Zugleich fällt das Gewicht der Argumentation auf die Ethik. Die Früchte zeigen, wo der Heilige Geist lehrt und wirkt. Die Standhaftigkeit, die der Schmied Angersbach an dem verfolgten Täuferführer Melchior Rinck beobachtet hatte, ist für ihn beredtes Zeugnis, daß dieser in der Wahrheit lehrt, d.h. vom Heiligen Geist geleitet ist. Das kann er bei den lutherischen Pfarrern so wenig erkennen wie bei den katholischen Priestern. Die Attraktivität der "Wieder"taufe und ihre biblische Rechtfertigung nach Apg 19 wurzeln letztlich in dem Gegensatz von Verheißung und Erfüllung: Die Säuglingstaufe ist Johannestaufe und damit keine christliche Taufe; die Gläubigentaufe ist Bekenntnis-, Glaubens-, Wasser- und Geisttaufe in einem.

8. Schlußbetrachtung

Die Diskussion, wie sie aus den hessischen Täuferakten vorgeführt wurde, ist eigenartig modern. Besonders die Darlegungen Georg Schnabels erinnern an die

[20]Vgl. dazu H.-J. Goertz, a.a.O., S. 67 ff.

[21]Wie Anm. 1, S. 43.

vielfältigen Aussagen zur Taufe, mit denen die sog. Lima-Erklärung der Kommission für Glauben und Kirchenverfassung des Ökumenischen Rats der Kirchen von 1982 aufwartete. Der große Reichtum der christologischen, ethischen, ekklesiologischen und eschatologischen Aspekte wird ausgebreitet (vgl. vor allem Nr. 2-10) und dabei auch der Versuch gemacht, zwischen den beiden Taufformen der Säuglings- und Gläubigentaufe zu vermitteln. Dazu gehört etwa, daß beide Initiationsformen in der Kirche als der Gemeinschaft der Glaubenden stattfinden, daß sowohl der Erwachsene als auch der Säugling nach der Taufe im Glauben wachsen müssen, wobei es in einem Fall um die Vertiefung des Glaubens, im anderen um eine Erziehung geht, die auf das Ablegen eines persönlichen Bekenntnisses gerichtet ist, daß beide Taufformen in der Treue Christi gründen und auf die Treue Gottes als dem Grund allen Lebens im Glauben verweisen, daß bei jeder Taufe die ganze Gemeinde ihren Glauben und ihre Verpflichtung zum Dienst neu bekräftigt, daß beide Taufformen sich der Initiative Gottes verdanken und als Antwort des Glaubens innerhalb der Glaubensgemeinschaft aufzufassen sind. Dennoch ist die Frage, ob jede Praxis einer "Wiedertaufe" um der sakramentalen Integrität einer Kirche vermieden werden kann, wie es die Lima-Erklärung will. Wenn Kirchen, die vornehmlich die Säuglingstaufe praktizieren, dies in unterschiedsloser Weise tun und sich ein Großteil der Getauften keinem lebenslangen Prozeß der Vertiefung im Glauben aussetzt, sondern ganz offensichtlich ein a-kirchliches Leben führt, dann sind die alten Fragen der Reformation nach den ethischen Konsequenzen sicher berechtigter als die "sakramentale Integrität" einer Kirche, die dazu verhilft, die christliche Taufe zu billig anzubieten.

Auch die Täuferkirchen müssen sich erneut den Fragen aussetzen, die das Neue Testament in seiner Vielfalt der Taufaussagen an sie stellt und die im ökumenischen Kontext durch die Lima-Konvergenzerklärung aufgeworfen sind. Die Praktizierung der Erwachsenentaufe allein genügt nicht.[22] Sie muß theologisch und praktisch gegründet sein im Heilsgeschehen Gottes für eine Welt voller Haß, Unfrieden, Krieg, Hunger und Katastrophen aller Art und im Zusammenhang mit der ökumenischen Nachbarschaft zu Kirchen mit Säuglingstaufe. Nicht zuletzt ist damit die Frage nach der Taufe als dem einigenden Band der Christenheit gestellt. Diese Frage ist aber damit nicht zu lösen, daß die Kirchen, die fast ausschließlich die Säuglingstaufe praktizieren, unter Umgehung der Täuferkirchen und ihrer berechtigten Anliegen so tun, als sei darin bereits ökumenische Einheit erzielt, wenn man wortreich die Taufe als Band der Einheit feiert.

---

[22]Vgl. aus baptistischer Sicht zuletzt: Thorwald Lorenzen, "Die Glaubenstaufe - ein Erfordernis für die Kirchen", in: Una Sancta 48, 1993, 14-24.

Peter Tesch, einer der in Marburg gefangenen Täufer, der mit Bucer disputierte und für die Kirche "gewonnen" wurde, faßte seine Meinung in einem Absatz zusammen, der auch heute noch nichts an Aktualität eingebüßt hat: "Vam kindertauf aber bekennen wir also, das wir diejenigen wilche kinder teufen ader lassen teufen, nit gedenken zu verdammen, sünderlich die sulches scheinen ze tun mit gudem gewissen als fur recht, deweil sei sich auf die beschnidung des alten testaments und auf die kirch der alten und auf gottes word gedenken zu gründen. Wiewol wir aber bis hieher und auch noch hüde sulches nit wissen mit ausgetruckter worheit für recht zu sprechen als gottes nutzlichste ordenung in der sach, glichwol so achten wir auch, das es dem kind nit schade, sunderlich so es anders zu dem gelehrt wirt getreuwelich, da mans in der tauf hingelobt und verpflicht hat. Ein jeder sehe aber und sei seines sinnes hie gewiss, damit nemants den minschen zu leib heuchele uber sein gewissen. Also gedenken wir auch ze tun und gegen ederman an dem ort gedult ze tragen, wilches wir auch wederum demutlich bitten und begeren van ederman dasselbige auch gegen uns gebrauchen willen, so doch das wir nit des sinnes seind, den missbrauch neben dem kindertauf umer mehr ze loben, sunder alwege lasteren, wilchen missbrauch wir auch nit begeren ze dulten an uns, deweil es nit allein heimlich, sunder offentlichen bescheltens und strafens werd ist, angesehen der misbrauch auch nit heimlich noch unwisslich, sünder offentlich und mit wissen geschicht, wilches auch zwar, deweil man sulches degelich sicht, weiss und lidet, die ganze substanz des kindertaufs nit wenich verdechtig macht."[23]

---

[23]Wie Anm. 1, S. 253.

"Rejoice and Be Glad, for Your Reward is Great in Heaven"

An Attempt at Solving the Structural Problem of Matt 5:11-12[1]

David Hellholm

1. A Proposal of a Series of Ten Makarisms in the Sermon on the Mount

In a close analysis of the beatitudes of the Sermon on the Mount [= SM; Sermon on the Plain = SP][2] it is pertinent to realize that we do not primarily have to do with one or more separate makarisms[3] but rather with a well-structured series of beatitudes,[4] and the relationship between the separate makarisms within that series.[5] This statement is valid even though there is no consensus about the exact structural building of the series.[6]

[1] This contribution to the Festschrift for my first New Testament teacher, Prof. Dr. Günter Wagner, is a small token of gratitude for what I, as a young student, learnt in his lectures on the Sermon on the Mount in the Rüschlikon Summer School in July – August 1959.

[2] See now the overview of both sermons in H. D. Betz 1992b.

[3] Mostly, however, makarisms appear as isolated sentences, see R. F. Collins 1992, 630.

[4] Cf. U. Luz 1985, 199: 'Die Seligpreisungen sind in sich geschlossen und durchkomponiert;' A. Kodjak 1986, 43: 'Because of this emphatic unification of the text, it must be perceived as a whole, as one system.'

[5] Betz 1985, 22: 'Mit dem Phänomen der Makarismenreihe hängt nun ebenfalls das Problem zusammen, wie die einzelnen Makarismen sich zueinander verhalten;' idem 1992a, 98; from a structuralistic point of view, see Kodjak 1986, 41-74; further Hellholm, 'Die Seligpreisungen der Bergpredigt als invertierte Makarismen', forthcoming.

[6] Series of makarisms are to be found above all in Jewish wisdom and apocalyptic literature, e.g. Ps 119:1-3; Sir 14:1f., 20-27; 25:7-10; Tob 13:14-16; 2 Enoch 42:6-14 and 52:1-14; Sib. Or. IV. 24-34. See K. Berger 1984, 190: 'Makarismen werden schon früh in Reihen überliefert, wobei aber in den älteren Texten das 'selig' selbst weniger oft wiederholt wird, als die Reihe Glieder hat, d.h. ein 'selig' steht für mehrere Dinge, die seligzupreisen sind'; one example is the series of nine beatitudes in Sir 25:7-10 introduced by the words: Ἐννέα ὑπονοήματα ἐμακάρισα ἐν καρδίᾳ καὶ τὸ δέκατον ἐρῶ ἐπὶ γλώσσης.

Contrary to most commentators,[7] Hans Dieter Betz has advocated an interpretation to the effect that the series in the Sermon on the Mount in reality encompasses altogether 10 makarisms in 5:3-12.[8] His arguments are primarily of two kinds: (1) The *number symbolism* in Jewish literature, in which the number ten is a frequently occurring principle of order symbolizing perfection; the ninth and tenth beatitudes (vv. 11-12) exhibit structures that deviate from the makarisms in the preceding rounded series of eight. Now, eight as well as seven are also symbols of perfection. For Betz all this amounts to an interpretation whereby the motif of perfection dominates the scene not only of the beatitudes but also of the entire SM.[9] (2) The *structures* of the concluding beatitudes differ considerably from the preceding eight in so far as they formally deviate, each in its own way,[10] from the previous ones, that they directly address the receivers in the 2nd person plural, and that the description of the situation is not expressed in the first line of the beatitude itself but in an expanded ὅταν-clause.[11]

2. Examination of the Proposal

When examining the proposal by Prof. Betz, it is first of all necessary to discuss briefly the symbolic value of the number ten, and then to investigate the structure of the beatitudes in the SM in order to confirm or invalidate a series of ten, which consequently means that his analysis of 5:11-12 will have to undergo a thorough testing.

2.1. The Symbolic Value of a Series of Ten Makarisms

It is, of course, true that *ten* is a number expressing completeness and thus perfection as is particularly true of the 'Ten commandments'[12] as well as of its

---

[7]See, however, below n. 40.

[8]Betz 1985, 22; idem 1992a, 97f.

[9]Betz 1985, 22: 'Die Vollkommenheit aber spielt als Theologoumenon für die Bergpredigt eine entscheidende Rolle [n. 19: vgl. Mt 5,48]'; idem 1992a, 98.

[10]See below § 2.3.

[11]Betz 1985, 23; idem 1992a, 99.

[12]Deut 4:13; 10:4; Exod 20:1-17; Deut 5:6-18.

usage in apocalyptic symbolism.[13] As far as the *number of makarisms* in series of beatitudes is concerned, however, it has not been possible to confirm a number of ten.[14] On the other hand a series of *seven* is found in *2 Enoch* 52:1-14[15] and a series of *nine* in *2 Enoch* 42:6-14 and in Sir 25:7-10.

From this state of affairs one has in connection with series of makarisms to make a distinction between a general numeric symbolism that is a *variable* and which can be utilized only on the level of *parole*, i.e. with regard to each individual series of any kind, and a specific numeric symbolism that is a *constant* in connection with a number of series of makarisms and which can be utilized on the level of *langue*. As far as I can see the only numeric symbolism that can be at work in series of Old Testament, Jewish, Graeco-Roman and Christian makarisms in general and in the series introducing the SM/SP in particular is the *parole*-conditioned, not however, the *langue*-determined, since the number of makarisms varies from text to text,[16] sometimes even within one and the same text corpus.[17] Thus, only a general numeric symbolism may play a role in the interpretation, not however, a symbolism specifically bound to a series of makarisms.

Under no circumstances should one allow the numeric symbolism to determine the analysis of the text. In those cases where it coincides with the general numeric symbolism it can constitute an important indication for a correct interpretation, when not, it has to yield to the text analysis as such.[18] Consequently, since the number ten in no way seems to be a constitutive element for any series of makarisms, I would suggest that the symbolic value of a proposed ten-series by all

[13]Dan 7:7, 20, 24; Rev 12:3, 13:1 17:3, 7, 12, 16. Cf. also Matt 25:1; Luke 19:12ff.

[14]So far Betz has not provided any example of a series of ten either. Cf. also S. T. Lachs 1987, 69: '...there are not ten beatitudes (the number of the original beatitudes is in doubt, but ten is certainly out of the question).' The *Gos. Thom.* has altogether ten beatitudes, but seven of them are isolated; thus even the *Gos.Thom.* does not secure a *series* of ten, see W. D. Davies/C. D. Allison 1988, 441.

[15]This series consists of altogether 7 makarisms and 7 curses in alternation.

[16]Cf. only the different number of makarisms in the SM and in the SP.

[17]Cf. the references to *2 Enoch* given above.

[18]Contra Betz as well as G. Strecker 1984, 30f., who makes an attempt at constructing a series of 3x3 beatitudes.

likelihood is very general and rather limited, esp. if the numeric structure is inconspicuous or even dubious.

2.2. The Structure of the Beatitudes in the Sermon on the Mount

Already upon a swift examination of the series of beatitudes it becomes obvious that the first part (vv. 3-10) constitutes a primary entity over against the second part (vv. 11-12):[19] the *apodosis* of the first and of the eighth makarism is made up of an identical causal clause: ὅτι αὐτῶν ἐστιν ἡ βασιλεία τῶν οὐρανῶν. In this way an *inclusio* is created with the first and the eighth makarisms as brackets.[20]

Another structural element of equal importance is made up of the adverbial qualifiers τὴν δικαιοσύνην and ἕνεκεν δικαιοσύνης respectively in the *protasis* of the fourth and of the eighth makarism. In this way the first four makarisms are bound together with the last four in the series of eight that are formulated in the third person plural.[21] The eighth occupies structurally in so far a key position as it contains both structural elements: 'Kingdom of Heaven' and 'Righteousness'. Already at the surface-level of the text-structure this is an indication that 'Kingdom of Heaven'[22] and 'Righteousness'[23] constitute central concepts first of

---

[19]The same is true of the fourth beatitude in Luke's SP, see S. Schultz 1972, 454f.; P. Hoffmann 1972, 73, 114, 147f.; D. Catchpole 1993, 91; D. Zeller 1992, 390: 'Die 4. Seligpreisung (Q 6,22f) etwa ist sicher hinzugewachsen ...;' Robinson 1992b, 369; see below nn. 36 and 84.

[20]So also J. C. Fenton 1959, 174ff.; D. J. Dupont 1958, 224; H.-Th. Wrege 1968, 27; N. A. Dahl 1973/82, 69; J. A. Fitzmyer 1981, 631; Betz 1985, 23; idem 1992a, 98; Lachs 1987, 77; J. Gnilka 1988, 115; D. Catchpole 1993, 17; otherwise Kodjak 1986, 70 when he writes: 'The eighth beatitude (5:10) introducing the second section of the Beatitudes ...; elsewhere Kodjak also realizes the inclusive character of the first and the eighth beatitude, see p. 45: '... they (sc. the first and eighth beatitude) frame the central six beatitudes (5:4-9) and separates them from the concluding, ninth one;' and p. 51: '... framing beatitudes (5:3 and 10) ....'

[21]The first four beatitudes constitute an entity of its own (a) in so far as they concern people who are short of something while the last four concern people who assume a certain attitude; (b) in addition the first four are formally kept together by means of π-alliteration.

[22]Betz 1985, 23, 25; idem 1992a, 98, 100.

all in the beatitudes but in addition also in the SM as a whole.[24] In addition, the eighth also paves the way semantically as well as pragmatically for the concluding vv. 11-12 as most of the important concepts both in the *protasis* and in the *apodosis* of vv. 11-12 are already anticipated in the *protasis* and *apodosis* of the eighth in v. 10.[25] Its function as a transitory makarism[26] is nicely summarized by W. Grundmann, when he writes: 'Der Schluß der Seligpreisung der Verfolgten führt auf den Anfang der Seligpreisungen zurück, während sie selbst zugleich zur folgenden Aussage überleitet.'[27] Of significance in view of the pragmatic situation is the usage of various tenses of the key-verb διώκω in vv. 10-12:

[23]Betz 1985, 46-48; idem 1992a, 124-26; Catchpole 1993, 20.

[24]Betz 1985, 83: 'Ein Hauptbegriff der Bergpredigt ist der Begriff 'Herrschaft der Himmel' (ἡ βασιλεία τῶν οὐρανῶν);' ibid. 107: 'Der übergeordnete theologische Begriff in der Bergpredigt ist der von der "Königsherrschaft der Himmel"...;' idem 1992a, 160 and 184; idem 1985, 47 n. 61: 'Der Begriff δικαιοσύνη, ganz im jüdischen Sinne verstanden, liegt der gesamten Bergpredigt zugrunde (Mt 5,6.10.20.45; 6,1.33; vgl. 7,13f.21-23)...;' idem 1992a, 124 n. 61; Luz 1985, 214: 'Δικαιοσύνη meint ein menschliches Verhalten. Nur deswegen, nicht wegen bloßer Sehnsucht nach (göttlicher) Gerechtigkeit, kann man verfolgt werden.'

[25]From a tradition-historical point of view, however, the eighth may be a later creation than the ninth, since the latter is a part of the Q-tradition, as has been suggested by O. H. Steck 1967, 21 n. 2; so also W. Schenk 1987, 196: '5,10 ist eine vorwegnehmende Dubl., wobei auch die Kausalpartikel ἕνεκα von V. 11 dupl. ist ....'

[26]See J. Wellhausen 1904, 15: V. 10 'soll den Übergang zu den beiden folgenden Versen machen;' Dupont 1973, 224: 'A la fois conclusion et introduction, la huitième béatitude fait donc figure de transition.' Cf. also the diachronic question raised by Lachs 1987, 77: 'The connection between v. 10 and vv. 11-12 has been the subject of much discussion and conjecture [with reference in n. 58 to D. R. A. Hare 1967, 118ff., 130ff.]. Is v. 10 a shortened form of vv. 11-12, or are vv. 11-12 an extension of v. 10?'

[27]W. Grundmann 1968, 132; Catchpole 1993, 83: 'Thus at one and the same time it rounds off the collection of short beatitudes and builds a bridge to the long one'. This is a more likely explanation for the occurrence of the eighth makarism than the 'triadic groupings' advocated by Davies/Allison 1988, 459; cf. also the explanation from the context of situation by Steck 1967, 21 n. 2: 'Offenbar bestand konkreter Anlaß, die Verfolgung als Konsequenz der δικαιοσύνη in die Reihe aufzunehmen; vgl. in diesem Zusammenhang das Part. Perf. δεδιωγμένοι, das bei der überlieferungsgeschichtlich späten Bildung von V. 10 kaum aus aramäischem Sprachgebrauch erklärt werden kann ....'

Noticeable is the *perfect* participle passiv δεδιωγμένοι in the eighth makarism (v. 10), which on the one hand 'entails that persecution is a fact of the past and of the present'[28] and on the other in accordance with the gnomic character of the first eight beatitudes 'hebt das in V 11f geschilderte aktuelle Ereignis der Verfolgung ins Allgemeine'.[29] The ninth makarism proper (vv. 11-12b) gives the verb in aorist subjunctive which is dependent upon the temporal conjunction ὅταν:[30] διώξωσιν, indicating a(n) (eventual and/or itinerated) future event,[31] which already has taken place at the time of fulfillment of the affirmation,[32] but not at the time of the pronouncement of the affirmation of felicity, thus constituting a *vaticinium ex eventu*-prophecy[33] 'oriented toward the specific situation of

---

[28]Davies/Allison 1988, 459; Dahl 1973/82, 69; Grundmann 1968, 132.

[29]Luz 1985, 214; ibid. 215. By no means should the perfect tense be characterized as 'ungeschickt', contra E. Klostermann 1927/71, 38; see Davies/Allison 1988, 461; cf. the abridged hybrid version (made up of the first beatitude in Luke 6:20 and the eighth in Matt 5:9) in Pol. *Phil.* 2:3 with the *present* part. passiv: μακάριοι οἱ πτωχοὶ καὶ οἱ διωκόμενοι ἕνεκεν δικαιοσύνης, ὅτι αὐτῶν ἐστιν ἡ βασιλεία τοῦ θεοῦ (sic!).

[30]See F. Blaß/A. Debrunner/F. Rehkopf 1976, § 382.3: 'ὅταν steht in der Regel mit Konj. (klass.), wenn eine Handlung in der Zukunft liegt (Eventualis), oder wenn eine Handlung häufig wiederkehrt (Iterativus), ...;' cf. Th. Zahn 1903, 194: '... denn nicht für den möglichen Fall, daß es geschehen werde (ἐάν), sondern in bezug auf alle Fälle, in welchen dies vorkommen mag (ὅταν), preist Jesus sie selig;' inexplicable H. Schürmann 1969, 336 n. 78 (with regard to the Lukan text): 'ὅταν mit Ind. Futur (sic !), nicht ἐάν, einen möglichen Fall meinend ...;' further F. Bovon 1989, 303 n. 63: ὅταν mit Konjunktiv Aorist in der Bedeutung "wenn es eintrifft, daß" (steht dem hypothetischen ἐάν nahe).'

[31]Blaß/Debrunner/Rehkopf 1976, § 363: 'Der Konjunktiv bezeichnet etwas noch nicht Eingetretenes, hat also futurischen Sinn, so daß der Konj. gelegentlich durch das Futur ersetzt werden kann;' regarding the Lukan version cf. Bovon 1989, 303: 'Der Bezug auf die Gegenwart ist anders als vorher, denn der selige Zustand hängt hier vom Eintreten der Verfolgung ab.'

[32]Cf. W. Bauer/A. Gingrich/F. Danker 1979, 588: 'ὅταν ... 1. ... b. w[ith] the aor. subj., when the action of the subordinate clause precedes that of the main clause ..., ὅταν ὀνειδίσωσιν *when they (have) revile(d)* Mt 5:11.'

persecution of the Christian community.'[34] In the concluding reasoning statement in v. 12c the tense is aor. ind. (ἐδίωξαν), since the grounds are given with reference to a historical parallel, the persecution of the prophets of old.[35]

2.3. The Structural Problem of VV. 11-12

As already mentioned above Prof. Betz, as others before him,[36] has noticed that these verses in many ways differ from the preceding eight beatitudes.[37] According to Betz, v. 11 constitutes a third type of beatitudes in the SM although it is also a *distich* as are the first eight: it is formulated in the 2nd person plural and is, in his view, not furnished with a specification of the addressees; the second line is made up of a ὅταν-clause describing three situations of perceived imminent persecution with reference to the addressees.[38]

V. 12 on the other hand is, according to Betz, a *tristich* but also formulated in the 2nd person plural: it begins with 'Rejoice and be glad', a variation of 'blessed are you'; the second line is a reasoning ὅτι-clause, consisting of a Jewish-dogmatic statement: 'Your reward is great in heaven', and the third line is another

---

[33]R. Bultmann 1964, 115; Strecker 1985, 45; W. Stegemann 1991, 119. The reason for the harassment 'indicates that those here envisaged are 'disciples' and that a time is in sight when Jesus is no longer physically present' as emphasized by J. D. Kingsbury 1988, 107 in connection with his discussion of the function of the five large speeches in Matthew.

[34]Kloppenborg 1987, 173.

[35]See the discussion below ad nn. 72f.

[36]Cf., e.g. Klostermann 1927/71, 34; Grundmann 1968, 119, 133; Dahl 1973/82, 66, 69; regarding Luke 6:20-23, see Schürmann 1969, 335: 'Der vierte Makarismus (bzw. Weheruf) bildet aber mit den ersten drei keine ursprüngliche Einheit;' further see above n. 19 and below n. 84.

[37]Cf. Kodjak 1986, 44: 'The uniformity of the Beatitudes is further evident in the balance between the two parts in the first eight beatitudes, from which the ninth again deviates ... The brevity of the first eight beatitudes is especially noticeable when compared with the ninth ....'

[38]Betz 1985, 23; idem 1992a, 99, where—in contrast to the original edition—ὅταν by mistake is replaced by ὅτι.

reasoning clause, this time introduced by οὕτως γάρ and in support of the second line: 'in the same way they persecuted the prophets before you'.[39]

As a consequence of his analysis of vv. 11-12 Betz arrives at the conclusion that these two verses in fact make up two separate makarisms or to be precise: one makarism and one chairism,[40] the first in v. 11 and the second in v. 12, thus creating *ten* makarisms in the SM, which according to Betz is not accidental but constitutive in view of the perfection motif discussed above.[41]

When investigating the structure of Matt 5:11-12 a text-*internal* analysis in comparison with the first eight makarisms in general and with the singular eighth makarism in particular will be performed, and subsequently a text-*external* comparison with other traditions inside and outside of the New Testament will be executed.

2.3.1. Text-internal Analysis of Matt 5:11-12

As stated above the *first eight* makarisms are all *distiches* made up of a *protasis*-line consisting of the adjective μακάριοι, functioning as a predicate attribute, followed by a substantivized adjective or participial construction, functioning as the subject of the *protasis*, but lacking a copula as predicate, thus being an elliptic

---

[39]Betz 1985, 23: 'Diese Zeile (sc. the ὅτι-clause) besteht aus einem jüdisch-dogmatischen Urteil: 'Euer Lohn ist groß im Himmel'. Dieses Urteil ist dann in der dritten Zeile mit einer Begründung versehen: 'denn in der gleichen Weise haben sie die Propheten, die vor euch lebten, verfolgt;' idem 1992a, 99; cf. already W. Trilling 1964, 81: 'Euer Lohn ist groß, denn auch die Propheten früher wurden (zu Unrecht) verfolgt (und waren doch gerecht und erbten Lohn).'

[40]Term coined by me. See in connection with the Lukan parallel already Steck 1967, 257: 'in Lk 6,22-23b liegt eine Fusion zweier Gattungen vor: ein Makarismus in der einfachen Form einer Verbindung von μακάριος mit einem Zustand oder Verhalten und ein Freudenaufruf mit folgender Begründung;' further with regard to Q 6:22-23, Kloppenborg 1987, 172f.: 'the first three are bipartite, consisting of a beatitude and a ὅτι clause but the fourth has a beatitude and an imperative with a motive clause ....'

[41]Betz 1985, 22; idem 1992a, 97.

construction;[42] this part of the *protasis* functions at the same time as a description of the *preconditioned situation* of those who are called 'blessed'.[43] The condition for their 'blessedness' is either their present situation or the result of a conditional change of situation or attitude, i.e. the conditional utterances regarding the 'blessedness' is either to be interpreted as *performative* or as *prescriptive* statements: 'Blessed are you, *since* you are...' or 'Blessed are you, *if* you change your status/remain in your status....'[44] Thus, depending upon the analysis of the *protasis*, the makarisms may be interpreted either as messages of salvation, i.e words of comfort[45] to people who are in need of comfort in one way or the other, or as ethical encouragements or exhortations to become what they are not or to remain as they are respectively, i.e. demands to conduct their lives in accordance with the subject part of each *protasis* as a condition for the realization of the affirmation given in the *apodosis*-line of each makarism.

The *apodosis*-line in all eight makarisms is made up of a causal clause introduced by the causal conjunction ὅτι; thereby the first and the last are—as we have seen—identical in formulation. In addition it is pertinent to observe that the causal connection in every instance is not with the subject part of the *protases* but throughout with the predicate attribute μακάριοι. Thus the *apodoses* render the reason for the affirmation of felicity, which in turn is the result of the preconditioned situation referred to in the subject part of the *protases*.

---

[42]Cf. Blaß/Debrunner/Rehkopf 1976, § 128,1. As a result of the elliptic construction the natural possibility of expressing *modi* is precluded, a fact that obscures the functional interpretation of the makarisms.

[43]See Betz 1985, 28: 'Das charakteristische Merkmal der ersten Zeile des Makarismus in Mt. 5:3 ist ... die Spezifizierung der Angeredeten;' idem 1992a, 104.

[44]The performative function is to make a *promise* by means of the affirmation, the prescriptive function is primarily not to make a promise but rather an *exhortation* by means of the makarism; secondarily it is, of course, also perfomative; cf. R. F. Collins 1992, 630; Luz 1985, 202-04; R. Guelich 1976.

[45]So Wrege 1968, 25.

The second part of the series (vv. 11-12) exhibits distinctive characteristics:[46] In v. 11 the audience, i.e. the disciples, is addressed directly: μακάριοί ἐστε ...; the change from the 3rd to the 2nd person plural bridges the transition from the introductory series of makarisms[47] to the following section (vv. 13-16): ὑμεῖς ἐστε...,[48] in this way these two sections are text-syntactically bound together, which is particularly important in view of the absence of a direct text-semantic and text-pragmatic connection.[49] The style is consequently also different: instead of a substantivized adjective or participial construction comprising the preconditioned situation of the addressees, we here encounter a temporal ὅταν-clause describing three situations of harassment with direct reference to the addressees;[50] on the other hand no reason for the affirmation of felicity is given, since the usual ὅτι-clause in the first part of the series is missing.

In v. 12 the audience is still addressed directly, this time, though, using a different set of words, viz. two verbs in the imperative modus: χαίρετε καὶ ἀγαλλιᾶσθε.

[46]Cf. Kodjak 1986, 44: '... the ninth beatitude violates almost all aspects of uniformity established in the preceding eight ...'

[47]So correctly Betz 1985, 24: 'Man hat anzunehmen, daß die Einleitung der Bergpredigt durch diese Makarismenreihe beabsichtigt ist'; idem 1992a, 99; Kodjak 1986, 42: 'The nine beatitudes, united into one indivisible text, function in two ways: to introduce the entire sermon poetically or formally and to establish the ideology of the following teaching.'

[48]Cf. Grundmann 1968, 133: 'Die Beibehaltung der Anrede hat aber einen anderen Grund als den der Treue zur Quelle; mit ihr wird übergeleitet zu den Anreden an die Jünger, die vom Sendungscharakter ihres Jüngerseins sprechen, und zwar durchgängig in der zweiten Person (5,13-16);' Dahl 1973/82, 66: 'V. 11f. that has the 2nd person plural holds a unique position and applies v. 10 to the audience (my transl.);' E. Schweizer 1973a, 56: 'Mit der Formulierung in zweiter Person ist schon der Übergang zu V. 13-16 gegeben;' Davies/Allison 1988, 461.

[49]Regarding the text-semantic/pragmatic connection, this is different if one interprets vv. 11-12 as introductions to the following section (vv. 13-16), see, e.g. Schenk 1987, 352f.: 'Durch die dir. Anrede, die Mt bis V. 16 fortsetzt, ist für ihn V. 11 nicht mehr wie in Q eine abschließende Anwendung der voranstehenden Makarismen, sd. hat eine neue Einleitungsfunktion für das Folgende bekommen ...;' ibid. 163f.; D. Patte 1987, 67f. Cf., however, above n. 20.

[50]Cf. Kodjak 1986, 44: 'The ninth beatitude violates the pattern of brevity further in its three references to human circumstances: ....'

However, neither a substantivized adjective or participial construction as in vv. 3-10, nor a temporal ὅταν-clause describing the situation under which the makarism is uttered, as is the case in v. 11, is present; on the other hand the ὅτι-clause, missing in v. 11, brings the motivation and reason for the affirmation of the addressees' confidence: ὅτι ὁ μισϑὸς ὑμῶν πολὺς ἐν τοῖς οὐρανοῖς. Thus, here we encounter a reason for the makarism or—according to Betz analysis—better: the chairism, but instead we miss a description of the situation. The description of the situation leading to the separate chairism can only be inferred from the additional and—as will be shown below—secondary sentence:[51] οὕτως γὰρ ἐδίωξαν τοὺς προφήτας τοὺς πρὸ ὑμῶν (v. 12c). These facts make one suspicious of the correctness of Prof. Betz's division of vv. 11-12 into two makarisms.

If in a synopsis (see Table 1) the eighth makarism in v. 10 is put opposite the concluding one(s) in vv. 11-12, it becomes, in my opinion, likely that these two verses do not contain two makarisms but rather constitute one single but expanded beatitude with an intercalated line of interpretation,[52] recapitulating the affirmation in the *protasis*, and functioning as a 'rejoinder':[53] χαίρετε καὶ ἀγαλλιᾶσϑε; the immediate pragmatic reason for the 'rejoinder' is, of course, the length of the ὅταν-clause.

If this interpretation is correct, the *protasis* is in fact furnished with a specification of the addressees, only this is done by means of a ὅταν-clause describing three possible situations of vexation including persecution with direct reference to the addressees and giving the *reason for the harassment* (ἕνεκεν ἐμοῦ);[54] once the

---

[51]For the secondary character of v. 12c, see below § 2.3.2.1.

[52]So Luz 1985, 215: 'V 12 nimmt μακάριοι interpretierend auf: Freude und Jubel soll in der Gemeinde über das Leiden herrschen.'

[53]So S. J. Patterson 1993, 51; see also below n. 56.

[54]Cf. *mutatis mutandis* Davies/Allison 1988, 459 regarding ἕνεκεν δικαιοσύνης: 'ἕνεκεν most naturally implies that "righteousness" is the occasion or cause of persecution ...;' L. Goppelt 1978, 305 n. 28. This reason for the harassment 'indicates that those here envisaged are 'disciples' and that a time is in sight when Jesus is no longer physically present' as is correctly pointed out by Kingsbury 1988, 107.

audience was directly addressed, the change of style was necessitated.[55] At the same time the *reason for the affirmation* of felicity is also given, since the usual ὅτι-clause is provided, only in this makarism after the recapitulation of the line of interpretation,[56] which, as a 'rejoinder', obtains the function of an αὔξησις or *amplificatio*[57] at the very end of the series of makarisms[58] by means of what I consider to be a *hendiadyoin*: χαίρετε καὶ ἀγαλλιᾶσθε.[59] Also in another sense this last makarism constitutes an amplification: The first eight beatitudes are gnomic in character, while the last is addressed to the disciples in view of the possibility of an impending harassment.[60] Even the description of harassment may take on an amplifying form by means of an *incrementum*:[61] reviling,

---

[55]With regard to the parallel in Luke 6:22-23, cf. Bovon 1989, 297.

[56]Cf. Kodjak 1986, 44: 'The ninth beatitude contains an additional restatement of the anaphora 'Blessed are ...' at the very beginning of the second verse (5:12), and only after this second statement of bliss, 'Rejoice and be glad ...,' does the right part (= the *apodosis* –DH) appear: 'for your reward is great in heaven.'" This is possible since, as in connection with μακάριος, also in connection with χαίρειν, the reason for joy can easily be given by ὅτι, see Bauer/Gingrich/Danker 1979, 873; regarding the Lukan text, see Bovon 1989, 304: 'V 23b [i.e. ἰδοὺ γάρ –DH] entspricht den ὅτι-Sätzen der anderen Seligpreisungen'.

[57]Cf. H. Lausberg 1976, 36 [§ 75]: 'Die Amplifikatio der *verba singula* (...) geschieht: ... durch parteiisch amplifizierende Synonymenwahl ....'

[58]Cf. Bovon 1989, 298 regarding Luke 6:22-23: 'Diese Seligpreisung steht an letzter Stelle, weil man nach einer bekannten Kompositionsregel in einer Logiensammlung mit Hilfe eines längeren Satzes einen guten Abschluß zu finden sucht;' ibid. 305: 'Die formale Breite erklärt sich aus der semitischen Rhetorik: Mit einem längeren Satz wird ein Abschluß ausgezeichnet;' further D. Daube 1956, 196-201, esp. 201: 'The form of the last beatitude is quite in order;' Wrege 1968, 20.

[59]Cf. Tob 13:13; *Par. Jer.* 6:20, but also 1 Pet 4:13; Rev 19:7; further *T. Levi* 18:5,14; see Dahl 1973/82, 69: 'The call to joy develops what is contained in "blessed"' (my transl.); R. Bultmann 1933, 19.

[60]Cf. Dahl 1973/82, 69; Kodjak 1986, 44, 46; Davies/Allison 1988, 461.

[61]See Lausberg 1976, 37 [§ 77]: 'Das *incrementum* besteht in der von unten graduell aufsteigenden sprachlichen Bezeichnung des zu amplifizierenden Gegenstandes. Die Skala kann gebildet werden: ... 4) durch sukzessive Aufzählung verschlimmernder (steigender) Umstände ....'

persecution and malediction;[62] this interpretation requires, of course, that ψευδόμενοι is a later (matthean?!) addition, when the original meaning was no longer understood. This formulation constitutes the more detailed description of the *preconditioned situation*, and notably so in the last makarism.

As in the eighth beatitude, so also in the ninth one has to distinguish between the reason given for the vexation in form of a prepositional attribute (ἕνεκεν ...) and the reason for the affirmation of the addressees' confidence given in form of a ὅτι-clause. Thus, a further argument for vv. 11-12 as one single makarism can be formulated as follows: While the phrases 'because of righteousness' (v. 10a) and 'because of me' (v. 11) do not motivate the disciples to realize the affirmation of felicity (v. 11a and 12a) nor to endure the harassment,[63] the statements of the *apodoses*: 'for theirs is the Kingdom of Heaven' (v. 10b) and 'for your reward is great in Heaven'(v.12b) do indeed in both instances give the reason for the affirmation; without the ὅτι-clause of the *apodosis*, the affirmation in v. 11 has no justification[64] and since all others (including Betz's tenth [v. 12]) do have, the interpretation given above is in my opinion preferable.

The last line is another reasoning clause, this time, however, introduced by οὕτως γάρ: 'for in the same way they persecuted the prophets before you', and—according to Betz—in support of the preceding ὅτι-clause: 'for your reward is great in heaven'. His understanding of this makarism is summarized in the following statement: 'Man muß das Argument sozusagen von hinten lesen. Das

---

[62]So Dahl 1973/82, 69: 'Does 'utter all kinds of evil against you' aim at accusations or curses? The last option gives the best climax and comes closest to the parallel in Luke' (my transl.); Schenk 1987, 164: 'Von der mt Wortfüllung her meint Mt 5,11 nicht allgemein 'üble Nachrede', sd. von vornherein 'Verteufelung';' ibid. 196; Bovon 1989, 304: 'Das letzte Verb bleibt unklar: Matthäus spricht von Schimpfworten, Lukas davon, daß die Feinde den Namen der Christen verfluchen. Das könnte sich aus zwei verschiedenen Übersetzungen erklären ... Matthäus denkt an magische Verfluchung, Lukas an ebenso gefährliche Verleumdung ....' The different word-order in D h k is certainly secondary. Cf. also the similar but differently conceived phenomenon in the Lukan version, see Schürmann 1969, 332.

[63]So Betz 1992a, 233.

[64]There are indeed such makarisms, see the examples below in § 2.3.2.2.

historische Urteil V. 12c führt zum dogmatischen Urteil in V. 12b, und beides zusammen bildet die Basis für den Makarismus V. 12a.'[65]

When Betz states that the ὅτι-clause in v. 12b is a 'Jewish-dogmatic statement'[66] this is only a paradigmatic and formal assertion but does not tell us anything about its syntagmatic function as a semantic and pragmatic justification for the affirmation of felicity indicated above. When he elsewhere states that v. 12c motivates the disciples 'to endure the harassment'[67] he is certainly correct, but this motivation does not—as he suggests—support the preceding ὅτι-clause,[68] i.e. the *apodosis*, but rather functions as a 'comment'[69] on or better: in support of the entire ninth makarism,[70] in particular its *protasis*;[71] in fact v. 12c presupposes

---

[65]Betz 1985, 23; idem 1992a, 99; cf. also Davies/Allison 1988, 463.

[66]Ibid.

[67]Betz 1992a, 233; so also Steck 1967, 259 n. 2: 'Dann wäre der Beziehungspunkt für γάρ zwischen V. 22b und c zu ergänzen (die mit γάρ begründete Aussage bleibt oft unausgesprochen, s. W. Bauer WB, Sp. 301 [= Bauer/Gingrich/Danker 1979, 152, s.v. 1.e. –DH]), also etwa: 'Verzagt in diesem Geschick nicht!'.' See further the argumentation given below in § 2.3.2.1 in connection with the text-external analysis of *Ioh. Ev. Apocr. Arab.* XXXII.3.

[68]See also with regard to the Lukan text Steck 1967, 258 n. 4: 'Die häufige Deutung 1 [sc. 'V. 23c begründet V. 23b' – ibid. n. 3] muß m.E. völlig ausscheiden; das eigentlich begründende Moment des Prophetenlohnes muß erst eingetragen werden ...;' cf. also Kloppenborg 1987, 173: 'Steck observes that v. 23c fits poorly with the logic of vv. 22-23b. It does not seem to undergird v. 23b (ὁ μισθὸς ὑμῶν πολὺς ἐν τῷ οὐρανῷ), which already provides an adequate motive clause for v. 23a;' cf. Luz 1985, 215: 'Inwiefern die Verfolgung der alttestamentlichen Propheten die Verheißung des himmlischen Lohns begründet, bleibt unklar.'

[69]Kodjak 1986, 44.

[70]Contra Steck 1967, 258f., who argues exclusively from inter-textual parallels, in which 'die auch dem gewaltsamen Geschick des Frommen geltende Heilszusage in der Tradition vom Leiden des Gerechten, der sie entstammt, nirgends begründet wird, sondern als autoritativer Zuspruch ergeht' (ibid. n. 4), and thus primarily paradigmatically; instead it is in my opinion essential to follow the argumentative character of this reasoning clause, which presupposes a syntagmatic analysis.

that vv. 11-12b constitute one single makarism without itself being a part of that makarism, since ἐδίωξαν takes up διώξωσιν in v. 11:[72] 'As persecuted the disciples stand in the tradition of the persecution of the prophets of old.'[73]

Before we turn to the text-*external* analysis, our text-*internal synchronic* investigation shall be substantiated by means of a brief text-*internal diachronic* remark, which will be further developed in the following section. Several scholars have argued that v. 12c is a secondary addition to the ninth beatitude (vv. 11-12b).[74] It is, of course, true that v. 12c only in a restricted sense fits with the logic of vv. 11-12b and does not really support the *apodosis* in v. 12b; only secondarily can it be said to justify the *protasis* of the ninth makarism. If v. 12a-b were a separate makarism/chairism, and if in addition v. 12c was added *after* the compilation of the chairism, then this chairism, both its *protasis* and its *apodosis*, would originally be without an information of a preconditioned situation,[75] which, as far as I can see, is singular i our literature.[76] Thus, it is preferable—as we have done—to take the chairism-line to be an interpretative 'rejoinder' with an amplifying function; in this way the ὅταν-clause of the *protasis* in v. 11 contributes the information of the preconditioned situation. This is—in my

---

[71] This interpretation comes close to Steck's 'Deutung 3', which he on paradigmatic grounds also rejects (1967, 258 n. 3); the reason for Steck's inability to recognize the existing connection in the extant text between v. 11 and v. 12c is his interpretation of vv. 11 and 12a-b as belonging to two different genres, and thus not constituting one single makarism, see the quotation above n. 40.

[72] Cf. Schenk 1987, 196: '5,12(+Q) [διώκω] parallelisiert es metonymisch für alle 3 Prädikate von V. 11 wiederum mit dem Prophetenschicksal ....'

[73] As Betz himself (1992a, 233) formulates the connection between vv. 11-12b and v. 12c. Cf. also Kodjak 1986, 47: 'Thus, the historical past blends with the future, and both lead to the kingdom of heaven, which is apparent also in the present;' further Patte 1987, 69: 'First, the evaluation of a *present* situation is correct only when it is done both in terms of the eschatological *future* (what will be in heaven, after the judgment) and in terms of a *past* sacred history and Scripture.'

[74] See below § 2.3.2.1.

[75] See below § 2.3.2.3.

[76] See below, ibid.

judgment—a good exampel of how a *diachronic* analysis can help us arrive at a correct *synchronic* interpretation of a difficult pericope.

2.3.2. A Text-external Analysis of Matt 5:11-12 (with its Parallels)

The forms of this beatitude/(these beatitudes) are multifarious and complicated as Table 2 below will show. The tradition-history is equally complicated, and this is also true of the tradition of literary sources, in which this beatitude/(these beatitudes) has/(have) been transmitted.[77]

The two versions of the makarism found in the Q-material of the synoptic Gospels (Matt 5:11-12//Luke 6:22-23) have parallels in the *Gos. Thom.* Logion 68 and 69, in *Clemens Alexandrinus Stromata* IV. 41.1-3 and in *Iohannis Evangelium Apocryphum Arabice* XXXII. 4.[78] A synopsis of these texts is provided in Table 2.

2.3.2.1. Matt 5:11-12b//Luke 6:22-23b in Relation to Matt 5:12c//Luke 6:23c

The external evidence speaks in favor of the internal analysis, substantiating the secondary character of v. 12c in our pericope. This second motivation in the SM has, as the synopsis reveals, its counter-part in the SP (Luke 6:23c), but it is as secondary there as in Matt.[79] In view of the trajectory of the Q-material this causes a rethinking of the traditio-historical development of the synoptic materials that were incorporated into our extant Gospels. The presence of the 'comment' in

[77]Regrettably these problems cannot be dealt with adequately within the scope of this essay.

[78]See the facsimile edition by G. Galbiati, *Iohannis Evangelium Apocryphum Arabice*, Milano 1957. The first transl. into a modern language is the one by O. Löfgren into Swedish 1967. I am most grateful to my long-time friend and colleague, Dr. Jan Hjärpe, Professor of Islamic Studies at the University of Lund, for help in philological matters concerning the Arabic text offered in a letter from 19 May 1993.

[79]See Steck 1967, 258f.; S. Schulz 1972, 456f. n. 404; K. Koch 1974, 54; Kloppenborg 1987, 173; A. Jacobson 1992, 100f. Otherwise Catchpole 1993, 91: '... within Q 6:23 there is evident competition and rivalry between two statements introduced by "for", that is, "for behold your reward is great in heaven" (Q 6:23b) and "for so their fathers did to the prophets" (Q 6:23c). Of these two it is the *former* while appears to be *secondary* (italic mine). In his reconstruction of the approximate content of the fourth beatitude in Q on p. 94 Catchpole, however, includes Q 6:23b as originally belonging to the makarism.

both Matt 5:12c and Luke 6:23c shows that it was a part of an early Q-tradition or even pre-Q-tradition. The most likely interpretation is that of Hans Dieter Betz, when he concludes that 'The SM and the SP were formulated first independently of Q as separate collections of sayings. At a later stage of Q's development they were joined to Q (SM to $Q^{Matt.}$; SP to Q^{Luke}).[80] If Betz, furthermore, is right in claiming that there is no place within the SM, where one can 'recognize sufficient reasons for assuming the interfering hand of the Gospel writer Matthew' to have been at work,[81] then Matthew cannot be responsible for the differences between Matt 5:11-12 and Luke 6:22-23 and consequently the secondary v. 12c//v. 23c must have been added at a later stage in the tradition of the sermons.[82] These differences must then be accounted for at a stage prior to the two sermons' incorporation into each of the two Gospels and in addition allow for a development from the original 'series of makarisms' (seven or eight in the SM and three in the SP), via the addition of the 'beatitude of the suffering of the righteous'[83] (i.e. the ninth in the SM [Matt 5:11-12b] and the fourth in the SP [Luke 6:22-23b])[84] to the 'deuteronomistic interpretation of the persecution of the

[80]Betz 1992a, 267; see further ibid. 249, 266-69 and 272: 'Moreover, I take it that there were two versions of Q: $Q^{Matt.}$ and Q^{Luke}. When they were included in the Gospels of Matthew and Luke, they were at an advanced stage of development and contained one of the sermons, the SM in $Q^{Matt.}$ and SP in Q^{Luke};' Cf. already J. M. Robinson 1971, 88 n. 47: 'Die Geschlossenheit der Sammlung legt nahe, daß die Bergpredigt und die Feldrede auf eine besondere mündliche oder schriftliche Sammlung zurückgehen und nicht auf verstreutes Material, das erst in Q zusammengestellt wurde;' idem 1992a, 186: 'Thus the disengaging of sapiential collections behind Q arrives at a position somewhat analogous to, though quite independent of, Hans Dieter Betz's claim that the Sermon on the Mount goes back behind Matthew to about 50 CE, that is prior to Q;' H. Koester 1990, 162-171.

[81]Betz 1992a, 272.

[82]See below n. 95. The extent to which Luke made alterations to the text of the SP cannot be discussed on this occasion. The differences can simply be due to separate traditions incorporated into the different versions of Q used by Matt and Luke respectively.

[83]Steck 1967, 258: 'Lk 6:22-23b erweist sich somit nach Gattung, Aussageführung und Formulierung als der Tradition vom Leiden des Gerechten zugehörig und hierin als ein völlig geschlossenes, keiner Ergänzung bedürftiges Ganzes;' Schulz 1972, 455f.; Jacobson 1992, 100f.

[84]See, e.g. Jacobson 1992, 99: 'Also generally accepted is the view that Luke 6:22-23//Matt 5:11-12 are later additions to the original beatitudes because they differ in form and content;' cf. above nn. 19 and 36.

prophets' in both sermons [Matt 5:12c and Luke 6:23c].[85] Jacobson summarizes the development as far as Q 6:22-23 is concerned pertinently, when he writes: 'If a shift in the understanding of the beatitudes was noticeable with the addition of Q 6:22-23b, another shift thus becomes apparent with the addition of Q 6:23c. The persecution mentioned in Q 6:22-23b is now no longer related simply to the situation of confession; it is put in the context of the persecution of the prophets.'[86] This rapid development must have taken place within a short period of time as Helmut Koester has pointed out: '... the entire development of Q, from the first collection of sayings of Jesus and their assembly into sapiential discourses to the apocalyptic redaction and, finally, the pre-Matthean redaction, must be dated within the first three decades after the death of Jesus.'[87] It must furthermore have taken place on two parallel tracks: the SM and the SP excluding a reconstruction first of all of one original sermon[88] and possibly also of one original Q-version, a 'Grundbestand Q'.[89] Thus, from a comparison between the SM and the SP it becomes clear that on the one hand neither Matt nor Luke can be responsible for the addition of the deuteronomistic interpretation and on the other that it in fact is not an original part of the 'beatitude of the suffering of the righteous' in either version.

The two different versions of the last beatitude in Matt and Luke can consequently be accounted for primarily on tradition-historical grounds and not on redaction-

[85]Cf., e.g. Steck 1967, 259f.; Kloppenborg 1987, 173: 'Verse 23c is a further expansion of vv. 22-23b, introducing the deuteronomistic motif of Israel's persecution of the prophets;' Jacobson 1992, 100f.: '... and the most distinctive editorial activity in 6:22-23 is the addition of the deuteronomistic idea of the persecution of the prophets.'

[86]Jacobson 1992, 101.

[87]Koester 1990, 170.

[88]See the pertinent deliberation by Betz 1992a, 249: 'If one assumes several stages of redaction in Q, the question is whether there ever was an earlier Q sermon or whether the SM and the SP were added at later stages of Q, the SM in $Q^{Matt.}$ and the SP in Q^{Luke}.' On the basis of Betz's analyses of the SM and the SP it is my proposal that in future investigations of the *Q-material* one should proceed methodologically in such a way that, when reconstructing the various strata of Q, the SM and the SP deliberately are left aside; only *after* having completed the stratification of the remaining Q-material should that result be compared with the SM and the SP respectively.

[89]Otherwise, e.g. Steck 1967, 27 and many others.

critical ones. Furthermore, it is not by accident that διώκω is missing in Luke 6:23c since it is also missing in the *protasis* of Luke 6:22; in fact—as was stated above—in the SM v. 12c presupposes that vv. 11-12b constitute one single makarism without itself being a part of that makarism, since ἐδίωξαν takes up διώξωσιν in v. 11; this is the link combining what Steck called the 'two parallel statements'.[90]

In addition to the Lukan parallel there are a few other very early Christian parallels to the persecution beatitude: *Gos. Thom.* 68 (see Table 2) and *Gos. Thom.* 69a (μακάριοι οἱ δεδιωγμένοι ἐν τῇ καρδίᾳ αὐτῶν ἐκεῖνοί εἰσιν οἱ γνόντες τὸν πατέρα ἐπ᾽ ἀληθείας[91])[92] and 1 Pet 4:14 (εἰ ὀνειδίζεσθε ἐν ὀνόματι Χριστοῦ, μακάριοι, ὅτι τὸ τῆς δόξης καὶ τὸ τοῦ θεοῦ πνεῦμα ἐφ᾽ ὑμᾶς ἀναπαύεται).[93] Characteristically enough none of these contains a phrase corresponding to Matt 5:12c//Luke 6:23c.[94] Noteworthy is also the absence of the

[90]Steck 1967, 259.

[91]Greek transl. from H. Greeven 1981, 30.

[92]Concerning the independence of the tradition in the *Gos. Thom.* from the canonical Gospels, see H. Koester quoted in: J. M. Robinson 1986, 145 and now Koester 1989, 42: 'A comparison with the Synoptic parallels (...) demonstrates that the forms of the sayings in the *GTh* are either more original than they or developed from forms which are more original'; idem 1990, 85: 'Those who assume that the Gospel of Thomas is dependent upon the Gospels of the New Testament have not been able to show that there is any concrete and consistent pattern of Thomas's dependence upon one particular gospels' version of the tradition of the sayings;' further P. Vielhauer 1975, 627f.; J. H. Sieber 1990, 64-73. Otherwise, e.g. W. Schrage 1964.

[93]See Steck 1967, 26 n. 4: 'Die letzte Seligpreisung hat demnach in einer älteren als der bei Mt und Lk vorliegenden Gestalt auf 1 Petr eingewirkt;' cf. further Goppelt 1978, 304-07.

[94]See spec. Steck 1967, 258-59; Schulz 1972, 456f. n. 404; Kloppenborg 1987, 173; Jacobson 1992, 100f.: 'This fragment i Q 6:23c seems to be directed, further, to the leaders of the community, the abused, rejected preachers who stand in the succession of the prophets. It is noteworthy that, though there are parallels to Q 6:22 in the Gospel of Thomas (saying 68) and 1 Pet 4:14, neither mentions the persecution of prophets. If, as is probable, GThom 68 and 1 Pet 4:14 independently attest the saying in Q 6:22, then Steck's

'deuteronomistic interpretation of the persecution of the prophets' in all of the different versions of the 'persecution beatitude' found in *Clem. Alex. Strom.* IV. 41.1-2a (μακάριοι οἱ δεδιωγμένοι ἕνεκεν δικαιοσύνης, ὅτι αὐτοὶ υἱοὶ θεοῦ κληθήσονται), IV. 41.2b (μακάριοι οἱ δεδιωγμένοι ὑπὲρ τῆς δικαιοσύνης, ὅτι αὐτοὶ ἔσονται τέλειοι), IV. 41.3a and 3b (see Table 2). These circumstances speak in favor of a relatively late addition of vv. 12c and 23c respectively to the preceding 'persecution beatitude',[95] which confirms my judgment from the text-*internal* analysis that vv. 11-12b must constitute one makarism,[96] since, in order for v. 12//v. 23 (i.e. Betz's tenth makarism) to function properly, the description of the situation leading to the separate chairism can only be inferred from the additional and—as the parallels just mentioned have confirmed—secondary sentence: οὕτως γὰρ ἐδίωξαν τοὺς προφήτας τοὺς πρὸ ὑμῶν (v. 12c//v. 23c). If, however, vv. 11-12b//vv. 22-23b make up one makarism, the description of the preconditioned situation is entailed in the ὅταν-clause of the *protasis* of the makarism in v. 11//v. 22, and each of the extended last makarisms could once have functioned perfectly well without the later addition.

Another, most interesting parallel is to be found in the *Arabic Apocryphal Gospel of John*, which probably obtained its final shape between 1000 and 1150 CE, but may go back even a few centuries more.[97] The text contains a whole series of makarisms, one of which is a close parallel to our text, viz. XXXII. 4 (see Table 2). This 'persecution makarism' seems to be some kind of mixture of the Matthean and the Lukan versions[98] including the intercalated line of interpretation as 'rejoinder' but without the additional 'deuteronomistic interpretation' (v. 12c//23c)

analysis is confirmed and the most distinctive editorial activity on Q 6:22-23 is the addition of the deuteronomistic idea of the persecution of the prophets'.

[95]This assertion causes further reflections with regard to the tradition-history of the Q-material and the SM/SP: if the SM and the SP were incorporated into Q[Matt] and Q[Luke] respectively (see above nn. 80 and 88), then v. 12c/v. 23c must either have been a part of SM//SP before they were incorporated into Q, or these vv. were added to the 'persecution beatitudes' independently of each other after they were already a part of each sermon. Since the latter solution seems rather unlikely, the tradition-history of these vv. seems to support Betz's assertion of a late incorporation of SM//SP into Q[Matt] and Q[Luke] respectively.

[96]See the discussion above § 2.3.1.

[97]See Löfgren 1967, XXIII.

[98]See the discussion of the makarism itself below *passim*.

indicating that the makarism was understood as one single beatitude. However, in v. 3, which immediately precedes the makarism in v. 4, we encounter a reference to the persecution of the prophets attesting that the author of *Ioh. Ev. Apocr. Arab.* knew of a tradition in which the 'two parallel statements'[99] were closely connected. Of equal importance is the fact that the motivation given in v. 3 is not 'reward' but, as explicitly mentioned, 'patience' (see text in Table 2), thus first of all confirming Steck's scepticism over against the connection between 'reward' in v. 12b and 'suffering of the prophets' in v. 12c[100] and then also confirming his interpretation of the point of relationship as an exhortation 'not to give up hope in this fatal moment'.[101] This formulation of v. 3 is a further—even though late—indication that Matt 5:12c//Luke 6:23c should not be taken to justify vv. 12b//23b.

2.3.2.2. Matt 5:12b and Parr.: The Apodosis-line

In view of the proposed ninth makarism in Matt 5:11 it is also essential to confirm the existance of beatitudes without a causal clause justifying the affirmation, i.e. makarisms consisting of only a 'propositional statement'.[102] In the Old Testament we find such makarisms in, e.g. Prov 3:13 (LXX: μακάροις ἄνθρωπος ὃς εὗρεν σοφίαν καὶ θνητὸς ὃς εἶδεν φρόνησιν); Eccl 10:17 (LXX: μακαρία σύ, γῆ, ἧς ὁ βασιλεύς σου υἱὸς ἐλευθέρων καὶ οἱ ἄρχοντές σου πρὸς καιρὸν φάγονται ἐν δυνάμει καὶ οὐκ αἰσχυνθήσονται); in early Jewish texts examples of such makarisms are *1 Enoch* 81:4 (*Blessed, is the man who dies righteous and upright, against whom no record of oppression has been written, and who received no judgment on that day*); 82:4 (*Blessed are the righteous ones*); Dan 12:12 (LXX: μακάριος ὁ ἐμμένων καὶ συνάξει εἰς ἡμέρας χιλίας τριακοσίας τριάκοντα πέντε); 4 Ezra 7:45 (*Beati qui praesentes et observantes quae a te constitutae sunt*); Sir 25:8 (μακάριος ὁ συνοικῶν γυναικὶ συνετῇ); such examples can also

---

[99]Steck 1967, 259.

[100]Steck 1967, 258 n. 4: '... soweit ich sehe, fehlt die Anwendung des Lohnmotivs auf die Propheten als solche im Spätjudentum überhaupt.' Reward for suffering, however, is well-known, even if it is given as thesis and not as statement of reason, ibid. 254ff.; 257 n. 7.

[101]Steck 1967, 259 n. 2 (my transl.).

[102]R. F. Collins 1992, 629 with examples: Ps. 2:12; 34:9; 41:2; 84:13; Job 5:17; Dan 12:12; see already E. Schweizer 1973b, 125.

be found in Greek literature, e.g. *Euripides, Ba.* 73ff. (ὧ μάκαρ, ὅστις εὐδαίμων τελετὰς θεῶν εἰδὼς βιοτὰν ἁγιστεύει καὶ θιασεύεται ψυχὰν)[103], in early Christian texts, e.g. 1 Pet 3:14 (ἀλλ᾽ εἰ καὶ πάσχοιτε διὰ δικαιοσύνην, μακάριοι);[104] Rev 22:7 (μακάροις ὁ τηρῶν τοὺς λόγους τῆς προφητείας τοῦ βιβλίου τούτου); *Gos. Thom.* 19 (*Blessed is he who came into being before he came into being*), and our pericope is in fact transmitted without its *apodosis* in *Clem. Alex. Strom.* IV. 41.3b (see text above Table 2). Furthermore, in a *series* of makarisms, beatitudes with and without an *apososis*-line can be mixed as is the case in *2 Enoch* 42:6ff., where the 2nd and the 6th makarism out of altogether nine is provided with a causal clause justifying the affirmation.[105] Due to these examples it cannot be ruled out completely that v. 11//v. 22 could constitute a separate makarism consisting only of the *protasis*-line.

Most makarisms, however, are made up of a *protasis*- and an *apodosis*-line. The *apodosis* can thereby be formulated in different ways: (a) either by means of an *asyndetic* period as in early Jewish texts like *Pss. Sol.* 4:23 (Μακάριοι οἱ φοβούμενοι τὸν κύριον ἐν ἀκακίᾳ αὐτῶν· ὁ κύριος ῥύσεται αὐτοὺς ἀπὸ ἀνθρώπων δολίων καὶ ἁμαρτωλῶν καὶ ῥύσεται ἡμᾶς ἀπὸ παντὸς σκανδάλου παρανόμου); in Greek texts like *Hom. Hymn to Demeter* 480-82 (ὄλβιος ὃς τάδ᾽ ὄπωπεν ἐπιχθονίων ἀνθρώπων· ὃς δ᾽ ἀτελὴς ἱερῶν, ὅς τ᾽ ἄμμορος, οὔ ποθ᾽ ὁμοίων αἶσαν ἔχει φθίμενός περ ὑπὸ ζόφῳ εὐρώεντι), and *Pindar, Fr.* 137[106] (ὄλβιος ὅστις ἰδὼν κεῖν᾽ εἶσ᾽ ὑπὸ χθόν· οἶδε μὲν βίου τελευτάν, οἶδεν δὲ διόσδοτον ἀρχάν); in early Christian texts like Rev 20:6 (μακάριος καὶ ἅγιος ὁ ἔχων μέρος ἐν τῇ ἀναστάσει τῇ πρώτῃ ἐπὶ τούτων ὁ δεύτερος θάνατος οὐκ ἔχει ἐξουσίαν, ...), or (b) by means of various *syndetic* constructions: (1) the causal conjunction ὅτι and its equivalents in Jewish texts, e.g. in: *1 Enoch* 58:2 (*Blessed are you righteous and elect ones, for glorious is*

---

[103]Cf. further *Eurip., Fr.* 910 N.2; *Aristoph., Frogs* 1482; *Vergil, Georgica II*, 490-92.

[104]As ἀλλά indicates, the motivation is to be found in the context; it is not to be found in an *apodosis*-line of the makarism itself. Regarding the optative, see the discussions in Goppelt 1978, 234 and N. Brox 1979, 158.

[105]Cf. also *Clem. Alex. Strom.* IV. 41.1-3.

[106]# 137 = B. Snell/H. Maehler 1975; # 121 = C. M. Bowra 1935.

your portion); *2 Enoch* 42:11 (*Happy is he who sows right seed*, for *he shall harvest it sevenfold*); in early Christian texts like: *Gos. Thom.* 49 (*Blessed are the solitary and elect*, for [ΧЄ] *you will find the kingdom [For* [ΧЄ] *you are from it, and to it you will return]*); *Clem. Alex. Strom.* IV. 41.1-2a, 2b, 3a (see text above § 2.3.2.1.); Jas 1:12 (μακάριος ἀνὴρ ὃς ὑπομένει πειρασμόν, ὅτι δόκιμος γενόμενος λήμψεται τὸν στέφανον τῆς ζωῆς ὃν ἐπηγγείλατο τοῖς ἀγαπῶσιν αὐτόν.);[107] 1 Pet 4:14 (see text above § 2.3.2.1.); Rev. 22:14 (μακάριοι οἱ πλύνοντες τὰς στολὰς αὐτῶν, ἵνα ἔσται ἡ ἐξουσία αὐτῶν ἐπὶ τὸ ξύλον τῆς ζωῆς καὶ τοῖς πυλῶσιν εἰσέλθωσιν εἰς τὴν πόλιν);[108] *Gos. Thom.* 69b (*Blessed are the hungry*, for [ϢΙΝⲀ] *the belly of him wo desires will be filled*);[109] furthermore, in a *series* of makarisms like Matt 5:3-10; Luke 6:20-21; (2) the causal conjunction γάρ and its equivalents in, e.g. 4 Macc 18:9 (... μακάριος μὲν ἐκεῖνος, τὸν γὰρ τῆς εὐτεκνίας βίον ἐπιζήσας ...); Luke 6:23b (see Table 2); Rev 1:3 (μακάριος ὁ ἀναγισώσκων καὶ οἱ ἀκούοντες τοὺς λόγους τῆς προφητείας καὶ τηροῦντες τὰ ἐν αὐτῇ γεγραμμένα, ὁ γὰρ καιρὸς ἐγγύς); (3) the connective conjunction καί and its equivalents in e.g. *1 Enoch* 103:5-6 (μακάριοι ἁμαρτωλοὶ πάσας τὰς ἡμέρας αὐτῶν, ὅσας εἴδοσαν ἐν τῇ ζωῇ αὐτῶν καὶ ἐνδόξως ἀπεθάνοσαν, καὶ κρίσις οὐκ ἐγενήθη ἐν τῇ ζωῇ αὐτῶν); *2 Enoch* 42:7 (*Happy is he who carries out righteous judgment, not for the sake of payment, but for justice, not expecting anything whatever as a result; and the result will be that judgment without favoritism will follow for him*); *Gos.*

---

[107]Regarding the connections between SM and James, see W. Popkes 1986,156-76; as to *Gos. Thom.* and James, see Patterson 1992,178-88.

[108]Blaß/Debrunner/Rehkopf 1976, § 456.2: 'Kausales ἵνα wird von den antiken Grammatikern vertreten, so erklärt Apollonius Dyscolus (ΠP) ἵνα φιλολογήσω παρεγενήθη Τρύφων als identisch mit διότι ἐφιλολόγησα (De synt. ΙΙΙ 28) ... Für das NT kommt allenfalls Apk 22,14 in Frage, wenn μακάριοι ... ἵνα = μακάριοι ... ὅτι von Mt 5,3ff ist ....'

[109]Thus the transl. by Th. O. Lambdin 1989, 81 which can be justified by reference to the Greek use of a causal ἵνα, for which see the previous note; cf. also Greeven's transl. into Greek (1981, 30): μακάριοι οἱ πεινῶντες, ὅτι χορτασθήσεται (ἵνα -ασθῇ?) ἡ κοιλία τοῦ θέλοντος. As a consequence the arguments from dissimilarity between Thomas and the synoptic versions—put forward by Patterson 1992, 52—should not be overestimated;

Thom. 18 (*Blessed is he who will take his place in the beginning*, and [ⲁ Ⲩ Ⲱ] *he will know the end and will not experience death*); *Gos. Thom.* 68 (see text above in Table 2; [ⲁ Ⲩ Ⲱ]); *Ioh. Ev. Apocr. Arab.* XXXII. 4 ('... and *know* ...;'[110] see text above in Table 2).

In spite of the possible construction of makarisms without an *apodosis*-line it seems to me safer to assume that all makarisms in the series in the SM as well as in the SP did contain an *apodosis*-line, and this so in light of the fact firstly that a majority (esp. in series of beatitudes in the synoptic gospels) contains such *apodoses* (of different syntactical constructions), and secondly that, with two exceptions (1 Pet 3:14; *Clem. Alex. Strom.* IV. 41.3b), all 'persecution makarisms' (Matt 5:11//Luke 6:22 not counted!) are provided with an *apodosis*-line. If this is the most likely conclusion even after the examination of the text-*external* parallels, then Matt 5:11-12b//Luke 6:22-23b by all likelihood constitutes only one, although considerably expanded, beatitude.

2.3.2.3. Matt 5:11 and Parr.: The ὅταν-clause as Description of Situation

The description of the situation of those who are called 'blessed' is usually entailed in that part of the *protasis* which consists of a substantivized adjective (e.g. οἱ πτωχοὶ [τῷ πνεύματι] ἁμαρτωλοί [Matt 5:3//Luke 6:20; *1 Enoch* 103:5]), a participial construction (e.g. οἱ πενθοῦντες, οἱ δεδιωγμένοι, ὁ συνοικῶν γυναικὶ συνετῇ [Matt 5:4; 5:10 and *Clem. Alex. Strom.* IV. 41.1-3a; Sir 25:8]) or a relative-clause (e.g. μακάριος ἄνθρωπος, ὃς εὗρεν σοφίαν; ὄλβιος ὃς ταδ᾽ ὄπωπεν ἐπιχθονίων ἀνθρώπων [Prov 3:13; *Hom. Hymn to Demeter* 480]).[111] It can, however, also be given in form of a subordinate circumstantial sentence as is the case in Matt 5:11; Luke 6:22; *Gos. Thom.* 68; *Clem. Alex. Strom.* IV. 41.3b

---

[110]Only the single *wa-* 'and' is written, without any causative or explanative meaning; (there is such an 'and', namely *fa-*)' [Hjärpe]. The examples with καί and its equivalents came very close to the asyndetic formulations.

[111]Cf. R. F. Collins 1992, 629: 'In form, the macarisms begin with the adjective *makarios*, followed by a relative or personal pronoun introducing a clause which describes a particular conduct or quality which prompted the praise of the person who is pronounced blessed.'

(see text above Table 2) and *Ioh. Ev. Apocr. Arab.* XXXII. 4 (see text above Table 2).[112]

As far as I have been able to discern, there are no or very few makarisms without a description of the preconditioned situation for the affirmation, be it performative or prescriptive. All of the examples given by Steck contain informations about the situational status of the addressees, either in the *protases* (Isa 14:29; 25:9f.; 54:1) or the *apodoses* (Isa 49:13) of the chairisms themselves, or in their immediate narrative contexts (Isa 61:10ff.; 66:10; Joel 2:21-23; Zech 2:14; 9:9).[113] This is also true of all the makarisms in the New Testament as well as of all nine found in the *Gos. Thom.* The same is also true of those cases where we have to do with chairisms rather than proper makarisms: in the *protasis* (Tob 13:13), in the *apodosis* (*Par. Jer.* 6:20; Rev 19:7), and in the narrative context (*T. Levi* 18:5, 14; 1 Pet 4:13). As far as those makarisms/chairisms are concerned, in which the immediate contexts provide the situational status, one has to make a distinction on the one hand between makarisms that are singular or part of a series of makarisms, and on the other makarisms that are incorporated into a narrative or argumentative framework, where the context can provide the situational background for the affirmation.

In for our deliberations relevant literature there are only those five texts just referred to, in which the description of the situation is given in form of a subordinate circumstantial sentence introduced by the temporal conjunction ὅταν,[114] all of which are formulated in the second person plural,[115] and all of

---

[112]Bovon 1989, 303: 'Der Bezug auf die Gegenwart ist anders als vorher, denn der selige Zustand hängt hier vom Eintreten der Verfolgung ab ... Sobald man auf die verschiedenen Fälle eingeht, tauchen immer neue Möglichkeiten auf: drei Verben plus ein Partizip bei Matthäus, vier Verben, die in zwei Wellen ... auftauchen, bei Lukas.'

[113]Steck 1967, 257 n. 3.

[114]See above n. 30. *Gos. Thom.* 68: ϨΟΤΑ[Ν]. *Ioh. Ev. Apocr. Arab.* XXXII. 4 has the temporal conj. *idhâ*, meaning 'whenever' [Hjärpe].

[115]The closest *formal* parallels in the NT are John 13:17 (εἰ ταῦτα οἴδατε, μακάριοι ἐστε ἐὰν ποιῆτε αὐτά; cf. Bultmann 1968, 363 n. 5: '... ἐάν = wenn in der Zukunft; Blaß/Debrunner/Rehkopf 1976, § 372 n. 1) and 1 Cor 7:40 (μακαριωτέρα δέ ἐστιν ἐὰν οὕτως μείνῃ ...) with the conditional ἐάν instead of the temporal ὅταν; regarding that difference, see above n. 30.

which are 'persecution beatitudes'.[116] Of these texts the synoptic examples constitute long climactic endings to series of makarisms as does the one in *Clem. Alex. Strom.* IV. 41.3b although differently, since it is the last and longest in a series of four 'persecution beatitudes' called κεφάλαιον for the 'disregard of death' (41.1), while the beatitude in *Gos. Thom.* 68 is the first in the only series of three in that Gospel; in the *Arab. Apocr. Gos. Joh.* this pericope is the introductory makarism in a series of 22 (17 of which are addressed to Simon!) in ch. XXXII: 'Jesus' Sermon on the Mount of Olives'. The detailed description is most developed in the texts that are a part of or reproduce the synoptic tradition, viz. first of all Matt 5:11 with its climatic structure described above,[117] but also the Lukan version (6:22) shows a similar but differently conceived climactic structure with one short ὅταν-clause and a tripartite second one;[118] the version in *Clem. Alex.*, which evidently is dependent upon the Lukan text, instead brings three ὅταν-clauses, leaving out the weakest harassment: ὀνειδίσωσιν and thus arriving at the climactic amplification: ὅταν μισήσωσιν, ὅταν ἀφορίσωσιν, ὅταν ἐκβάλωσιν τὸ ὄνομα ὑμῶν ὡς πονηρόν. Also the *Arab. Apocr. Gosp. Joh.* has a tripartite series of harassments following—like in Matthew—upon only one temporal conjunction: 'whenever', but the order is different from all the others: *persecute you, revile you, and say lies against you*; the version that deviates the most, however, is *Gos. Thom.* 68 since it has only two lines: ὅταν μισήσωσιν ὑμᾶς καὶ διώξωσιν ὑμας, and yet being climactic in structure.[119]

With the exception of Luke 6:22 and its reproduction in *Clem. Alex. Strom.* IV. 41.3b all versions, including the three preceding beatitudes in *Clem. Alex. Strom.* 41 contain the verb διώκω, indicating that the original notion behind these

---

[116]Cf. the last woe in the series of woes in the SP (Luke 6:26), in which the preconditoned situation is also expressed with help of a ὅταν-clause, see I. Broer 1986, 21f. Regarding the parallelism between the last makarism and the last woe in Luke 6, see also Stegemann 1991, 123f. and Catchpole 1993, 91-94.

[117]See above ad n. 62.

[118]Schürmann 1969, 332: 'Die beiden ὅταν-Sätze bilden einen klimaktischen Parallelismus, sich von einer Widrigkeit im 1. Glied zu der dreifachen des 2. Gliedes steigernd.'

[119]See below ad n. 125.

makarisms is indeed reflecting a real situation of vexation,[120] which in the tradition has been actualized and reinterpreted to suit new situations of harassment and persecution at different times.[121] In all these texts the preconditioned situation is expanded and thus thematized in a way foreign to the gnomic macarisms in their immediate contexts.

2.3.2.4. Matt 5:12a and Parr.: The 'Rejoinder'-clause as Amplification

The interpretative 'rejoinder'-clause is found in three of the five 'persecution beatitudes' containing a description of the situation in form of a ὅταν-clause. The easiest exception to account for is *Clem. Alex. Strom.* IV. 41.3b, since this version also misses the *apodosis*-line of 'reward', which does not fit this section on the 'sum of all virtue' (41.1), and consequently the 'rejoinder'-line becomes superfluous. The diverging formulation in *Gos. Thom.* 68 is the only one without a 'rejoinder' but with an *apodosis*; that no 'rejoinder' was felt necessary is, of course, due to the very short ὅταν-clause consisting of only two statements of harassments as we have noticed already; this is, in addition, also—with the exception of *Clem. Alex. Strom.* IV. 41.3a[122]—the only *apodosis* repeating the verb διώκω/ⲆⲒⲰⲔⲈ from the *protasis*; in this way the *protasis* and the *apodosis* are kept as close together as possible. Noteworthy is also the fact that the *protasis* deviates from the synoptic versions in such a way that ⲘⲈⳲⲦⲈ

---

[120]Cf. Koester 1990, 137: '... But because *Gos. Thom.* 68 and 69a also blesses the disciples when they are persecuted, the persecuted were most likely also mentioned in the blessings of Q;' M. Fieger 1991, 198: 'Log 68 des ThEv setzt wohl konkrete Verfolgungssituationen voraus. In Log 69a dagegen it von einer übertragenen Verfolgung 'im Herzen' die Rede.' Regarding the absence of διώκω in Luke 6:22f., see esp. Stegemann 1991, 114-20.

[121]This can be seen not only in the various formulations in the *protasis*-part but also in the different and sometimes difficult interpretation of the *apodosis*-parts, cf., e.g. *Gos. Thom.* 68b (hereto, e.g. E. Haenchen 1962, 19-29; Schrage 1964, 148; K. Toyoshima 1983, 235-41; Fieger 1991, 198; Patterson 1992, 136 n. 69) with *Clem. Alex. Strom.* IV. 41.3a (see ibid.). It can also be indicated by lexical choices as in *Ioh. Ev. Apocr. Arab.* XXXII. 4, where the word for 'people' in the *protasis* is *'al-umam*, which can mean '[religious] communities' (i.e. 'people' in the sense of 'those who belong to a certain religion' ... Accordingly, it cannot be *'anthropoi'* [Hjärpe].

[122]Here the *protasis*-clause is made up not of a ὅταν-clause but of a participial construction similar to the eighth makarism in Matt 5:10.

corresponds to Luke's μισέω and ⲆⲒⲰⲔⲈ to Matthew's διώκω, while the only verb shared by Matt and Luke ὀνειδίζω is missing; in addition one should notice that the reference to the reason for the harassment (ἕνεκεν δικαιοσύνης, ἕνεκεν ἐμοῦ,[123] ἕνεκα τοῦ υἱοῦ τοῦ ἀνθρώπου,[124] *for my name's sake*) is mentioned in all of the 'persecution beatitudes' except for the one in the *Gos. Thom.* 68 and 69: These facts 'may serve to confirm what our tradition-historical analysis has already indicated: not only is Thomas unaware of the synoptic texts themselves, it seems to be independent of their source, Q, as well', says Patterson in his analysis of Logion 68.[125]

The conclusion to be drawn from this comparative analysis with regard to the structure of the 'persecution beatitudes' is that whenever the *protasis*-line is long and complicated and is followed by an *apodosis*-line, an interpretative line in form of a 'rejoinder' functioning as a climactic amplification is provided. In those cases when either the *apodosis*-line is missing or the *protasis* is short and simple the 'rejoinder'-line is left out or not inserted.

The way in which the chairism-line functions as an amplifying 'rejoinder' is pretty much the same in all three texts in spite of the stylistic variations and differences in wording: (a) in Matthew the connection is asyndetic and the implicit reference in the *hendiadyoin* is primarily anaphoric to the time of persecution mentioned in the *protasis* v. 11,[126] not kataphoric to the eschatological end-time of reception

---

[123]Cf. Betz 1992a, 233; Kingsbury 1988, 107.

[124]Cf. Robinson 1992b, 369: 'The fourth Beatitude (Q 6,22-23) was secondarily appended … to refer specifically to those whose hardship is not due to fate, but due to support of Jesus;' idem 1992a, 189; Jacobson 1992a, 101; idem 1992b, 417; see also P. Hoffmann 1972, 96, 146 f.; idem 1992, *passim*.

[125]See Patterson 1992, 52.

[126]Steck 1967, 24: 'In der Mt-Fassung entspricht dem Zuspruch, daß die Angeredeten in ihrem Geschick (jetzt) selig zu preisen sind …;' Wrege 1968, 23: 'Dort (sc. Matt. 5:12) bezieht sich nämlich das Jubeln auf die Gegenwart der Verfolgten, die wegen des himmlischen Lohns schon jetzt seliggepriesen werden;' Luz 1985, 215: 'Freude und Jubel soll in der Gemeinde über das Leiden herrschen;' contra, e.g. Schulz 1972, 453 n. 380; Strecker 1985, 48.

of the reward in the *apodosis*;[127] the present imperative (χαίρετε καὶ ἀγαλλιᾶσθε)[128] corresponds to more general and less specific, durative or iterative situations described in the ὅταν-clause.[129] (b) In Luke the connection is likewise asyndetic but the reference in the 'rejoinder'-line is here explicitly formulated by means of a temporal indication:[130] ἐν ἐκείνῃ τῇ ἡμέρᾳ also referring back to the time of persecution mentioned in the *protasis*-section in v. 22,[131] but being more specific than the one in SM,[132] not to the eschatological

[127]Steck, ibid.: '... der Aufruf, sich im Blick auf den künftigen Lohn (jetzt schon) zu freuen und zu jubeln;' Dahl 1973/82, 69: 'The meaning is not directly that they shall rejoice because of the reward, but that they shall rejoice because of the persecutions in assurance of the reward' (my transl.); Luz, ibid.: 'Der Grund zur Freude liegt in der Umkehr der Verhältnisse, die die Zukunft bringen wird ....'

[128]Cf. Blaß/Debrunner/Rehkopf 1976, § 335.

[129]See Luz 1985, 214 who—presupposing Matthean redaction—points out that the formulation in Matt 5:11 can be used in very many different situations: 'Statt ἀφορίζω und ἐκβάλλω τὸ ὄνομα hat er das viel allgemeinere διώκω und λέγω πονηρόν. Mit Schmähung und Verfolgung muß die Gemeinde grundsätzlich rechnen.'

[130]Cf. the similar anaphoric reference in Tob. 13:13: τότε χάρηθι καὶ ἀγαλλίασαι (χάρηθι following La, G I).

[131]Schürmann 1969, 334: 'Solch Verfolgungsschicksal, besonders wohl das Ereignis des Synagogenausschlusses, sollen die Jünger zum Anlaß nehmen, noch am gleichen Tag ein Freudenfest mit Tanz zu veranstalten;' Koch 1974, 54: 'Der Evangelist (sc. Lukas) setzt hinzu 'an jenem Tag' (vgl. den Einsatz 'jetzt' V. 12), um die Entstehung der Freude im Augenblick der Bedrängnis hervorzuheben;' Fitzmyer 1981, 635: 'The time of persecution will become a time of joy and festive dancing;' Betz 1992a, 228: 'The faithful are filled with joy now (6:23) because they can expect Paradise and adoption as 'sons of God' (6:20b-23, 35);' Bovon 1989, 304: 'Da ich ἐν ἐκείνῃ τῇ ἡμέρᾳ nicht eschatologisch als letzte Zeit, sondern geschichtlich als Zeit der Verfolgung verstehe (nur so wird ἰδοὺ γάρ in V 23b verständlich), sehe ich im Wechsel vom präsentischen zum aoristischen Imperativ nur eine stilistische Verbesserung;' Stegemann 1991, 119: 'An jenem Tage, an dem die vorausgesagten Ereignisse eintreffen werden - der Gerichtstag ist natürlich nicht gemeint -, sollen sich die Betroffenen freuen und "hüpfen".'

[132]Cf. Kloppenborg 1987, 173: '... 6:22-23 is oriented toward the specific situation of persecution of the Christian community;' Jacobson 1992, 100f.; Stegemann pleads for an interpretation of Luke 6:22f. as not being a 'persecution beatitude' but rather a beatitude, in

end-time[133] or the *parousia* of Christ[134] or 'ein menschlicher Gerichtstag'[135] in the *apodosis*-part; the aor. imperative (χάρητε ... καὶ σκιρτήσατε)[136] corresponds to the more specified time of persecution indicated partly by the harassments mentioned in the ὅταν-clause, partly by the dating in the 'rejoinder'.[137] (c) In *Ioh. Ev. Apocr. Arab.* XXXII. 4 the connection is established by means of an explanative 'and' (*fa-*)[138] and as in Luke the 'rejoinder'-line is here also explicitly formulated by means of the temporal indication: '*in that moment*' also referring back to the time of persecution mentioned in the preceding

which 'es ... um die Erfahrung der Ablehnung (geht), die durch verbale Verunglimpfungen und die Störung bzw. Aufhebung von Gemeinschaftsbeziehungen näherhin umschrieben wird' (1991, 123f.).

[133]Contra H. E. Tödt 1963, 115: 'Vers 23 zeigt, daß es sich dabei um die Verheißung von Freude und Lohn an *jenem Tage* im Himmel handelt;' Wrege 1968, 23; Jeremias 1980, 139: 'Die Wendung ἐκείνη ἡ ἡμέρα (ἡ ἡμερα ἐκείνη) im Singular mit eschatologischer Bedeutung, ein im Urchristentum gängiger Sprachgebrauch ...;' Steck 1967, 24: 'bei Lk ... ist die Seligpreisung solchen Geschicks abgesetzt von der Freude am eschatologischen Tag;' Steck's (as well as Jeremias's) argumentation that ἐκείνα ἡ ἡμέρα ein stehender Ausdruck traditionell eschatologischen Gehalts ist ... und so auch in synoptischer Tradition verwendet wird' (Steck, ibid. n. 4) is not convincing, since it is exclusively paradigmatic and not syntagmatic in character; see Schürmann 1965, 334 n. 62: 'Die ἡμέρα ἐκείνη muß nicht immer ... den Gerichtstag meinen.'

[134]Thus Betz 1992a, 226: 'the term 'on that day' (6:23: ἐν ἐκείνη τῇ ἡμέρᾳ) presumably refers to the day of the Parousia of the Son of Man (6:22);' see however, ibid. 228 quoted above n. 131.

[135]So Grundmann 1981, 144.

[136]See above n. 128; The formulation in the SP is not a *hendiadyoin* as in the SM; see further Klostermann 1929/75, 79: 'χάρητε ... καὶ σκιρτήσατε (luk., Steigerung gegen Mt 12 ἀγαλλιᾶσθε?).'

[137]Klostermann 1929/75, 79: 'Imperative des Aorists (gegen Mt) wegen des wohl sekundären ἐν ἐκείνη τῇ ἡμέρᾳ;' Schürmann 1969, 334 n. 62: 'Die Zeitbestimmung bewirkt (diff Mt) den bestimmteren Imp. Aor.;' H. Conzelmann 1973, 359 n. 84: 'Der Aor entspricht dem pointierenden Zusatz ἐν ἐκείνη τῇ ἡμέρᾳ, der durch Ag 5,41 kommentiert wird.' Contra Bovon 1989, 304, see quotation above n. 131.

[138]See above n. 110.

protasis-section.[139] Thus, the late arabic translation in a two-fold way supports the interpretation of the 'day of joy' as the day of vexation.

For our statement of the structural problem of Matt 5:11-12 this means that the chairism-line in all the instances we have discussed refers back to the preceding description of the harassment and consequently cannot constitute the opening *protasis* of a new makarism in v. 12, but on the contrary serves as an amplifying and connecting interpretation of the *protasis* of the one and single but considerably expanded last makarism (vv. 11-12b) in the series of the SM as is likewise the case in the corresponding beatitude (vv. 22-23b) in Luke's SP.

3. Conclusion

In our investigation of the structure of the last two verses in the series of makarisms introducing the SM we have on text-*internal* grounds come to the conclusion that vv. 11-12 do not make up two separate but one coherent makarism and that for the following reasons: if we first remove v. 12c as secondary and then remove v. 11 as a separate makarism, then v. 12a-b will be without any form of description of the preconditioned situation leading to the affirmation or exhortation in v. 12a (which would be singular in our literature!), since neither the *protasis* of such a separate chairism nor the *apodosis* gives any clue as to who the addressees are or why they are promised the reward in heaven. Now, v. 12c is shown to be a secondary addition to the SM before the sermon was incorporated into Q^{Matt}, and consequently the *protasis* of v. 11 was once the only section providing information about the situation of those addressed, thus being a necessary part of the makarism; later when the 'deuteronomistic interpretation' was added, it restated and reinforced the specification of the situation. If, on the other hand, v. 11 were a separate makarism, it would lack an *apodosis*-line providing the reason for the affirmation, which is not a singular phenomenon in general but nonetheless so in the series of makarisms in the SM, the SP as well as in most other instances. Positively the chairism-line can be accounted for both semantically and pragmatically, since it functions as a semantic 'rejoinder' of the *protasis* and the *apodosis* after the long and intensifying ὅταν-clause and pragmatically as a amplifying restatement of the affirmation by means of a *hendiadyoin*. Accordingly, there are strong text-*internal* reasons for taking vv. 11-

---

[139]'"Moment' can hardly be interpreted eschatologically but should rather be understood as referring to the 'moment of persecution', esp. since the verb 'know' here is *'alama*, with the nuance that one possesses transmitted knowledge, such knowledge which one has learnt and is informed about' [Hjärpe].

12b as a unity, constituting a long and comprehensive beatitude concluding the series of nine beatitudes at the beginning of the SM.

The text-*external* evidence from the Old Testament and Jewish tradition, from Graeco-Roman literature, and from early Christian traditions confirms the *internal* analysis. Firstly, the secondary character of v. 12c is substantiated by the parallel Lukan version and esp. by the different placement and wording of the motivation found in the late Arabic tradition as well as by its absence from other early Christian text, none of which contains a phrase corresponding to vv. 12c//23c. Secondly, most makarism, esp. in the synoptic material, are made up of a *protasis* and an *apodosis*, even though there are many examples—not only in Jewish and Christian texts but also in the Graeco-Roman material—in which a makarisms is lacking an *apodosis*. Since—with two exceptions—all 'persecution beatitudes' are provided with an *apodosis*, the evidence speaks in favor of interpreting the last makarism in the series as a complete one with a *protasis*- as well as an *apodosis*-part. Thirdly, the scrutiny of literary parallels has lead to the result that there are very few, if any examples at all of makarisms without a description of the situation into which the affirmation is spoken. All texts in which the situation of those addressed is provided by means of an amplifying temporal clause thematizing the preconditioned situation are 'persecution beatitudes' reflecting a real situation of harassment. A tenth beatitude consisting of v. 12a-b would be lacking any form of indication about the situation into which it was spoken, which again speaks in favor of our text-*internal* interpretation. Fourthly, with regard to the connecting 'rejoinder'-clause found in three of the five 'persecution beatitudes' we observed that whenever the *protasis* is long and comprehensive and is followed by an *apodosis,* a chairism-line is provided. In those cases, however, when either the *apodosis* is missing or the *protasis* is short and simple the chairism-line is missing. In view of the structural composition of our text we also made the pertinent observation that the chairism-line here-as in all the relevant texts discussed above-refers back to the preceding description of harassment in v. 11b and consequently cannot constitute the opening *protasis* of a new makarism or chairism in v. 12, but can only function as an amplifying restatement of the affirmation of felicity given in the μακάριοί ἐστε of v. 11a.

These observations taken together decisively point to an understanding of vv. 11-12 as being one comprehensive makarism and so the number of makarisms remains nine instead of ten. The notion of completeness and perfection in the SM is thereby not called in question, only the numeric symbolism of ten that is supposed to substantiate it; for that purpose the eight gnomic makarisms forming an *inclusio* should be sufficient.

Table 1

Matthew 5:10	Matthew 5:11-12
(P) μακάριοι οἱ <u>δεδιωγμένοι</u> ἕνεκεν δικαιοσύνης	(P) μακάριοί **ἐστε ὅταν** ὀνειδίσωσιν ὑμᾶς καὶ <u>διώξωσιν</u> καὶ εἴπωσιν πᾶν πονηρὸν καθ᾽ ὑμῶν [[ψευδόμενοι]] ἕνεκεν ἐμοῦ·
	χαίρετε καὶ ἀγαλλιᾶσθε,
(A) ὅτι αὐτῶν ἐστιν ἡ βασιλεία τῶν οὐρανῶν.	(A) ὅτι ὁ μισθὸς ὑμῶν πολὺς ἐν τοῖς οὐρανοῖς·
	οὕτως γὰρ <u>ἐδίωξαν</u> τοὺς προφήτας τοὺς πρὸ ὑμῶν.

Table 2

Matthew 5:11-12	Luke 6:22-23	Gospel of Thomas 68	Clem. Alex. Strom. IV.41.3a	Clem. Alex. Strom. IV.41.3b	Ioh. Ev. Apocr. Arab. XXXII.4
(P) μακάριοί ἐστε ὅταν ὀνειδίσωσιν ὑμᾶς καὶ διώξωσιν καὶ εἴπωσιν πᾶν πονηρὸν καθ᾽ ὑμῶν [ψευδόμενοι] ἕνεκεν ἐμοῦ·	(P) μακάριοί ἐστε ὅταν μισήσωσιν ὑμᾶς οἱ ἄνθρωποι, καὶ ὅταν ἀφορίσωσιν καὶ ὀνειδίσωσιν καὶ ἐκβάλωσιν τὸ ὄνομα ὑμῶν ὡς πονηρὸν ἕνεκα τοῦ υἱοῦ τοῦ ἀνθρώπου·	(P) μακάριοί ἐστε ὅταν μισήσωσιν ὑμᾶς καὶ διώξωσιν ὑμᾶς·	(P) μακάριοι οἱ δεδιωγμένοι ἕνεκα ἐμοῦ·	(P) μακάριοί ἐστε ὅταν οἱ ἄνθρωποι μισήσωσιν ὑμᾶς, ὅταν ἀφορίσωσιν, ὅταν ἐκβάλωσι τὸ ὄνομα ὑμῶν ὡς πονηρὸν ἕνεκα τοῦ υἱοῦ τοῦ ἀνθρώπου·	(P) Blessed are you, whenever people (= rel. communities) persecute you, revile you and say lies against you for my name's sake;
χαίρετε καὶ ἀγαλλιάσθε,	χάρητε ἐν ἐκείνῃ τῇ ἡμέρᾳ καὶ σκιρτήσατε·				and see in that moment you may rejoice
(A) ὅτι ὁ μισθὸς ὑμῶν πολὺς ἐν τοῖς οὐρανοῖς·	(A) ἰδοὺ γὰρ μισθὸς ὑμῶν πολὺς ἐν τῷ οὐρανῷ·	(A) καὶ οὐχ εὑρεθήσεται ὁ(?) τόπος ὅπου ἐδίωξαν ὑμᾶς·	(A) ὅτι ἕξουσι τόπον ὅπου οὐ διωχθήσονται.		(A) and know that your reward is great in heaven.
οὕτως γὰρ ἐδίωξαν τοὺς προφήτας τοὺς πρὸ ὑμῶν.	κατὰ τὰ αὐτὰ γὰρ ἐποίουν τοῖς προφήταις οἱ πατέρες αὐτῶν.				Show patience, for the prophets who were before you, were persecuted and mistreated, but they endured with patience. (n.b. XXXII: 3fin.)

4. Bibliography

4.1. Editions and Translations

Aland, K. 1965: *Synopsis Quattuor Evangeliorum*, Stuttgart [3]1965.

Bowra, C. M. 1985: *Pindari Carmina*, Oxford 1935.

Black, M. 1970: *Apocalypsis Henochi Graece* (PsVTGr III), Leiden 1970.

Charlesworth, J. H. (ed.) 1983: *The Old Testament Pseudepigrapha, Vol. I:* Apocalyptic Literature & Testaments, Garden City, N.Y. 1983.

Charlesworth, J. H. (ed.) 1985: *The Old Testament Pseudepigrapha, Vol. II:* Expansions of the 'Old Testament' and Legends, Wisdom and Philosophical Literature, Prayers, Psalms and Odes, Fragments of lost Judeo-Hellenistic Works, Garden City, N.Y. 1985.

Dodds, E. R.1960: *Euripides' Bacchae*. Edited with Introduction and Commentary, Oxford [2]1960.

Fairclough, H. R.1935: *Vergil, Georgica II*, (LCL), Cambridge, MA/ London 1935.

Galbiati, G. 1957: *Iohannis Evangelium Apocryphum Arabice*, Milan 1957.

Geffcken, J. 1902/67: *Die Oracula Sibyllina*, Leipzig 1967 [= 1902].

Greeven, H. 1981: *Synopse der drei ersten Evangelien*, Tübingen [13]1981.

de Jonge, M. 1978: *The Testaments of the Twelve Patriarchs. A Critical Edition of the Greek Text* (PsVTGr I,2), Leiden 1978.

Klijn, A. F. J. 1983: *Der lateinische Text der Apokalypse des Esra* (TU 131), Berlin 1983.

Kloppenborg, J. S. 1988: *Q-Parallels*. Synopsis, Critical Notes & Concordance (Foundations & Facets), Sonoma, CA 1988.

Lambdin, Th. O. 1989: 'The Gospel According to Thomas. Text and Translation', in: B. Layton (ed.), *Nag Hammadi Codex II, 2-7, Vol. I* (NHS XX), Leiden/New York/København/Köln 1989, 52-93.

Lindemann, A./Paulsen, H. (eds.) 1992: *Die Apostolischen Väter. Griechisch-deutsche Parallelausgabe*, Tübingen 1992.

Löfgren, O. 1967: *Det apokryfiska Johannesevangeliet* (Apokryfiska evangelier I), Stockholm 1967.

Nestle, E./Aland, K. 1979: *Novum Testamentum Graece*, Stuttgart [26]1979.

Purintun, A.-E. 1972: *Paraleipomena Jeremiou* (Texts and Translations 1. Pseudepigrapha Series 1), Missoula, MT 1972.

Rogers, B. B. 1924: Aristophanes, *Frogs* (LCL), Cambridge, MA/London 1924.

Rahlfs, A. 1935: *Septuaginta. Editio octava, Vol. I-II*, Stuttgart 1935.

Richardson, N. J. 1974: *The Homeric Hymn to Demeter*, Oxford 1974.

Snell, B./Maehler, H. 1975: *Pindarus. Pars II: Fragmenta. Indices* (B. Teub.), Leipzig [4]1975.

Stählin, O. 1960: *Clemens Alexandrinus, Stromata Buch I-VI, Vol. 2*, Berlin [3]1960.

4.2. Grammers and Lexica

Bauer, W./Aland, B. & K 1988: *Griechisch-deutsches Wörterbuch zu den Schriften des Neuen Testaments und der frühchristlichen Literatur*, Berlin/New York [6]1988.

Bauer, W./Arndt, W. F./Gingrich, F. W./Danker, W. 1979: *A Greek-English Lexicon of the New Testament and Other Early Christian Literature*, Chicago/London [2]1979.

Blaß, F./Debrunner, A./Rehkopf, F. 1976: *Grammatik des neutestamentlichen Griechisch*, Göttingen [14]1976.

4.3. Literature

Berger, Kl. 1984: *Formgeschichte des Neuen Testaments*, Heidelberg 1984.

Betz, H. D. 1985: *Studien zur Bergpredigt*, Tübingen 1985.

Betz, H. D. 1992a: *Synoptische Studien. Gesammelte Aufsätze II*, Tübingen 1992.

Betz, H. D. 1992b: 'Sermon on the Mount/Plain', in: *Anchor Bible Dictionary*, *Vol. 5*, New York/London/Toronto/Sidney/Aukland 1992, 1106-12.

Bovon, F. 1989: *Das Evangelium nach Lukas. 1. Teilband Lk 1,1-9,50* (EKK III/1), Zürich/Neukirchen 1989.

Broer, J. 1986: *Die Seligpreisungen der Bergpredigt*. Studien zu ihrer Überlieferung und Interpretation (BBB 61), Königstein/Bonn 1986.

Brox, N. 1979: *Der erste Petrusbrief* (EKK XXI), Zürich/Neukirchen-Vluyn 1979.

Bultmann, R.1933: 'ἀγαλλιάομαι', in: *ThWNT, Vol. I,* Stuttgart 1933, 18-20.

Bultmann, R.1964: *Die Geschichte der synoptischen Tradition* (FRLANT 29), Göttingen [6]1964.

Bultmann, R. 1968: *Das Evangelium des Johannes* (KEK II), Göttingen [19]1968.

Catchpole, D. 1993: *The Quest For Q,* Edinburgh 1993.

Conzelmann, H. 1973: 'χαίρω κτλ', in: *ThWNT, Vol. IX,* Stuttgart 1973, 350-62.

Collins, R. F. 1992: 'Beatitudes', in: *Anchor Bible Dictionary, Vol. 1,* New York/London/Toronto/Sidney/Aukland 1992, 629-31.

Dahl, Nils Alstrup 1973/82: *Matteusevangeliet, Del 1,* Oslo/Bergen/Tromsø [3]1982.

Daube, D. 1956: *The New Testament and Rabbinic Judaism,* London 1956.

Davies, W. D./Allison, D. C. 1988: *The Gospel According to Saint Matthew, Vol. I,* (ICC), Edinburgh 1988.

Dupont, D. J. 1958/69/73: *Les Béatitudes* I and II, Paris 1958/ [2]1969; III Paris 1973.

Fenton, J. C. 1959: 'Inclusio and Chiasmus in Matthew', in: *Studia Evangelica* (TU 73), Berlin 1959, 174-179.

Fieger, M. 1991: *Das Thomasevangelium.* Einleitung, Kommentar und Systematik (NA 22), Münster 1991.

Fitzmyer, J. A. 1981: *The Gospel of Luke, Vol. I,* Garden City, N.Y. 1983.

Goppelt, L. 1978: *Der erste Petrusbrief* (KEK XII/1), Göttingen 1978.

Gnilka, J. 1988: *Das Matthäusevangelium I. Teil* (HThK I/1), Freiburg/Basel/Wien [2]1989.

Grundmann, W. 1968: *Das Evangelium nach Matthäus* (ThHK 1), Berlin 1968.

Grundmann, W. 1981: *Das Evangelium nach Lukas* (ThHK 3), Berlin [9]1981.

Guelich, R. A. 1976: 'The Matthean Beatitudes: 'Entrance-Requirements' or Eschatological Blessings?', in: *JBL* 95 (1976) 415-34.

Haenchen, E. 1962: 'Spruch 68 des Thomasevangeliums', in: *Muséon* 75 (1962) 19-29.

Hare, D. R. A. 1967: *The Theme of Jewish Persecution of Christians in the Gospel of St. Matthew* (SNTS.MS 6), Cambridge 1967.

Hoffmann, P. 1972: Studien zur Theologie der Logienquelle (NA 8), Münster 1972.

Hoffmann, P. 1992: 'QR und der Menschensohn. Eine vorläufige Skizze', in: F. Van Segbroeck/C. M. Tucket/G. Van Belle/J. Verheyden (eds.), *The Four Gospels 1992. Festschrift Frans Neirynck. Vol. I* (BEThL 100-A), Leuven 1992, 421-56.

Jacobson, A. D. 1992a: *The First Gospel. An Introduction to Q* (Foundations & Facets), Sonoma, CA 1992.

Jacobson, A. D. 1992b: 'Apocalyptic and the Synoptic Sayings Source Q', in: F. Van Segbroeck/C. M. Tucket/G. Van Belle/J. Verheyden (eds.), *The Four Gospels 1992. Festschrift Frans Neirynck. Vol. I* (BEThL 100-A), Leuven 1992, 403-19.

Jeremias, J. 1980: *Die Sprache des Lukasevangeliums.* Redaktion und Tradition im Nicht-Markusstoff des dritten Evangeliums (KEK. Sonderband), Göttingen 1980.

Kingsbury, J. D. 1988: *Matthew as Story*, Philadelphia, PA [2]1988.

Kloppenborg, J. S. 1987: *The Formation of Q.* Trajectories in Ancient Wisdom Collections (Studies in Antiquity & Christianity), Philadelphia, PA 1987.

Klostermann, E. 1927/71: *Das Matthäusevangelium* (HNT 3), Tübingen [4]1971 [= [3]1927], Tübingen 1971.

Klostermann, E. 1929/75: *Das Lukasevangelium* (HNT 5), Tübingen [3]1975 [= [2]1929], Tübingen 1975.

Koch, Kl. 1974: *Was ist Formgeschichte?* Methoden der Bibelexegese, Neukirchen-Vluyn [3]1974.

Kodjak, A. 1986: *A Structural Analysis of the Sermon on the Mount* (Religion and Reason 34), Berlin/New York/Amsterdam 1986.

Koester, H. 1989: 'The Gospel According to Thomas. Introduction', in: B. Layton (ed.), *Nag Hammadi Codex II, 2-7, Vol. I* (NHS XX), Leiden/New York/København/Köln 1989, 38-49.

Koester, H. 1990: *Ancient Christian Gospels.* Their History and Development, Philadelphia, PA 1990.

Lachs, S.T. 1987: *A Rabbinic Commentary on the New Testament*, New York 1987.

Lausberg, H. 1976: *Elemente der literarischen Rhetorik*, München [5]1976.

Lührmann, D. 1969: *Die Redaktion der Logienquelle* (WMANT 33), Neukirchen-Vluyn 1969.

Luz, U. 1985: *Das Evangelium nach Matthäus* (EKK I/1), Zürich/Neukirchen-Vluyn 1985.

Patte, D. 1987: *The Gospel According to Matthew*. A Structural Commentary on Matthew's Faith, Philadelphia, PA 1987.

Patterson, S. J. 1992: *The Gospel of Thomas and Jesus* (Foundations & Facets), Sonoma, CA 1992.

Popkes, W. 1986: *Adressaten, Situation und Form des Jakobusbriefes* (SBS125/126), Stuttgart 1986.

Robinson, J. M. 1971: 'LOGOI SOPHON: Zur Gattung der Spruchquelle Q', in: H. Koester/J. M. Robinson, *Entwicklungslinien durch die Welt des frühen Christentums*, Tübingen 1971, 67-106.

Robinson, J. M. 1986: 'On Bridging the Gulf from Q to the Gospel of Thomas (or Vice Versa)', in: Ch. W. Hedrick/R. Hodgson, Jr. (eds.), *Nag Hammadi, Gnosticism, & Early Christianity*, Peabody, MA 1986, 127-75.

Robinson, J. M. 1992a: 'The Q Trajectory: Between John and Matthew via Jesus', in: B. A. Pearson (ed.), *The Future of Early Christianity. Essays in Honor of Helmut Koester*, Minneapolis, MN 1992, 173-94.

Robinson, J. M 1992b: 'The Sayings Gospel Q', in: F. Van Segbroeck/C. M. Tucket/G. Van Belle/J. Verheyden (eds.), *The Four Gospels 1992. Festschrift Frans Neirynck. Vol. I* (BEThL 100-A), Leuven 1992, 361-88.

Schenk, W. 1987: *Die Sprache des Matthäus*. Die Text-Konstituenten in ihren makro- und mikrostrukturellen Relationen, Göttingen 1987.

Schrage, W. 1964: *Das Verhältnis des Thomas-Evangeliums zur synoptischen Tradition und zu den koptischen Evangelienübersetzungen*. Zugleich ein Beitrag zur gnostischen Synoptikerdeutung (BZNW 29), Berlin 1964.`

Schürmann, H. 1969: *Das Lukasevangelium. Erster Teil*. Kommentar zu Kap. 1,1-9,50 (HThK III), Freiburg/Basel/Wien 1969.

Schulz, S. 1972: *Q: Die Sprache der Evangelisten*, Zürich 1972.

Schweizer, E. 1973a: *Das Evangelium nach Matthäus* (NTD 2), Göttingen 1973.

Schweizer, E. 1973b: 'Formgeschichtliches zu den Seligpreisungen Jesu', in: *NTS* 19 (1973) 121-26.

Sieber, J. H. 1990: 'The Gospel of Thomas and the New Testament', in: J. E. Goehring/Ch. W. Hedrik/J. T. Sanders/H. D. Betz (eds.), *Gospel Origins & Christian Beginnings. In Honor of James M. Robinson* (Forum Fascicles), Sonoma, CA 1990, 64-73.

Steck, O. H. 1967: *Israel und das gewaltsamme Geschick der Propheten.* Untersuchungen zur Überlieferung des deuteronomistischen Geschichtsbildes im Alten Testament, Spätjudentum und Urchristentum (WMANT 23), Neukirchen-Vluyn 1967.

Stegemann, W. 1991: *Zwischen Synagoge und Obrigkeit. Zur historischen Situation der lukanischen Christen* (FRLANT 152), Göttingen 1991.

Strecker, G. 1984: *Die Bergpredigt. Ein exegetischer Kommentar*, Göttingen 1984.

Tödt, H. E. 1963: *Der Menschensohn in der synoptischen Überlieferung*, Gütersloh [2]1963.

Toyoshima, K. 1983: 'Neue Vorschläge zur Lesung und Übersetzung von Thomasevangelium Log. 21, 103 und 68b', in: *Annual of the Japanese Biblical Institute* 9 (1983) 230-41.

Trilling, W. 1964: *Das wahre Israel: Studien zur Theologie des Matthäus-Evangeliums* (StANT 10), München [3]1964.

Vielhauer, Ph. 1975: *Geschichte der urchristlichen Literatur* (de Gruyter Lehrbuch), Berlin 1975.

Wellhausen, J. 1904: *Das Evangelium Matthaei*, Berlin 1904.

Wrege, H.-Th. 1968: *Die Überlieferungsgeschichte der Bergpredigt* (WUNT 9), Tübingen 1968.

Zahn, Th. 1903: *Das Evangelium des Matthäus* (KNT I), Leipzig 1903.

Zeller, D. 1992: 'Eine weisheitliche Grundschrift in der Logienquelle', in: F. Van Segbroeck/C. M. Tucket/G. Van Belle/J. Verheyden (eds.), *The Four Gospels 1992. Festschrift Frans Neirynck. Vol. I* (BEThL 100-A), Leuven 1992, 389-401.

Resurrection and Discipleship

Thorwald Lorenzen

1. Locating the Issue

The inter-relationship between the resurrection of Christ and Christian disciple-ship is controversial in theological discussions and in Christian *praxis*. Most theologians agree with the apostle Paul that the resurrection of Christ is the *irreplaceable foundational event* for the Christian faith: "... if Christ has not been raised, then our preaching is in vain and your faith is in vain" (1 Cor 15:14)! It becomes difficult and controversial, however, when one asks how this foundational event can be recognised *as such*, how it can be *known and understood*. Again, there is a general consensus that the object of inquiry, in our case the resurrection of Christ, must determine the way of knowing. This hermeneutical principle reminds us that in our search for an adequate way of knowing and understanding we must give procedural priority to the reality of the resurrection as it is manifest in the earliest sources. We want to understand the reality that has given rise to the earliest texts and to which these texts witness. But is that possible? Can we use a method of enquiry that distances the text sufficiently from us, so that we do not simply use it to confirm our own notions? Is there a method of understanding that does not predetermine the results of our enquiry?

Many Christians would ask, for instance, whether this is a problem at all. Does not the New Testament teach clearly that the resurrection of Christ is a *historical event*; and has not the church through the centuries and around the world accepted it as such? If it is a historical event, so the argument continues, then it must be accessible to *historical reason and its methods*. And indeed, up to the present day there have been Christian apologists who have argued on rational scientific grounds that the tomb, into which the dead Jesus had been laid, was found empty, and that therefore Jesus must have been bodily raised from the dead.

Nevertheless, a few questions directed to us from the primary sources in the New Testament immediately problematise these traditional answers. Is there a difference between the resurrection of Jesus on the one hand, and of the narrated resurrections of Lazarus (John 11), the widow's son at Nain (Luke 7:11-17) or the daughter of Jairus (Mark 5:35-43) on the other? Paul certainly implies this when he insists "that *Christ* being raised from the dead *will never die again*; death no longer has dominion over him" (Rom 6:9f., emphasis mine). Christ therefore has been taken out of the realm of death altogether, while Lazarus and the others would have to die again. This raises a further question: how can we, who live in the process of history, and as such live under the shadow of death, know and understand a reality that is no longer determined or affected by the reality of death? And there is a further question that has not been given adequate recognition. How in our theological reflection can we adequately recognise that according to the biblical testimony it was the *crucified* Christ who was raised from the dead? The theological challenge is, therefore, to locate and describe a way of knowing that is adequate to the resurrection of the crucified Christ as an act of God.

2. The Epistemological Challenge

This is not a new problem for theology. Most contemporary theologians, while maintaining the historical thrust of the resurrection, insist that *faith* is the proper mode to receive the reality of the resurrection. The earliest Christian confessions declared: "*we believe* that God raised Jesus from the dead." This knowledge of faith has soteriological significance: "if you confess with your lips that Jesus is Lord and believe in your heart that God raised him from the dead, *you will be saved*" (Rom 10:9, emphasis mine). The New Testament does not speak of any unbelievers witnessing to the resurrection. And the major creeds and confessions of the church continue to portray this interlocking of the resurrection and faith: "*I believe* in God .... And in Jesus Christ ..., Who ... on the third day rose again from the dead ...." (Apostles' Creed); "*We believe* in one God .... And in one Lord Jesus Christ .... He suffered and the third day he rose, and ascended into heaven ...." (Creed of Nicea); "*We believe* in one God .... And in one Lord Jesus Christ .... He was crucified for us ..., and suffered and was buried, and rose on the third day ...." (Constantinopolitan Creed).

It is indeed fundamental to recognise this interlocking of faith and the resurrection. But this interlocking must become apparent! It must be clear that the witness of faith forms indeed an analogy to the reality and the content of the resurrection of the crucified Christ. This assurance is not given with the modern concept of faith. "Faith" has become widely misunderstood.[1] The general

---

[1]Paul Tillich's "Introductory Remarks" to *Dynamics of Faith* (1957) deserve to be repeated: "There is hardly a word in the religious language ... which is subject to more misunderstandings, distortions and questionable definitions than the word 'faith.' It belongs to those terms which need healing before they can be used for the healing of men. Today the term 'faith' is more productive of disease than of health. It confuses, misleads, creates alternately skepticism and fanaticism, intellectual resistance and emotional surrender, rejection of genuine religion and subjection to substitutes." (in: Carl Heinz Ratschow, ed., *Paul Tillich: Main Works / Hauptwerke.* Vol. 5 / Bd. 5 [Berlin/New York: De Gruyter, 1988, pp. 231-290], p. 231).

understanding of faith no longer guarantees that it is the *crucified* Christ who through the resurrection and in the power of the Spirit is present in the event of faith. It is therefore imperative to make the *content* of Christian faith explicit. And that is better accomplished with the concept of *discipleship*.[2]

3. "Discipleship" as a historical and theological Problem

Why has there been such hesitancy in Protestant theology to interrelate the Resurrection and Discipleship?[3]   Hesitation has been expressed on two fronts. *Firstly*, there has been the fear that a focus on discipleship would lead to a *distortion of "sola gratia"* and possibly even to the heresy of *synergism* (from the Greek word *sunergeîn* = "co-operating"). Then, *secondly*, it was suspected that discipleship may suggest a *distortion of the "sola fide"*, and lead to an *ethicising or moralisation of faith*.[4]   Both dangers must be acknowledged and avoided.

---

[2]Regrettably, in this brief essay, we cannot develop the content of Christian discipleship. The reader is reminded of the works of a teacher and of a student of Günter Wagner: Eduard Schweizer, *Lordship and Discipleship*. SBT (London: SCM, 1960 [1955]); Eduard Schweizer, "Discipleship and Church," in: *The Beginnings of the Church in the New Testament* (Edinburgh: Saint Andrew Press, 1970 [1967]), pp. 85-104; Athol Gill, *Life on the Road. The Gospel Basis for a Messianic Lifestyle* (Scottdale, Pa.: Herald Press, 1992 [1989]); Athol Gill, *The Fringes of Freedom. Following Jesus, Living Together. Working for Justice* (Homebush West: Lancer, 1990).   Further: Ferdinand Hahn, "Pre-Easter Discipleship," in: *The Beginnings of the Church in the New Testament* (Edinburgh: Saint Andrew Press, 1970 [1967]), pp. 9-39; Martin Hengel, *The Charismatic Leader and His Followers* (Edinburgh: Clark, 1981); August Strobel, "Discipleship in the Light of the Easter-event," in: *The Beginnings of the Church in the New Testament* (Edinburgh: Saint Andrew Press, 1970 [1967]), pp. 40-84; Segundo Galilea, *Following Jesus* (Maryknoll, NY: Orbis, 1981); Reiner Strunk, *Nachfolge Christi. Erinnerungen an eine evangelische Provokation* (München: Kaiser, 1981); and the literature mentioned below.

[3]This hesitancy is lamented by Karl Barth (see below footnotes 10, 11 and 12), Dietrich Bonhoeffer (*The Cost of Discipleship* [New York: MacMillan, 1963 [1937]], chapter 1 on "Costly Grace"), Jürgen Moltmann ("Einführung," in: Jürgen Moltmann, ed., *Nachfolge und Bergpredigt* [München: Kaiser, [2]1982] pp. 8f.; *The Way of Jesus Christ. Christology in Messianic Dimensions* [London: SCM, 1990 [1989]], pp. 116-119), and Reiner Strunk (*Nachfolge Christi. Erinnerungen an eine evangelische Provokation* [München: Kaiser, 1981], pp. 174, 189f.).

[4]So Gerhard Ebeling's criticism of Karl Barth's theology: "Karl Barths Ringen mit Luther," in: *Lutherstudien*, Band III: Begriffsuntersuchungen - Textinterpretationen - Wirkungsgeschichtliches (Tübingen: Mohr, 1985), pp. 428-573, explicitely pp. 550f., 557f.;

Synergism is suspect because it questions the soteriological sufficiency of *sola gratia* by maintaining that the human being "co-operates" with God in the work of salvation. And if faith is dissolved into ethics or morality then its justifying and liberating character is being lost.

However, is it not equally true that the constant awareness of, indeed even fascination with, these dangers, coupled with individual and ecclesiastical self-interest, has led to an ideology of *sola gratia* and *sola fide* by which it is no longer evident *who* the God is, who freely shares his grace with us, and thereby invites to a life of faith?

4. A Historical Reminder

Already during the Reformation the so-called *Anabaptists* suspected a reduction of the Gospel when the magisterial reformers made a distinction between justification and sanctification, and when they located the presence of Christ in the word and in the (proper) administration of the sacraments. They agreed with the magisterial reformers in their insistence on *sola gratia*, *sola fide* and *sola scriptura*, but they insisted that faith means more than the individual and personal appropriation of salvation. It means "*following Jesus*" in the context of an *intentional Christian community*. They criticised the reformers' understanding of faith as being superficial and shallow.[5] In their understanding the reformers preached "a sinful sweet Christ",[6] who does not lead to a "betterment of life".[7]

compare also Gerhard Ebeling, "Über die Reformation hinaus? Zur Luther-Kritik Karl Barths," *ZThK*. B 6 (1986, pp. 33-75), pp. 57, 66-75. In the same volume see Eberhard Jüngel's response, and defense of Barth's position: "Zum Verhältnis von Kirche und Staat nach Karl Barth," *ibid.*, pp. 76-135.

[5]Conrad Grebel, "Letters to Thomas Müntzer," in: *Spiritual and Anabaptist Writers*. The Library of Christian Classics (Philadelphia: Westminster, 1957, pp. 73-85), p. 74.

[6]Conrad Grebel, "Letters to Thomas Müntzer," in: *Spiritual and Anabaptist Writers* (1957), pp. 78f.

[7]Balthasar Hubmaier writes: "Faith alone makes us holy (frumm = fromm) before God ... Such faith can not remain passive but must break out (ausbrechen) to God in thanksgiving and to mankind in all kinds of works of brotherly love." ("Eighteen Theses" (1524), in: W. Estep, ed., *Anabaptist Beginnings* [1523-1533]. A Source Book [Nieuwkoop: B. De Graaf, 1976], p. 24); Conrad Grebel writes to Thomas Müntzer: "... today ... every man wants to be saved by superficial faith, without fruits of faith, without baptism of trial and probation, without love and hope, without right Christian practices, and wants to persist in all the old

In our century *Dietrich Bonhoeffer* has spoken out most clearly - backing up his words with a life of credible witness - that "the outcome of the Reformation was the victory, not of Luther's perception of grace in all its purity and costliness, but of the vigilant religious instinct of man for the place where grace is to be obtained at the cheapest price."[8] When *Christ* calls persons, so Bonhoeffer insists in ever new variations, he *frees them* "from all man-made dogmas, from every burden and oppression, from every anxiety and torture which afflicts the conscience."[9] But this is only possible when the person hears the call and obeys it by following *him* in radical discipleship.

Karl Barth has acknowledged the importance of Bonhoeffer's contribution and has wholeheartedly agreed with his emphasis.[10] In all of his writings Barth seeks to maintain that God's freely given grace implies and therefore includes the call to radical discipleship. God's very being, the fact that in the humanity of Christ he *is* for us, liberates the believer to active obedience.[11] The content of this

---

manner of personal vices ...." (C. Grebel, "Letters to Thomas Müntzer," in: *Spiritual and Anabaptist Writers* [1957], p. 74); Jakob Kautz challenged the Protestant clergy of the city of Worms on June 13, 1527 by insisting: "Jesus Christ of Nazareth did not suffer for us and has not satisfied (for our sins) in any other way but this: that we have to stand in his footsteps and have to walk the way which he has blazed for us first, and that we obey the commandments of the Father and the Son, everyone according to his measure. He who speaks differently of Christ makes an idol of Christ." (Cited from R. Friedmann, *The Theology of Anabaptism. An Interpretation* [Scottdale, Pa.: Herald Press, 1973], p.85); perhaps Hans (John) Denck has most clearly expressed this concern: "... none may truly know (Christ) unless he follow after him with his life. And no one can follow after him except in so far as one previously knows (*erkennet*) him." ("Whether God is the Cause of Evil," [1526], in: *Spiritual and Anabaptist Writers* [1957], pp. 88-111], p.108).

[8]Dietrich Bonhoeffer. *The Cost of Discipleship* (1963 [1937]), pp. 52f., see further, for instance, the "Introduction" and chapter 1 on "Costly Grace". In a sermon on the Magnificat in Luke 1:46-55 Bonhoeffer says that we can only adequately know the Christian story of Advent if we cease to be spectators and become active participants in God's dealings with humanity. (*Predigten, Auslegungen, Meditationen I, 1925-1935* [München: Kaiser, 1984], p. 412, cited from Bertold Klappert, "Die Rechts-, Freiheits- und Befreiungsgeschichte Gottes mit dem Menschen. Erwägungen zum Verständnis der Auferstehung in Karl Barths Versöhnungslehre (KD IV/1-3)," *EvTh* 49 [1989, pp. 460-478], pp. 472f.).

[9]*The Cost of Discipleship* (1963 [1937]), p. 40.

[10]*Church Dogmatics* IV/2 (Edinburgh: T. & T. Clark, 1958 [1955]), pp. 533-553.

[11]Karl Barth emphasizes, for instance, that the activity of God "kann ja als vollzogen gar

discipleship is given by the humanity of Christ through whom God has revealed and thereby confirmed his partiality for the poor and oppressed.[12]

5. The Resurrection as an "Open" Event.[13]

The essential interlocking between the resurrection and our faith and discipleship becomes evident when we recognise that the earliest Christians narrated the resurrection as an *open event* - open to the future, seeking to create faith, through it to shape history, and thus to determine the future.

This openness of the resurrection toward its future fulfilment finds expression in the careful wording of one of the oldest confessional formulas in *1 Corinthians 15:3-5*: "Christ died (aorist tense) ... he was buried (aorist tense) ... *he has been raised (perfect* tense) ... he appeared (aorist tense) ...." The use of the perfect tense to describe the resurrection stands out. It is intentionally used to distinguish the resurrection of Jesus Christ from his death, his burial and his appearance. It is used to underline the "continuing effect"[14] of the event of resurrection. In the

---

nicht anders als in seinem *tätigen Nachvollzug* erkannt werden" (*Kirchliche Dogmatik* IV/1 [1953], p. 111, [emphasis mine]; the English translation is inadequate at this point). The same idea is contained in the subsequent sentences: "God is not idle but active. ... therefore, man must be active too." (*Church Dogmatics* IV/1 [New York: Charles Scribner's Sons, 1956 [1953]], p. 103). Compare further the important essays "Gospel and Law" (1935) and "Church and State" (1938), both in: Karl Barth, *Community, State, and Church. Three Essays* (Gloucester, Mass.: Peter Smith, 1968), pp. 71-100, 101-148. *Barmen 2* may serve as a summary statement: "As Jesus Christ is God's comforting verdict (*Zuspruch*) of the forgiveness of all our sins, so, *and with equal seriousness*, he is also God's vigorous announcement of his claim (*Anspruch*) upon our whole life. Through him there comes to us joyful liberation from the godless ties of this world for free, grateful service to his creatures." ("The Barmen Theological Declaration," [1934], § 2, emphasis mine).

[12]*Church Dogmatics* IV/2 (1958 [1955]), §64,3 (pp. 154-264), explicitly for instance on p. 166: Jesus "exists analogously to the mode of existence of God." Therefore the "royal man shares ... the strange destiny which falls on God ... to be the One who is ignored and forgotten and despised and discounted by men" (p. 167). Jesus manifested the partiality of God in that "He ignored all those who are high and mighty and wealthy in the world in favour of the weak and meek and lowly" (p. 168).

[13]In 1969 Günter Wagner assigned to me the following topic for a "Three Day Paper", being part of the requirement for the "Master of Theology" degree: "In which sense does Christ's resurrection 'include' man's resurrection? A study in Pauline soteriology".

[14]F. Blass and A. Debrunner, *A Greek Grammar of the New Testament and other early*

earliest churches the risen Christ was therefore called "the *first fruits* of those who have fallen asleep" or "the *first-born* from the dead" (1 Cor 15:20,23; Col 1:18; Rev 1:5; compare Matt 27:52f.). But how can we, who are part of the historical process, understand an event that is "open"? An event that aims at the fulfilment, when the Son has ultimately triumphed over the estranging forces of death, and when he will hand back his God given authority to the Father, so that God will truly be what he is (1 Cor 15:20-28). How can we know and communicate the resurrection of the crucified Christ as a unique and eschatological event, and yet as an event that has changed the world, that is changing the world, and that will change the world?

To portray the openness of the resurrection Jürgen Moltmann has retrieved the biblical-theological concept of *"promise"*.[15]　He understands promise as a "language event" of a special kind: it remembers, and as such preserves history, and at the same time it aims at the concrete historical actualisation of this promise in the shaping and in the anticipation of the future.[16]

The resurrection of Jesus Christ therefore calls for a *way of knowing* that avoids the extremes of a *historical positivism* on the one hand, and *historical existentialism* on the other. *Historical positivism* tends to *absolutise the past* by freezing an event into its so-called objective past. The emphasis is on what actually happened, and the response is a theoretical affirmation or denial of that fact. *Historical existentialism* tends to *absolutise the present* by being primarily interested in the effect of an event on the present existence of the enquirers and their life-situation.

The concept of "promise" reminds us that a historical event, which we qualify as an act of God, cannot be properly understood by merely making a theoretical affirmation that the event has happened in the past; nor is it sufficient to experience the subjective, existential or psychological significance of such an event for

Christian Literature. A Translation and Revision of the ninth-tenth German edition incorporating supplementary notes of A. Debrunner, by Robert W. Funk (Cambridge: University Press, Chicago: University of Chicago Press, 1961), p. 176 (§ 342).

[15]Compare especially: Jürgen Moltmann, *Theology of Hope. On the Ground and the Implications of a Christian Eschatology* (London: SCM, 1967).

[16]Jürgen Moltmann, "Verkündigung als Problem der Exegese," (1963) in: *Perspektiven der Theologie. Gesammelte Aufsätze* (München: Kaiser, 1968, pp. 113-127), p. 126: "Eine Verheissung ist ein 'Sprachereignis', aber ein solches, das Geschichte erinnernd aufbewahrt und das auf die zukünftige Wirklichkeit geschichtlicher Erfüllung hinzielt."

our life. Beyond this objective-intellectual and subjective-existential knowledge, the reality and the content of the event itself calls for a holistic response in which it becomes evident that it is *God* who calls to the obedience of faith, and at the same time it must become manifest *who* this calling God is. We affirm such an event as true by tuning our life into the history which that event is creating and shaping. This is the knowledge of the *praxis* of discipleship, not of theory.[17] To be unwilling to engage in such discipleship or to consider such discipleship to be an optional extra is to question the truth and reliability of the event.

The resurrection is an act of God. As such it is neither a historical event that can be captured with historical reason, nor is it an unhistorical myth that alludes to general resurrection phenomena in nature and human existence. It is a "promise" that is anchored in the Christ-event, but it is calling for people who will, like Moses, Abraham and Paul, stake their life on God's promise and thereby participate with God in shaping the future.[18] The resurrection is a *history creating event*. The controversial theological issue is not the resurrection as such. What is controversial is how we can know it as an *act of God*, and that this God is the One who reveals his power by raising the *crucified* Christ from the dead.

6. The Resurrection of the *Crucified* Christ

Having recognised the resurrection of Christ as an "open" event, which as such must be spoken of in terms of "promise" rather than "fact", we must now retrieve the *content* of the resurrection. Here it is of interest that the Gospels insist that with the resurrection, the poverty of Jesus' life and the agony of his arrest, trial and death were not left behind. The slogan "from cross to crown" is misleading. It is the product of religious self-interest and religious projection. It is not grounded in the biblical story. It promises a crown without a cross. It speaks of a salvation that does not necessarily include the call to follow Jesus. It seeks the en-

---

[17]Dietrich Bonhoeffer says: "The response of the disciples is an act of obedience, not a confession of faith in Jesus" (*The Cost of Discipleship* [1963 [1937]], p. 61.).

[18]Those who suspect here a reduction or a distortion of *sola gratia* may be reminded of 1 Corinthians 3:9 where Paul assigns theological status to the human being as God's partner. Grace does not bypass human response and human activity, but calls it into being! Wolf Krötke has reminded us that this theological concept is central to the theology of Karl Barth: "Gott und Mensch als 'Partner'. Zur Bedeutung einer zentralen Kategorie in Karl Barths Kirchlicher Dogmatik," *ZThK*. B 6 (1986), pp. 158-175. This is noteworthy because Barth has often been accused of dissolving the freedom and dignity of the human person into the all encompassing grace and sovereignty of God.

joyment of religion, but it forgets about the poverty of Jesus.

In contrast, the resurrection narratives in the Gospels insist that it was the *crucified* Christ who was raised from the dead. The risen Christ displays his identity by pointing to the marks of his crucifixion (Luke 24:36-39; John 20:20,25,27). The apostle Paul has understood this when, in criticism of his opponents in Galatia and Corinth, he emphasised that the resurrection does not eliminate or relativise human weakness, but that the resurrection-power of God is at work in human weakness. While his opponents could not associate human weakness with God; while they described Paul's weakness as a "messenger of Satan", and while they located the power of God in good looks, good oratory, and demonstrative miracles, Paul locates the presence of the risen Christ in his life by saying: "... when I am weak, then I am strong" (2 Cor 12:10). And this "weakness" is not merely referring to sickness or tiredness, it includes "insults, hardships, persecutions, and calamities" (2 Cor 12:10), all of which are the direct result of his discipleship. So when Paul speaks about the resurrection of the crucified Christ, he does so not in the triumphant terms of his opponents, who prided themselves on being "super-apostles", participating in the reign of Christ already, but he speaks about his relationship to Christ in terms of suffering service in the world: "I die every day!" (1 Cor 15:31); and this death is not that of a martyr, nor does it refer to some kind of spiritual death, but it is the concrete consequence of a life of service as a disciple and apostle of the crucified and risen Christ: sleepless nights, hunger, thirst, ill clad, buffeted, reviled, persecuted, afflic-ted, beaten, imprisoned, homeless, insulted, hard work ... (1 Cor 4:8-13; 2 Cor 1:3-7, 6:1-10; 10-13; Gal 4:12-20, 6:17).

The death and resurrection of Jesus Christ therefore seeks to find analogies in the existence of the believer. This found a moving expression in the poetic couplets by which the apostle portrays the inter-relationship between the death and resurrection of Jesus Christ on the one hand and the life of the Christian believer on the other:

Cross	Resurrection
We are afflicted in every way,	*but not crushed;*
perplexed,	*but not driven to despair;*
persecuted,	*but not forsaken;*
struck down,	*but not destroyed;*

| always carrying in the body the death of Jesus, | *so that the life of Jesus may* |
| *also* | *be manifested in our bodies.* |

(2 Cor 4:8-10)

7. Discipleship - as the most adequate human response to the resurrection of the crucified Christ

How does one respond to the resurrection as an *open* event? And how does it become clear in this response that it was the *crucified* Christ who was raised from the dead? At this point we must remind ourselves that in early Christianity it was not primarily the word, the kerygma, that was the bearer of the Christian message, but especially the "*witness*". The word group "witness/testimony" is found in major biblical traditions, it is used in philosophical and hermeneutical discussions, and it has also been adopted in theological reflections.[19] It is important to retrieve this emphasis in order to safeguard faith against its individualistic and ecclesiastical distortions.

As an "open" event, the risen Christ *calls for a corresponding witness and testimony* in order to keep the event alive in the ongoing process of history. The event needs the testimony and the witness, and the testimony and witness live from the event.

The testimony is given in the *present*, but it lives from the *past*. Through the testimony, a past event becomes real in and for the present. A testimony gathers up an event of the past and makes it manifest in the present. It helps us to interpret and modify the present, and thereby aids in shaping the *future*.

Without such testimony and witness an event is lost. It disappears in the abyss of history. The event therefore calls for a testimony in order to have a *Wirkungsgeschichte* - an effect and influence on the ongoing historical process. Through an

---

[19]Compare for instance: Allison A. Trites, *The New Testament Concept of Witness* (Cambridge: University Press, 1977); Paul Ricoeur, "The Hermeneutics of Testimony," (1972), in: Paul Ricoeur, *Essays on Biblical Interpretation*, ed. with an introduction by Lewis S. Mudge (Philadelphia: Fortress, 1980), pp. 119-154; Klaus Kienzler, *Logik der Auferstehung. Eine Untersuchung zu Rudolf Bultmann, Gerhard Ebeling und Wolfhart Pannenberg* (Freiburg: Herder, 1976); Francis Schüssler Fiorenza, *Foundational Theology: Jesus and the Church* (New York: Crossroad, 1986), chapters 1, 2 and 11.

adequate testimony people at all times and in all situations can share in the reality of a past event.

The testimony must therefore *re-present the event*. It gathers up (it "remembers") the event and faithfully manifests it in the present. This is done with *language and* with an *existence* that gives substance and credibility to the language.

Bringing an event out of the past into the present normally happens through *language*. Words are used, a narrative or a confession for instance, to re-present a past event and relate it to the present. Testimony therefore has a word or language character. *Jesus*, therefore, related the power of the "Kingdom of God" to the world in *parables*. For the apostle *Paul* the saving and liberating power of the gospel was present in the *word of preaching* that aimed to create faith in the hearer (e.g. Rom 1:16f., 10:17). Also for the *fourth evangelist* it was the *word* that brought eternal life to the hearer (John 5:24).

But words alone are not enough to witness to the reality in which they are anchored! The *word of testimony* must be related to, and must be authenticated by, the *existence of the witness*. Therefore the unconditional love of God and his accepting grace became an event not only in Jesus' parables, but also in his healing ministry and in his concrete fellowship with "publicans and sinners". The same is true for the apostle Paul whose theology of the cross was essentially related to a "crucified" existence (2 Cor 4: 6; 10-13). So also in the fourth gospel we hear Jesus saying: "My food is to do the will of him who sent me, and to accomplish his work" (John 4:34).

Both, therefore, the *truth* of a testimony and the *adequacy* of re-presenting an event, are at stake in the existence of the witness. For an adequate *Wirkungsgeschichte*, events call not only for words, but also for an existence that responsibly re-presents the message. If the existence of the witness does not cohere with the content of the testimony then the testimony is "broken", it is distorted.

Therefore the words of a testimony must not only reflect the event that is testified, they must also be related to the one who makes the testimony. Persons who make the testimony are responsible for its truth with their existence. The truth of the testimony is at stake in the existence of the witnesses, and the credibility of the witnesses is dependent on the adequacy of their representation of the event. The witnesses must be willing to suffer for their testimony. Paul Ricoeur says it well: "Testimony is ... the engagement of the pure heart and an engagement to the death. It belongs to the tragic destiny of truth."[20] Therefore the testimony and the existence of the witness, the one who testifies, belong together. Human witness belongs to the reality that makes a past event present through language and existence.

The witnesses do not testify to an abstract fact *that* Jesus has been raised from the dead, but the witnesses and their testimony are a necessary part of the communicative event which brings the reality of the risen Christ into the present. The risen One is present in the life of the believer. Paul defines this presence as "carrying in the body (i.e. in his existence) the death of Jesus" (2 Cor 4:10). Appropriate testimony to the resurrection is therefore not a theoretical or propositional dogmatic statement, it is also not a charismatic religious experience, but it calls for a life of discipleship in which it is existentially manifested that the risen Lord makes himself known under the shadow of the cross.[21]

It suggests a false alternative, i.e. an alternative that is inadequate to the nature of the event, if one is asked to make a choice whether the resurrection of Christ is communicated through a pure kerygma, which as such does not need any historical support, or a message that is supported by historical evidence. The reality of the resurrection suggests a way of faith beyond these alternatives. The resurrection of the crucified Christ is not properly guarded by an existential decision or a rational construct, but by a credible life of following Jesus.

The resurrection of Jesus Christ is therefore on one hand essentially linked to the *life and death of Jesus*, and on the other hand to the *life of the witness and the witnessing community*, and, through the witness and the community, to the *life and future of the world*. We recognise and affirm the *unity of the Christ-event* when we realise that our faith in the risen Christ cannot by-pass the fact that during his life Jesus ministered to, and showed solidarity with, the outcast, the

---

[20]Paul Ricoeur, "The Hermeneutics of Testimony," (1980 [1972]), p. 130. The following words are written in the same context: "The witness is capable of suffering and dying for what he believes" (p. 129). "The witness is the man who is identified with the just cause which the crowd and the great hate and who, for this just cause, risks his life" (p. 129). In this context we must also recall that the Greek word for "witness" is *mártys* from which the English word "martyr" derives.

[21]A classical paradigm is the encounter between Jesus and Peter at Caesarea Philippi as presented by Mark: Mark 8:27-9:1. It is not merely the orthodox confession "You are the Christ" (v. 29), but the concrete life of discipleship, following the suffering One, that is the appropriate response to Jesus as the Christ (vv. 34-38).

poor, the oppressed, and the sick. With them he shared the colourful grace of God. It is therefore in our concrete engagement for the needs of the world in our time that we show whether we believe in the Jesus who lived a certain life, who was killed because of it, and who was raised from the dead to demonstrate that his vision of reality is true. This partiality of God for those who are lost and broken must become evident in the witness to the resurrection. Otherwise the event is distorted.

At the same time it must be emphasised that although the reality of the resurrection of Christ flows over into the existence of the believer and constitutes the believer as a witness, the resurrection is *not dissolved* into the existence of the believer. The *difference and the distance* between Christ and the believer remains. Christ has been raised from the dead, while the witnesses walk in newness of life (Rom 6:4). There is a clear distinction between Christ and the believer. He is risen, not the believer. He manifests the power of the resurrection by empowering the believer to a newness of life. This newness of life cannot mean withdrawal from responsibility for the world because in it it must become evident that it was the crucified Christ who was raised from the dead.

If we keep in mind that the *witness to the risen Christ is grounded in the event of the resurrection*, and remember the essential inter-relationship between event and witness, then we will avoid the following *distortions*. We will not *objectify* the resurrection of Christ, but remember that it aims for a concrete manifestation in our life and in the world. We will not reduce the reality of the resurrection to our *experience* of it, but remember that it is Jesus Christ, not ourselves, who is risen and who wants to shape our life. We will not limit verification to a *theoretical proof*, but we will remember that we must confess our allegiance to Christ with our whole existence. The category of witness therefore enables us to think of the resurrection of Jesus Christ as determining our life and our future, without being dissolved into our experience.[22]

---

[22]Klaus Kienzler comments: "Allein der Begriff Zeugnis gewährleistet auch, daß die Erscheinungen des Auferstandenen weder als in sich eindeutige Ereignisse, die die Auferstehung beweisen, interpretiert noch mit dem eigentlichen Geschehen der Auferstehung identifiziert werden und so für die Aussage stehen, daß Jesus ins 'Kerygma' auferstanden sei. Im Zeugnis begründen die Erscheinungen vielmehr die geschichtliche Erfahrbarkeit und Aussagbarkeit der Auferstehung, ohne daß sie Beweis der Auferstehung oder gar diese selbst wären." (*Logik der Auferstehung* [1976], p. 254).

8. Conclusion

Can one *really* understand the meaning of a dance apart from dancing it? Will one ever *really* know the fascination of a football game apart from having played it? Of course, one can know the structure of a dance and the rules of a game. One may have been a spectator on many occasions. But the inner movement and meaning of a game or a dance, their melody, their dynamic and fascination, can only be known by participating in them.

It is true, of course, that the dance and the game exist apart from the participants. We know their content and their rules. And yet the dance *must* be danced to become what it is, and the game *must* be played. The dancer and the player are necessary for the dance and the game to become what they are! The dancer does not create the *Flamenco*, but she is necessary to portray it. And what is a football game without it being played. It is a useless abstraction.

The dancers must decide to dance, and the players must decide to play. Their participation takes place within given parameters. They follow certain rules. But within these given parameters and rules they freely shape the game and interpret the dance. Indeed the *telos* of the game and the dance is fulfilled if the participant becomes so much a part of the proceedings that the dance or the game take over and determine the existence of the participant.[23]

With the resurrection of the crucified Christ, God has spoken a concrete and life-giving word into history. This word aims to be heard, and being heard, it creates the concrete obedience of faith which we call discipleship. Not individual piety or doctrinal orthodoxy but the concrete following of Jesus in our everyday life is the most adequate response to the resurrection of Jesus Christ.

The resurrection of the crucified Christ calls for Christian discipleship so that the identity of Christian faith is preserved; Christian discipleship needs the reality of the resurrection so that its liberating manifestation of the gospel is not reduced to sterile moralism.

---

[23]These reflections are adopted from Hans-Georg Gadamer, *Truth and Method* (London: Sheed and Ward, 1975 [1960]), pp. 91-119.

THE HOLY SPIRIT IN AFRICAN INDEPENDENT CHURCHES

John Mbiti

1. Introduction

African Independent Churches (AICs) are those which have separated themselves from overseas and mission-founded Churches and from one another. This phenomenon began in Sierra Leone in 1819 and grew slowly at first. As the continent became more evangelized and the Bible more available in African languages, the momentum of Independent Church movement also increased. In 1993 we reckon that there are some 8,000 independent Churches with some 45 million members (or 14% of total Christian population), found in practically every country of Africa. The figures are proportionally higher in individual countries in central and southern Africa.[1] Literature on the Independent Church Movement is enormous.[2] Many features characterize the Independent Churches, among which their occupation with the Holy Spirit is very prominent. We examine here briefly some of their experiences of and concepts about the Holy Spirit.

Many names of Independent Churches incorporate aspects of the Holy Spirit. For example, in 1973 there were 200 AICs in Kenya, among which the following bore names that incorporated aspects of the Holy Spirit: African Church Holy Spirit Independent, African Church of the Holy Spirit, African Eden Roho {Spirit} Society or African Roho Mission, African Evangelist Fellowship Healing, African God New Covenant Holy Ghost Church, African God Worshippers Fellowship Society, African Holy Ghost Christian Church, African Independent Pentecostal Church of Africa, African Mission of Holy Ghost Church, African Nabi Roho

---

[1]Cf. D.B. Barrett and T.J. Padwick, *Rise Up And Walk!*, Nairobi, Oxford 1989, p. 9. Higher figures are cited by M.L. Daneel, "African Independent Church Pneumatology And The Salvation Of All Creation", *International Review of Mission*, Vol. LXXXII No. 326, Geneva, April 1993, p. 144.

[2]There is an enormous literature on African Independent Churches. Among others: D.B. Barrett, *Schism and Renewal in Africa*, Nairobi, Oxford 1968; H.-J. Becken, *Wo der Glaube noch jung ist*, Erlangen, Germany 1985; W. Korte, *Wir sind die Kirchen der unteren Klassen*, Bern, Frankfurt 1978; R.C. Mitchell and H.W. Turner, *A Bibliography of Modern African Religious Movements*, Evanston (U.S.A.) 1966 (with over 1300 items up to that time); B.G.M. Sundkler, *Bantupropheten in Südafrika*, Stuttgart 1964; H.W. Turner, *African Independent Church.* 2 vols., Oxford 1967; F.B. Welbourn, *East African Rebels*, London 1961. The Interact Research Centre in Birmingham, England assembles all available material on AICs.

Maler *{African Prophet Holy Spirit}*, African Revelation Church St. Mission, African Spiritual Israel Church or Roho *{Spirit}* Church of God of Israel, All Africa Nation of Holy Ghost Church Israel, A-Nabii Church or Church of the Prophets, Apostolic Fellowship Church of God, Bible Fellowship Church, Chosen Church of the Holy Spirit in Kenya, Christian Holy Ghost Church of East Africa, Church of Holy Communion of God, Church of Spirit in Grace and Truth in Africa, Church of the Holy Spirit of God in Africa, Communion Church of Africa, Dini ya Misambwa *{Religion of the Spirits}*, East African Pentecostal Churches, East African Church Roho *{Spirit}* Israel, Eldoret Christian Fellowship Church, Friends of the Holy Spirit (2x), Full Gospel Fellowship Mission of Africa, God's Word and Holy Ghost Church, Gospel Holy Spirit of East Africa, Holy Ghost Church of Kenya, Holy Spirit Brotherhood Church, Dini ya Roho *{Religion of the Spirit}*, Holy Spirit Church of Zayun *(Zion)*, Independent Pentecost Evangelistic Fellowship, International Church of God Evangelistic Fellowship, International Fellowship for Christ, International Pentecost Church of Christian Fellowship, International Pentecostal Assemblies (or Pentecostal Evangelistic Fellowship of Africa), Israel Holy Ghost Church of Kenya, Kendu Roho *{Spirit}* Church Mission, Kenya Full Gospel Fellowship, Kenya Pentecostal Fellowship, Magina Pentecostal Church in Africa, Miracle Revival Fellowship Pentecostal Church, etc.[3]

This is a long (howbeit incomplete) list of names. It reveals immediately the great weight that Independent Churches put onto the Holy Spirit. He is central in their Churchmanship. He is essential for their existence, identity and dignity. For that reason He is mentioned in the names of the Churches, indicating their identification with Him and the status He thereby confers upon them. In these names lies the essence of their being, and that is the Holy Spirit or aspects of Him.

2. The Spirit in African Cosmology

African sensitivity to the Spirit is traceable to the traditional African Religion which is found in various forms in each people *{tribe}*. In African Religion God is clearly understood as Spirit, even when people use anthropomorphic terms to describe him (her). Everywhere it is understood that God is a spiritual being and cannot be portrayed in physical ways. It is remarkable that no physical representations of the One God, Creator of all things, has been found in Africa. In some areas God is compared to the wind or air, and people say that he is invisible and everywhere. Some of the traditional prayers call upon him as Spirit. We take

---

[3]D.B. Barrett, a.o., ed., *Kenya Churches Handbook*, Kisumu, Kenya 1973, pp. 229 ff.

one example from the Shona people of Zimbabwe, who thus pray in praise of God the Great Spirit:

Great Spirit! / Piler up of the rocks into towering mountains! / When thou stampest on the stone, / The dust rises and fills the land. / Hardness of the precipice; / Waters of the pool that turn / Into misty rain when stirred.

Vessel overflowing with oil! / Father of Runji, / Who seweth the heavens like cloth: / Let him knit together that which is below. / Caller forth of the branching trees: / Thou bringest forth the shoots / That they stand erect. / Thou hast filled the land with mankind, / The dust rises on high, oh Lord!

Wonderful One, thou livest / In the midst of the sheltering rocks, / Thou givest of rain to mankind:

We pray to thee, / Hear us, Lord! / Show mercy when we beseech thee, Lord. / Thou art on high with the spirits of the great / Thou raisest the grass-covered hills / Above the earth, and createst the rivers, / Gracious One."[4]

In African cosmology there are other spirits, but these are not God and are subject to Him. Some are the spirits of the departed human beings. Others are those attributed to nature or natural objects and phenomena which have been personified. It is clear that in this context of African Religion the Christian teaching about the Holy Spirit does not offend the religious sensitivities and insights of African peoples. It is not something strange which descends upon them out of the blue. Without major difficulties they accept it as an essential part of the Christian message and something valuable which goes deep into their religiosity.

When we look at African languages it seems as though the double expression "Holy Spirit" is a distinctly Christian usage. There are, naturally, African words for "Holy" and "Spirit". But the combination which gives us the "Holy Spirit" as part of the Trinity, is a specifically Christian heritage, as far as I have been able to find out in East African languages. Through Christian teaching and usage, the two words have been joined and applied to the Third Person of the Trinity, thus 'forcing' or 'achieving' a new theological concept in African languages. This does not mean that the doctrine of the Trinity is easy to comprehend, even though the new concept has been planted successfully into African languages.

---

[4] J.S. Mbiti, *The Prayers of African Religion*, London and New York 1975, pp. 148 f.

3. African Experience of the Holy Spirit

Christian teaching about the Holy Spirit has found a fertile ground in Africa. Unconsciously it affirms and confirms an important part of African worldview, and thereby becomes very meaningful in the religious experiences. Insights from African Religion make it easier for this teaching to penetrate into the thinking and feelings of the people, which in turn makes it readily acceptable and assimilable. Christians feel free to solicit the presence of the Holy Spirit in different situations of their life. They experience Him in ways that are similar to those of the early Church in the New Testament.

Speaking broadly and generally, Jesus Christ is the concrete physical and human dimension (incarnation) of God, on the one hand. The Holy Spirit stands for that other dimension of God, the spiritual (versus the physical), on the other hand. He thus speaks to or meets the longing of the 'spirit' in African worldview. Here we can clearly discern the ground for the development of a strongly pneumatological ecclesiology in the AICs in comparison with Mission-Churches which have a more (or strictly?) christological ecclesiology very much like that of their counterpart Churches in Europe and America. Naturally, both tendencies belong to the New Testament spectrum of the Church, but one has generally struck deeper roots in the AICs. The above list of names from Kenya is a good example of something rarely found in names of Mission-Churches.

4. Speaking in tongues (Glossolalia), visions, prophesyings and revelations

There are many expressions of experiencing or being filled with the Holy Spirit, which are widely spread in AICs. These include speaking in tongues (glossolalia), visions, prophesyings, revelations and dreams. The experiences are seen as originating from the Spirit and are highly valued. They are particularly important for the founders and leaders of AICs, though ordinary members may and do also have them. They confer greater authenticity and credibility upon the founders and leaders than would otherwise be the case. These in turn can then, with authority, inform their Church members and sometimes the public about their experiences, or pass on to them the messages they have thereby received. That adds weight to the leaders and to their Churches in a way that Jesus Christ 'alone does not do'. The Holy Spirit is, in this respect, more active in them than is Jesus Christ. Church members are in Jesus Christ through Faith, but in addition the Holy Spirit is actively in them. One designation of the AICs is 'Prophetic Churches' and many of their founders are commonly known as 'Prophets and Prophetesses'. This is partly due to the fact of their being filled with the Holy Spirit as manifested through these reportedly 'spirit filled or originating' experiences.

In Nigeria for example, "Ecstatic Prophecy and supernormal Experiences" take place during Church services and prayer meetings. "One of the indispensable signs that one has been called to be a prophet or a leader, is the ability to see visions, talk in strange tongues, dream dreams, and hear extraordinary voices. The presence of the healing power is also an unmistakable sign of a divine call... The prophet-leaders are no doubt regarded as 'men of God', and therefore sacrosanct. It is regarded as dangerous to offend them or to call into question the authenticity of their oracles. There is in most of the prophetic Churches a mad rush to acquire these supernatural powers and to experience the divine... In these movements, there is complete freedom to make use of spiritual gifts thus acquired, and one may freely leave oneself to the promptings of the Spirit."[5]

Through prophecy the Holy Spirit warns against sinful life, calls to repentance and condemns unrighteousness in the country's government or in society. Such prophecies move people to prayer in which they ask God to remove the pending catastrophe. Visions serve as vehicles of the most important messages. One prophet, Caleb, in Nigeria explained it to Dr. Nathaniel Ndiokwere that visions come "after a long prayer. The body becomes 'charged' by the Spirit. The visionary is as it were intoxicated. He no longer sees with the material eye, but by the power of the international *{internal?}* mind - the third eye. He also hears internal words - a 'still voice' which no one else but he alone hears." Another prophet, Theo, explained that: "Visions are the photostat of what God intends doing or has done, handed down to us by his angels..."[6]

During Church services and prophetic assemblies, the Holy Spirit manifests himself in various ways, including the shaking of the body, charismatic addresses and speaking in tongues, or even through sneezing. Some Churches take such experiences as fulfilling the prophecy of Joel 2:28-32 in which God promises to "pour out my Spirit on all flesh" (cf. Acts 2:16-21).

Possession by the Holy Spirit is reported all over Africa. It happens to the prophets or other members of the Churches, or even to the whole congregation together. This phenomenon is heightened by powerful dancing. An example can be cited from the 'Khaki Movement' (known to be a "congregation of the Spirit") in Zaire, in which "many of the adherents were known to have performed acrobatic movements. Seized by the Spirit while in the Church, they would begin to jump up

---

[5]N. Ndiokwere, *Prophecy and Revolution*, SPCK London 1981, p. 77.

[6]Ndiokwere, op. cit., 79 f.

and down, with violent shaking and rushing out, and even climbing to the top of trees..." The feeling on the possessed person is as though he is no longer the normal himself or herself but another person.[7] This is the same as or similar to the feeling experienced in African Religion.

Less dynamic but equally important, is the Baptism through the Holy Spirit, which is practised by many (but not all) Independent Churches. The most classical example is the Kimbangu Church in Zaire, which has dispensed with water Baptism altogether, replacing it with that of the Holy Spirit. In this Church it is understood that God is at work in the Baptism, in which His Spirit comes into the Church member and changes him or her. Baptism is not carried out on children before they reach the age of 12 years. The Kimbangu Church bases its Baptism with the Holy Spirit on biblical texts like that in which John the Baptist says that: "I baptize you with water for repentance, but He Who is coming after me is mightier than I... He will baptize you with the Holy Spirit..." (Matt 3:11; cf. Mark 1:8, Luke 3:16; John 1:33 f.). The Kimbangu Church teaches categorically, that "Jesus did not baptize with water because He baptized with the Holy Spirit. In other words, for Kimbanguist theology Jesus marks the end of the former practice of baptism with water and the coming of the era of baptism with the Holy Spirit... If God sends down His Holy Spirit on someone {Acts 10:44-48}, is it absolutely necessary to baptize that person with water, since nothing God does is imperfect?"[8] The Kimbangu Church puts a lot of weight upon personal decision for Faith and the challenges involved in Christian life.

Some of the Dreams (or Visions) of the founders and leaders of AICs are seen as expressions of God's revelation. Countless numbers of Church ministers, pastors, priests, founders and leaders of AICs (as well others in Mission-Churches) tell how, through dreams or visions, God called them to take up Church work.

---

[7]Ndiokwere, op. cit., 87 ff.

[8]P. Manicom, introducer, *Out of Africa Kimbanguism*, CEM London, 1979, pp. 37 f., part of "The Essence of Kimbanguist Theology". For a fuller discussion of Baptism by the Holy Spirit, see Christine Lienemann-Perrin, "Taufe und Kirchenzugehörigkeit in der Kimbanguistenkirche (Zaire)", in C. Lienemann-Perrin, ed.: *Taufe und Kirchenzugehörigkeit*, Chr. Kaiser, München 1983, pp. 389-416.

5. Ecumenical Relations

It is reported in Zimbabwe for example, that the Spirit-oriented AICs have criticized other Churches as not being truly Christian, and this constitutes "a formidable stumbling block in the way of ecumenical cooperation."[9] Nevertheless ecumenical cooperation is generally on the increase everywhere in Africa, as members of the different Churches get to study or work together and know one another better. We have already cited the case of the Kimbangu Church which baptizes with the Holy Spirit and not with water. It was accepted into membership of the World Council of Churches in 1969. A deeper understanding of the doctrine of the Holy Spirit among the AICs should also help to open them more for ecumenical cooperation.

In his book, *Prophecy and Revolution*, London 1981, Dr. Nathaniel Ndiokwere questions which Spirit is at work in AICs. He charges that there is a "general confusion caused by misunderstanding of the biblical meaning of the Holy Spirit" and that this is "liable to be disheartening." He is very sceptical about the claim of the AICs to be possessed by the Holy Spirit: "The general confusion caused by misunderstanding of the biblical meaning of the Holy Spirit in the Independent Churches is liable to be disheartening. Which 'spirit' is it that moves, possesses, and instils confusion in worship, and often drives men to madness? Is it the personal spirit, the 'ancestor', or the Holy Spirit of the Scriptures? Some would question whether it is the Holy Spirit that is at work if it 'knocks people about and makes them fall over', and it is asserted that the true Spirit gives people messages rather than makes them roll about. On this view, all possession would be an occasion for exorcism, but very few have arrived at this advanced conclusion.

"In any case whatever may be their achievements, it could still be said that the prophetic vocation in the Independent African Churches exhibits a dubious character. Our observation may no doubt be seen as 'flogging a dead horse', since most of our critics have already made up their minds concerning the character of this phenomenon in Africa!"[10]

---

[9]M.L. Daneel, *Fambidzano, Ecumenical Movement of Zimbabwean Independent Churches*, Gweru 1989, p. 19 f.

[10]Ndiokwere, op. cit., p. 257, quoting directly from H.W. *Turner, African Independent Church*, Vol. 2, Oxford 1967, p. 134.

Very clearly Dr. Ndiokwere is overstating his criticism of the AICs and their experience of the Holy Spirit. In some respects he exhibits the stand of his Roman Catholic Church which has generally been critical of AICs or not officially open towards them. He also rushes into criticizing the experience of the Holy Spirit in the charismatic movement: "One cannot fail to be surprised by the rate at which 'the spirit' moves people and 'throws confusion' into the gatherings of charismatics all over Europe and America" (p. 257). Is this strong criticism called for?

Professor M.L. Daneel who has devoted many years to the study of Independent Churches especially in Zimbabwe, states that they clearly distinguish the Holy Spirit from the spirits of the departed. He writes: "I pointed out that the Holy Spirit was predominantly perceived as a person and that his demands in the all-important faith-healing activities of the prophetic healers were more in the nature of a *confrontation* with and *opposition* to the traditional spirit world than an *accommodation* of and *compromise* with the old beliefs." Comments made by members of these Churches are very clear. For example, one states: "'I learnt that the Holy Spirit gives one strength to preach the Word of God. We see in the New Testament that it was after the outpouring of the Holy Spirit that Peter started preaching and healing...'"[11] This is in complete contrast with the scepticism expressed by Father Dr. Ndiokwere. Professor Daneel states categorically what has already become widely accepted, namely that: "I consider the AICs on the whole to be *integral to the mainstream of Christianity*. Most of them accept and apply scripture as literally and fundamentally normative. Belief in a triune God, the reign and closeness of a creator father, the saviourhood and mediation of Christ and the pervasive presence of an indwelling Holy Spirit, together with the regular or intermittent practice of the sacraments of baptism and holy communion, are common key features of these churches."[12] A good number of Independent Churches are members of ecumenical bodies like national Christian Councils of their respective countries, the All Africa Conference of Churches and the World Council of Churches. In these ecumenical bodies they show themselves to be mutually open towards and accepting "main stream Churches". Many have also their own ecumenical councils, of which the Organisation of African Instituted Churches with headquarters in Nairobi, Kenya is the continental body. The AICs have all along sought ecumenical conciliarism, even if other Churches were not

[11]Daneel, op. cit., p. 339, his italics.

[12]Daneel, op. cit., in footnote 1 supra, p. 143.

quick to reciprocate in a brotherly and sisterly fashion.[13] They nevertheless share more and more common concerns with other Churches, such as justice, freedom, peace, environment, fight against corruption and abuse of human rights, and evangelisation. It can be expected that their occupation with the Holy Spirit will have some impact on other Churches, though this is not yet so evident. In comparison, the "main stream Churches" have a weaker Pneumatology, just as some Independent Churches have a weaker Christology.

While it is important to view the role of the Holy Spirit in the African Independent Churches with scholarly objectivity and caution, we cannot *in toto* dismiss that role or call it 'confusion'. It is clear that the Holy Spirit as we understand and see Him at work in the Bible, is also at work in the AICs. At the same time these are human Churches and institutions and some 'excessive' (or over enthusiastic) interpretations and claims in their teaching and practice cannot be ruled out. Perhaps these belong to the process of growing up in Jesus Christ through the Holy Spirit (Ephesians 2:21 f.; 4:15 f.).

6. Conclusion

While there is still much to investigate about Pneumatology in the African Independent Churches, we may draw some tentative conclusions out of our short survey.

(i) The fact that the Independent Churches have highlighted the Person and work of the Holy Spirit is a common, perhaps uniting, point of strength on their part. It deserves to be taken seriously and with appreciation. It is a challenge to 'main stream Churches' and unveils the fact that in comparison, the latter have largely neglected, or are in danger of neglecting the Third Person of the Trinity.

(ii) The AICs put greater weight on the Holy Spirit than on Jesus Christ in their ecclesiology and in their practice of Christian life. They have thus a more pneumatological than christological ecclesiology, though we must not push this distinction too far. However, in the healing practices which are so important in the AICs, Jesus Christ is more prominent than the Holy Spirit, while the latter features more strongly in ecstatic experiences like visions, prophesying, possession, revelations, prophetic dreams and glossolalia. These experiences of the Holy Spirit are

---

[13]See: "A Chronology of Conciliarism and the African Indigenous Churches 1815-1987" in D.B. Barrett and T.J. Padwick, *Rise Up And Walk!*, Oxford University Press, Nairobi 1989, pp. 55-90.

not in contradiction to either the Bible or experiences of the Church in course of its history. They are also not essentially different from experiences in the Pentecostal and Charismatic movements.

(iii) These manifestations of the Holy Spirit in or through the Independent Churches are an enrichment to the Church in Africa. It makes more theological sense to attribute them to the working of the Holy Spirit than to that of the devil or other agencies.

(iv) The life of Jesus was filled with the Holy Spirit. He healed the sick, drove out evil spirits, experienced visions and made prophecies. What we do not hear about Him, is whether He experienced ecstatic Spirit possessions, had revelatory dreams, or spoke in tongues. Nevertheless, all these manifestations of the Holy Spirit are mentioned in the early Church. They are also more or less present in the Jewish Bible (Old Testament).

(v) Whether or not all the African Independent Churches put great weight on the Holy Spirit, they are in general a dynamic witness to the presence of Christianity in Africa. They contribute to the religious life and the theological development of the Church. That which is positive can only be attributed to God. The Holy Spirit is at work through and in them, just as He is at work in the Mission-Churches which, seemingly, have a different understanding of Him. Moreover, emphasis on the Holy Spirit comes or grows with time and does not start on the day the Churches are founded. This shift is also linked to wider understanding of Christian doctrines.

(vi) The Independent Churches are widening their understanding of the work of the Holy Spirit beyond the level of providing ecstatic experiences. He is also at work in other areas of practical life. An example of this is mentioned in Zimbabwe, where it is said that: "Having delivered His people from political bondage, the Holy Spirit was now increasingly seen as the liberator from poverty and economic despair, as one intimately involved... in nation building."[14] Is this an overstatement? How far we can go along with this sentiment is for me an open question. In any case the Holy Spirit Who, at the beginning, moved over the face of the waters" as the earth was "without form and void" and changed chaos into

---

[14]Daneel, op. cit. (note 1 supra), p. 159. In this article Professor Daneel attributes to "the AIC prophets" that they "are starting to conceive of and respond to the Holy Spirit as the *earthkeeping Spirit*... As this conviction grows... the Churches are being mobilized into ecologically liberating action" (pp. 160 ff., his own italics).

meaningful shape, continues to move over the face of our human history, in and outside the Church. We must remain open to His transforming work through whichever means, method, persons or natural phenomena He may use, to the glory of the Triune God.

FORM UND NORM

Geschichtlichkeit und Verbindlichkeit

DAMASKINOS PAPANDREOU

Wenn man von Form spricht, dann versteht man darunter meistens einen vielfältigen, legitimen, theologischen oder liturgischen Ausdruck des Wesens, d.h. der geoffenbarten Wahrheit, die wir nur durch Teilnahme und Teilhabe am Leben der Kirche erfahren können.

Wesen und *Form* verhalten sich zueinander wie Einheit in der Vielfalt. Hierzu möchte ich Blaise Pascal zitieren: "Die Vielheit, die sich auf keine Einheit zurückführen lässt, ist Wirrwarr; die Einheit, die nicht von der Vielfalt abhängt, ist Tyrannei."

Es wäre tatsächlich bequem und nicht zweckmässig, eine Einheit ohne Vielfalt anzustreben. Die Einheit in der Vielfalt und die Vielfalt in der Einheit kennzeichnen jene lebendige Kirche Christi, die in organischer Beziehung zur Welt und zur Geschichte stehen soll und die um der Erlösung des Menschen willen der Wahrheit des Evangeliums das Fleisch des Hier und Jetzt gibt, ohne ihre wesentliche Kontinuität anzutasten. Das geschichtliche Gewand, welches die inkarnierte Wahrheit in jeder Epoche annimmt, ändert nichts am Wesen der Wahrheit.

Einheit und Quellentreue der Kirche einerseits, Vielgestaltigkeit und kontinuierliche Inkarnierung der Wahrheit anderseits sind die Früchte des Heiligen Geistes, der immer in der Geschichte lebt, damit die Wahrheit der Kirche, die mit dem fleischgewordenen Logos Gottes identisch ist, nicht verraten wird, wenn sie in jeder geschichtlichen Epoche neu inkarniert wird; sie wird eher dann verraten, wenn sie wie eine Reliquie oder ein Museumsstück aufbewahrt wird - aus Angst, sie könnte von der Geschichte angetastet werden.

Das Drama der Kirche besteht darin, dass es in ihr Glieder gibt, die zwischen Wesen und Form nicht mehr zu unterscheiden verstehen. Die Folge ist, dass sie formale Gesichtspunkte für wesentlich halten - der Fehler des Traditionalismus - oder die zentrale Wesenheit relativieren - der Fehler des falsch verstandenen Reformismus.

Wie bekannt, wurde die geoffenbarte Wahrheit im Osten und im Westen verschieden empfangen, gelebt und verstanden. Diese Verschiedenheiten der Theologie wurden als vereinbar innerhalb eines selben Glaubens aufgefasst, um so mehr, als ein wacher Sinn für die Transzendenz des Mysteriums und den vorwiegend apophatischen Charakter, den sein menschlicher Ausdruck anzunehmen hat, freies Feld einem legitimen Pluralismus der Theologien im Schosse desselben traditionellen Glaubens liess. Eine entgegengesetzte Bewegung entstand dann auf beiden Seiten, mehr noch im Westen als im Osten. Diese hat dazu geneigt, den Glauben und seinen Ausdruck mit besonderen Theologien zu identifizieren und in den Bereich, auf dem notwendigerweise Übereinstimmung verlangt wird, so manche Aspekte des christlichen Denkens einzubeziehen, die vordem als legitime Versuche der Theologen, das Mysterium anzugehen oder auszudrücken, betrachtet worden waren.

So hat man oft die Form, d.h. die verschiedenen theologischen Traditionen, die den verschiedenen Kulturen entsprachen, ausschliesslich mit dem Wesen identifiziert, d.h. mit dem von der lebendigen apostolischen Tradition getragenen Glauben. In diesem Falle wurde die Form zur Norm. Eine solche Einstellung bringt natürlich Gefahren mit sich, die man aus dem Leben der Kirche kennt und von denen man sich befreien muss, wenn man einen wesentlichen Beitrag zur Überwindung der Trennung leisten will.

Die Verabsolutierung der Form - ohne Unterscheidung zwischen dem Glauben und seinem legitimen Ausdruck - begegnet uns in der Geschichte der Kirche auch in einer anderen Form von Verabsolutierungen von Teilwahrheiten der geoffenbarten Wahrheit, die ebenfalls Gefahren mit sich bringt, auf die wir auch kurz hinweisen möchten.

1. "Form" als Norm

Wenn man von den heutigen Erscheinungsformen der orthodoxen Kirche ausgeht, dann stellt man oft fest, dass Orthodoxie und Orthopraxie nicht immer zusammengehen, obwohl sie zusammengehören. Es gibt z.B. *Orthodoxe*, die das Wesen des apostolischen Glaubens und seinen Ausdruck mit der Form und mit den Partikular-Traditionen auf eine ausschliessliche Art und Weise identifizieren. Für sie wird dann die Form zur Norm für die Bewertung aller anderen nicht-orthodoxen Erscheinungsformen des christlichen Glaubens und der christlichen Frömmigkeit, die sie - sowieso ausserhalb von ihren formellen Grenzen - nicht in der Lage sind, zu entdecken, geschweige denn kennenzulernen oder anzuerkennen. Ich meine damit die Fundamentalisten, die heute in allen Kirchen anzutreffen sind. Um ein Beispiel anzugeben, wären die Altkalendarier in Griechenland zu nennen, für die der alte Kalender - d.h. in diesem Falle eine Form -, der nicht einmal den genauen astronomischen Gegebenheiten angepasst worden ist, zum Kriterium der Bewertung der Orthodoxie geworden ist.

Meine Ausführungen möchte ich mit einigen Beispielen aus der *römisch-katholischen* Kirche und der Alten, ungeteilten Kirche belegen. Betrachtet man jene römisch-katholischen Dogmen in ihrer geschichtlichen Entwicklung, die die Letzten Dinge betreffen wie auch die Sakramente, die Rechtfertigung, den gleichzeitigen, vernünftigen und selbstlosen Charakter des Glaubensaktes, so unterscheidet man zwischen dem Wesen, was den Inhalt dieser Dogmen anbetrifft, und zwischen den philosophischen und theologischen Formen, in die sich diese Dogmen wegen der westlichen Kulturwelt, in der sie kraft der geschichtlichen Umstände erarbeitet wurden, gekleidet haben.

Diese Definitionen haben nur festhalten wollen, was schon vom Konsensus der östlichen wie der westlichen Väter gelehrt worden war. Angesichts der neuen Fragen, die sich damals der Kirche im Westen stellten, haben sie den Glaubensgehalt festhalten wollen. Was diese Fragen anbetrifft, so dürfte von den Orthodoxen nicht mehr verlangt werden, als dass sie sich davon enthalten, die Form, die der Westen seinem Bekenntnis geben musste, um es in einer bestimmten Epoche zu verteidigen, als illegitim zu verwerfen. Hier gilt, was Papst Paul VI. in der Patriarchalkirche St. Georg im Phanar betont hat: "Auch hierin muss uns übrigens die Liebe behilflich sein, wie sie Hilarius und Athanasius zur Zeit, da schwerwiegende Differenzen den Episkopat spalteten, behilflich war, über die Unterschiedlichkeiten des Vokabulars hinweg die Identität des Glaubens wahrzunehmen. Verteidigte nicht der heilige Basilius in seiner Hirtenliebe den wahren Glauben an den Heiligen Geist, indem er es vermied, sich gewisser Worte zu bedienen, die, so zutreffend sie auch sein mochten, doch für einen Teil des christlichen Volkes zu Ärgernis Anlass geben konnten? Und war der heilige Cyrill von Alexandrien nicht 433 damit einverstanden, seine so schöne Theologie beiseite zu lassen, um mit Johannes von Antiochien Frieden zu schliessen, nachdem feststand, dass trotz unterschiedlicher Ausdrucksweisen ihr Glaube der gleiche war?"[1]

Zu den Fragen, die sich auf die Pneumatologie und die Epiklese beziehen, könnte man behaupten, dass die im Westen ausgearbeiteten Lehrausdrücke nicht als widersprüchlich zu den Lehren des Ostens interpretiert werden dürfen. Man kann und man muss einerseits die Formeln der griechischen, andererseits die der lateinischen Väter und das Filioque erklären, indem man ihre Übereinstimmung unter völliger Beachtung ihrer jeweiligen Originalität aufweist. Seit dem 4. Jahrhundert gab es in der westlichen Tradition das Filioque, und dies wurde

---

[1]Ansprache Papst Pauls VI. bei Patriarch Athenagoras am 25. Juli 1967. In: Tomos Agapis, hg. i. A. des Stiftungsfonds PRO ORIENTE, Wein 1978, 113f.

solange nie als Hindernis zur Gemeinschaft betrachtet - bis diese Gemeinschaft aus anderen Gründen zerbrach.

Vom orthodoxen Standpunkt aus anstössig ist es jedoch, dass durch die Einfügung des Filioque das Nizäno-Konstantinopolitanische Glaubensbekenntnis verändert worden ist trotz der ausdrücklichen Ablehnung und Verurteilung jedweder Veränderung durch die Ökumenischen Konzile.

Es sollte jedenfalls hier unterschieden werden zwischen der Einfügung des Filioque in das Nizäno-Konstantinopolitanum und den verschiedenen Pneumatologien, die im Osten und Westen entwickelt worden sind. Die Rückkehr auf den normativen Glaubensausdruck des II. Ökumenischen Konzils wäre die beste Art und Weise, das 1600jährige Jubiläum zu feiern. Dies habe ich bereits im Jahre 1981 in Rom betont. Was die verschiedenen pneumatologischen Entwicklungen angeht, so sollten die Römisch-Katholischen und die Orthodoxen voneinander nur verlangen, sich zunächst davon zu enthalten, die Formulierungen des anderen als illegitim zu verwerfen. Sie sollten ihre Bezeugung bekräftigen, dass der Weg, der dem Bewusstsein dieser Konvergenz Vertiefung und Ausdruck ermöglicht, der Dialog zwischen den beiden Kirchen ist.

Was die Definitionen der Unbefleckten Empfängnis der Seligen Jungfrau Maria und ihrer Aufnahme in den Himmel betrifft, so stossen sie sich nicht am Wesen des orthodoxen Glaubens und widersprechen auch nicht den Symbolen der Ökumenischen Konzile. Was dort von der römisch-katholischen Kirche kanonisiert worden ist, ist allein das, was die Substanz dessen ausmacht, was der Osten selber, namentlich in seinen traditionellen Liturgien, seit der Väterzeit von der unvergleichlichen Heiligkeit der Seligen Jungfrau Maria seit dem Beginn ihrer Existenz und von ihrer Vollendung mit ihrem auferstandenen und verherrlichten Sohn glaubt. Als offizieller Ausdruck, der aus geschichtlichen Gründen der Verehrung der Gottesmutter im christlichen Volk des Westens auferlegt worden war, werden diese Definitionen von den orthodoxen Gläubigen respektiert, selbst wenn sie nicht sehen, wie die katholische Formulierung sich mit der Lehre von der Erbsünde vereinbaren lässt oder eine Begründung in der Heiligen Schrift und der Tradition haben kann. Mehr noch: was allgemein die negative Reaktion hervorgerufen hat, ist die Art und Weise, auf die diese neuen Dogmen von der Kirche des Westens proklamiert worden sind, d.h. ohne Befragung der orthodoxen Kirche.

Auch hier müsste gefordert werden, dass im Zusammenhang mit der Wiederaufnahme normaler Beziehungen zwischen den beiden Kirchen nicht a priori die Möglichkeit ausgeschlossen wird, in der Formulierung dieser Wahrheiten eine Übereinstimmung zu finden.

Die "Form" als unersetzbarer normativer Ausdruck des Glaubens

Neben den vielen "Formen", die als legitime Entfaltungen des einen Glaubens betrachtet werden können, gibt es auch "Formen", die als "unersetzbarer" normativer Glaubensausdruck betrachtet werden müssen. Dies gilt z.B. für das *Nizäno-Konstantinopolitanum.*

Angesichts der heutigen Wirklichkeit ist oft die Rede von einem ökumenischen Glaubensbekenntnis, das die alten Symbole eventuell ersetzen könnte. Ein künftiges ökumenisches Glaubensbekenntnis hätte vor allem dann einen Sinn, wenn es die Einheit im Glauben, also die Einheit der Kirche - welche das Ziel des Ökumenismus ist - ausdrücken würde. Es sollte dann in einer Weise verbindliche Lehrautorität besitzen, so dass es in allen Kirchen und an allen Orten angenommen würde. Es wäre keine intellektuelle, rationale Schöpfung der kirchlichen Institution, sondern ein lebendiger Ausdruck des gemeinsamen Glaubens, der durch seine spirituelle Klangfarbe seinen rechten doxologischen Platz im Leben der Kirche einnehmen würde.

Damit ist natürlich nicht gesagt, dass die Kirche nicht die Lehrautorität hätte, ein neues Glaubensbekenntnis auszuarbeiten, wenn dies durch das Hier und Jetzt erforderlich würde. Die Kirche ist der Ort der ununterbrochenen Inkarnation der Wahrheit durch den Heiligen Geist.

Was ein ökumenisches Glaubensbekenntnis anbetrifft, so bezweifle ich jedoch die Möglichkeit und die Notwendigkeit, ein solches zu schaffen - und zwar aus *folgenden Gründen*:
1. Es fehlt ein allgemeingültiges, universelles "Lehramt", das für die gesamte Christenheit verpflichtend sprechen könnte. Ein solches wäre nur *nach* Wiederherstellung der Einheit denkbar.
2. Ausserdem bezieht sich die dringende heutige Not nicht auf die eine oder andere christliche Lehre, die in Zweifel gezogen wird, sondern auf unseren gemeinsamen christlichen Glauben als solchen, der vollzugs- und inhaltsmässig in Frage gestellt wird.
3. Was sollte schliesslich in einem eventuellen künftigen ökumenischen Glaubensbekenntnis, welches alle Christen ansprechen und kurz gefasst sein sollte, ausgesagt und weggelassen werden? Welches wären seine entscheidenden Elemente? Jedenfalls ist in keinem Glaubensbekenntnis der Alten, ungeteilten

Kirche alles gesagt worden, was zum Glauben gehört - und es ist auch nie nötig gewesen.

4. Ich glaube nicht, dass man unsere heutige Situation der Trennung durch lehramtliche Definitionen überwinden kann. Das Zweite Vatikanische Konzil hat mit Recht keinen Versuch in dieser Richtung unternommen.

5. Damit ist nicht gesagt, dass die Kirche nicht nach verschiedenen Ausdrucksformen des Glaubens suchen könnte, um die Heilsbotschaft in den verschiedenen Situationen zur Sprache zu bringen.

6. Nicht die Formulierung eines ökumenischen Glaubensbekenntnisses ist meines Erachtens das Wesentliche, sondern die Entdeckung des einen Glaubensbekenntnisses in den vielen Bekenntnissen.

Was die "Form", d.h. die Gestalt des Nizäno-Konstantinopolitanischen Glaubensbekenntnisses anbetrifft, so möchte ich mit M. Farantos

> "einige Ansichten von namhaften westlichen Dogmatikern der Gegenwart anführen. So spricht J. Ratzinger über 'das durch nichts aufzuhebende Recht des Griechischen im Christlichen. Ich bin der Überzeugung, dass es im tiefsten kein blosser Zufall war, dass die christliche Botschaft bei ihrer Gestaltwerdung zuerst in die griechische Welt eintrat und sich hier mit der Frage nach dem Verstehen, nach der Wahrheit verschmolzen hat'.[2] Den Beitrag des griechischen Geistes zum Christentum unterstreicht auch J. Auer, der betont: 1. dass der Eingottglaube nur durch die grosse philosophische Reflexion der Griechen aus den Banden des jüdischen Nationalismus sich befreien konnte;[3] 2. dass die grossen Werke der Theologie, die in der Vergangenheit hervorgebracht wurden, 'ohne den Dienst der grossen griechischen Philosophie' nicht möglich gewesen wären;[4] und 3. dass 'die Rede von der Hellenisierung des Christentums durch die Väter im ganzen schief und grossenteils falsch' ist .[5]

> Hinsichtlich unseres Themas jedoch sind die Bemerkungen von H. Thielicke nützlich, die im übrigen nicht unbekannt sind; er behauptet nämlich, dass die griechischen Wörter und die philosophischen Begriffe in den alten Glaubensbekenntnissen nicht zufälligerweise ausgewählt worden

---

[2] J. Ratzinger, Einführung in das Christentum. Vorlesungen über das Apostolische Glaubensbekenntnis, 1968, 51.

[3] J. Auer, Kleine Katholische Dogmatic, Bd. 2, 1978, 437.

[4] Ebd. 439.

[5] Ebd. 448.

sind, sondern weil ihr Inhalt 'schon von Haus eine gewisse Affinität zu den Bedeutungsgehalten, in deren Dienst sie gestellt werden', hat. Trotz des 'Bedeutungswandels', dem sich diese Wörter und Begriffe bei ihrem Eintritt in das Christliche unterziehen, und trotz der 'Preisgabe ihrer Identität, die sie als 'neue Schöpfung' erleiden, bleibt bei ihnen genau so wie beim Getauften die Kontinuität zur früheren Existenz ja *erhalten'*. 'Natürlich ist der Bedeutungswandel nicht total'. Diese Begriffe, wie z.B. Logos, Ousia, Hypostase usw., haben in der göttlichen Offenbarung wie auch in der christlichen Theologie 'doch eine spezielle Qualifikation für die *neue* Funktion, die ihnen zugemutet wird'; sie wurden 'nicht beliebig' und 'nicht willkürlich' ausgewählt, und daher sind sie auch nicht 'beliebig austauschbar'.[6]

Diese Tatsache muss auch mit einer anderen in Verbindung gebracht werden, nämlich dass wir heute in einer Zeit leben, die von der Säkularisierung bestimmt wird, die durch den 'Prozess der Modernisierung als Industrialisierung und Bürokratisierung des Lebens mit all den daraus erwachsenden Folgen in der abendländischen westlichen Kultur dazu geführt hat, dass die Sinnfrage jeder öffentlichen Geltung beraubt und in die Sphäre des Privaten abgedrängt worden ist', wie W. Pannenberg in bezug auf das bekannte Buch von Peter Berger 'The homeless Mind' berichtet.[7]

Was insbesondere die Sprache unserer Zeit charakterisiert, ist ihre Entartung zu einer technischen Sprache, zu einer Sprache des Messens und Kalkulierens, zu einer Sprache, die den Sinn der menschlichen Existenz nicht mehr in einer dialogischen Begegnung mit den Tiefen des Seins sucht; sie ist eine Sprache mathematischer Berechnungen und Informationen. 'Deshalb verstummt das Zeugnis von Gott da, wo Sprache nur noch Technik der Mitteilung von 'etwas' ist. Im logistischen Kalkül kommt Gott nicht vor. Vielleicht rührt unsere Schwierigkeit, heute von Gott zu reden, gerade davon her, dass unsere Sprache immer mehr dahin tendiert, zum reinen Kalkül zu werden, dass sie immer mehr blosse Signifikation technischer Mitteilung wird und immer weniger Berührung im Logos des gemeinsamen Seins ist, in der so der Grund aller Dinge ahnend oder bewusst mitberührt wird'.[8]

Auf Grund des oben Ausgeführten können die 'einzelnen Formulierungen des apostolischen Bekenntnisses' und folglich auch des Nizäno-

---

[6]H. Thielicke, Der Evangelische Glaube, Bd. 1, 1968, 88-89.

[7]W. Pannenberg, in: HK (1981) 183.

[8]J. Ratzinger, a.a.O. 66.

Konstantinopolitanums nicht 'durch andere, vermeintlich zeitgemässere Formeln ersetzt (werden), die auch im besten Falle nie die Funktion erfüllen können, die die alten Bekenntnisformulierungen tatsächlich haben, dass nämlich durch sie der einzelne Christ sich in die Gemeinschaft der ganzen Christenheit einreihen kann'. Daher stimme ich auch im Grunde mit Pannenbergs Ansicht überein, dass nämlich 'das heute so verbreitete Unverständnis für die Bekenntnisformulierungen nicht nach ihrer Abschaffung (ruft), sondern nach ihrer Erklärung'.[9]"[10]

Zur Überwindung des ausschliesslichen Festhaltens an "Formen" gerufen

Überwinden wir nicht das Festhalten an "Formen", so können wir nicht auf eine konstruktive Art und Weise gemeinsam die Frage beantworten, "ob unsere Trennungen - zum grossen Teil wenigstens - nicht eher Unterschiede verschiedener Denk- und Sprachformen, unterschiedlicher Spiritualität und somit Ausdruck legitimer Pluralität in der Glaubensüberlieferung seien als wirkliche, sich ausschliessende Trennungen in der Überlieferung des einen und verpflichtenden Glaubens selbst. Man beruft sich dabei auf den wachen Sinn der östlichen Theologie für die Transzendenz des Mysteriums und den vorwiegend apophatischen Charakter, den sein menschlicher Ausdruck anzunehmen hat. Diese Weisheit[11] des Ostens ist auch zumindest in der grossen Theologie des Westens nicht vergessen worden; es gilt sie nur neu zu entdecken. So sagt z.B. Thomas von Aquin, dass der Glaubensakt sich nicht auf die Glaubensformel beziehe, sondern auf die Wirklichkeit Gottes und seines Heilshandelns, der gegenüber jedes menschliche Wort immer zu kurz greift.[12] Die Anerkennung dieses "an sich" so selbstverständlichen "Sachverhaltes" wird vor einer sich selbst absolut setzenden Eindimensionalität theologischen Denkens bewahren und schafft Raum für die Anerkenntnis von Komplementärformen theologischer Rede, in denen sich erst das nie ganz aussagbare Ganze des Glaubens - annäherungsweise - bricht."[13]

---

[9]W. Pannenberg, Das Glaubensbekenntnis, 1974, 22.

[10]M. Farantos, Bemerkungen zur Trinitäts- und Geisteslehre des Glaubensbekenntnisses von Nizäa-Konstantinopel. In: Le IIe Concile oecuménique. Signification et actualité pour le monde chrétien d'aujourd'hui, Chambésy 1982, 237-238 (Etudes théologique 2).

[11]Vgl. D. Papandreou, in: KuD 29 (1983) 100-13; hier: 109-11.

[12]Vgl. Thomas von Aquin, Sth II-II, 1,2.

In dieser Richtung gibt es einige wesentliche *ökumenische Fragen*, die heute gemeinsam neu durchdacht werden müssen.
1. Wie verhalten sich akademische theologische Arbeit und kirchlicher Auftrag zueinander, damit weder die akademische Tätigkeit eine trockene intellektuelle Schöpfung ist noch der kirchliche Auftrag von den akademischen Lehrinstitutionen getrennt wird?
2. Wie verhalten sich in unserer akademischen und kirchlichen Botschaft, die wir übermitteln wollen, Inhalt und Form zueinander, damit weder die wesentliche Botschaft relativiert wird - unter dem Vorwand einer angeblichen Anpassung unseres Zeugnisses an unsere konkrete Wirklichkeit hier und jetzt - noch legitime formelle Gesichtspunkte verabsolutiert werden, was eine Gefahr für den heutigen Fundamentalismus und Traditionalismus zu sein scheint?
3. Wie verhalten sich Glaube und Liebe zueinander, wenn man vor allem davon ausgehen muss und soll, dass Glaube ohne Liebe ein starrer Intellektualismus und Liebe ohne Glaube ein leerer Emotionalismus sein kann? "τὸ ὅλον ἐστὶν πίστις καὶ ἀγάπη ὧν οὐδέτερον προκέκριται" (Klemens von Alexandrien) - d.h. das untrennbare Ganze (τὸ ὅλον) ist Glaube *und* Liebe, und keines kann vorgezogen werden.
4. Wie bildet man neue theologische Kräfte aus, die das Glaubenszeugnis heute übermitteln können, ohne sein Wesen zu verraten? Wir brauchen Theologen, die fähig sind, dem Zeugnis des Evangeliums das Fleisch der Geschichte im Hier und Jetzt zu geben, ohne die Kontinuität des Zeugnisses, was sein Wesen anbetrifft, abzubrechen. Wir brauchen Leute, die dem Heiligen Geist verfügbar und gleichzeitig der apostolischen Tradition der Kirche treu sein können.

Das Festhalten an "Formen" ist oft die Folge einer unechten Gemeinschaft der Christen mit dem Haupt der Kirche, d.h. mit Christus. Die Priorität hat aber das Wesen und nicht die Wörter. Leben erzeugt Leben und der *Geist* den *Buchstaben*. Niemals umgekehrt der Buchstabe den Geist oder das Tote das Lebendige.

Im Rahmen der Kirche und der orthodoxen Theologie ist eine Unterwerfung "unter den Buchstaben"[14] nicht gerechtfertigt. Die Auslegungsart, die sich auf den Buchstaben beschränkt, kam den jüdischen Schriftgelehrten gelegen, deren statische Auffassung vom Gesetz sich in scharfem Gegensatz zum dynamischen Leben der Kirche befand und die die "Vollkommenheit durch Zusätze"[15] zu

---

[13]F.-L. Hossfeld, Ansprachen aus Anlass der Ehrenpromotion Sr. Eminenz Damaskinos Papandreou, Bonn 1988, 11f.

[14]Gregor von Nazianz, Über den Heiligen Geist: PG 36, 160 B.

erreichen suchten. Der Sinn für das Wachstum, das die lebendige Realität der Kirche voraussetzt, war dem unfruchtbaren Geist der Gesetzeslehrer fremd, und ihnen gleichen jene Orthodoxen, die sich im Kreise bewegen und "das Ungeschriebene"[16] verurteilen. "Die verborgene Schönheit",[17] d.h. die Fülle der göttlichen Wahrheit, die sich hinter dem Buchstaben der Heiligen Schrift verbirgt, wird durch Teilnahme und Teilhabe am Leben der Kirche verbürgt.

"Wir behaupten nicht, dass die Erkenntnis bloss in Begriffen bestehe, sondern sagen, dass sie ein göttliches Wissen und jenes Licht sei, das infolge des Gehorsams gegen Gott in der Seele entzündet wird, ein Licht, das dem Menschen alles offenbart und ihn lehrt, sich selbst zu erkennen und Gottes teilhaftig zu werden."[18]

Nicht der Buchstabe der christlichen Lehre ist es, der die Heiden bekehrt, sondern die ins Leben umgesetzte christliche Lehre. Justin erzählt von sich selbst und anderen, dass er wie diese durch unmittelbare Anschauung christlicher Lebensführung für das Christentum gewonnen worden seien.[19]

Die Apostel übermitteln die christliche Lehre durch göttliche Kraft und nicht, wie Origenes bemerkt, durch blosse Begriffe:

> "Wer das Wirken der Apostel Jesu verständig und ohne Vorurteil zu betrachten vermag, kommt zu der Ansicht, dass sie mit göttlicher Kraft das Christentum lehrten und es so erreichten, die Menschen dem Worte Gottes zu gewinnen. Denn es war bei ihnen nicht der Besitz jener Redegewandtheit und schönen Ordnung des Ausdrucks, wie die dialektische oder rhetorische Kunst der Griechen es fordert, was ihre Zuhörer gefangen nahm. Und ich bin der Meinung, wenn Jesus zur Verkündigung seiner Lehre Männer ausgewählt hätte, die nach der Auffassung der grossen Menge weise und geeignet waren, nach Gefallen des Volkes zu denken und zu reden, so würde man wohl mit Fug und Recht geargwöhnt haben, Jesus habe sich eines ähnlichen Verfahrens bedient wie die Gründer einer Philosophenschule; es wäre dann auch die Erfüllung der Verheissung von

[15]Ebd. PG 36, 161 C.

[16]Ebd. PG 36, 156 C.

[17]Ebd. PG 36, 156 D.

[18]Klemens von Alexandrien, Stromata III, 5: PG 8, 1148 B.

[19]Justin, Apologie 12,1.

der Göttlichkeit seiner Lehre nicht mehr sichtbar zutage getreten, da 'das Wort und die Verkündigung' in 'Überredungskunst der Weisheit' bestanden hätte, die sich auf Ausdruck und Darstellung stützt, und so würde dann 'der Glaube' geradeso wie es bei dem Glauben der Weltweisen an ihre Lehren der Fall ist, auf 'Menschen-Weisheit' und nicht auf 'Gottes-Kraft' sich gründen. Wenn man aber sieht, wie 'Fischer' und 'Zöllner', welche 'nicht einmal die Anfangsgründe der Wissenschaft kennen' - so schildert sie uns das Evangelium, und Celsus glaubt ihnen darin, dass sie nämlich die Wahrheit sagen, wenn sie sich als ungelehrte Leute bezeichnen -, unerschrockenen Mutes nicht nur vor Juden vom Glauben an Jesus reden, sondern ihn auch bei den übrigen Völkern mit Erfolg verkündigen, wird man dann nicht fragen, woher die überzeugende Kraft ihrer Worte stammte, da sie doch anders geartet war als die bei der grossen Menge geltende? Wer wollte auch in Abrede stellen, dass Jesus das Wort: 'Folget mir nach, und ich will euch zu Menschenfischern machen', durch eine göttliche Kraft an seine Aposteln erfüllt hat?... Deshalb werden auch die, welche das mit Kraft verkündete Wort hören, selbst mit Kraft erfüllt und erweisen diese durch ihre Gesinnung und ihr Leben und ihr Kämpfen für die Wahrheit bis zum Tode."[20]

Nicht der tote Buchstabe, sondern "Geist und Kraft" sind es, die das Christentum ausweisen, wie Origenes gegen Celsus unterstreicht,[21] der nichts Gutes in der Bibel fand, was nicht auch schon eine Menge von Philosophen und Dichtern gesagt hätte.

Es ist nicht möglich, dass sich die Kirche von einem "Gefäss der Wahrheit" in ein "Gefäss des Buchstabens" verwandelt. Der Heilige Geist, der die Kirche schuf, inspirierte sowohl die Verfassung der Heiligen Schrift als auch die Schaffung der Theologie. Solange die Kirche der lebendigen Gegenwart dieses Geistes sicher ist, der das Werk des Herrn fortsetzt, wird sie die Fesseln des Buchstabens sprengen und die Schönheit der Wahrheit erfahren. Sie wird nicht davor zurückschrecken, dieser Schönheit der Wahrheit Ausdruck zu verleihen, selbst wenn sie nicht im Buchstaben der Schrift festgelegt ist. Solange die Theologie ein Ausdruck der einen und katholischen Wahrheit ist, ein Ausdruck also des Geheimnisses der heiligsten Dreieinigkeit und ihrer Heilsökonomie, wird die Kirche wahrhaftig wachsen - wachsen in Christus durch den Heiligen Geist. "Der Herr wird durch uns selbst oder durch andere die Erfüllung des noch fehlenden geben gemäss der Erkenntnis, die der Geist denen, die seiner würdig sind, gewährt."[22]

[20]Origenes, Contra Celsum I, 62.

[21]Ebd. III, 68.

2. Teilwahrheiten und die "gesamte" Wahrheit

Die Stellung der orthodoxen Kirche

Die orthodoxe Kirche setzt in ihrem Glauben und in ihrer Theologie die *Tradition der ungeteilten Kirche* fort. Sie inkarniert auf eine harmonische Art und Weise die Menschwerdung Gottes und die Vergöttlichung des Menschen, Schrift und Tradition, Wort und Sakrament, Kontemplation und Aktion, Gottesfrage und Menschenfrage. Ihr Zugang zu der Liebe und zur Betrachtung der geistigen Schönheit erlaubte der Orthodoxie, die Wahrheit symphonisch zu betrachten - in ihrer ganzheitlichen, untrennbaren Synthese von Aspekten des christlichen Pluralismus, der oft die Gemeinschaft des Glaubens und der Liebe bereichert.

Die Orthodoxie ist weder eine selbstgenügsam isolierte Ortskirche noch eine blosse Summe von nebeneinander stehenden Ortskirchen. Sie ist auch nicht eine universalistisch strukturierte Kirche, die die lokalen Kirchen als "de iure" und "de facto" untergeordnete Teile der einen Kirche auffasst, noch ist sie eine Art Föderation von Ortskirchen, sondern sie ist eine Gemeinschaft von fünfzehn autokephalen und autonomen Ortskirchen, die jede für sich den Anspruch erheben kann, die ein, heilige, katholische und apostolische Kirche fortzusetzen - unter der Voraussetzung, dass sie in Gemeinschaft mit den anderen Lokalkirchen steht.

Diese Gemeinschaft bedeutet keine Uniformität in der liturgischen Ordnung und in den kirchlichen Gebräuchen, sondern sie kommt darin zum Ausdruck, dass die beteiligten Kirchen die je geschichtlich gewordene legitime Entfaltung des einen Glaubens der Alten und ungeteilten Kirche bewahren. Diese Gemeinschaft bedingt auch nicht die Unterwerfung der einen Kirche mit ihrer Tradition unter die andere, denn dies würde der Wirklichkeit der Gemeinschaft geradezu widersprechen.

Die orthodoxe Kirche ist die Trägerin der konstitutiven Elemente des *christlichen Erbes Europas*, und da sie fest daran glaubt, dass sie die eine, heilige, katholische und apostolische Kirche fortsetzt, hat sie einen besonderen Beitrag aus ihrer Tradition heraus zu leisten. Die interne Konkurrenz zwischen den verschiedenen Elementen einer Zivilisation ist in der Tat ein fortwährender dialektischer Gegensatz zwischen den "Teilen" und dem "Ganzen", denn der periodische Dynamismus des "Teiles" subsistiert bekanntlich im "Ganzen" und zwar indem in

---

[22]Basilius von Cäsarea, Über den Heiligen Geist, XXX, 79. Übers. v. M. Blum, Freiburg/Br. 1967, 117.

prozesshafter Weise die Funktion der anderen Komponenten der kulturellen Identität neutralisiert wird. Der Begriff des "Ganzen" wird in jeder Zivilisation durch die Fülle der Elemente definiert, die sie ausmachen und die die Hierarchie der Werte bestimmen. Der Begriff "Teil" ist mit einer selektiven oder einseitigen Sicht der Elemente verbunden, welche ihrerseits nach und nach die Hierarchie der Werte neu bestimmen.

Die orthodoxe Kirche hat die Aufgabe, daran zu erinnern, dass die Teilaspekte und Teilwahrheiten niemals verabsolutiert werden dürfen. Unser Beitrag z.B. zur Integration Europas muss begründet sein

a) auf die Wiederherstellung des Gleichgewichts zwischen allen fundamental geistigen Elementen der europäischen Zivilisation, so wie sie sich herausgebildet haben und zu allen Zeiten der europäischen Geschichte massgebend waren, nämlich das griechische Denken, der römische Geist und der christliche Glaube, wobei darauf insistiert werden muss, dass sich der moderne Geist Europas in seiner diachronischen Dimension in diese Synthese inkorporieren muss;
b) auf den Prozess der Reinigung des geschichtlichen Gedächtnisses der europäischen Völker, welches durch die Vergangenheit beeinträchtigt wurde, wobei diejenigen Elemente, die die jeweilige nationale Identität und religiöse Eigenheit ausmachen, nicht eliminiert werden dürfen;
c) auf der klugen Wiederaufwertung aller institutionellen Manifestationen des geistigen Erbes Europas wie z.B. Staat, Kirche, Erziehung, Denken usw., damit alle Elemente dieses geistigen Erbes wieder neu belebt werden können.

Wie oft *"Teilwahrheiten"* verabsolutiert werden, kennen wir aus der Geschichte der Kirche. Christus, die Quelle unseres immer wieder erneuernden und kontinuierlichen Handelns ist "derselbe gestern, heute und in Ewigkeit". Jede wesentliche Abweichung von der christologischen Lehre würde auch eine Abweichung des soteriologischen Lebens mit sich bringen. Jede Untreue zu der Menschheit und Gottheit des Sohnes in der einen Person des Gott-Menschen würde gewisse Konsequenzen auf anthropologischem, ekklesiologischem und soteriologischem Gebiet nach sich ziehen. Die Untreue könnte dadurch ausgedrückt werden, dass man die eine oder andere Teilwahrheit aus dem Glaubensbekenntnis herausgreift, mit der Tendenz, sie zu verabsolutieren. Eine solche Teilwahrheit ist z.B. die - für uns sicher verständlichere - Menschheit Christi. Der mit Mühsal und Leiden beladene Mensch klammert sich an die menschliche Natur des leidenden Jesus von Nazareth und hält sich daran fest, die unfassbare Natur Gottes aber "entschwindet von ihnen" (cf. Lk 24:31b). Man denkt nur an den Menschen Jesus.

Eine andere Teilwahrheit wird oft ebenfalls isoliert. Es ist die Gottheit Christi, die unser Menschsein und unsere Beziehung zur Welt bestimmen soll. Das, wovon man sich ansprechen lässt, darf man nicht überbetonen und verabsolutieren, so als ob die Frage wäre: menschliche oder göttliche Natur, Humanismus oder Theokratie, Kreuz oder Auferstehung.

Man kann das eine nicht gegen das andere ausspielen, auch nicht das eine hinter dem anderen suchen und so voneinander trennen, sondern alles gehört zusammen. Das eine ist im andern.

Auch die Kirche ist christologisch zu verstehen. Sie ist der "Leib Christi". Die Gott-Menschheit Christi bildet die Form der Kirche, das ontologische Gesetz ihre Struktur. "Christus totus in capite et in corpore".

Geht man ebenfalls nicht in seinen ekklesiologischen Voraussetzungen von der untrennbaren Einheit von Gottheit und Menschheit Christi aus, so wird die Kirche entweder als eine bloss soziologische oder menschliche Organisation und Institution oder als eine bloss weltfremde Gesellschaft verstanden, je nach der Teilwahrheit, die man herausgreift und bewusst oder unbewusst verabsolutiert.

Sind wir dem geoffenbarten Christus-Bild treu, so werden wir die konkrete heutige Situation berücksichtigen durch eine gleichwertige Bestimmung unserer *vertikalen* und *horizontalen Beziehung* zu Gott.

Die Vertikalität bestimmt die Beziehung des Menschen zu Gott. Der Mensch schwingt sich in die göttliche Transzendenz, um darin aufzugehen. Der Liebestausch zwischen Schöpfung und Schöpfer vollzieht sich gleichzeitig von unten nach oben und von oben nach unten. Die Horizontalität bestimmt die Beziehungen des Menschen zu seinen Brüdern und Schwestern. In ihnen liebt und dient er Gott, den er nicht sieht. Die Brüder und Schwestern sieht er aber nicht nur im Blick auf ihre ewige Berufung, sondern auch im Blick auf ihre zeitliche Situation. Er sieht oft "den Nächsten als einen zweiten Gott, nach dem einen und einzigartigen Gott". Die Gefahr der Vertikalität ist das Vergessen unserer Brüder und Schwestern beim Bestreben, uns in Gott zu versenken. Die Gefahr der Horizontalität ist das Vergessen Gottes unter dem Vorwand des Dienstes an unseren Brüdern und Schwestern.

Auf die letzte Gefahr müssen wir hier hinweisen: dass die Kirchen, um in der Welt zu wirken, schliesslich selber verweltlichen. Aber Kirche muss auch da Kirche bleiben, wo sie für die Armen, Verfolgten und Hungernden Partei ergreift.

Indem sie es tut, soll sie den Menschen dieser Zeit den einen ungeteilten Christus und nur ihn verkündigen und ihnen sein Heil überbringen.

Es ist wahr, dass Jesus denjenigen, die am Rande der Gesellschaft stehen, eine ganz besondere Liebe und Nähe zeigt, den Kranken, den Armen, aber auch den Fehlbaren und den Schuldigen. Auch ergreift er Partei für jene, die alle gegen sich haben und steht auf der Seite der Schwachen und Rechtlosen.

Soll das aber heissen, dass man Gott mit den Unterdrückten und die Botschaft des Evangeliums mit der Überwindung von Gewalt und Ungerechtigkeit identifizieren soll?

Die Gerechtigkeit darf nicht mit der Rechtfertigung verwechselt werden, auch nicht die politische Befreiung und der Sieg über die Armut mit der Erlösung..

Berdjajew sagt, dass die Frage nach meinem eigenen Brot eine materielle Frage ist, während die Frage nach dem Brot meines Nächsten eine spirituelle ist. Es liegt etwas Wahres darin. Derjenige, der sich nicht spontan einsetzt, um den Menschen in seinen konkreten Lieden zu helfen, kann ebenso der Häresie schuldig werden wie derjenige, der diese oder jene Glaubenswahrheit ablehnt.

Zur Überwindung von Teilwahrheiten berufen

Wenn wir als Christen dazu beitragen wollen, dass sich der "Teil" und das "Ganze" miteinander vereinbaren lassen, so müssen wir wieder zusammen lernen, den Absolutismus und den Exklusivismus in unseren partikularen Traditionen zu überwinden. Nur diese Haltung wird uns erlauben, Schwestern und Brüder ausserhalb unserer eigenen konfessionellen Grenzen zu entdecken, ja sogar Kirchen ausserhalb unserer eigenen kirchlichen Grenzen anzuerkennen, denn sehr oft wurden diese in bezug auf das Heil in exklusiver Weise mit der einen, heiligen, katholischen und apostolischen Kirche identifiziert.

Wir müssen unsere Dualismen und unsere Polarisierungen überwinden, die die Geschichte Europas deutlich gekennzeichnet haben. Kardinal Ratzinger verweist zu Recht auf folgendes: "Als Inbegriff der Neuzeit erscheint schliesslich zu Unrecht jene vollkommen autonomisierte Vernunft, die nur noch sich selbst kennt, damit aber blind geworden ist und in der Zerstörung ihres Grundes inhuman und schöpfungsfeindlich wird. Diese Art von Vernunftautonomie ist zwar Produkt des europäischen Geistes, aber zugleich ihrem Wesen nach als post-europäisch, ja anti-europäisch anzusehen, als die innere Zerstörung dessen, was nicht nur für Europa konstitutiv, sondern überhaupt Voraussetzung einer humanen Gesellschaft ist."[23] Diese Trennung war sicherlich eine Folge der Ideen der neuen europäischen Rechtssysteme: Diese hielten sich "deshalb für universalisierbar..., weil sie sich als Aufklärungrecht aus der christlichen Grundlage gelöst hatten und nun als reines Vernunftrecht auftraten... Diese Rechtssysteme (müssen) gerade deshalb als gottlos und glaubenswidrig empfunden werden. Angesichts der Einheit des Ethischen und des Religiösen erscheinen sie als ein zugleich ethischer und religiöser Angriff, als Entfremdung nicht nur vom Eigenen, sondern vom Eigentlichen."[24]

Wir müssen zusammen die Beziehung zwischen dem "Ganzen" und dem "Teil" überdenken, und zwar so, dass wir gleichzeitig unseren Wurzeln treu und für neue Möglichkeiten verfügbar bleiben.

Ob aber die Menschen genügend Brot zum Leben haben werden, das wird davon abhängen, ob genügend Menschen erkennen, dass der Mensch nicht vom Brot allein lebt. Es wäre falsch, hier die Vertikale gegen die Horizontale auszuspielen. Alle Dimensionen gehören zusammen. Es gibt keine strenge Trennung zwischen Heilsgeschichte und Weltgeschichte. Natürlich ist die Kirche nicht nur der Arzt am Krankenbett der Gesellschaft. Denn wir leben in der Gesellschaft, wir können mit ihr krank sein, kämpfen und verzweifeln.

Es ist schwer, das Gleichgewicht zwischen den beiden verschiedenen Tendenzen zu finden: zwischen der Horizontalen und der Vertikalen, zwischen der Menschlichkeit Gottes und der Vergöttlichung des Menschen. Unsere Generation hat noch jene "guten Christen" gekannt, deren Ideal es war, der Welt zu entfliehen, obwohl sie sich darin manchmal sogar recht häuslich niedergelassen hatten. Heute leiden wir an der entgegengesetzten Versuchung; weil sie sich ganz dem Dienst an den Brüdern und Schwestern widmen wollen, gelangen viele Christen heute zu einem Vergessen der Transzendenz Gottes und wollen nur mehr seine Immanenz in den Menschen wahrhaben.

Unsere Sendungsvergessenheit ist oft mit einer einseitigen theologischen Orientierung verbunden. Wir sollten um des Menschen und der Welt willen theologisch etwas treuer werden: nicht im Sinne einer Restauration toter Formen und statischer Traditionen, sondern im Sinne einer dynamischen Wiedererlangung der lebendigen Wahrheit der Kirche, die mit dem Fleischgewordenen Logos

---

[23]J. Ratzinger, Kirche, Ökumene und Politik, Eisiedeln 1987, 207, Anm.2.

[24]Ebd. 200.

128

gleichzusetzen ist, im Sinne einer Theologie, die nicht vom Leben und der Doxologie zu trennen ist und die nicht für ihren Inhalt vor der Ratio des Menschen verantwortlich sein will, einer Theologie, die im täglichen Leben ihre harmonische Anwendung finden kann, die gerade das fruchtbare Paradoxon unseres Glaubens, das Zusammentreffen der Horizontalen mit der Vertikalen berücksichtigt, welches die Originalität des Christentums unter allen Religionen ausmacht, einer Theologie also, die zu vergegenwärtigen versteht, was wir in den letzten Tagen erfahren werden: die Kohäsion des Ganzen, die Harmonie des Alls.

Wenn wir also tiefer "theologisch" werden in dem Sinne, dass der Dienst am Menschen nicht vom Gottesdienst abzutrennen ist, dann wird uns unsere Liebe zu Gott zu unseren Mitbrüdern und -schwestern führen und die Liebe zu unseren Mitbrüdern und -schwestern zu Gott; dann werden wir unsere Solidarität mit der Welt gleichsam automatisch und selbstverständlich bekunden, dann wird das vertikal empfangene Christusgeschehen horizontale Folgen im ethischen und sozialen Bereich haben.

Denn auch der heutige verweltlichte Mensch, um den es geht, wird seine Orientierung wiederfinden, wenn er auf das Geheimnis hingewiesen wird, dass Gott Mensch wird, um der Erlösung des Menschen willen, wenn also der Mensch das Prinzip des paradoxen Gleichgewichts zwischen göttlichem und menschlichem Element, zwischen Transzendenz und Immanenz wiedergewinnen kann.

Es bleiben nun noch *einige Fragen* offen, die zum Schluss gestellt werden sollen: Wie verhalten sich Teilkirche und Gesamtkirche oder anders gesagt Teilkirche und Einheit und Katholizität der einen Kirche Christi zueinander? Wie konkretisiert man die Überwindung der Polarisierung zwischen dem ekklesiologischen Selbstbewusstsein der orthodoxen Kirche, nachdem sie die eine, heilige, katholische und apostolische Kirche fortsetzt, und der Stellungnahme der Kongregation für die Glaubenslehre, nach der die orthodoxen Kirchen als "jene ehrwürdigen christlichen Gemeinschaften" bezeichnet werden, die "auf Grund ihrer derzeitigen Situation in ihrem Teilkirchesein verwundet" sind, da "die Gemeinschaft mit der durch den Nachfolger Petri repräsentierten Gesamtkirche nicht eine äussere Zutat zur Teilkirche ist, sondern eines ihrer inneren Wesenselemente"?[25]

---

[25]Schreiben an die Bischöfe der katholischen Kirche über einige Aspekte der Kirche als *Communio*, Vatikanstadt, 1992, Par.17, p.18.

Wie es auch sein mag, der Osten und der Westen können sich nur dann begegnen und zueinander finden, wenn sie sich an ihre ursprüngliche Verwandtschaft in einer gemeinsamen Vergangenheit erinnern. Der erste Schritt dazu ist, dass sie sich wieder bewusst werden müssen, dass der Osten und der Westen trotz ihrer Eigenheiten organisch zur einen Christenheit gehören.

The Law of Liberty (James 1:25; 2:12)

Wiard Popkes

I. Introduction

The syntagma "law of liberty" is found in James 1:25; 2:12 only, nowhere else in the New Testament and even in all the ancient Greek writings which we know.[1] What does James mean and want to convey with his unusual formulation? He seems to presuppose though that his readers can make sense of it, after all; he appears to imply that it is not entirely unfamiliar to them.[2]

In 1:22-25 James contrasts the person who hears the word but does not do it, to someone "who leans over looking into a/the perfect law, that of freedom, and who perseveres", being not a forgetful hearer, hence a blessed person. In 2:12 James describes (or urges; *laleite, poieite* can be indicative or imperative) his readers as (or to be) people "who are about to be judged by a/the law of freedom". In both instances "law" is used without an article. What is James referring to? Why is it a law of liberty to which these qualities and functions can be ascribed? In 1:25 the apposition to "law", i.e. "that of freedom", bears a special emphasis; the sentence would make sense without it; but as it stands, "that of freedom" is made the more conspicuous. 2:12 obviously picks up the reference to the "royal law" in v.8, which is identified with the commandment to love the neighbour. Is this reference an explanation of the "law of liberty", and if so: why and how?

What kind of genitive does "of liberty" denote? Strangely enough, few commentators actually bother very much about this question.[3] The most common

---

[1]Cf. e.g. R. Schnackenburg, Die sittliche Botschaft des Neuen Testaments, Neubearbeitung, II (HThK, S II), Freiburg 1988, 213; further material: W. Popkes, Adressaten, Situation und Form des Jakobusbriefes (=Adressaten, SBS 125/126), Stuttgart 1986, 68.

[2]Cf. e.g. P. Davids, The Epistle of James (NIGTC), Grand Rapids 1982, 99; M. Dibelius, Der Brief des Jakobus (=Jak, KEK XV, mit Ergänzungen von H. Greeven, 6. Aufl. dieser Auslegung mit einem Literaturverzeichnis und Nachtrag hrsg. von F. Hahn), Göttingen 1984, 148ff.

[3]R. Fabris, Legge della liberta in Giacomo (RivBib, S 8), Brescia 1977; S. Vollenweider, Freiheit als neue Schöpfung. Eine Untersuchung zur Eleutheria bei Paulus und in seiner Umwelt (FRLANT 147), Göttingen 1989, 184ff.; et al.

interpretation reads: "the law which leads to, or grants, liberty".[4] Schnackenburg considers it to be a genitive of quality ("a law which is liberal in nature") or a genitive of purpose and direction ("a law leading to freedom"); he thinks, however, that this need not be an alternative.[5] Hort interprets: "the law characterised by freedom" which makes us "feel free".[6] We should exert caution, however, in resolving the formulation too rapidly. After all, James does not write *nomos eleutheroon* (active participle, "a liberating law"). He might have meant just as well "a law defined by liberty, a law originating in liberty" (genitivus subjectivus or originis, equivalent to *nomos eleuthéroon*, genitivus pluralis, "law of free people"[7]). In any case, the interpretation must not start with pretending to know what as yet has to be disclosed.

II. Arguments

The meaning of "law of liberty" can be approached from four angles, using a method safer than an untimely interpretation of the genitive: (1) the direction of the arguments in Jas 1:25 and 2:12, including the frame of reference; (2) analogous formulations of "law" with a genitive; (3) the nearest parallels in the New Testament with regard to "freedom"; (4) other syntactical combinations between *eleuther-* and "law".

(1) In Jas 1:25 "that of liberty" seems to qualify "perfect"; the perfection of the law is to be found in its very relation to freedom. But what does "perfect law" mean? Again, this syntagma is much disputed.[8] The main interpretations are: The law is perfect "since it is from God"[9]; "because it protects human dignity"[10]; it is perfect

---

[4]I.e. as genitivus obiectivus: Dibelius, Jak 148ff.; Davids, James 99: G. Delling, *telos ktl*: ThWNT VIII 75; H. Hübner, *teleioo*: EWNT III 824; et al. This is meant also by D.E. Hiebert, The Epistle of James. Test of a Living Faith, Chicago 1979, 137: "...denoting that this law produces the experience of freedom...", although he calls it a subjective genitive.

[5]Sittliche Botschaft II 213.

[6]F.J.A. Hort, The Epistle of St James, London 1909, 178.

[7]Cf. Dibelius, Jak 152.

[8]Cf. Hübner, EWNT III 824; Vollenweider (s. note 3) 185.

[9]F. Schnider, Der Jakobusbrief (RNT), Regensburg 1987, 51; cf. Fabris (s. note 3) 154ff. 180f.

in contrast to the imperfect OT (ritual) law[11]; in its wholeness over against single commandments;[12] "as it claims man totally for his creator"[13]; since it is the law promised by Jeremiah and Ezechiel, planted by God into our hearts[14]; because it is "an inclusive concept, embracing the preceptive teaching of both the Old Testament and the New Testament"[15]; as an eschatological law, anchored in the *telos*.[16] We are thus faced by another unclarity to be resolved.

"Perfect law", approached on the *synchronic* level in James, relates to several instances where "perfect" occurs: 1:4 (perfect work, complete and mature people); 1:17 (God's perfect and good gift); 3:2 (perfect is who does not even fail with his tongue); the verb is found in 2:8 (fulfill the law diligently and faithfully). "Perfect" means for James something unsurpassable and in this sense eschatological; it is a term denoting supreme quality. James does not indicate (in 1:25; 2:12) a contrast to what could be called an "imperfect law" nor a reference to Old Testament scriptures. It appears that the genitive "of liberty" itself is the most important interpretative element of "perfect law". The law is unsurpassable by its very relation to freedom.

---

[10]Schnider, Jak 51.

[11]Vollenweider (s. note 3) 185; F. Mußner, Der Jakobusbrief (= Jak, HThK XIII/1), Freiburg [4]1981, 109.

[12]W. Schrage, Ethik des Neuen Testaments (NTD, E 4), Göttingen 1982, 273; S. Schulz, Neutestamentliche Ethik, Zürich 1987, 645; cf. S. Laws, A Commentary on The Epistle of James (=James, BNTC), London 1980, 87.

[13]L. Goppelt, Theologie des Neuen Testaments, Göttingen [3]1978, 535; cf. K. Niederwimmer, *eleutheros ktl*: EWNT I 1058.

[14]Fabris (s. note 3) passim; Hübner, EWNT III 824.

[15]P.J. du Plessis, *TELEIOS*. The Idea of Perfection in the New Testament, Kampen 1959, 237 (referring to Pss 19 and 119).

[16]H. Preisker, Das Ethos des Urchristentums, Gütersloh [2]1949, 133.

Studying "perfect law" from a *diachronic* vantage-point, we are led to the early Christian instruction or catechism of neophytes.[17] Here "perfect (law)" means the best possible foundation of life, the true framework of dicipleship, leading to Christian maturity. "Perfection, completeness" is an important goal for the Christian and the Christian way of life (cf. Matt 5:48; Heb 5:14; Phil 3:15; 1 Thess 5:23; also 1 Cor 2:6; 3:1ff.; Phil 1:6-11; Eph 4:13; Jas 1:4). Perfection is understood as maturity, which becomes manifest in the ability to discern God's will and to teach others as well as in the capability to receive deeper insight in God's ways and to strive for peace and righteousness. Since Christ is the perfect image of God, his instruction is perfect in its quality, leading us to where God wants us to be. This is on the same line as the close connection between "perfect law" and "word of truth" (1:18) and "implanted word" (1:21) in James' text.

In Jas 2 we find a notion similar to the relation between "law of liberty", "perfect" and "(law of) freedom" in Jas 1: "law of liberty" is related to "royal law".[18] Again this syntagma has found a variety of explanations, such as: a law of royal authority; given by a king; destined for kings; the supreme, most important law; ruling law; law of God's kingdom; law of Jesus Christ, the king.[19] Proceeding on the *synchronic* level, the propinquity to "kingdom" in 2:5 (the only other occurrance of *basil-* in James) suggests an interpretation like "law of God's kingdom". This finds support from a *diachronic* viewpoint. Although "royal law" is no fixed concept in secular and Jewish Greek literature, it indicates the supreme origin and eminent importance of (a) law, the general intention of a ruler. Again, as in the case of "perfection", the early Christian tradition, as reflected in Jas 2, seems to have had its "Sitz im Leben" in the instruction of the neophytes; they were told that they became "heirs of the kingdom"[20] and were to follow "the law

[17]Cf. W. Popkes, Adressaten, 136ff.; Die Gerechtigkeitstradition im Matthäus-Evangelium: ZNW 80 (1989) 1-23; Zum Charakter von Galater 6,1-10: Theol. Gespräch 1/1992 (Festgabe A. Pohl), 8-14; New Testament Principles of Wholeness: EvQ 64 (1992) 319-332.

[18]Mußner, Jak 126; Schnackenburg (s.note 1) 211.

[19]Cf. the commentaries. Greek and other background material is found in the dictionaries by Liddell-Scott-Jones and Bauer-Aland; C.H. Dodd, The Bible and the Greeks, London [2]1954; K.L. Schmidt, *basileus ktl*: ThWNT I 593; J.B. Mayor, The Epistle of St. James, London [2]1897, 87; A. Deissmann, Licht vom Osten, Tübingen [4]1923, 310.

[20]Cf. G. Haufe, Reich Gottes bei Paulus und in der Jesustradition: NTS 31 (1958) 467-472; K. Donfried, The Kingdom of God in Paul, in: W. Willis (ed.), The Kingdom of God

of Christ" (Gal 6:2), which is the commandment to love one's neighbour (as also in Jas 2:8).

Both "perfect law" (1:25) and "royal law" (2:8) then are references to a specific early Christian tradition, indicating the foundation, path, guidance and goal of dicipleship. The relation to Christian maturity and to mutual love denotes the content of the law. James goes on to underline, in 1:25, the necessity of having a permanent relationship with the law of liberty. This is James' very intention and interest: unles someone perseveres, i.e. exerts continuity and stability, there is no valuable result. Endurance is requested; a momentary encounter is soon forgotten; it does not effect any activity. Genuine Christian discipleship, however, will bear fruit, in particular loving concern for the needy; it will stand the test for an appropriate relation to the law of liberty. This becomes obvious in 1:26f. and even more extensively in Jas 2, describing the very test of social behaviour. Partiality is, as demonstrated by James, a violation of the royal law (2:9). The law of liberty will turn against its own adherents who are about or even "intend" (*melloo* may have a notion of wilfulness, in distinction to the mere future tense[21]) to be judged by the law of liberty. The law itself will be an active factor (*dia* is instrumental: "by, through", not just "according to") in the last judgment.[22] Apparently the law of liberty is regarded as valid law, both by James and his readers. James underlines: You will have to see where you end up when you are going to be judged by this very law! An element of warning cannot be overlooked. James addresses people who claim that they are followers of the "royal law" and the "law of liberty", referring to the commandment of love. But how do they practice it? Their claim seems to have become little more than a pretence. They interpret love and liberty according to their own - unsocial - preferences.

(2) Formulations of the pattern "law plus genitive" are found quite often in ancient literature.[23] They may denote persons by or for whom a law is given, the genitive being an auctoris, possessivus or subjectivus. There are also more complex formulations, some even of a reciprocal nature, in particular when the genitive denotes something abstract. "Law of a town" e.g. may mean the law which a

in 20th-Century Interpretation, Peabody 1987, 175-190; Popkes, ZNW 1989 (s. note 17) 14-17.

[21]Cf. Popkes, Adressaten, 69.

[22]Cf. Laws, James, 116.

[23]For details: H. Kleinknecht, *nomos ktl*: ThWNT IV 1017; Bauer-Aland, Wörterbuch zum NT 1097; Vollenweider (s. note 3) 358.

certain habitation developed, which is characteristic for that town, and which also determines and shapes life there. In the NT it is primarily Paul who uses such (abstract) formulations, most of them in Rom:[24] the law of works and faith (3:27), of the mind (7:23), of sin (7:23,25) and death (8:20), of the spirit of life (8:2a) and righteousness (9:31). Eph 2:15 and Heb 7:16 have "law of the commandment(s)". The instances demonstrate a variety in the usage of the genitive. The double genitive in Rom 8:2 indicates character, quality and power on the one hand (spirit/sin), result and consequences on the other (life/death).[25] In 3:27 "works/faith" signify the character of the law; the consequence (righteousness) follows in 3:28 (cf. 9:31).

What does all of this mean for the "law of liberty" in James? Certainly our survey demonstrates that the usual interpretation "law which grants freedom" is not the only possible or even the most probable solution. On the contrary, Jas 2:12 emphasizes that such a law does not necessarily lead into freedom but can become an instrument of judgment. Jas 1:25 requests endurance as the way towards blessedness. The survey suggests that the genitive may just as well, and even more appropriately, denote the character, the decisive influence upon and the origin of that law (genitivus qualitatis and originis). The "law of liberty" then would mean a law which has its origin in liberty, which stands under the decisive influence of freedom, and the very nature of which is determined by freedom.

(3) The nearest parallels in the NT with regard to "freedom" are found in Paul's letters. Paul does not use the formulation "law of liberty", but he comes close to it. Furthermore, Paul can be regarded as the preacher of freedom in the NT.[26] John 8:30ff. mentions freedom but not law; where John speaks of the new law, that of love (John 13:34; 15:12; 1 John 2:7f. et al.), he does not refer to freedom. Paul underlines liberation by Christ as an essential element of salvation (Gal 5:1,13; Rom 6:18,22; 2 Cor 3:17). The most conspicuous parallel to James is Rom 8:2: "For the law of the spirit of life in Christ Jesus liberated you from the law of sin and death". One law abrogates the other, which is an act of liberation. Here indeed we find the concept of a liberating law, which as such is not alien to ancient Greek

---

[24]There is a sharp debate about the meaning of *nomos* here between U. Wilckens, Der Brief an die Römer (=Röm, EKK VI), Neukirchen-Zürich I 1978, 245, II 1980 122f., and Vollenweider (s. note 3) 358.

[25]Cf. Wilckens, Röm II 123; F.St. Jones, "Freiheit" in den Briefen des Apostels Paulus. Eine historische, exegetische und religionsgeschichtliche Studie, Göttingen 1987, 123.

[26]Cf. Vollenweider (s. note 3) passim.

literature; but this does not compel us to interpret James' statements in the same way.

The use and understanding of "law" in Paul is a much debated matter.[27] It seems that Paul was or became aware of the fact that his message of freedom was misunderstood by some as a call to a law-less life, i.e. to libertinism.[28] Paul counter-acted by stressing the obligation to Christ (Rom 6:16; 7:6). This obligation can be interpreted (by quoting earliest Christian tradition) as the commandment to serve one another in love (Gal 5:13; Rom 13:8-10; cf. 1 Cor 9:19; 2 Cor 4:15), which is the fulfilment of the whole law, the "law of Christ" (Gal 6:2; cf. 1 Cor 9:21).

In the early reception of Pauline tradition (which as such has to be presupposed for James, cf. 2:14-26) people seem to have inferred from Paul's statements that he preached not only freedom from the old law, that of Moses, but also something like a new law of liberty which is identical with the commandment to love one's neighbour - a law of supreme, unsurpassable quality and dignity. If this observation holds true, not only Jas 2:14-26 but also 2:8ff. (and with it 1:25) has to be interpreted on the background of the reception of Pauline tradition.[29] The reception had taken a direction, however, which became more and more a distortion of Paul's intention. Paul was made the proclaimer of a "law of liberty" (in the same way as he was made the advocate of "faith only" without

---

[27]St. Westerholm, Israel's Law and the Church's Faith: Paul and His Recent Interpreters, Grand Rapids 1988; L. Gaston, Paul and the Torah, Vancouver 1987; H. Räisänen, Paul and the Law, Tübingen 1983; The Torah and Christ, Helsinki 1986; U. Wilckens, Zur Entwicklung des paulinischen Gesetzesverständnisses: NTS 28 (1982) 154-190; E.P. Sanders, Paul and Palestinian Judaism. A Comparison of Patterns of Religion, London 1977; Paul, the Law, and the Jewish People, Philadelphia 1983; O. Merk, Paulus-Forschung 1936-1985: ThR 53 (1988) 1-81; H. Hübner, Das Gesetz bei Paulus, Göttingen ³1982; Paulus-Forschung seit 1945: ANRW II 25.4 (1987) 2649ff.; Methodologie und Theologie. Zu neuen methodischen Ansätzen in der Paulusforschung: KuD 33 (1987) 150-176; 303-329; K. Kertelge (Hrsg.), Das Gesetz im Neuen Testament, Freiburg 1986; Autorität des Gesetzes und Autorität Jesu bei Paulus, in: Festschrift J. Gnilka (Vom Urchristentum zu Jesus), Freiburg 1989, 358-376; T.L. Donaldson, Zealot and Convert: The Origin of Paul's Christ-Torah Antithesis: CBQ 51 (1989) 655-682; F. Thielman, From Plight to Solution: A Jewish Framework for Understanding Paul's View of the Law in Galatians and Romans (NovT, S 61), Leiden 1989; B.L. Martin, Christ and the Law in Paul (NovT, S 62), Leiden 1989.

[28]Cf. e.g. K.H. Schelkle, Paulus (EdF 152), Darmstadt 1981, 213; H.D. Betz, Galatians. A Commentary on Paul's Letter to the Churches in Galatia (Hermeneia), Philadelphia 1979, 272f.; Vollenweider (s. note 3) 327ff. (on Rom 6).

consequences) which had little more substance than a general call to act "in freedom", meaning "as you please", its contents (the call to love) becoming more and more evaporated, receiving the character of a shallow slogan. The actual practice of the "law of liberty" turned out to be virtually a contradiction to what was meant originally. The development may be compared with some extreme sort of "situation ethics" in modern times, operating with very loose concepts of liberty and love, getting into the danger of disregarding the essentials of social and personal ethics, ending up in little more than permissiveness.

"Law of liberty", on this background, then has to be understood as a "Pauline" formulation, "Pauline" at least in the opinion of those who regarded themselves as heirs of Paul's tradition. If this is so, the syntagma "(perfect) law of liberty" originally denotes the quality and character of that law. It is the law of people who were set free by Christ and live according to that law. This law has its origin in liberty and is an expression of Christian freedom. In this sense it has eschatological quality. Such a concept stands behind Jas 1:25; 2:12, interpreted and (ab)used, however, in a distorted form which provokes James' critique.

(4) Which other (i.e. other than in James and Paul) syntactical combinations between "law" and *eleuther-* could shed light upon "law of liberty"? The very concept of freedom is rooted in Greek culture; the Hebrew experience and approach follows a different line.[30] The basic Greek statement reads: "Free is who lives as he wants."[31] This statement was coined first about the polis, later also

---

[29]Cf. Popkes, Adressaten, 68-70.

[30]H. Schlier, *eleutheros ktl*: ThWNT II 484-500, contains rich material about the Greek-Hellenistic heritage, but nothing about OT and Judaism. Extensive exposition in Vollenweider (s. note 3). On the history of NT research: Jones (s. note 25). Cf. also the articles on "freedom" by H.W. Bartsch, TRE XI 497; R. Heiligenthal, TRE XI 499; D. Nestle, RAC VIII 286; furthermore G. Bornkamm, Das urchristliche Verständnis von der Freiheit (Neckarer Hefte 8), Heidelberg 1961 (7 et al.); H.-J. Hermission, Gottes Freiheit - Spielraum des Menschen. Alttestamentliche Aspekte eines biblisch-theologischen Themas: ZThK 82 (1985) 129-152. For literature on Judaism cf. Vollenweider 123 note 87. - Attempts to derive "law of liberty" from Jewish heritage (as made by Fabris, s. note 3, et al.) lack a firm enough basis; cf. Jones 220f. note 67. Usually Pirqe Aboth 6,2 is quoted (Ex 32,16 should be read as *cheruth*=freedom, "for there is no free man for you except the one who is busy studying the torah"); but this instance is rather late. Other texts (as ExR 12,2 "He led them out of darkness and the shadow of death, from the iron yoke to the yoke of the torah, out of slavery into freedom") underline first of all the intimate connection between exodus and freedom.

about the individual.[32] The core idea of freedom is self-determination. The question "Where am I free?" was answered by distinguishing between ""what is at our disposal" and what is not (e.g. physical conditions).[33] The question "How can I be free?" was answered by the reference to the logos which grants true insight into the "laws" of[1] life. Freedom has to be regulated and protected by law.[34] It is wisdom's task to find the true law of life, the divine logos-nomos of the kosmos.[35] The law then is the mode of freedom, the basis and frame for the wise to live in freedom. Judaism developed similar ideas, though less connected with "liberty".[36] The pious (=wise) follows God's torah (=wisdom) which enables him a life acceptable to God.[37] Both Greeks and Jews tried to find the true law (logos,

[31]For a detailed presentation cf. the studies mentioned in note 30: Schlier 484ff.; Bartsch 505; Vollenweider 30ff.; Jones 124f. The most often quoted passages are from Aristotle Politeia and Epictetus Diss.

[32]Cf. Schlier (s. note 30) 484-487 on the polis; on the Stoa cf. ibid. 486. 489; Vollenweider 23ff.

[33]Schlier 490; Vollenweider 33-35.

[34]Schlier 485. There was quite a debate about the relation between law and freedom (cf. Vollenweider 87-96; Jones 79f.), depending on the understanding of law, whether it is the authentic "divine" logos-nomos or man-made restrictions. Plato e.g. argued that true free reason needs no laws; Sophists and Cynics criticized laws from an "enthusiastic" vantage-point, which in turn was counter-criticized by Epictetus et al. The Romans suspected Greek *eleutheria* of leading to licentia, not libertas. Also the distinction between written and unwritten laws exerted considerable importance. By and large, however, the Greek tradition was not antinomal, though often law-critical; Greek thinking is not oriented by chaos but by *kosmos*, i.e. by good and proper order which requires laws, rules and regulations.

[35]The close relation between wisdom, logos and nomos is pre-eminent. The wise person brings logos, nomos and freedom into harmony. Cf. Schlier 490f. on peace, comfort of the soul, inward certitude etc; Vollenweider 35ff. on the metaphysical and religious dimension (also 97ff. on "Gottessohnschaft"), *pronoia, oikeosis, paideia* etc.; Nestle, RAC VIII 275; Dibelius, Jak, 148f.

[36]Cf. Vollenweider 123ff. Important texts as Aristeas, Sapientia, Joseph and Aseneth do not use the word *eleutheria*, 4 Macc only in 14:2.

[37]Philo, in an early writing, treats the theme "That every good person is free". Freedom means to act "reasonably" (*phronimoos*, 59). Philo goes on to combine this approach with the torah of Moses, being the epitome of the true order of the kosmos. The principle "they

wisdom) in the original, undistorted form of the kosmos (creation), thus looking backwards to the status incorruptus of both the world and the human beings.[38]

Judaism did not develop a concept of a "new law of freedom" on the basis of Jer 31 or Ez 36, i.e. a law corresponding to the "new covenant", a law out of freedom and for people set free by God's eschatological intervention. This is, however, what early Christianity developed, in particular under the influence of Paul. Pauline tradition contributed the concept to what James can presuppose. It is a concept that looks forward, anticipating the eschaton.[39] It is on this background that the formulation "law of liberty" could be found and pronounced. It may not be without reason and not at random that this syntagma is found nowhere else in ancient documents.

The survey supports what the previous investigations suggested. The background of Jas 1:25; 2:12 is not found in general Greek ideas about the relationship between law and freedom. The texts do reveal, however, that the interpretation "law which grants liberty, which liberates" has much less evidence than is often asserted. Even in the Greek tradition law is more the basis and mode of liberty than its cause. More important, however, is the theological setting of the NT formulations. Freedom in the NT understanding refers to God's action in Christ. The "law of liberty" denotes the way how people can live according to what God has done. James and his addressees received these ideas mainly from the Pauline tradition, albeit in such a form that misunderstandings had to be corrected.

who live with the law are free" (Quod omnis 45) is, in its proper sense, valid for the Jews only.- Hellenistic Judaism picks up several lines of Greek ideas about freedom. Josephus e.g. describes parts of Israel's history as a history of liberation, though he criticizes the zealots. Josephus' intention is a fundamental concern of (diaspora) Judaism at that time, living under a foreign government, viz. to secure the freedom of worshipping God.- Another aspect, of a more philosophical nature, is the discussion among Jews and their "parties" about the relation between fate and free will. Here the major theological concern is human responsibility to God and the free choice of obedience or disobedience.

[38]This is emphasized by Vollenweider 95. There is, however, also an eschatological expectation of freedom, especially since the Maccabean times, translating the concept of exodus into the future (again by expounding Ex 32:16); cf. ibid. 138-145. These ideas are, however, not directly related to the question of law.

[39]Vollenweider's emphasis again, 95.

III. Conclusion

Neither "law" (Jas 1:25; 2:8,9,10,11,12; 4:11) nor "freedom" (only 1:25; 2:12) are typical for James' vocabulary. With the exception of 4:11 he uses the two words in combination. He does not explain what he means by either of them, and even less so what he means by the "law of liberty". Apparently he can presume that his readers know what the terms mean and what he means by using them. The terms serve as elements of communication; evidently they function as a means of reference to something known.

The meaning of "law of liberty" has to be disclosed from the argumentation in James, and here again from the process of tradition, reception of tradition and re-interpretation of tradition. The usual approach - i.e. a rash definition of the genitive and a reference to Hellenistic, Stoic ideas - falls short. The context, both in terms of argument and of situation, decides about the meaning.

Two fundamental aspects have to be considered in interpreting James' epistle, in my regard. First, James is dealing with a distorted Pauline tradition and church - not only in 2:14-26 but also in several other parts. Second, James refers his readers back to the common, fundamental instruction of the Christian way of life (instruction to neophytes; cf. the resemblances between James, 1 Peter and Matt 5-7).[40] These two elements play a vital role also in the section here under consideration.

In 1:18 James began[41] treating the theme "the Christian and the Word". God brought us to life through the word of truth. We must be eager to listen, slow to speak. The implanted, saving word must be received with meekness.[42] James refers back to baptismal instruction. The neophyte-tradition knows also about the dangers of living with the word, mainly anger and lack of action. Using that tradition, James reinforces his argument by reminding his readers of self-

---

[40]Cf. Popkes, Adressaten, part III.

[41]Most commentators see a new section begin with 1:19. In that case, however, the double reference to the "word" 1:18,21 (working in spiritual birth and salvation) is split. It seems to me that James is drawing on a section of neophyte theology and instruction, beginning with 1:18, concentrating on the "word", after having treated the aspect of "temptation" in 1:2ff. with 1:16f. as a conclusion.

[42]The comma in Jas 1:21 should be placed before, not after "in meekness" (against Nestle-Aland 26th edition).

deception. More and more then James turns to the problems on the side of his readers, mainly: unsocial behaviour, even in the church. This is James' pivotal concern: Christian faith must not deceive itself, but be active in love! This is what is emphasized in the last part of the first and throughout the second chapter (and later, too).

The very problem on the side of the readers is that they cover their deficiencies by references to what seems to be good Pauline tradition: the emphasis on faith, liberty, justification and the "royal law". The "church of the Word" becomes a "church of mere words"; faith is evaporated to mere monotheism; and even the commandment to love is distorted to serve for escaping from true social concern. The "law of liberty" has been abused, just as the "sola fide" has, as an instrument for self-centered ambitions.

James criticizes and corrects such a position; he warns and threatens his readers. He points back to true Christian beginnings, which should be familiar to them indeed. He warns about self-deception and empty words. He confronts the recipients with what they will have to face in the last judgment: the very law of liberty, speaking against them. They have made this law an easy-going theological slogan; but they do not actually live in it with endurance. James wants to correct this abuse. His rhetoric includes elements of polemic and even of sarcasm and irony. James wants the law of liberty to become again what it is meant to be: an expression of the freedom accomplished and granted by Christ, and a rule of life which reflects this liberation, with all its positive consequences, in particular genuine social concern and love which is worth its name.

THE MAGNA CHARTA OF SPIRITUAL GIFTS

A Re-reading of 1 Corinthians 12, 1-11

Jannes Reiling

Ever since in the early years of the Baptist Theological Seminary of the Netherlands a student told me that he had been baptized with the Holy Spirit and could speak in tongues the question of the Holy Spirit in general and the spiritual gifts in particular has been on my theological and exegetical agenda, to the extent that my dear friend and colleague Günter Wagner (to whom I shall return at the end of this article) at one time called me *"unseren Pneumatologen"* ("our pneumatologist"). Contributing to this Festschrift at the occasion of his retirement gives me an opportunity to get even with his verdict and write on a "pneumatological" text I have been reading and studying for over thirty years.

Different levels

Biblical texts are read on three different levels, historical, theological and applicative. At the historical level we try to reconstruct the historical situation in its contemparary context, at the theological level we attempt to discover the place of the text in the thought of its author and to relate it to the central message of the NT, the gospel of Jesus Christ. At the applicative level, however, the text is read, not as a reconstruction or an interpretation but as a norm and rule for the present.

Proper exegesis is bound to begin working at the first level. Its first task is to reconstruct as carefully as possible the situation in which the text is written and read. It does not avoid the second level, since the exegete realizes that it is the preaching of the gospel which created the Christian church and all the situations therein to which the texts relate.

It is, however, at the third level that biblical texts are read and studied by the majority of the readers. Their conclusions interact with their own experience. Sometimes their experience leads to a new understanding of biblical texts which hitherto had not been discovered by exegetes and biblical theologians. On the other hand Bible study at the applicative, or prescriptive, level may easily overlook the historical dimension of biblical texts and treat historically determined statements as timeless words of God. This applies also to texts that inspired and inspire pentecostal and charismatic Christians. Their contributions to the understanding of these texts are considerable.[1] But they tend to read them

---

[1] Cf. My farewell lecture at the university of Utrecht, May 25, 1988: *"Aangaande de geestelijke gaven"* , (Utrecht 1988).

primarily within the framework of their own experiences. When that happens a re-reading of the texts is necessary and it is the task of historical exegetes to undertake that. This is what I intend to do in the present contribution with regard to a text much cherished among our charismatic fellow-Christians, viz. 1 Corinthians 12: 1-11.

Paul's letters are to be read in the first place as parts of a process of communication. They are the only part of the process that is accessible and from which the process as a whole must be reconstructed. Within this process his letters are means to inform and to persuade the readers to accept a certain behaviour. In the last three decades this insight has been rediscovered and many scholars have turned to the books of the ancient rhetoricians and tried to investigate how the rules of persuasive rhetoric have been applied by Paul (and the other writers of the NT). Interesting though this may be, I do not think that this approach is in the end very fruitful. In the first place it is doubtful whether there was a rhetorical theory of letter writing in Paul's time[2] and secondly the rhetorical nature of his letters cannot be determined by checking them against the theory-books but by comparing them to writings of the same nature. Rhetorical analysis is not question of rules applied but of intention and structure discovered [3]

It is from this point of view that we shall attempt to re-read 1 Cor 12: 1-11. This text is part of the section covering ch. 12, 13 and 14. Its opening is determined by the introductory *peri de tôn pneumatikôn* (12: 1), possibly a reference to the letter of the church to Paul (cf. 7: 1; 8: 1; 16:1); its close is determined by the concluding injunction of 14, 39, introduced by *hôste, adelphoi*. This text summarizes the whole of ch. 14 and at the same time indicates what the Corinthians had brought before Paul *peri tôn pneumatikôn*: what is the place and importance of glossolalia and prophecy in the life and the meetings of the congregation? It is clear from ch. 14 what Paul's answer is. It is aptly summarized in the closing words of the section: be eager to prophesy and do not forbid speaking in tongues. Prophecy, the speaking of the intelligible word of God directly inspired by the Holy Spirit [4]holds the first place, glossolalia, the uttering of unintelligible speech, also inspired by the Spirit, is of less importance but should not be forbidden. The same verdict is, albeit less explicitly, already given in

[2]Cf. P.L. Schmidt,*Epistolographie*, Der kleine Pauly 2 München 1979 325.

[3]A model of rhetorical analysis in this sense is Barnabas Lindars, *The rhetorical structure of Hebrews*, NTS 35 (1989) 382-406.

[4]Cf my *Prophecy, the Spirit and the Church*, in J. Panagopoulos (ed.), *Prophetic Vocation in the NT and Today* (Leiden 1977) 58-76.

the opening verse of ch. 14 - which makes this chapter an *inclusio*, a sustained argument. This argument would have been sufficient if the problem of the Corinthians was confined to prophecy and glossolalia. Yet it comes after two preceding chapters of which ch. 12 deals with the Holy Spirit and ch. 13 with love excelling all gifts of the Spirit. For some reason Paul thinks it necessary to place this before his treatment of the questions of the Corinthians.

As far as ch. 13 is concerned Paul's intention is clear. It is in a sense an interruption in his argument on the Spirit, but more than just that: a subsumption of all that has been said and yet is to be said about the Holy Spirit under the superstructure of love, the *kath' huperbolèn hodos* (12: 31b). This is the rhetorical function of ch. 13 vis à vis ch. 14 and implicitly also vis à vis the Corinthian question: to remind them that, whatever is going to be said on prophecy and glossolalia, is overarched by the superstructure which is love.

But why thinks Paul it necessary to write so extensively about the Spirit and the body of Christ before embarking upon his dealing with the Corinthian questions? In other words: why ch. 12 before ch. 14? It is true that prophecy and glossolalia are mentioned already here (12, 10.28.29f.), and in such a way that the verdict of ch. 14 is already foreshadowed. But that is as it were only in passing. It is not the main point of the argument. There must have been a reason for elaborating so extensively on the Spirit before coming to grips with the actual problems of the church in Corinth.

I submit that this reason is to be found in 2: 6 - 3: 4. The first part of that passage, 2: 6-16, is the second of Paul's arguments in dealing with the divisions in the church (1: 10ff.), the first being that of the wisdom of the cross (1: 18 - 2: 5). This wisdom is revealed through the Spirit. The esoteric terminology which he uses in 2: 6-16 is probably that favoured by the (or some) Corinthians. He uses it only to continue in 3: 1-4 that what he said about the Spirit and the *pneumatikos*, the man of the Spirit, does not apply to them since their behaviour towards one another shows that they are not *pneumatikoi* at all[5]

The Corinthians' questions about glossolalia and prophecy provide an oppertunity for Paul to return to the theme of the Spirit, this time not in the esoteric language which the Corinthians are so fond of, but in clear statements which deal with the basics of pneumatology and prepare the way for the treatment of the Corinthian

---

[5].For a full exegesis of 2: 6-16 see my *Wisdom and the Spirit,* in T. Baarda *e.a.* (ed.), *Text and Testimony, Essays in honour of A.F.J. Klijn* (Kampen 1988) 200-211.

problems. Is ch. 13 the superstructure of Paul's argument, ch. 12 is the substructure, the ground on which any discussion on the work of the Spirit is to be based.

After these preliminary observations let us now follow the text more closely. The structure of 12: 1-11 is clear: vv. 1-3 is the fundamental introduction, as such characterized by the various *verba cognoscendi: ou thelô humas agnoein, oidate* and *gnôrizô*. Then follows the section 4-11, an *inclusio* defined by *to ..auto pneuma* in v. 4 and *to hen kai to auto pneuma* in v. 11[6].

12: 1-3

The thematic opening *peri de tôn pneumatikôn* (cf. *supra*) is followed by the well known phrase *ou thelô humas agnoein* but, unlike 10: 1; Rom 1: 13; 11: 25; 1 Thess 4: 13, not with an object (sentence or noun). Instead of saying what he wants the Corinthians to know Paul , as it were, interrupts himself and turns to what his readers already know and presumably must keep in mind just now. They should remember that once they were *ethnê*, pagans, and used to be carried away to the dumb pagan gods. This is the general gist of the sentence but the text has several grammatical and textual problems: *hoti hote*, in some manuscripts simplified to either *hote* or *hoti,* must be retained as the *lectio difficilior*; the problem is then which verb goes with *hoti:* when *êgesthe* (which would be the natural choice after *ête* , what about *hôs an* preceding it and what is then the meaning of *apagomenoi?* When *apagomenoi*, the participle would have to be complemented by another *ête* (omitted as a haplography?) and *hôs an êgesthe* would be a case of an iterative in past time[7]. This is probably the better solution. The placing of *êgesthe* and *apagomenoi* side by side has the effect emphasizing it as the characteristic of their life as pagans[8]. It was a religion without conscious control[9]. It is precisely the opposite which Paul will introduce in the next verse.

---

[6]12: 12-27 is also an *inclusio*, defined by the word *sôma* in vv. 12 and 27, and at the same time a continuation of the argument of vv. 4-11 as shown by the connection between *hen pneuma* and *hen sôma* in vv. 13.

[7]Cf. Blass-Debrunner-Rehkopf,*Grammatik des neutestamentlichen Griechisch* (Göttingen 1975[14]) § 367.

[8]Cf. Seneca, *Ep. Morales* 23, 8: (of people who do not follow reason) *eorum more quae fluminibus innatant, non eunt sed feruntur.*

[9]Whether Paul thinks of ecstatic religion is not sure and for Paul's argument irrelevant, cf. Conzelmann, *Der erste Brief an die Korinther* (Göttingen 1969) 242.

The opening verb of v. 3 *gnôrizô* takes up *ou thelô humas agnoein* of v. 1 and introduces the information which Paul wants the Corinthians to know. This information is expressed in two corresponding antithetical statements of which the latter appears to be clear and the former is, to say the least, ambiguous and problematic. It is not possible to deal with all the problems involved within the compass of this article. The clue to an acceptable interpretation of the verse as a whole is to be found in the contrast between vs. 2 and vs. 3: in the past a religion without control, now a religion governed by *Kurios Iêsous*. The fundamental truth of this new religion is expressed in this confession, the essence of the revelation which God had given through the Spirit (cf. 2: 10ff.). The content of this confession is expressed in Rom 4: 25:'...who was put to death for our tresspasses and raised for our justification', and its impact in Rom 14: 8: 'If we live, we live to the Lord, and if we die, we die to the Lord; so then, whether we live or whether we die, we are the Lord's'. This confession is the way to salvation (cf. Rom 10: 9f.). Its source is the Holy Spirit.

This the heart of the new situation in which the Christians live in full contrast to their past. This is the overarching antithesis of vv. 1-3. Remains the antithesis within v. 3 itself. There is no reason to connect the words 'Jesus curse!' with the main antithesis for this would mean that they refer to their pagan past. In that case any reference to the Spirit, positive of negative, would be out of place. It is so to speak an interior antithesis within v. 3 and within the Christian situation. The second part of that antithesis describes that situation in an inverted negative way: 'nobody...except by the Spirit'. The idiom of the first part is straight negative: 'nobody..'. The common element in the two is 'speak under the influence of the Spirit', and the first sentence says what is not said under the influence of the Spirit and the second what is said. Both statements are in the indicative: they do not prescribe but describe. The question is: is the antithesis purely rhetoric and is the only function of the first part to strengthen the force of the second? Or does it refer to words actually spoken by Christians? If the latter, then the next question is: are there Christians of the first generation who are reported to have used words like *anathema Iêsous*?

There is no good answer to this question, for the simple reason that we do not know of such people. So we are in no position to verify any interpretation of *anathema Iêsous* against its actual use. Within these limits the interpretation of my predecessor, the late Professor Willem C. van Unnik, commends itself because it is consistently based on the use of *anathema* (and the related *katara* in Gal 3: 13) in Paul's letters (Gal 1: 8; 1 Cor 16: 22; Rom 9: 3). His conclusion is that *anathema Iêsous* refers to Jesus' vicarious death on the cross. To call Jesus a curse means an implicit denial of his resurrection and the confession *Kurios Iêsous* is the explicit acknowledgement of his resurrection and exaltation. The former cannot be said under the influence of the Spirit, the latter cannot be said but for the influence of the Spirit[10].

Whether or not the words *anathema Iêsous* were actually spoken, in the juxtaposition with *Kurios Iêsous* they serve to strengthen the force of that confession over against the pagan past of the Corinthians: they are now under his lordship and as the Spirit makes people say *Abba* (Rom 8: 15), so the Spirit makes them confess 'Jesus is Lord'.

The emphatic closing words of v. 3 *en pneumati hagiô* remind us of the fact that Paul is embarking on the theme *peri tôn pneumatikôn*. If the confession of Jesus' lordship is due to the Holy Spirit, then the area of the Spirit is also under the same lordship. The area of the Spirit is not beyond or above the area of faith.

12: 4-6

The next section is determined by two words, viz. *diaireseis* and *to auto/ho autos*, both repeated three times. The semantic contrast between the two is the main message of the section. Whatever the exact meaning of *diaireseis*, it certainly has the connotation of variety[11]. Since the thought of vs. 4-6 is repeated and summarized in the closing words of v. 11: *to auto pneuma diairoun idia hekastô kathôs bouletai*, it is appropriate to interpret *diaireseis* in vv. 4-6 in the same sense: 'allotments', 'distributions', and *pneuma, kurios* and *theos* are understood to be the distributing agents of the 'gifts', 'services' and 'acts of power[12]' The triadic formula in the second parts of the three sentences points to a divine diversity which is balanced by the closing phrase of vs. 6: *(theos) ho energôn ta panta en pasin*, where the all-embracing unity of divine actions is stressed.

---

[10]W.C. van Unnik, *Jesus: Anathema or Kyrios (1 Cor 12: 3)?*, in B. Lindars and S.S. Smalley (*ed.*), *Christ and the Spirit, Studies in honour of C.F.D. Moule* (Cambridge 1973) 113-126.

[11]Of the long list of possible meaning of *diairesis* in Liddell & Scott, *Greek-English Lexicon* I (Oxford 1940) 395, only two suit the context, viz. 'dividing', 'distribution' and 'distinction'.

[12]*Energêmata* is to be understood with *dunameôn* as in v. 10, the only two occurrences of the word in the NT.

All this has a bearing on the three nouns in the first parts of the three sentences: they belong together like Spirit, Lord and God belong together. They cannot be taken apart and understood as the special areas of Spirit, Lord and God respectively. As v. 11 shows, what is said in v. 6 of God's activity can just as adequately be said of the Spirit. Of the three words the rare *energêma* is used because a noun to go with *diaireseis* was necessary but the cognate verb *energeô* is not resticted to God as the agent[13]. *Diakonia* is too general a term to be considered as one distinct area of action connected with *Kurios*. *Charisma* too does not always refer explicitly to the area of the Spirit[14].

The upshot of these observations is that vv. 4-6 are not to be interpreted analytically but comprehensively. Paul's message is this: whatever gifts, services, acts of power there are, their common source and force is God, whether they are ascribed to the Spirit, the Lord Jesus Christ or to God himself. This is the second step in Paul's argument. The next step leads the argument more into detail.

12: 7-11

V. 7 is the opening of the new section and consists of four parts which between them reflect the structure of vv. 4-11. The four elements are: (a) *hê phanerôsis tou pneumatos;* (b) *didotai;* (c) *hekastô;* (d) *pros to sumpheron.*

(a) *Phanerôsis* is best understood as 'manifestation', rather than 'revelation'[15], and *tou pneumatos* is subjective genitive: the Spirit manifests. But is there an objective genitive to be understood with *phanerôsis?* In v. 11 it is said explicitly that the Spirit 'works', i.e. 'produces' or 'makes happen' all the things that are mentioned in vv. 8-10. The Spirit is their source and agent. V. 7 however is different: the gifts are not made manifest by the Spirit, they happen and can be observed by everyone present[16]. It is the Spirit which is manifested in them. The *nomen actionis phanerôsis* does not stand for an active verb *phaneroi* but for reflexive *phaneroutai.*

---

[13]For other agents than God cf. *e.g.* Rom 7: 5; 2 Cor 4: 12; Eph 2: 2.

[14]Cf Rom 5: 15f.; 6: 23; 11: 29; 2 Cor 1: 11.

[15]Against Bultmann/Lührmann, *TWNT* IX (Stuttgart 1973) who make no distinction between this place and 2 Cor 4: 2.

[16]As contrasted with the fruit of the Spirit (Gal 5: 22) which consists of attitudes not recognisable as acts of the Spirit.

(b) *Didotai*, 'is given'. This verb is repeated in v. 8 and understood with all nominatives in vv. 8-10. It expresses that all things to be mentioned are gifts of the Spirit, not possessions. They belong to the Spirit which manifests itself in them.

(c) *Hekastô*, 'to everyone'. This is repeated in the concluding v. 11. The manifestation of the Spirit is not limited to a select number of *pneumatikoi* within the church but reaches out to everyone. The whole church is the area where the Spirit manifests itself.

(d) *Pros to sumpheron*, 'for the common good'. This short phrase at the end of the sentence is the main thrust of the statement. It is a widely used expression[17]. The community where the Spirit manifests itself must benefit from it. What this benefit would be is not explained until 14: 12-26: *pros tên oikodomên tês ekklêsias* , 'for the upbuilding of the church'. This is the specific contribution of v. 7 and the third step in the argument as a whole.

The following verses 8-10 have exercised a tremendous influence in pentacostal and charismatic movements through the centuries. They have come to be considered as the definite and normative list of the gifts of the Spirit. This could only be done by taking them from their context and setting them apart as a *magna charta*. When they are read and interpreted within their context, viz. as part of Paul's argument, they appear to have a more modest function.

The introductory *gar* and the repetition of *didotai* show that the long sentence of vv. 8-10 is a continuation of v. 7. The references to 'the same Spirit' in vv. 8 and 9 connect it with the inclusive theme of vv. 4-6 and v. 10 and make clear that the rhetorical function of vv. 8-10 is to elaborate and support the main theme of vv. 4-11, viz. the Holy Spirit as the one source of the variety of gifts. The gifts here mentioned are samples, not a more or less complete list, let alone an authoritative canon of the gifts.

This view of vv. 8-10 is not only supported by the fact that there are other and different enumerations of spiritual gifts[18] but also by a careful exegesis of the text and an investigation of the gifts that are mentioned here and the structure in which they are presented. This structure is determined by a series of datives that take up *hekastô* in v. 7. Some commentators take the beginning *hô men* and

---

[17]Cf. Bauer-Aland, *Wörterbuch zum Neuen Testament* (Berlin 1988[6])1557.

[18]Cf. 12: 28-30; Rom 12: 6-8; Eph 4: 11.

heterô in vv. 9 and 10 as the heading of a group of gifts and *allô* as indicating subdivisions in each group[19]. This view presupposes that *hô men* and *heterô* are in the same semantic class and semantically different from *allô*. Neither is, however, the case. From Homer on *heteros* and *allos* have been used alternatively in enumerations[20]. There is therefore no reason to assume that *hô men* corresponds exclusively to *heterô* and not to *allô*. It is not Paul's intention to present a structured list of gifts of the Spirit but to convince the Corinthian church that all so called gifts come from the same Spirit.

The first two gifts mentioned are *logos sophias* and *logos gnôseôs*. The common element *logos* indicates that they belong together. They do no reappear in any of the other lists of spiritual gifts. Some exegetes connect them with the apostles and teachers who are not mentioned here but appear in vv. 28 and 29 where these gifts are not mentioned. But the apostles and teachers are mentioned in one breath with the prophets and in vv. 8-10 prophecy appears near the end of the list and not in connection with the 'word of wisdom' and the 'word of knowledge'.

When we look more closely at the use and the distribution of the three words *logos, sophia* and *gnôsis* in Paul's letters in general and in 1 Corinthians in particular, another interpretation suggests itself. The meaning of *logos* is clear: it is the act and content of speech in one[21]. The subsequent genitives refer to the content. In his *captatio benevolentiae* (1: 4-9) Paul mentions *logos* and *gnôsis* as the richness of the Corinthians. We may assume that he uses terms that are favourites of his readers. Yet in 4: 9 he is not a little sceptic about the *logos* of some or all members and in 8: 1 he states bluntly that *gnôsis* 'inflates'. Apparently these words are ambivalent: they are valued by the Corinthians but their valuation is critically examined by Paul. The same is true of *sophia*. It occurs 17 times in 1 Corinthians against one in Romans and 2 Corinthians! Paul's criticism of wisdom in 1: 18 -3: 23 in the context of his dealing with the Corinthian divisions (1: 10-17) suggests that it was one of the issues in the conflict. The word does not reappear in the letter except here. It is therefore very probable that both *logos sophias* and *logos gnôseôs* are concepts dear to the Corinthians but less so to Paul and that he places them at the beginning of his exposition of the manifold gifts because he is sure of their agreement. It is a well known expedient of the rhetoric

---

[19]Cf. e.g. Robertson-Plummer, *A Critical and Exegetical Commentary of the First Epistle of St Paul to the Corinthians* (Edinburgh 1914[2]) 265.

[20]Cf. Liddell & Scott, *op. cit.* s.v *heteros* I 2; Bauer-Aland, *op. cit.* 638.

[21]Like 'word of truth' (2 Cor 6:7) and 'word of reconciliation' (2 Cor 5: 19).

of persuasion[22] and serves as a minute *captatio benevolentiae* at the beginning of the argument.

If this interpretation is correct there is no need to search for Paul's own understanding of *logos sophias* and *logos gnôseôs* on the basis of other texts in the Corpus Paulinum. Paul does not present his own interpretation to his readers but takes their favourite words and utilizes them in his argument.

We dwelt on this question at some length because so much energy and ingenuity have been invested in trying to find out what the distinctive content of these two gifts could be[23], without convincing results. Once the rhetoric nature of Paul's arguing is perceived and the persuasive function of v. 8 is recognized it is clear why no convincing solution is found. The Corinthians had their own ideas about them and Paul does not care to correct them.

This has a bearing on the interpretation of what follows. In the first place it shows that it is not necessary to dwell on the distinctions between the prepositional phrases in vv. 8-9: *dia, kata* and *en* are not meant to express different relationships between the gifts and the Spirit. They are used for the sake of variety. Between them they carry the main weight of the argument: *dia tou pneumatos* takes up *tou pneumatos* in v. 7; *kata to auto pneuma, en tô autô pneumati* and *en tô heni pneumati* take up *dia tou pneumatos* and emphasize that it is the same Spirit. This is again underlined in the peroration in v. 11.

Of the gifts mentioned in vv. 9-10 *pistis* is the notorious *crux interpretum*. The use of this word in an enumeration of spiritual gifts is exceptional in Paul. Faith is primariliy faith in...and as such it belongs to every Christian[24] and is not a gift bestowed on some. Hence the appearance of *pistis* seems to be un-pauline[25] It is worth investigating whether it is a Corinthian favourite like the preceding two.

---

[22]Cf. Aristotle, *Rhetorica* I ii 3; H. Lausberg, *Elemente der literarische Rhetorik* (München 1963) 34: "Herstellung einer affektischen Zustimmung"; R. Volkmann, *Die Rhetorik der Griechen und Römer* (repr. Leipzig 1963) 176f., 190ff.

[23]See my farewell lecture (n. 1) *passim*.

[24]Cf. R. Bultmann, *TWNT* VI (Stuttgart 1959) 218-224

[25]Cf. however Gal 5: 22 where *pistis* appears in a catalogue of virtues that are the fruit of the Spirit. Its meaning in that -traditional- context is probably not 'faith' but 'faithfulness' ,cf. H.D. Betz, *Galatians* (Philadelphia 1979) 288.

In 2 Cor. 8: 7, in a clearly persuasive context, Paul refers to the Corinthians as abounding in faith, speech and knowledge (*pistei kai logô kai gnôsei*). This is very similar to his praise in 1 Cor. 1: 5 (see *supra*). Both texts are a *captatio benevolentiae*. The words they contain are words dear to the Corinthians and it makes sense to include *pistis* in the mentioning of gifts which are peculiar to the Corinthians. It is they who boast about *pistis* as a power to accomplish mighty acts. In 13: 2 Paul pushes to the extreme the gifts which the Corinthians value most[26]. He mentions faith as the power to move mountains. Presumably that was the mood in which his readers felt about *pistis* as a special gift of the Spirit. In Paul's argument it is utilized in support of his thesis 'many gifts, one Spirit'.

The next gift mentioned, viz. the 'gifts of healing', is the last that is modified by a reference to the Spirit (*en heni pneumati*). The remaining three immediately follow one another, not because they belong together but because Paul changes his style and moves into *staccato*.

It should be noted that both nouns of the phrase *charismata iamatôn* are in the plural (also in vv. 28 and 30). Whether this means that each act of healing was regarded as an incidental charisma (Plummer: "gifts that result in healing") or that for each sort of illness there was a specific gift of healing cannot be decided on the strength of the words and is as far as Paul's argument is concerned not relevant. No charismatic healings are mentioned in 1 Corinthians. Quite to the contrary Paul refers to the many weak and sick people in the church and the death of many (11: 30). Probably the Corinthians had little or no experience of charismatic healings. Healings are reported only in Acts (apart from the gospels, naturally) and what healings are mentioned there are due to the apostles[27] and no mention is made of a specific gift of healing (nor, for that matter, in Mark 16: 17f.). The connection between the Spirit and healing goes back to the ministry of Jesus himself (cf. Matt 12: 28) and the OT promise of which He knew himself to be the fulfilment[28]. It seems then that the gift of healing did not have a prominent place in the life of the church in Corinth nor in the churches to which the other letters are addressed. Is it perhaps traditional to refer to the gift of healing?

Even more general than the wording of this gift is the next: *energêmata dunameôn*. The first word occurs only in v. 6 (without qualifying addition) and

---

[26]N.B. *panta* and *pasan* (twice)!

[27]Cf. Acts 3: 6ff.; 5: 15f.; 8: 7; 9: 18; 16: 18; 20: 10; 28: 9.

[28]Cf. Isa 61: 1ff.; Matt 11: 2-6par.; Luke 4: 16-30.

here; in vv 28 and 29 Paul writes *dunameis* for short. The phrase refers to 'acts of power' without further specifications. What acts he has in mind he does not say because that is not important in the present argument. The relationship between miracles and the Spirit is well attested in the NT[29].

The last two gifts are prophecy, together with the distinguishing of the spirits that speak through the prophets, and glossolalia, together with the gift of translating. In the summaries of v. 28 and v. 29f. prophecy is at the top and glossolalia at the bottom like here. That they are treated here together is probably due to the fact that their manifestations in the congregation cause problems and are therefore brought before Paul. In ch. 14 he tackles these problems and deals with prophecy and glossolalia extensively. There is no reason to go into the subject here[30].

The 'list' then consists of: (a) three popular Corinthian items: wisdom, knowledge and faith; (b) two general statements that have no direct connection with the church in Corinth: healings, acts of power; (c) the two specific gifts which cause problems in that church: prophecy, glossolalia. But however different in value or experience, all have one and the same source: the Holy Spirit.

V. 11 sums up this message as a conclusion of the whole argument. Several words in the preceding verses return: *panta..tauta* epitomizes the gifts mentioned above; *energei* takes up *energôn* in v. 6; *to hen kai to auto pneuma* embraces all previous statements on the Spirit: *hekastô* reflects *hekastô in v. 7; diairoun* resumes *diaireseis* in vv. 4-6. Together these elements create an impressive peroration of vv. 4-10 and emphasize the message of the text: not a list of gifts but what gifts there are, they are gifts of the one Holy Spirit.

These observations are dedicated to Günter Wagner at his retirement as Professor in the New Testament of the Baptist Theological Seminary in Rüschlikon as a token of long-standing friendship. It started well before we became teachers of the New Testament, in 1950 when he as a young student of the then new seminary came to the Netherlands to attend a youth leaders conference. It has continued till today. The fact that we both worked in the same field has deepened and extended our friendship. He was the first representative of Rüschlikon I ever met. He has been faithful to Rüschlikon for better and worse till today. The apostle Paul -with

---

[29]Cf Acts 2: 43f.; 6: 8; 2 Cor 12: 12; Rom 15: 19; Hebr 2: 4, mostly in connection with the preaching of the gospel.

[30]Cf. my *Hermas and Christian Prophecy* (Leiden 1973) and J. Panagopoulos, *op.cit.* (n. 4).

whom we both spent the best years of our lives as teachers- wrote once that what matters for a steward of God's mysteries -such as a teacher of the New Testament- is *hina pistos tis heurethê* (1 Cor 4: 2). With great respect I apply these words to Günter Wagner, faithful to his calling, his scholarship, his seminary and his numerous friends.

Where Are We Today in the Life-of-Jesus Research?

Eduard Schweizer

1991 "Faith and Order" issued a statement of around 100 pages on **"Confessing the One Faith"**[1] as the result of a team work of many years, to which **Günter Wagner** has contributed quite a bit. On pp. 45-48 the problems of the earthly ministry of Jesus are discussed. Whereas "the unity of Jesus Christ as Son with the eternal God" was clear to the Church Fathers, "modern exegetical scholarship considers (the respective biblical testimonies) as more ambiguous" and "that seems to create a tension between this approach and the 'Nicene' approach", but "the two approaches are compatible and may even enrich each other", because "from the earliest stages of the tradition there has been present implicitly that which only later became explicitly stated". Whether this statement would be signed by the "Jesus-Seminar", I am not so sure. This seminar meets in California in some continuity. Scholars discuss specific sayings of Jesus and vote at the end of the sessions by means of differently coloured ballots for different degrees of probability of authenticity or inauthenticity. The results are spread by the media and create some agitation.

Thus, it makes sense to ask again where we can find our positions in the field of modern "life-of-Jesus-research". This is a wider formulation than "research of the historical Jesus". The latter term means, strictly speaking, "the Jesus whom we can 'recover' and examine by using the scientific tools of modern historical research".[2] The "real Jesus" was, of course, much more than that as, for instance, my mother was much more than what could be detected by such tools. Any historian has to combine the facts of which he or she is sure to a convincing portrait of a living person. As long as he or she is doing so in "honest objectivity", necessarily personally engaged, but cautioning him- or herself against all presuppositions of sympathy or antipathy to the subject of his or her work, this is a fruitful and unavoidable part of the work. In this sense, we try to see what modern research has to say to us.

1. A living Christ without a life of Jesus?

As early as 1906 **Albert Schweitzer** showed that a life of Jesus, in the usual sense of the word, can no longer be reconstructed. There is almost nothing to learn about his family, his inner and outer development, the teachers, parents and

---

[1]Faith and Order Paper No. 153, Geneva: WCC.

[2]John P. Meier, A Marginal Jew. Rethinking the Historical Jesus I, New York: Doubleday 1991, 25.

friends that influenced him, etc. The evangelists are not primarily interested in a historically accurate report, but rather in the proclamation of their faith in Jesus.[3] **Rudolf Bultmann** accepted this result without any reserve. If it is the faith of the early church that is proclaimed even in the gospels, then it is this faith, grounded on the Easter event, that we have to start from. Thus, "Jesus has risen into (not: in!) the kerygma". [4] What he means is the fact that we find Jesus after Easter only in the preaching of the church and that it is only this preaching that understands Jesus correctly. This is undoubtedly true for all believers. Bultmann would even admit that there is something like an implicit christology in the ministry of Jesus; that means: that Jesus in his words and deeds claimed to be the definitive revelation of God. Yet, whether this was so or not, and in what way he may have claimed to be that, is theologically not decisive for Bultmann. Our faith does not depend on the facts of the life of Jesus. To believe does not mean to take this or that fact for granted; it means to be touched in one's innermost self, to see oneself as one is, and to get the justification from God himself, the acceptance as his child, forgiveness of sins and a new life. It means that we do no longer find our real lives in our works, in what we perform and accomplish, nor in our belief, in what we accept as a dogmatic statement of the church. We find our lives in their givenness only, in what we receive and accept as a gift of God. Faith is not a matter of sacrificing our intelligence. It is change of our self-understanding.

Bultmann's solution was fascinating. It gave his students a limitless freedom of historical-critical research and, at the same time, the possibility to accept the confessions of the church about Jesus Christ, the Son of God and redeemer from all our sins. Whether Jesus thought of being the messiah and dying as an atonement for the sins of the world was irrelevant, since we knew that he was the messiah and that his death brought about our salvation. He freed the world indeed from their trusting in their own works or in their religious convictions. He enabled the world to accept the grace of God. We needed no more than the mere "that": namely that Jesus had once lived and died on the cross.

All this got clearer features in Bultmann's program of "demythologization",[5] of a translation of all mythical language of times gone into modern, intelligible

---

[3]Geschichte der Leben-Jesu-Forschung, Tübingen: Mohr 1906.

[4]R. Bultmann, Exegetica, Tübingen: Mohr 1967, 469.

[5]Neues Testament und Mythologie, in: Offenbarung und Heilsgeschehen, München: Kaiser 1941, 27-69. The further discussion is summarized in P. J. Achtemeier, An Introduction to the New Hermeneutic, Philadelphia: Westminster 1969, 55-70 (esp. 56-63); English literature ib. 169-171.

language. For Bultmann this meant: a language dealing with our existence, an existential language. What the Bible describes as the fight of God against Satan or of the spirit against the flesh, modern language describes as the almost ineradicable human desire to "boast", to prove ourselves superior to others, physically or psychicly, in terms of wealth or art or even religion. This can only be overcome by acceptance of the grace of God, by the insight that all we can accomplish is **given** to us. It is the battle in ourselves that really matters.

Even as a student in Marburg, I had asked Bultmann why then we needed Jesus? Was he simply the motivation that led us to accept the same philosophy that he was living from? Would it not be enough just to take over this view of ourselves from the gospels, from Paul or from modern philosophers without any need to know more about Jesus, as we can take over the philosophy of Plato without knowing anything about life and death of Plato? When Bultmann spoke of demythologization, quite some theologians asked: Why then stop at God? Should we not translate this term also in modern language and speak of our innermost self, which teaches us to understand life as a gift?

2. The relevance of history

In a famous paper that he read 1953 in the group of the Bultmannians, **Ernst Käsemann** set up the battle cry.[6] The vulnerable spot in Bultmann's position was obviously his difficulty to show why and how Jesus was more than a teacher, an example or a model of the insight that life is, primarily, gift and not based on our achievements. If salvation means not more than a change in our self-understanding (in the terms of Bultmann) or our conversion (in the terms of the traditional church), then we believe actually in our own believing, we trust in our own trusting. Then salvation is reduced to an idea, which reigns over our lives, but which also participates in all the ups and downs of our devotion to that idea. But the Bible proclaims the good deeds of God, which are unconditioned by our behaviour and attitude. The gospels are narratives, and the same is true of most parts of the Old Testament. They tell of God's acts, by which he has guided his people, and of Jesus, the one in whom God came to us, has reconciled us and made us his children. This has happened long before we did anything for him, and it was mere grace that no human philosophy could have expected. God acted "outside of us", as the Reformers say.

In many ways, one could bypass the problem. In 1959 **James Robinson** spoke of

---

[6]Das Problem des historischen Jesus, in idem, Exegetische Versuche und Besinnungen, Göttingen: Vandenhoeck u.Ruprecht 1967, I 187-214.

"A New Quest of the Historical Jesus",[7] stressing both sides of the truth: the gospels are no biographies, but rather sermons proclaiming the grace of God, a grace that has become true in an earthly life and death which can be dated within the history and geography of our world. Thus, what we find in the gospels is the faith of the four evangelists, a faith shaped by the whole ministry of Jesus, including his death. This faith certainly presupposes the resurrection, which is important to the authors of the gospels, but important as God's vindication of the earthly ministry of Jesus. It is the narrative of a human life and death in which we find the revelation of God.

Would that mean that we could do without the resurrection of Jesus? It seems to be so with **Herbert Braun**.[8] He restored Bultmann's view, and Bultmann accepted it, but Braun founded it on the ministry of Jesus, not on the faith of the post-Easter church. It is, according to him, the earthly Jesus who liberated his hearers to seeing themselves as loved and accepted by God and, therefore, also to loving others. The resurrection added nothing to this central new understanding of oneself. Braun even argued that the continuity of the whole New Testament was exactly this new understanding of man, anthropology, not the understanding of Jesus as the Christ, christology. Even God seemed to disappear; according to Braun seeing one's brother is seeing God.[9]

1967 **Dorothee Sölle** replaced God by Jesus. What God used to be for people, Jesus is now, because God is dead. Resurrection might mean a newly reached oneness and identity of all people. In a society without class distinctions God might come alive again.[10] She certainly said so against a very conservative position, in which God became a mere object, the existence of which one simply had to take for granted without really getting engaged with his or her total existence. I know few theologians who try to think and to speak as seriously and honestly as Braun and Sölle. For both Jesus is central, though he teaches and lives how, on principle, every human being could do. Nonetheless, is their Jesus without God as his father and Lord not like an ambassador, who still holds his office, though his country has ceased to exist long ago?

[7]SBT 25, London: SCM.

[8]Jesus, Stuttgart: Kreuz-Verlag 1969.

[9]Idem, ZThK 54 (1957) 368-371, 57 (1960) 18.

[10]Stellvertretung:ein Kapitel Theologie nach dem "Tode Gottes", Stuttgart:Kreuz-Verlag 1967,175,181,190, cf. M. Machovec, A Marxist Looks at Jesus, Philadelphia: Fortress 1976. For more detailed references to notes 3-10 cf. E. Schweizer, Jesus Christ, Macon, GA: Mercer Univ. Press 1987, 1-6.

More modern is the trend, remarkable since the publication of **E. P. Sanders'** books at the end of the seventies,[11] to place Jesus and, to some degree, also the earliest church into Judaism. This approach focuses, like that of Braun and Sölle on the earthly ministry of Jesus of Nazareth (without emphasizing his resurrection and his role in the post-Easter church); differently from them, the uniqueness of this ministry is rather toned down. The last monography I know that "reclaims" Jesus for Judaism and tries to bring him home to Israel is that of **Maurice Casey**.[12] According to him, Jesus was a Jewish prophet, who did never use any title like messiah, son of God or Lord as a self-identification, who humbly spoke of himself as "son of man" in a general sense, more or less as we use "one". He expected the imminent end of the world and the final coming of the kingdom of God. Therefore, he intensified the commands of the Mosaic law, with emphasis on the love of one's neighbour. With regard to himself, he expected his death and his vindication by God. Since, however, his disciples and all those who shared their beliefs had to find their identity after Easter over against the Jews that did not accept these beliefs, they needed a miracle like Jesus' exaltation to heaven (as it had happened to Enoch and Elija according to the scriptures) and a new focus of their faith: Jesus instead of the law. Not yet with Paul, but with John, Jesus was consecutively even called "God", and this remained the position of the church from the council of Chalcedon on.

3. The Jewishness of Jesus and the early church

Jesus was certainly a Jew, and this is important. The same is true for most of the authors of the New Testament, and this, again, is also important. One of the principal difficulties in the dialogue of Jews and Christians and in the modern approach to a belief in Jesus Christ is our thinking **in terms of substance,** which we inherited from the Greeks, especially from Aristotle. This way of thinking has become, if not wrong, at least questionable today. In modern natural science everything has become motion and energy so that terms like "matter" are no longer going without saying. Sure, even in the Jerusalem of the times of Jesus Hellenistic views prevailed for almost three centuries, and Greek was spoken by many Jews there, perhaps even by Jesus, though it remains improbable that any of his words reported in the gospels were originally spoken in Greek.[13] Yet, in the

[11]Paul and Palestinian Judaism 1977 - Paul, the Law and the Jewish People 1983 - Jesus and Judaism 1985 (all: Philadelphia: Fortress).

[12]From Jewish Prophet to Gentile God, Cambridge: Clark 1991 (my review TLZ 117 [1992] 353-356).

[13]J. P. Meier, 258-262.

areas in which the Hebrew Bible was of first importance, and this includes the whole sphere of religious life, its way of thinking was clearly influencing the understanding. For instance, when a Jewish Christian confessed Jesus as the son of God, he did so in the way his Bible taught him. The king became son of God when he acceeded the throne of Israel (Ps 2:7). From then on he represented God. It was God who spoke through him and acted through him. In a similar way, Israel as God's chosen people or the pious Israelites could be called sons of God. This is the way in which a Jewish Christian understood Jesus to be the son of God. In and through Jesus God spoke to him, acted with him, saved him.

Let us consider this statement and clear as much as possible what it does mean and what not. In a first reflection, we should admit that this is, indeed, the only language in which we can speak of God correctly. Even outside of any religious area, as soon as we speak of a living being, of a person or an animal, we cannot really define him, her or it. Terms of substance do not really help. If you asked me who my wife is, you would not expect me to tell you that she consists of so and so many pounds of bones or of fat or of muscles and of so and so many liters of water and of blood. You would expect me to narrate, to give you an account of where she was born, what schools she had gone through, what calling she has chosen, how she brought up our children, what sports she practiced, how she laughs, what hobbies she has, etc. In the same way, or even more so, I cannot furnish a definition of God, but I can narrate how he proved himself the living God, calling us, saving us, speaking to us, acting with us. The same is true for Jesus. When I confess that he is indeed the son of God, I do not mean that his body is of a different substance than our bodies, that, for instance, his blood was mere water, as many people in that time believed of the blood of Alexander the Great. I mean that in his life, his death and his resurrection God himself lived, acted, spoke with and to us. Thus, his titles, be it messiah or son of God or any other description of his unique dignity, are basically of a narrative character. This is central for understanding the New Testament.

In a second round, however, we have to discuss whether this is all that we want to convey to our partners in the dialogue. We certainly do not mean, and the Jewish Christians in the time of the earliest church did not mean, that Jesus was on the same level as any Jewish king or even as any pious Jew. How can we express, in our language, that Jesus is, for us, unique among all those who might have been called sons of God? We cannot do so by mere comparatives. He is not simply "more" of a son of God than David or John the Baptist. He is son of God in a different way. Here, we cannot avoid using mythical language, on the contrary. Again, even when we tell others about a loved friend or spouse, strictly rational words of a language of mere information defy us. We have to convey our experiences of love to the hearers, or rather all the expressions of the life of our friend or spouse that caused these our experiences. We cannot do so without resorting to imagery that might awake similar experiences in our hearers. The same is true when we try to show a picture gallery to our child or to help him or her to listen to good music. As little as we can explain rationally the experience of love, of art, of music as little or much less can we do with regard to our experience of God. As **Kurt Niederwimmer** once wrote, our subconscious life, more important than the rational one, expresses itself precisely in mythological imagery.

Rudolf Bultmann emphasized that we should not remove mythological statements of the Bible, but translate them into intelligible modern language. Unfortunately, he used in his introduction the example of modern people who no longer light oil lamps, but switch on the electric light and expect as a matter of course that the electric current causes the bulb to shine.[14] This was wide open to the misunderstanding of demythologization being a reduction of all mythical imagery to mere rational expressions. However, what we can do and must do is to translate the mythology of the first into that of the twentieth century, for instance by speaking of "transcendence" instead of "heaven". "Transcendence" cannot rationally define what we mean, but the term has, in a long discussion of philosophers, won a certain "band-width", within which the truth is to be found. It is better secured against misunderstandings to the left and to the right than the old term "heaven". Nonetheless it does not simply provide a definition that we could take over without really getting engaged ourselves with all our experiences. Thus, speaking of God needs, by necessity, mythological language.

All this would certainly not reconcile Jewish and Christian views of Jesus. First, we have to admit that there are passages in the New Testament that speak of him as the son of God in a way which is closer to the language of Aristotle or Plato than to that of the Psalms and the Prophets. We would have to interpret them from their contexts, and I think that almost all of them would not understand the divine nature of Jesus as a physical difference from other people, but rather as the manifestation of the fact that Jesus lived in a total openness to God or is, after Easter, now living in a total community with God, which cannot be defined by human conceptions. Even in some questionable formulations the background is the conviction that God encounters the world in Jesus Christ, speaking and acting through him. Second, we interpret these passages as we interpret the many other images of the New Testament, as linguistic attempts to describe the uniqueness of this sonship of Jesus. For a Christian Jesus is the "eschatological" son of God, who fulfills definitively what God's people or its kings or its righteous ones ever

[14]R. Bultmann, Neues Testament 34-42 und 14.

had been and done as representatives of God. And at this point a Jew could not agree. He would, however, at least understand what we mean, when we speak of the son of God as the acting representative of God.

4. Should we resign?

Have we come to a blind alley? **Either** we side with Bultmann's original position: then we decide to accept the faith of the early church in a decision of faith that cannot be argued this or that way, and the problem arises what the role of Jesus, of his life, his death and his resurrection is. **Or** we side with Käsemann: then the ugly problem of the historian faces us; if history is of eminent importance, who tells us whether Jesus was a preacher of existentialism, as Braun sees him, or of left wing politics, as Sölle or Machovec understands him, or a psychotherapist, as Niederwimmer might say, or a Jewish prophet, as Casey suggests, or still somebody else?

Let us consider both alternatives. If we follow **Bultmann,** he certainly offers full freedom for any historical critical research, and its results are not threatening our faith, whatever they may be. But why would we need Jesus? Bultmann would answer that the theologian, in contrast to the philosopher, knows about the weight of sin and knows, therefore, that we need more than a mere philosophy. This means that the life and death of Jesus could motivate us to the necessary change of self-understanding. Is this enough? The really saving event would still be this change, in traditional terms: our innermost conversion, to which Jesus helps us as a teacher and a model. Would we, in this case, then believe in our believing? In our own religiousness? But our religious life, our experiences of God are never stable. Would our faith not change with all the ups and downs of our religious feelings? As long as we are spinning around ourselves we are lost. And it makes no great difference whether we turn around our morally good and pious deeds like the Pharisees or around our sins and pseudo-sins like a well trained protestant, around the religious experiences of our souls or around the daring atheistic thoughts of our rational minds. Years ago, we swam down the Rhine river. In front of me one after the other of my comrades disappeared in an eddy, which was rather bewildering, but all of them came up again, which was more gratifying. Then the same happened to me. If the whirlpool had really drowned me for good, nobody would have asked whether the whirl turned clockwise or anti-clockwise. Thus, in what ever way we spin around ourselves in our faith, we are lost. In the Bible Jesus is more than a motivating teacher or model. The New Testament says that he has saved us, long before we could hear him and decide to listen to him. Salvation has happened "outside of us", "extra nos" as the Reformers emphasized. Therefore, history is of first importance for Christianity. But if we accept that and follow **Käsemann,** where do we find security about the historical facts?

Let us start with some general reflections. First, in these times of insecurity, we yearn after security, and many fundamentalist movements offer it in many religions or pseudo-religions. But it is, by necessity, a sham-security. The most important facts in our world are facts that we cannot detect without getting involved ourselves. If a boy tests all available girls by some totally objective criteria and finally chooses the girl with the highest score, he will, probably never detect what love is. Since faith is much more than just accepting some proven facts, since it implies a personal relation to the one in whom we believe, we cannot dodge the adventure of a personal response. What we find in Jesus is **not a security** that could be proved by photographs or by experiments that could be repeated by everybody whenever wanted; it is **the certitude** of love, of being loved and loving, the certitude that gives shelter and warmth, not the cold security of indubitable proof. If a husband wanted proof of the love of his wife and got her shadowed by a private eye, 365 excellent daily reports a year would certainly not be the beginning of real love, but very probably its end. Therefore, we need the imagery of mythical language to express this certitude of engaged relation to Jesus.

Second, the gospels are written in the time after Easter in a retrospect influenced by this event. However, every historian needs to know about the development of the past; otherwise he could not select the facts he describes. The famous tea party of December 17, 1773 in Boston seemed to be not more than a prank of some hoodlums. The historian reports it, because he knows that it was the beginning of the fight for independence of the USA. Every historian has to get engaged in his subject, otherwise he can't understand the facts. This is especially true when he describes the life of an artist or a political genius. As long as he knows about the presuppositions in his mind for or against the subject of his story and checks them time and again against the facts he knows, this is helpful for his work. It was only after Easter that what Jesus had achieved became visible. To accept that as God's good will does not blind us to the facts of the history of Jesus, as long as we remain open to them. It will, on the contrary, open our minds for the depth of what has happened in the ministry of Jesus and in its aftereffects.

Third, **security in all details is never possible**. Classical historians sometimes grin at the scruples of their New Testament colleagues; if they investigated the antique history as critically as we do, they would find about nothing. Even in the life of my mother there are very few details that are beyond any doubt. My sister often tells a story quite differently from how I remember it. Yet, there is an overall picture of her life that cannot be doubted. This makes the method of the

Jesus Seminar disputable. When going from detail to detail we are in danger to fail to see the forest by looking at hundreds of single trees with all their problems.

However, do we possess some criteria for investigating the ministry of Jesus?

5. Criteria

John P. Meier[15] discusses the five criteria[16] that are still valid: 1. "Embarrassment": actions or sayings of Jesus that are difficult for the early church, for instance his baptism by John or his ignorance of day and hour of the parousia. 2. "Discontinuity": Whatever cannot be explained as originating from Judaism or the early church is probably authentic. This is, today, the most disputed criterion, since a Jesus who is no longer Jewish or shares nothing with the faith of his followers would be a caricature. However, if we are aware of the fact that this leads to a mere minimum of genuine Jesus tradition, this dissimilarity is still helpful. 3. "Multiple attestation" favours authenticity, but could also come from common oral post-Easter tradition. 4. "Coherence" is more important. Whatever fits well into the minimum resulting from criterion 2, may, tentatively, be accepted as genuine. 5. "Rejection": Jesus has been rejected and finally crucified. Why? Actions and sayings that can explain this, are with some probability historic facts.

Not one of these points leads to 100%-security, which is not attainable to historical reconstruction. But if we use all of these criteria in a cautious way, we come to a general picture of the ministry and death of Jesus and the immediately following development, which is much clearer than that of almost all persons in antiquity. We may add extra-biblical testimonies like that of Josephus (in its original core) and Tacitus, which prove the crucifixion of Jesus and the existence of a group of believers.

Apocryphal gospels like that of Peter and Thomas, favoured by **J. D. Crossan** and **H. Koester** are, in my view[17], of no help.

---

[15]J. P. Meier 167-195.

[16]Ibidem 178-183 dubious criteria: Aramaisms, Palestinian Environment, Vividness of Narration, Tendencies of the Synoptists, Historical Presumption. For the limited value of form-criticism and its crisis cf. E. Schweizer, TZ 47 (1991) 195f.

[17]Also in the view of J. P. Meier (139), who carefully discusses all extra-biblical sources on pp. 56-166.

Even if Jesus had never called himself Christ or son of God, his call of twelve disciples as a claim to the whole of the twelve tribes of Israel, his conviction of the presence of the kingdom of God in his parables, in his healings and in his table fellowships as manifestations of God's forgiveness of sins, his "I say to you" that contrasted the word of the scriptures and his prayer to God as his "abba" described him as surpassing all messianic expectations.

If, therefore, we stress the relevance of history in our faith, with **Käsemann** and also with **Karl Barth**, we take seriously the position of almost all of the New Testament authors: In Jesus God has brought his history of salvation, inaugurated in Israel, to its goal. This has become true "outside" of our assent, even our knowledge. Our salvation is God's doing. It is not created by our change of self-understanding and not dependent on its quality. Jesus' death is more than the motif for our conversion, and his resurrection more than a mere vindication of the dead Jesus. Jesus is certainly an example and model (John 13:15), but he is much more than that (13:8). This "more" is asserted in the language of faith of the New Testament in very different images: that of the final, "eschatological" quality of the Jesus event (e.g. Luke 11:20; Mark 14:25), of solidarity to the utmost limit (Luke 23:40f), of a ransom paid for a debt (Mark 10:45) of a vicarious (John 11:50-52) or sacrificial death (Mark 14:22-24).

If we want a cooling swim on a hot day, having no thermometer to check the temperature of the water, we may have to jump. If we want the experience of faith, we have to jump - into the ocean of God's love, manifested in these images.

THE WOMEN OF THE FOURTH GOSPEL:
PARADIGMS OF DISCIPLESHIP OR PARAGONS OF VIRTUE?

Martin Scott

1. INTRODUCTION

There is a profound sense of irony for the reader of the Fourth Gospel, that the presence of stories of women apparently functioning as paradigms of discipleship for the community to whom the Evangelist writes seems to raise more problems than it solves - no matter where the reader stands on the theological spectrum. For the entrenched dinosaur still locked into support of the patriarchal structures of ecclesial life, the presence of such potentially powerful pictures of women in a first-century writing offers enormous threat: the thin edge of a wedge which would rend tradition asunder. From a totally different perspective, however, their presence may be equally irksome to the committed feminist, for despite what many may have written about the 'liberated' nature of their role,[1] the suspicion remains that they are chosen as paradigms precisely because no one better illustrates servanthood (an apparent Johannine characteristic of discipleship) than those in the lowliest position - women! They may, therefore, be seen not so much as breaking the mould of tradition as reinforcing its patriarchal modes of submission. Perhaps the women of the Fourth Gospel are not so much paradigms of discipleship as paragons of virtue.

Up to this point, this particular feminist critique has not been expressed in writing directly in relation to the theme of women as 'disciples' in the Fourth Gospel. It has, however, been a matter which I have discussed at some length with several colleagues and friends, who have spurred me to re-evaluate the material I had already written on the Johannine women and to add some additional points to the arguments in my book, *Sophia and the Johannine Jesus*. Given that it has, however, been discussed in relation to other pictures of women in the biblical tradition,[2] this seems an apt moment to pick up the subject and give it an initial

---

[1] Cf. Brown,R.E., *The Community of the Beloved Disciple* (London: Geoffrey Chapman,1979) pp. 183-198; Schneiders,S.M., "Women in the Fourth Gospel and the Role of Women in the Contemporary Church" *BibThBull* 12 (1982) pp. 35-45; Collins,A.Y., "New Testament Perspectives: the Gospel of John" JSOT 22 (1982) 47-53; Fiorenza,E.S., *In Memory of Her* (London: SCM Press,1983) pp. 323-333; Scott,M., *Sophia and the Johannine Jesus* (Sheffield: Sheffield Academic Press,1992; JSNTS Monograph Series, 71) pp. 174-240.

[2] Cf. the volume of seminar papers, G.Brooke (ed.) *Women in the Biblical Tradition* (Lewiston,NY/Lampeter: Edwin Mellen Press,1992; *Studies in Women and Religion*, 31), in particular the article by Mary Cotes, "Women, Silence and Fear (Mark 16:8)", pp. 150-166.

airing. It is also appropriate in the context of this present *Festschrift*, since it was in the cut and thrust of a New Testament seminar on *Women in the Gospels*, chaired by Prof. Günter Wagner in 1981, that my interest in the subject was first stimulated. In common with other contributors to this volume, I remain indebted to him for awakening a desire to follow through some of the challenges of critical New Testament study - even if he should not be held responsible for the limitations of this present article!.

That there is a problem surrounding the appearance of women in the Johannine stories is perhaps illustrated best with reference to a description of the nature of patriarchy. For Elisabeth Schüssler Fiorenza, "what constitutes the heart of patriarchy" is "dependence on and control by men. Obedience is the essence of patriarchy".[3] Now it is immediately clear that all of the women of the Fourth Gospel, beginning with the Mother of Jesus at Cana and ending with Mary of Magdala in the garden, act in an obedient and submissive manner towards the Johannine Jesus. His Mother silently accepts her son's rebuke, even if she then goes on to assume authority in the situation. The Samaritan Woman trots off to bring in the 'harvest' while Jesus and the μαθηταί[4] discuss its implications, despite the fact that she has earlier sat quite forcibly discussing theology. On her first appearance, Mary of Bethany immediately obeys the summons of the Johannine Jesus (11:29 - ἠγέρθη ταχὺ καὶ ἤρχετο πρὸς αὐτόν) and falls at his feet on arrival. She then goes on to anoint his feet in great humility - the event for which she is apparently best remembered (11:2 - ἦν δὲ Μαριὰμ ἡ ἀλείψασα τὸν κύριον μύρῳ καὶ ἐκμάξασα τοὺς πόδας αὐτοῦ ταῖς θριξὶν αὐτῆς). Her sister Martha, though portrayed as a strong figure in chapter 11, does the classic domestic task of serving while her brother and Jesus lounge at the table. Jesus' Mother passes from his control to that of another man, the Beloved Disciple, at the foot of the cross. Finally Mary of Magdala obeys the command of the risen Jesus

---

[3]Fiorenza,E.S., "Patriarchal Structures and the Discipleship of Equals" in: *Discipleship of Equals: a Critical Feminist Ekklesia-logy of Liberation* (London: SCM Press,1993) p.213.

[4]I have chosen to retain the Greek μαθηταί to designate the group of (presumably) *male* 'disciples' who appear at various points in the Gospel and show a distinct lack of perception with regard to the nature and mission of the Johannine Jesus. This allows for a distinction to be made between them and others, including the women, who function in the role of disciples. The Fourth Evangelist only uses the term 'twelve' (δώδεκα) to describe the traditional male group of disciples known from the Synoptic tradition on two occasions in Jn 6:70-71.

to 'go and tell', an action which appears to have had remarkably little effect on the male μαθηται. If obedience really is the essence of patriarchy, the women of the Fourth Gospel are clearly off to a difficult start!

Before examining this material in some more detail, it is necessary to outline some presuppositions, the argumentation for which is far beyond the scope of this current article, but which may be available to the reader in other places. First, I work with the basic premise that the most significant formative influence on Johannine christology was that of the Jewish figure Wisdom, Sophia.[5] The Prologue to the Gospel introduces Jesus as Sophia incarnate by use of the synonymous term Logos, this being the more appropriate because of its masculine gender.[6] The influence of Sophia, however, extends not only to the christological presentation, but also to the understanding of discipleship and its models within the Gospel.[7] It is therefore a significant factor in any discussion of the role of women in the Fourth Gospel.

Second, the relationship of the Fourth Gospel to the Synoptic tradition is important for the direction of this paper, not least in relation to the discussion of the βασιλεια του θεου. It is my assumption that the author knew at least Mark in written form and probably also Luke's reinterpretation of the Markan story. However, it is clear that the Fourth Evangelist felt sufficiently at liberty from the constraints of tradition to be able to use that material in a free and creative manner.[8]

Third, the characterisation of the Johannine community, out of which the present Gospel emerged, as a community under threat, wracked by schism and in some measure on the margins of wider ecclesial life at the end of the first century of the Christian era, seems to be an appropriate one, given the evidence of the Johannine corpus as a whole.[9] This would be significant particularly for the discussion of

[5]For a full argumentation of this see, Scott, *Sophia and the Johannine Jesus*, passim, but particularly pp.83-173.

[6]Scott, *Sophia and the Johannine Jesus*, pp.170-173.

[7]Scott, *Sophia and the Johannine Jesus*, pp.174-240.

[8]Perhaps the most obvious example of this is the story of the Anointing of Jesus by a woman, which in the Fourth Evangelist's telling combines both Markan and Lukan elements in the framework of a thoroughly Johannine narrative.

[9]The material written on the Johannine community is now vast. Most influentially see:

the context in which and out of which the Johannine picture of women as disciples is to be understood.

2. THE DISCIPLESHIP OF WOMEN IN JOHN

So to the material involving women in discipleship roles in the Fourth Gospel. We have already noted the presence of five principal characters who, at least on one level, appear to function under the control, or in submission to the Johannine Jesus. We shall now, in the briefest terms outline the role which these women play within the various narratives before then setting their function against the background of the language of community within the Fourth Gospel as a whole.

2.1 THE MOTHER OF JESUS.

The first female figure we encounter in the Gospel is Jesus' Mother, who becomes involved in the wine miracle at a wedding in Cana (Jn 2:1-11). Since this is the first of the σημεῖα, so important in John's dramatic framework, it is already striking to find a woman in a prominent role, rather than the μαθηταί, who are introduced in the opening verse, but remain in the background, only emerging to express some faith in Jesus *after* the event. As the story unfolds her exemplary discipleship is demonstrated both in her knowledge of where to go when the wine runs out (to Jesus, Sophia incarnate), and in her demonstrated faith *before* the σημεῖον takes place.[10] Despite what appears to be a deliberate distancing between Jesus and his mother -Τί ἐμοὶ καὶ σοί, γύναι; (2:4) - we find that she nevertheless perseveres in the expectation that Jesus will be able to supply the necessary wine for the occasion.[11] Her faith is demonstrated in the command to the house servants to follow the instructions of Jesus, and this prepares the way in

Martyn,J.L., "Glimpses into the History of the Johannine community" in: *The Gospel of John in Christian History* (1978) pp.90-121; Brown, *Community*, passim; Wengst,K., Bedrängte Gemeinde und verherrlichter Christus (Neukirchen-Vluyn: Neukirchener Verlag,1983); Rensberger,D., *Overcoming the World. Politics and Community in the Gospel of John* (London: SPCK,1988).

[10]Cf Jn 20:29 - μακάριοι οἱ μὴ ἰδόντες καὶ πιστεύσαντες

[11] It is significant to note that Jesus' Mother does not ask for anything in the narrative. She simply remarks οἶνον οὐκ ἔχουσιν. Wine is one of the gifts of Sophia to her followers (eg. Prov 9:5) and this particular disciple knows the source from which more wine is likely to come. Cf. Scott, *Sophia and the Johannine Jesus*, pp.178-179.

the dramatic unfolding of the narrative for the σημεῖον to take place.

This story makes clear at the opening of the public ministry of the Johannine Jesus that a disciple's importance for the community is not based on her family ties to Jesus, but on the *quality* of her discipleship. Far from her exerting influence upon Jesus or gaining recognition because she is his mother, she becomes prominent because of the faith and insight which she demonstrates before any action takes place. This stands in contrast to the μαθηταί, who only come to believe as a result of the 'sign' itself (2:11).

In the case of Jesus' Mother, this point is reinforced in her second appearance in Jn 19:25-27. Here at the foot of the cross along with other women who have faithfully followed to the end, Jesus' Mother is recognised as belonging to a new family in which mother and son are given to one another in a relationship of equality. By placing Jesus' Mother at the foot of the cross along with the Beloved Disciple, the Fourth Evangelist allows two of the great unnamed, symbolic figures of the Gospel to be seen in their true light as exemplary disciples - they 'abide' to the end, again in stark contrast to the group of μαθηταί who have abandoned him to his fate.   Thus the Mother of Jesus frames the beginning and the completion of the ministry of Jesus Sophia as an example of the disciple who remains faithful to the end.

2.2 THE SAMARITAN WOMAN.

The story of the encounter between Jesus Sophia and a Samaritan woman at the well of Jacob provides the second example of a woman in a significant role in the Fourth Gospel. The story is unique in NT terms in that it openly identifies the woman's *sex* as an issue in the narrative. While the discussion initially points out the conflict between Jews and Samaritans as a potential barrier to conversation (4:9), the μαθηταί, on returning from their excursion into the Samaritan village, remark on the inappropriateness of Jesus' public conversation with a *woman* (4:27).

The conversation itself is illuminating in terms of the narrative development of the Johannine understanding of discipleship. Following on from a series of stories set *within* the boundaries of Israel, John 4 moves the question of discipleship *outside* into the region of Samaria. Just as the Jewish reaction to the presence of Jesus, Sophia incarnate, has ranged from disbelief (2:23-25), through misunderstanding and incomplete faith (Nicodemus 3:1-21), to the exemplary faith of John the Baptist (3:30 - ἐκεῖνον δεῖ αὐξάνειν, ἐμὲ δὲ ἐλαττοῦσθαι), so too the Samaritan woman demonstrates this same pattern in her encounter with Jesus Sophia. Initially she shows a total lack of understanding in her request for the practical benefits of 'everlasting water' (4:15),but she then goes on to show both a knowledge of her religious traditions, and a developing, though as yet incomplete, understanding of who this man is (4:19 - Κύριε, θεωρῶ ὅτι προφήτης εἶ σύ) In the end she receives a direct revelation of the messianic character of her interlocutor (4:26 - Ἐγώ εἰμι, ὁ λαλῶν σοι) which apparently leads her to a position of active faith.

That she has reached such a position is borne out by her subsequent behaviour. Firstly, she immediately leaves her water jar and goes off to the city to report what has happened. This is a precise parallel to the action of the *male* followers of Jesus in the Synoptic tradition - they leave the tools of their trade at once to take up the task of discipleship.[12] Since the Samaritan woman's journey to the well was surely a regular daily task, her abandonment of her jar must be seen as an exact parallel to the behaviour of those Synoptic disciples.

Secondly, on reaching the village she bears witness to what she has seen and heard, and calls others to come and meet this man for themselves. In all the Gospel traditions this is seen as a primary function of the true disciple, but particularly in John, where the language of *'come and see'* is used by both Jesus and others to draw outsiders in. Indeed, the assumption of this role as a natural and vital part of discipleship is underlined by the great prayer of John 17, where mention is made of those who will come to belief through the witness of the followers of Jesus Sophia.

Thirdly, we note that the outcome of the Samaritan woman's witness is precisely parallel to that of John the Baptist in 3:30 and completely within the parameters of the Johannine understanding of the role of an active disciple. Having called the villagers to an encounter with Jesus Sophia, the woman's role as witness is superseded by that encounter. While the people have come to faith through the witness of this woman, they now believe the more so because they have also seen and heard for themselves. This is not intended as a demeaning of the value of the witness of the disciple (whether female or male),[13] but is rather a reflection of the

[12] It is interesting to note that the Fourth Evangelist, while reporting the call of disciples in the opening chapter of the Gospel, does not make any reference to their leaving of nets. Apparently the Samaritan woman replaces the Synoptic disciples in this role.

[13]This is in stark contrast to the misogyny of Calvin, who thinks that the 'untrustworthy' word of a woman is replaced by the trustworthy word of Jesus! Calvin, J., *The Gospel*

power of the encounter with the δόξα of Jesus Sophia. The subsequent confession by the villagers reflects the end of the process by which disciples are called and confirmed in the Johannine tradition.

As in the story of the wine miracle at Cana, we must also observe the contrasting *passive* role of the μαθηταί. Not only do they do nothing towards the work of witness (a point emphasised in the dialogue - ἄλλοι κεκοπιάκασιν καὶ ὑμεῖς εἰς τὸν κόπον αὐτῶν εἰσεληλύθατε [4:38]), but they also show a marked lack of understanding of the words of Jesus Sophia. Once again it is the woman who is marked out as the true paradigm of discipleship, while the male μαθηταί, disturbed even by her sex, focus the attention on misunderstanding.

2.3 MARTHA AND MARY.

The women of Bethany, Martha and Mary, form the focus of two significant stories, which draw the Johannine narrative on towards the end of the 'Book of Signs' and into the farewell and glorification of Jesus Sophia. Although the characters are known by name from the Synoptic tradition of Luke (Lk 10:38-42), the Johannine portrayal of them is, as always, very individual in its approach. The addition of the brother, Lazarus, does nothing to diminish the role which the women play in the stories, even although he is the subject of a startling 'sign'.

It is that 'sign', the raising of Lazarus, which provides the stage for Martha's discipleship to be acted out. Having sent a message to Jesus Sophia indicating the deteriorating health of her brother, Martha comes out to meet his arrival some days later with the sad news of Lazarus' death. Despite her grief, Martha already shows in this initial encounter with Jesus that she has faith in his good judgment - καὶ νῦν οἶδα ὅτι ὅσα ἂν αἰτήσῃ τὸν θεὸν δώσει σοι ὁ θεός (11:22). Thus, when confronted with the statement that her brother will rise from the dead, Martha is not disturbed, but offers a theologically literate response. As with the Samaritan woman, however, Martha has to be pushed further to extend her horizons beyond the traditional views of her religious contemporaries through a direct revelation of Jesus Sophia - Ἐγώ εἰμι ἡ ἀνάστασις καὶ ἡ ζωή (11:25).

This self-revelation of Jesus Sophia opens up the possibility of a new kind of belief for Martha, one to which she gladly responds. What follows is one of the most astonishing pieces of reinterpretation of Jesus-tradition in the Gospels, as Martha

According to St John (Trans. E.H.L.Parker: Edinburgh: Oliver & Bond, 1959) p.110.

takes into her mouth the words of confession associated in the Synoptics with Peter at Caesarea Philippi - σὺ εἶ ὁ χριστὸς ὁ υἱὸς τοῦ θεοῦ (11:27). This is highly significant in itself, being a further pointer to the ongoing polemic between the Johannine disciples, largely though not exclusively represented by women, and the male group (μαθηταί) known also from the Synoptic tradition, whose chief representative is Peter. However, Martha's confession is also very important in *Johannine* terms, being the community confession *par excellence*. This can be seen from a quick comparison with the stated aim of the writer in Jn 20:31, where precisely the words on Martha's lips become the confession by which the reader is identified as being at one with the community. Since Martha's use of this confession is the only one within the Gospel, usurping Peter's traditional role and anticipating within the narrative structure the post-resurrection conclusion of the community, it surely places Martha in a most prominent and exemplary position of discipleship for the reader.

Martha's confession is also significant for the reader in relation to discipleship because of its position in the unfolding drama of chapter 11. Like the Mother of Jesus at Cana, Martha also demonstrates her faith *in anticipation* of the 'sign', rather than in response to it. Her faith is thus truly Johannine in its dependence on the *word* of Jesus Sophia rather than the *sign*. It stands once more in dramatic contrast to the dim-witted μαθηταί, who cannot even grasp the fact that Lazarus is dead (11:14), never mind offer a confession of faith which is not dependent on 'signs'!

Mary's role in the same story is but a cameo in comparison with that of her sister, but it prepares the way for her main appearance in the following chapter. Despite the quite unjustified tendency of some commentators to see Mary's reaction as weak over against Martha's,[14] she also demonstrates qualities of discipleship not seen in her male counterparts. In coming out and falling at the feet of Jesus Sophia, Mary shows her insight into who this person is, acknowledging by her action what Martha has confessed in word. In doing so she provokes a deeply sympathetic reaction from Jesus, whose weeping is surely an open expression of the 'agape' which was noted at the opening of the story (11:5), and which even the watching, normally unsympathetic 'Jews' recognise (11:36).[15]

[14] It is astonishing how both translators and commentators alike see a contrast in the behaviour of Mary and Martha in this story. A proper reading of the text reveals that both characters use exactly the same words in their initial address to Jesus Sophia.

[15] Although the verb φιλεῖν and not ἀγαπᾶν is used in 11:36, this makes no difference, since the two terms are clearly interchangeable in John (see also later footnotes).

It is in the second story set at Bethany that we find Mary playing a major role, as she anoints the feet of Jesus Sophia in an act of the greatest devotion (12:1-8). The Johannine version of this story has often puzzled commentators because of its peculiar mix of Synoptic traditions, C.K.Barrett remarking that "John's narrative is confused wherever it came from".[16] However, by taking it in its overall Johannine context it is far from confused. While retaining its Markan purpose as an anointing for burial (Jn 12:7), the Fourth Evangelist deliberately changes to the Lukan version of anointing feet rather than head. This has a two-fold effect on the role of Mary in the account. Firstly, she is enabled to display her prior understanding of true discipleship by anointing feet in anticipation of the footwashing scene which follows in chapter 13. Secondly, she is further able to demonstrate her insight into the nature of the call to community which Jesus Sophia makes by avoiding any hint of kingship, which might be implied in anointing Jesus' head.

While this second point will only become clear when we look in more detail at the language of community used in the Fourth Gospel, we can nevertheless note again in this story the contrast between the exemplary discipleship of Mary and the stupidity of the μαθηταί. By performing the act of true discipleship before seeing Jesus Sophia enact it,[17] Mary not only stands in stark relief to the male μαθητής Judas, rebuked in 12:4-7, but also compares most favourably to the misunderstanding and downright ignorance of the archetypal male disciple Peter in 13:6-10.

In a reversal of the role pattern of chapter 11, Martha plays the small part in the anointing story. It is worth noting, however, that her work is described as διακονία (12:2 - καὶ ἡ Μάρθα διηκόνει). Given that this Gospel was almost certainly written towards the end of the first century CE, the reader can hardly escape the ecclesiastical inference of this word - a term barely used elsewhere in the Johannine corpus.[18] Given the explanation of such 'service' as 'discipleship'

[16]Barrett,C.K., *The Gospel According to St John* (London: SPCK,1978[2]) p.409.

[17]That this action of Mary is truly one of discipleship is clear from Jn 13:14-15, where Jesus Sophia commands his followers to take up the example he has set them in washing their feet.

[18]The verb διακονεῖν appears only in Jn 12:2,26(x2); the nominal form διακονία only in Rev 2:19; the other cognate noun διάκονος only in Jn 2:5,9;12:26.

only a few verses later (Jn 12:26), the reader builds a picture of Martha as a prior exemplar.

2.4 MARY OF MAGDALA.

The witness to the presence of Mary of Magdala at the tomb of Jesus is one of the few elements of tradition which all four Gospels hold in common. However, as so often proves to be the case, the Johannine picture of her role there is markedly different from the others. At best, in the Synoptics, she goes with the other women to report the angel's message to the male disciples (Matthew), while at worst she either goes off without saying anything (Mark), or is seen as the co-bearer of an 'idle tale' (Luke 24:11 - λῆρος τὰ ῥήματα ταῦτα). For the Fourth Evangelist, Mary takes on the most significant of roles as the sole witness to the risen Jesus Sophia at the tomb.

In the addition to the empty tomb narrative of a story involving both Peter and the Beloved Disciple, the author had a golden opportunity to allow a male figure to act as the authoritative witness to the resurrection for the community. Thus it is all the more striking that this opportunity is set aside in favour of a single focus on Mary of Magdala. Having discovered the empty tomb and failed to comprehend its meaning, Mary initially goes to fetch these two apparent authority figures. Although we hear of their rather absurd race to the tomb and even of the 'belief' of the Beloved Disciple (20:8), the reader of this narrative who awaits the triumphant return of these male witnesses to the rest of the group is sadly disappointed. Whatever 'belief' may have been engendered seems to have had little effect upon them!

Following their departure from the tomb, Mary is left alone, weeping. Her comprehension of what has happened has not been helped by the male visitors, nor does it seem to be given a boost by the angelic messenger whom she encounters in the tomb. Even the appearance of Jesus does not initially break through her grief. Only when she is called by name, in a dramatic acting out of the parable of the Good Shepherd, does she finally recognise that this is none other than the risen Jesus Sophia, who knows his sheep and calls them by name.[19] Like the Samaritan woman before her, Mary now begins on the journey of faith as she calls Jesus 'Teacher' (ῥαββουνί - 20:16). That her understanding (πίστις) is not yet complete is indicated both by the use of this title instead of either κύριος

---

[19]On this motif, see further, Scott, *Sophia and the Johannine Jesus*,121-125,231-234.

(20:18) or possibly even θεός (20:28), and by her 'clinging' to Jesus as though it were possible to hold onto the past. However, following the command to go and tell the male followers (20:17), Mary shows the final movement towards faith in her confession 'I have seen the Lord' (ἑώρακα τὸν κύριον - 20:18).

It is this confession which marks out Mary of Magdala as an apostolic witness. In going to tell the μαθηταί of her discovery, which at least in the narrative structure is assumed to be a novelty, Mary becomes the Apostola Apostolorum, using the classic apostolic formulation.[20] Her reaction to the appearance of Jesus Sophia is again contrasted with the failure of the μαθηταί to believe her words with any conviction. Thus, when Jesus finally does appear to them, they are huddled together in the secrecy of a locked room, not out telling the good news as Mary has done. One of them, Thomas, even needs the further proof of touching the wounds to be convinced, evoking through his little faith the phrase by which true discipleship within both Gospel and subsequently community may be judged - Ὁ κύριός μου καὶ ὁ θεός μου (20:28). Clearly the word of witness of the woman, Mary, whom the risen Jesus Sophia entrusted with the good news, was not sufficient for the men to whom she went. The Fourth Evangelist would remind readers that it ought to be sufficient for them!

3. THE LANGUAGE OF COMMUNITY

So much for an outline of stories concerning women in the Gospel. These stories do not exist merely in a vacuum, but grow out of community and are written for reading in community. The essence of community lies in the willingness and ability of people involved in it to communicate, to be in relationship, however unsatisfactory or filled with tension that process may be. Essential to the act and art of communication is the medium of language, which both reflects the attitudes and outlook of those who use it and at the same time delineates the boundaries of their relationships. Just as the community constructs its own language, so also language constructs community. In the question of the function of the stories involving women in the Fourth Gospel, the language of community is therefore a highly significant factor.

In his interesting analysis of *John as Storyteller*, Mark Stibbe has identified two different approaches to understanding the sociological function of the Johannine language of community. On the one hand, he notes the techniques of J.L.Martyn

---

[20] Compare this with Paul's definition of his apostolic role in 1 Cor 9:1.

and D.Rensberger who regard "the behaviour of Jesus as an allegory of actual or idealised community history".[21] Stibbe's own approach, on the other hand, shows him to be "more interested in the way the language in John (18-19) operates as an index of the community's value-system".[22] Since it would appear from a simple reading of the Fourth Gospel, that the value-system of the community is precisely what brings it into conflict with others, whether Jewish, Roman or even other Christian authority groups, the value of Stibbe's approach should be self-evident.

A very brief comparison between the language of community used in the Synoptics and in John provides some illuminating contrasts. While John frequently talks of Jesus' followers as 'friends' (φίλοι), Matthew and Luke only place this term in the mouths of Jesus' critics - τελωνῶν φίλος καὶ ἁμαρτωλῶν (Mt 11:19; Lk 7:34). Again, the Johannine description of the relationship between Jesus and his followers frequently uses terms of deepest affection, particularly words from the group ἀγαπᾶν, while this language is virtually absent from the Synoptics. Instead, the communities of the Synoptic tradition are primary defined in terms of 'servanthood in the work of the Kingdom'.[23] While 'servanthood' is to some extent used within the Fourth Gospel, it is usually qualified, as we shall see, by reference to 'friendship'. 'Kingdom', however, is a concept which is at best marginal to the Johannine tradition and at worst, we shall show, runs counter to its value-system. Let us, then, turn to look at John's language in more detail.

3.1 'FRIENDS WHO REMAIN TO THE END'

There are many characteristics which denote the practice of proper discipleship in the Fourth Gospel, some of which we have already noted as being illustrated in the action of the Johannine women. The disciple has an *encounter* with Jesus Sophia, which leads to a *decision to follow*. This following is characterised by a desire to bear *witness* to the encounter which the disciple has had, and this ultimately leads to a *confession* of Jesus as the Christ. The disciple is always *known intimately* by

---

[21]Stibbe,M., *John as Storyteller. Narrative Criticism and the Fourth Gospel* (Cambridge: CUP,1992; SNTS Monograph Series) p.150.

[22]Stibbe,M., *John as Storyteller*, p.150.

[23] Perhaps this tendency in the Synoptic tradition is best illustrated with reference to some of the parables, which often seek to describe the Kingdom in terms of Master/Servant relationships. Cf. Matt 18:23-35; Matt 21:33-43 (=Mk 12:1-11/Lk 20:9-17); Matt 22:1-14 (=Lk 14:15-24); Matt 24:45-51 (=Lk 12:41-46); Matt 25:14-30 (=Mk 13:34/Lk 19:11-27).

Jesus Sophia, who can call followers by *name* in the clear knowledge that they will *hear* and *respond*.

In addition to these characteristics, however, there are some *qualities* of discipleship which mark the Johannine picture out from that of the Synoptics. These are summed up by two particular words, the first μένειν, and the second to which we have already alluded, ἀγαπᾶν. In the unfolding dramatic narrative of the gospel, the Johannine Jesus actually points directly to both as constitutive marks of discipleship.[24] In the context of an acrimonious dispute with the 'Jews' over the question of his origins, Jesus responds to some who 'believe' in him by stressing the quality of 'abiding' as a measure of the depth of their discipleship: Ἐὰν ὑμεῖς μείνητε ἐν τῷ λόγῳ τῷ ἐμῷ, ἀληθῶς μαθηταί μού ἐστε (Jn 8:31). Then later in the Gospel, after Jesus Sophia has taken leave of the world and is trying to communicate the essence of discipleship to a fairly obtuse set of μαθηταί, he stresses the importance of relationship as a witness of genuine commitment amongst his followers: (13:34) ἐντολὴν καινὴν δίδωμι ὑμῖν, ἵνα ἀγαπᾶτε ἀλλήλους, καθὼς ἠγάπησα ὑμᾶς ἵνα καὶ ὑμεῖς ἀγαπᾶτε ἀλλήλους. (13:35) ἐν τούτῳ γνώσονται πάντες ὅτι ἐμοὶ μαθηταί ἐστε, ἐὰν ἀγάπην ἔχητε ἐν ἀλλήλοις.

The essence of 'abiding' is illustrated in the picture of the Vine and the Branches in John 15. Above all, this places the emphasis on a reciprocal relationship which can be defined as 'friendship'. Commenting on this passage, Bultmann says:

> "Μενειν is persistence in the life of faith; it is loyal steadfastness to the cause only in the sense of always allowing oneself to be encompassed, of allowing oneself to receive. . . . It is not the holding of a position, but allowing oneself to be held, corresponding to the relationship of the κλῆμα to the ἄμπελος. In this sense the relationship can be a reciprocal one; indeed it *must* be".[25]

[24]Cf. Schnackenburg,R., *The Gospel According to St John*, vol. III (London: Burns & Oates,1982) 203-217.

[25]Bultmann,R., *The Gospel of John* (trans.G.Beasley-Murray, Oxford: Basil Blackwell,1970) pp.535-536.

This attitude of 'give and take' is fundamental to the Johannine understanding of community, a point amply illustrated by the insistence of Jesus Sophia that Peter cannot be a true disciple without allowing the washing of his feet (Jn 13:8). The mark of belonging in community is the willingness of disciples both to give themselves to others and to allow them to reciprocate. This is also underlined as being an outworking in community of the relationship which exists between Jesus Sophia and God (Jn 14:10-11,20-21), this again being defined as a matter of 'abiding' (ὁ δὲ πατὴρ ἐν ἐμοὶ μένων ποιεῖ τὰ ἔργα αὐτοῦ - Jn 14:10b). Brown comments:

> Common indwelling, life and love are but different facets of the basic unity binding Father, Son and believer. Divine indwelling is an intimate union that expresses itself in a way of life lived in love.[26]

It is in this context that the Fourth Evangelist offers a qualification of the language of 'servanthood' which has been used at various points throughout the Gospel. While Jesus Sophia may still talk of 'commands' (ἃ ἐγὼ ἐντέλλομαι ὑμῖν - 15:14), these are given in the context of being called 'friends' (φίλοι) rather than 'servants' (δοῦλοι). Since the 'command' of which Jesus Sophia speaks is that of reciprocal love (13:34-35; 15:12), it can scarcely be understood as the hierarchical claim of a master upon a servant. Any suggestion of the reinforcement of traditional stereotypes of 'Master-Servant' relationships as the model for discipleship are dispensed with at this point in the narrative. For 'servant' the reader must now substitute 'friend'.

A similar situation exists with the use of ἀγαπᾶν[27] to describe the reciprocity of relationship expected of the members of the Johannine community. Using the model which the Wisdom writers had previously outlined of the relationship between God, Sophia and her disciples (Prov 8:17; Wis 7:28; Sir 4:14)[28], the

---

[26] Brown,R.E., *The Gospel According to John 1* (New York: Doubleday, 1966) p.511

[27] I include within this discussion also the use of φιλεῖν, which is often used synonymously in the Fourth Gospel. For a concise summary of this discussion see, Brown, *John 1*, pp.497-499.

[28] For further discussion and documentation see, Scott, *Sophia and the Johannine Jesus*, pp.199-200,214-216.

Fourth Evangelist frequently speaks of the love which God has for Jesus Sophia, which love is shared with the disciples as they share it with each other. For the community to which this Gospel is addressed, the essence of discipleship may be captured in the notion of a loving friendship, based on the model of Jesus Sophia, which persists to the end.

Now if we ask where this is best illustrated in the Gospel narrative, the women of the community again feature prominently. With the exception of the unnamed 'Beloved Disciple'[29], only the women of the Gospel offer models of consistent, persistent love. It is they who are the 'friends who remain to the end', each of them in turn displaying something of the required characteristic of persistence in devotion, and one of them even becomes a model for reciprocal community life at the foot of the cross (19:25-27).

The Mother of Jesus illustrates her persistence in faith (μένειν) as she tells the house servants to be obedient to the demand of her son, whom she has recognised as Sophia incarnate, the supplier of the wine. Her reward is two-fold, in the provision of the need for wine and in the subsequent expression of 'faith' from the onlooking μαθηταί. Her subsequent singling out as a community role-model at the foot of the cross must also appear as a mark of significant persistent devotion (ἀγαπᾶν).

The persistence of the Samaritan woman can hardly be doubted, both in her questioning leading to a faith encounter, and in her subsequent witness to the Christ present in Jesus Sophia at the well. The dramatic structure of the narrative invites the reader to feel the resentment of the μαθηταί as they return to find Jesus Sophia in conversation with her (4:27), but also presents her faithfulness to the task of witness as she leaves her common task and calls others to an encounter similar to her own.

Martha and Mary are specifically introduced as those with whom Jesus Sophia shares an intimate relationship (ἀγαπᾶν - 11:5). This theme is developed throughout the course of both the stories of the women at Bethany, with even the hardest enemies of Jesus Sophia recognising the depth of relationship as he weeps by the tomb (11:35-36). Again we find that both women display the kind of persistence which is characteristic of an 'abiding' disciple: Martha expressing her

[29]Incidentally, the 'Beloved' tag can be applied using either ἀγαπᾶν (13:23 et al.) or φίλειν (20:2).

utter confidence in the resurrection power of Jesus Sophia even in the face of death; Mary continuing with her loving, anticipatory act of anointing despite the ignorant criticism of one of the onlooking male μαθηταί.

Mary Magdalene demonstrates her quality as a 'friend who remained to the end' in her presence at both cross and tomb. Whatever the danger of being identified as a close friend of an executed criminal, Mary and the other women are the ones who join with the 'Beloved Disciple' at the foot of the cross rather than the traditional male μαθηταί. She it is also who arrives alone to express her ἀγάπη for the dead Jesus, only to be filled with joy at the finding of the risen Jesus Sophia. This is the one who calls her by name, who knows her with an intimacy and love which goes beyond death and offers hope to the community left behind, to whom she is gladly sent with the good news.

In all this the male μαθηταί remain silent: dumb onlookers in every sense! These men are more concerned with matters of pride, honour, kingship and position, none of which enter the Johannine picture of discipleship. It is the women, who by their may of living and giving, by their unaffected acceptance of the reciprocal love of Jesus Sophia, illustrate for the reader the essence of community as the 'loving friends who remain to the end'.

3.2 THE ABSENCE OF THE ΒΑΣΙΛΕΙΑ ΤΟΥ ΘΕΟΥ

Just as the language of 'friends who remain to the end' is striking by the frequency of its occurrence in the Fourth Gospel, so too is the language of 'servants of the Kingdom' notable for its virtual absence. Now it might be argued that this is simply a question of style and that the Fourth Evangelist prefers to tell the story in an individual way, but given the prominence of 'kingdom' language in the Synoptic tradition and the likelihood that John knew the Synoptics in some form, this seems a weak argument. Much more likely is the possibility that the Evangelist has deliberately omitted reference to βασιλεία τοῦ θεοῦ.

The phrase βασιλεία τοῦ θεοῦ is used only twice in the Fourth Gospel, both times in the context of a dialogue between Jesus Sophia and Nicodemus (3:3,5). In addition, the word βασιλεία is used three times in the interchange between Pilate and Jesus Sophia during the trial sequence, all in the space of one verse (18:36). There are several instances (16) of Jesus Sophia being called βασιλεύς in the Gospel, but the vast majority appear in the mockery of the soldiers and the ascription of Pilate in the Passion Narrative (12 times). Of the four instances in the Book of Signs, two relate to the quotation from Zech 9:9 in the story of the Entry into Jerusalem (12:13,15). This leaves only two of any real significance in 1:49 (Nathaniel) and 6:15, where the crowd wish to make him 'king'.

Let us briefly examine the way in which these words are used in the main instances we have noted. Firstly, the references to Jesus as βασιλεύς. In the first chapter of John, Nathanael has been brought to meet Jesus Sophia by Philip. The encounter between them leads Nathanael to acclaim Jesus as 'the King of Israel'. The response which Nathanael receives does nothing to suggest that the title is one which the Johannine Jesus is either seeking, or is willing to accept. Indeed, Jesus' reply is at least ironic, if not comic - "Do you believe because you have seen these things?" - suggesting that the whole response of Nathanael is at best inadequate.

That Nathanael has used a title which Jesus Sophia does not wish to acknowledge is borne out by the next occurrence of βασιλεύς in 6:15. Following the bread miracle, the crowd are reported as having made an attempt to force Jesus to be their king. However, his reaction is to slip away as quickly as possible, rejecting their advances. The very fact that the crowd would need to "seize" (ἁρπάζειν) him, shows the inappropriateness of their action in the Johannine narrative framework.

The reference to Jesus as 'king' in the story of the Entry into Jerusalem is somewhat ambiguous. At first sight the narrative appears to accept that 'kingship' is an appropriate category for addressing him, since reference is made to the initial *mis*understanding of the μαθηταί and their subsequent enlightening in the post-resurrection period (12:16). On the other hand, in contrast to the Synoptic tradition, the Fourth Evangelist juxtaposes the stories of the Anointing and the Entry into Jerusalem.[30] This is surely a deliberate piece of redactional work on the part of the Fourth Evangelist, who chooses to place the attack on the Temple at the *outset* of the ministry of Jesus Sophia. We have already noted that the striking feature of John's account of the Anointing is the fact that *feet* and not *head* are anointed. While the primary purpose of this change is surely to point to the exemplary discipleship of Mary in advance of the footwashing story, it also

---

[30]Both the Anointing stories in Mk 14:3-9 and Matt 26:6-13 are separated from the Entry into Jerusalem (Mk 11:1-10; Matt 21:1-9), which account is instead connected in both instances to the attack of Jesus on the Temple. Luke contains the rather different account of the anointing by 'a woman from the city' in Lk 7:36-50, but like Mark and Matthew, he connects the Entry story (Lk 19:28-40) with the Temple incident.

functions as a means of dispensing with the idea, alluded to in the Synoptics, that the anointing of the *head* is a sign of Jesus' coming *kingship*.[31]   Rather, John places the Anointing and Entry side by side to allow the reader the possibility of offering a critique of the crowd's response to Jesus Sophia, and perhaps even to reveal something of the continuing misunderstanding of the post-resurrection μαθηταί.

The use of the phrases βασιλεία τοῦ θεοῦ and βασιλεία ἡ ἐμή appears, at least on one level, to be related in the dramatic structure of the Fourth Gospel.   The Johannine Jesus talks to both Nicodemus and Pilate in language which ought to be comprehensible to them.   He uses a concept to which they can, in their own different ways relate: *'kingdom'*.   But in both cases the Johannine Jesus is redefining the boundaries of what 'kingdom' might mean precisely in order to dispense with it.

In 3:3,5 the use of βασιλεία τοῦ θεοῦ is related to 'water and spirit', where 'water' represents baptism into the new community, the character of which is summed up in the paradigms of discipleship chiefly offered by the women of the Gospel stories, and represented in the words of 13:33-34.   Beasley-Murray comments that,

> despite the fact that the expression βασιλεία τοῦ θεοῦ occurs
> only in John 3:3 and 5, the whole Gospel is concerned with the
> kingship of God in Jesus.[32]

He misses the point, however, that the very thing which the Fourth Evangelist wants to *avoid* is the language of 'kingship, kingdom, king'.   Having passed up the opportunity to introduce the language of 'kingdom' in the interchange with Nathanael, the Johannine Jesus now talks to the Pharisee, Nicodemus, in terms which he might be expected to understand. One might, therefore, paraphrase the story of the dialogue between Nicodemus and the Johannine Jesus by saying: "that thing which you might think of as 'kingdom' is actually a new kind of community, marked by the baptism of water and spirit (3:5-6), characterised by the self-giving love of God (3:14-16), which seeks not to destroy but to redeem humanity (3:17)". For such a community the motif of monarchy is quite inappropriate, as the later

---

[31]The anointing of the king's head during the enthronement ceremony was a common feature of ANE life. For a biblical example see 1 Sam 10:1.

[32]Beasley-Murray,G., *John* (Waco: Word Books,1987) p.330.

description of the character of community relationships defined in chapter 15 will show.

The rejection of the 'kingdom' motif becomes clearer still in the dialogue between Pilate and the Johannine Jesus in 18:33-38, a crucial passage for the definition of the Fourth Evangelist's purpose in avoiding such language. It is vital to note that *Pilate* and not the Johannine Jesus introduces the title 'king' (18:33). In character with other cases of displaying intimate knowledge of the motives of other people in the Gospel, Jesus Sophia sees through Pilate's question and calls his bluff: "Is that your question or have others suggested it to you?" (18:34). This leads to a somewhat enigmatic statement in the mouth of Jesus Sophia, in which he declares that his βασιλεία is not ἐκ τοῦ κόσμου τούτου. There is much discussion amongst commentators as to the meaning of this phrase[33]. Barrett relates it to the similar phrase in 8:23, where Jesus Sophia indicates that his origin is "from above" (ἐγὼ ἐκ τῶν ἄνω εἰμί), thus suggesting that the authority of Jesus' "kingdom" is derived from the place of his origin, and not from a worldly powerbase.[34] This seems to make sense, given that Jesus' reply differentiates between the worldly 'king', who has armed followers, and his own situatuon in which his true followers have no such weaponry.[35]

If, then, the Johannine Jesus wishes to reject the language of 'kingdom', why does he use it in response to Pilate. The most obvious answer is that he picks up Pilate's terminology and uses it against him and his 'Jewish' accusers. Since he nowhere else takes 'kingdom' as a model for the community of disciples, there is no reason to think that he is suddenly adopting it here.

The language of the βασιλεία τοῦ θεοῦ is almost completely absent from the teaching and discourses of the Johannine Jesus. In the isolated instances we have noted, such language stems from the person whom Jesus Sophia is addressing. In 18:36, he simply replies in the terms which Pilate has introduced and can understand, and in doing so he seeks to subvert the concept of 'kingdom' which Pilate holds. Community is not built on force or position ('king'), but rather on

[33]See most recently the discussion in Beasley-Murray, *John*, 330-331.

[34]Cf. Barrett, *John*, 536.

[35]Note that the Johannine Jesus has already rejected armed struggle as an option in the account of Peter cutting off the ear of Malchus in 18:10-11. This incident shows once more the lack of understanding which the group of μαθηταί have of Jesus Sophia's intentions.

the kind of relationship already outlined in the Gospel: it is a community led by a Shepherd, not by a king. There may still be a qualitative difference expressed between the position of this shepherding figure and those who are led, but the politically charged language of kingship cannot express it for this community. The relationship intended to exist amongst the followers of Jesus Sophia is one of true equality, based on the qualities summed up in the words ἀγαπᾶν and μένειν.

The relationship is best and most often illustrated by the women of the Gospel and not by the men, who, typified by Peter's action in cutting off the ear of Malchus, the High Priest's servant, still see force and the 'Pilate' view of 'kingdom' as the model to adopt.

4. CONCLUSIONS

So we return to the starting point of this paper: are the women of the Fourth Gospel paradigms of discipleship, or are they merely paragons of virtue, chosen because of their lowly position and reinforced in it by the narrative shape of the Gospel? I shall attempt to offer an answer to this by bringing together some of the observations we have made in the two main sections of this paper.

Firstly, we have noted that there is some measure of ambiguity in the role of women as disciples of Jesus Sophia. On one level they can be viewed as exercising a role which is typical of the patriarchal expectations of the day: they remain somewhat under the control of Jesus and defer to him. It is difficult to argue that they are a precursor of the liberated feminist of the twentieth century. To expect this, however, is as anachronistic as the attempts to show that Jesus was really a feminist! On another level, however, these women illustrate for the reader (both then and now), what true discipleship is all about. They *are* the paradigms of discipleship for the community to whom the Gospel is addressed and function as such for new communities which seek to be faithful to the love commandment preserved for us by the Fourth Evangelist.

Secondly, we note that the women do stand in deliberate contrast to the male group of disciples, known also from the Synoptics, whom we have continued to call the μαθηταί. Schnackenburg proposes that, on one level this male group represents "the later believers in that they are challenged and tempted and their faith is inadequate".[36] If he is correct in this observation, then their position in relation to the *female* disciples is all the more interesting. It would appear that the Fourth Gospel then allows the reader to find a contrast between how things are

[36]Schnackenburg, *John III*, p.207.

and how they might be. Inadequate, often dim-witted male disciples are set in opposition to the responsive, quick-witted female disciples, who offer not an *idealised* picture of discipleship, but a *real alternative* upon which all may, and ought to build. For the reader of the Fourth Gospel, the Johannine women embody not only some stereotypical characteristics of discipleship, but their lifestyles offer an illustration of the true *qualities* of discipleship: a deep and loving friendship which remains to the end.

Thirdly, at this point the *language* of the community becomes particularly important. If Mark Stibbe is correct in his observation that the language of the Gospel "operates as an index of the community's value system"[37], then here we have an early Christian community which wishes to stake its future on a model of community which is best represented by the lifestyles and behaviour of women rather than of men. Ideas of hierarchy, or of power exercised through force and manipulation are rejected as inappropriate for the community which follows in the footsteps of Jesus, Sophia incarnate. Since such ideas belong almost exclusively to the world of male politics and power games, the men of the Gospel, with the exception of the unnamed Beloved Disciple, fail to grasp what true Johannine discipleship is all about. Instead, the women express the value-system which the community wishes to espouse, not because they are mere paragons of virtue who are patronisingly allowed to fulfil a male stereotype, but because their lifestyle makes them the authentic leaders of the community of Jesus Sophia.

It is highly significant that the Johannine community value-system has been so submerged as to be barely noticable in the history of the Christian church, despite the fact that Johannine christology became foundational for the creeds of the second and subsequent centuries. The male models of hierarchy, and the militaristic language of the 'kingdom' have overwhelmingly dominated the thinking and value-system of church to the present day. What the women of the Fourth Gospel show us is that it need not have been so, and certainly need not be so now. If we treat them as mere paragons of virtue, they may still be patted on the head and told that they do not understand the realities of life. One the other hand, perhaps if we take seriously the paradigm of discipleship which they offer us, not out of weakness, but out of the strength of real community, there may yet be hope for a church which truly follows in the footsteps of Jesus Sophia.

---

[37] Stibbe, *John as Storyteller*, p.150.

Some Reflections on ὤφθη (I Cor 15:5) on the Background of Ezek 1

Jean Marcel Vincent

Introduction

One of the highlights of theological studies at the Baptist Theological Seminary was Günther Wagner's Exegesis Class on I Corinthians. As students we were fascinated by his deep knowledge and careful presentation of both the English and German literature and by his concern to make the texts relevant for our faith in an ecumenical context.

I remember well his interpretation of I Cor 15:3-8, a *locus classicus* for the reconstruction of the so-called kerygma of the early Church. Günther Wagner exposed at length the scholarly discussion about the original language of the creed (Semitic or Greek?), the limit of the pre-Paulinian tradition (v. 5 or 7?) and the duality of the appearance sequences (conflation of a Petrine and Jacobine tradition?).[1] He addressed the hermeneutical questions being discussed in the mid-1960's about the relation of faith to historical facts (is christian faith totally independent of history?) and the role of witnesses.[2] His position was marked by openness and moderation: the resurrection does not prove an act of God, but points to it. The μωρία of the message of the cross is, on one side, that faith is bound to an event that can be dated in history; on the other, that the own inner significance and meaning of the message cannot be grasped by our own understanding: it can only be recognized by faith, when man responds to the message of the gospel.

In honour of my former teacher, I propose here some reflections on one aspect of this creed (I) in the light of Ezek 1 (II) with a look at some intermediary texts (III).

---

[1] See P. Winter, I Corinthians XV 3b-7, in: NOVT 2, 1958, pp. 142-152; J. Jeremias, *Die Abendmahlworte Jesu,* Göttingen 1960³, pp. 95-97; H. Conzelmann, Zur Analyse der Bekenntnisformel I Kor 15:3-5, in: EvT 1965, pp. 1-10.

[2] See R. Bultmann, Karl Barth, "Die Auferstehung der Toten" [1926], in: Idem, *Glauben und Verstehen I,* Tübingen 1961⁴, pp. 38-64; and E. Fuchs, Die Auferstehungsgewissheit nach 1. Korinther 15, in: Idem, *Zum hermeneutischen Problem in der Theologie,* Tübingen 1959, 197-210.

1." Ὤφθη---- in I Cor. 15:5

My interpretation of ὤφθη in I Cor 15:5 will be restricted to five observations.

1) In the passage I Cor 15:1-11 taken as a whole, the verb ὤφθη, which is repeated no less than four times (vv. 5,6,7,8), is most significant, in particular for Paul's own understanding of his ministry. In 9:1 he claimed, as a warrant of his apostolic authority, that he had seen Jesus (οὐχὶ Ἰησοῦν τὸν κύριον ἡμῶν ἑόρακα;). Now he binds this personal experience (ὤφθη κἀμοί - I Cor 15:8) to the foundational story of God's revelation in the Christ event, such as expressed in the creed (vv. 3b-5), with the effect that «Paul's apostolic mission is a constitutive part of the gospel».[3] In the context of I Corinthians it becomes evident that for Paul the christophany was not simply a kind of notarial function to attest the fact of the resurrection; it has a heuristic function: thanks to the ὤφθη, Paul discovers that the crucified is «the Lord of Glory» (2:8). This is the μωρία and σκάνδαλον of the message of the cross (1:18-23).

2) Does ὤφθη have a similar significance in the pre-paulinian creed (vv. 3b-5) itself? H. Conzelmann (1965) had argued against J. Jeremias (19603) that the creed has two strophes with each the characteristic κατὰ τὰς γραφάς. Consequently the four verbs of the creed are not of equal value: ἐτάφη and ὤφθη are subordinated to the main verbs, respectively ἀπέφανεν and ἐγήγερται. However this observation should not be overaccentuated, for ἐτάφη and ὤφθη are not participles which qualify the preceding verbs, but full verbs dependent on παρέλαβον and introduced with ὅτι. Stylistically κατὰ τὰς γραφάς, situated in between, permeates all four verbs.[4] Furthermore a certain accent should be

---

[3]So C. C. Newman, *Paul's Glory-Christology. Tradition and Rhetoric*, NOVT Suppl LXIX, Leiden 1992, pp. 187f. This Paulinian claim, which is already implied in I Cor 2:6-20, will be developed in the reflections on Paul's ministry in the Deutero-Paulinians, Col 1:23-28 and specially Eph 3:1-13.

[4]This should be said also against R. Liebers' *«Wie geschrieben steht. Studien zu einer besonderen Art frühchristlichen Schriftbezugs»*, Berlin 1993. According to him, the function of ἐτάφη and ὤφθη is to «secure the fact» of the preceding verbs («he died», «he was raised»), as the function of κατὰ τὰς γραφάς is to secure «the meaning» of Christ's death and resurrection (p. 250). This is a reduction of the evidence which

recognized on ὤφθη as the last proposition of the confession.

3) ῎Ωφθη (aorist passive) will not be translated by «he has been seen» (the construction is not with ὑπό «by»). Nor do we have a *passivum divinum* («he has been made visible», i.e. by God - as is the case for ἐγήγερται). The meaning is «he appeared to» (intransitive with dative). The accent is not primarily on the witnesses, but on the event of the apparition of Christ, an event which indeed legitimates those who have seen Christ, so that they are part of the Christ event, not because they have seen him, but because Christ has revealed himself to them.

4) I contend that already in the creed, as it is evident for Paul, the subject of ὤφθη is the Exalted One. The creed is not a summary of resurrection narratives. Rather: these narratives are built on the creed, as can be shown in Mk 16:1-8, a text which definitively describes the appearance as a theophany. Indeed, «he appeared to», in the context of Old Testament theophanic language (see for instance Gen 12:7 ὤφθη κύριος τῷ Αβραμ), and in the light of other confessional formulations of the early church (see for instance I Tim 3:16 ὤφθη ἀγγέλοις), implies that this christophany has the quality of a theophany. To «appear» as God does, Christ must share divine authority and power. As God revealed himself and called to a particular ministry, so does Christ.

5) ῎Ωφθη follows and expands the affirmation that Christ has been resurrected by God (ἐγήγερται) and this in the light of the Scriptures (κατὰ τὰς γραφάς). That he reveals himself confirms of course that he is resurrected, but this is only one side. The other side is that the appearance sheds a decisive light on the resurrection: the resurrection was not a simple return to life, but an act of glorification and, in the light of Scriptures (κατὰ τὰς γραφάς) the eschatological realisation of God's plan of salvation, the triumph of God's reign, the inauguration of a new creation.[5]

This extraordinary event is expressed in nuce in this simple ὤφθη of I Cor 15:5.

impoverishes his further extremely well informed and instructive study on possible Old Testament references meant by κατὰ τὰς γραφάς.

[5] With C. Wolff, *Der erste Brief des Paulus an die Korinther,* THKNT VII/2, Berlin 1990[3], pp. 160 and 165; against Liebers (op. cit.), who limits the reference to the motive of the suffering righteous one (p. 367).

2. Ezek 1

The most sensational description of the apparition of God in the Scriptures is certainly to be found in Ezek 1, a text which belongs to a complete different literary genre from I Cor 15,3b-5. This chapter has been the object of numerous studies on its text, the traditions it uses, its redaction and its very complex *Wirkungsgeschichte* in Judaism and Christianity, and more specially on the language of christophanies.

1) Biblical interpretation, especially in this field of studies on the use of Ezekiel's throne vision in early Christianity, often alternates between two extremes. On the one side we find scholars who insist on very precise literary critical analysis of the texts in their original context and who recognize an influence only when an exact literal dependence can be traced. On the other side we find scholars who are extremely generous in discovering parallels. The first group risks viewing the evidence too narrowly and missing the forest by paying exclusive attention to the leaves. The second group risks amalgamating phenomena which do not really belong together, disqualifying the whole enterprise. Interpretation has to navigate between these Scylla and Charybdis.

2) It must be recognized that Old Testament scholars place difficulties before their colleagues of the New Testament field who want to utilize their results on Ezek 1, in oder to build on a solid exegetical ground. There seems to be no consensus among Old Testament scholars on textual-, literary- and redaction-critical problems. The search for a «purified» *Grundtext* has led by and large to a *cul de sac*.[6] Indeed the text is evidently overloaded and at places difficult to understand. The question is whether these difficulties can and should be solved through text- and literary-critical methods which, in the end, threaten to dissolve the text itself.

Two recommendations may help us out of this dilemma. First, at the text-critical level, the LXX should be used with more care than has been the case in the reconstruction of the *Grundtext* of Ezek 1. There are two reasons for this: a)

---

[6]With a consequent yet moderate use of text- and literary-critical method, as they are common in German scholarship, W. Zimmerli (*Ezechiel*, BKAT XIII/1, Neukirchen 1969, pp. 23-30) arrives at a *Grundtext* which contains vv. 4aα,5-6b,11b-12a, 12bβ, 13aα,22a,26-28a. With the same type of arguments H. F. Fuhs (*Ezechiel* 1-24, NEB Lfg. 7, Würzburg 1986[2], pp. 21f) proposes: vv. 4aα, 5a, 22a, 26-28. K.-F. Pohlmann (*Ezechielstudien*, BZAW 202, Berlin 1992, p. 95) reduces the *Ursprungstext* to V. 3b*.

shorter texts are not necessarily more original than longer ones,[7] specially in the *translation* of such a complex description as Ezek 1; b) the Greek version of the vision has its own literary form and integrity which must be respected as such,[8] and this might already be true of the *Vorlage* which the translators used in comparison to our masoretic text.[9] Second, at the literary-critical level, we should not be too quick to suppress words and word-groups as glosses on the ground that they are unnecessary, unlogical, repetitious etc., before we have discovered the precise nature of the text,[10] and before we have made a detailed analysis of the complex structure of the text in its final form in order to appreciate its own inner logic. Is there not some arrogance and a kind of cultural imperialism in the pretention to reconstruct a «purified» text based on unconscious criteria of Greek and Latin literary aesthetics?[11]

3) It is not possible to present here the complex structure of the vision and I can only refer to the various observations made by A. Sole, H. van Dyke Parunak, M. Greenberg, B. Tidiman and L. C. Allen.[12] I summarize as follows. «I saw» (וָאֶרְאֶ[ה]) forms a perfect *inclusio* between end (v. 28bαi) and beginning (v. 4aα) of

---

[7]See: W. A. Lind, A Text-critical Note to Ezechiel 1: Are Shorter Readings Really Preferable to Longer?, in: *JETS* 27, 1984, pp. 135-139.

[8]See this frequent remark in D. Barthelémy's *Critique textuelle de l'Ancien Testament, 3: Ezéchiel, Daniel et les 12 Prophètes,* OBO 50/3, Fribourg and Göttingen 1992.

[9]See the articles of J. Lust, P.-M. Bogaert and M. Dijkstra in: J. Lust (ed.), *Ezekiel and his Book. Textual and Literary Criticism and their Interrelation,* BETL LXXIV, Leuven 1986.

[10]See also the critical remarks of D. I. Block, Text and Emotion: A Study of the «Corruptions» in Ezekiel's Inaugural Vision (Ezekiel 1:4-28), in: *CBQ* 50, 1988, pp. 418-442.

[11]In that respect there is much to win from modern Jewish scholarship as can be appreciated in M. Greenberg's commentary, *Ezekiel 1-20,* AB 22, Garden City 1983, and in D. Barthelémy's op. cit. [n. 8].

[12]See: A. Sole, The Structure of Chapter 1 in the Book of Ezekiel, in: *Bêth Miqrâ* 23/72, 1977/78, pp. 73-79 (hebr.; engl. summary, p. 125); H. van Dyke Parunak, The Literary Architecture of Ezekiel's mar'ôt 'elohim, in: *JBL* 99, 1980, pp. 61-74; M. Greenberg (commentary ad loc.); B. Tidiman; *Le livre d'Ezéchiel,* tome 1, CEB 4, Vaux-sur-Seine 1985, pp. 73-91; and L. C. Allen, The Structure and Intention of Ezekiel I, in: VT 43, 1993, pp. 145-161.

the vision. The verb «see» רָאָה has a structuring function, as it recurs also in v. 15 and 27. V. 4 and vv. 27f form clearly an envelope for the entire narrative, as can be seen in the recurrence of «cloud» (עָנָן), «fire» (אֵשׁ), «it was surrounded by a radiance» (וְנֹגַהּ לוֹ סָבִיב) and «like the brillance of » (כְּעֵין הַחַשְׁמַל). The introduction v. 4 presents the leading themes of the whole: a perception of extreme blending brilliance. Then follow four sections which describe: a) the «four living creatures» (vv. 5-14), b) their relation to the «wheels» (vv. 15-21), and c) their relation to the «firmament» (רָקִיעַ) (vv. 22-25). The fourth section (vv. 26-28) points to the «throne» and above it to the «figure with the appearance of a man» and concludes with the final affirmation: «That was the appearance of the figure of the Glory of YHWH». Each section has clear subdivisions with an introduction, a brief presentation of a new element of the vision and then a detailed description of some aspects of it. The fact that each section is bound to the previous one through catchwords, and that, when a new element is introduced, it is related to the preceding description to enrich it with new details on the details, makes the whole very complex. But by and large, we can say that the vision is straightforward, as O. Keel has noted.[13] There is even no convincing reason to take out the description of the wheels (vv. 15-21), as these verses bring in fact further details on the description of the living creatures and their movements.[14] Many repetitions are not at all due to clumsy glosses or scribal errors: they belong to the peculiar logic of the description, which we should not «correct», but understand and respect.

4) Much useful research has clarified the imagery used in Ezek 1 to describe the heavenly world. Great attention has been especially paid to the Ancient Near Eastern iconography.[15] The conclusion is that every element of the vision has its

---

[13]*Jahwe-Visionen und Siegelkunst*, SBS 84-85, Stuttgart 1977, p. 141.

[14]This has been recognized by D. Viehweger, *Die Spezifik der Berufungsberichte Jeremias und Ezechiels im Umfeld ähnlicher Einheiten des Alten Testaments*, BEATAJ 6, Frankfurt a.M. / New York 1986, p. 58. Furthermore Ezek 10 presupposes this description of the wheels (the possibility of a secondary influence of Ezek 10 on Ezek 1:15-21 has been abandoned for good reasons), as well as the conclusion Ezek 3:12-15.

[15]See the above [note 13] mentioned study of O. Keel (1977, pp. 125-273); M. Greenberg, Ezekiel's Vision. Literary and Iconographic Aspects, in: H. Tadmor and M. Weinfeld (eds), *History, Historiography and Interpretation. Studies in Biblical and Cuneiform Literatures*, Jerusalem 1983, pp. 159-168); and a summary in R. Klein's *Ezekiel. The Prophet and His Message*, University of South Carolina 1988, pp. 18-24.

background in the religious imagery of the Ancient Near East - including of course Israel - (e.g. the imagery of the deity riding on the clouds and coming from the North, the accompanying effects of the theophany, the living creatures with their wings and multiple faces, as bearers of the throne and keepers of the holy space), but the combination of these elements in Ezek 1 is totally unique. It could be shown that Israelite (for instance Isa 6; I Kings 6:27-37), Mesopotamian and Egyptian[16] elements have been purposely and eclectically mixed with the paradoxical effect that the richness of details rather than clarifying it has made the image nebulous. Such a technique belongs specifically to the use of imagery in the book of Ezekiel (see e.g. chaps 40f). R. Hoeps has enriched recently the apperception of the throne-vision by the use of categories based on the hermeneutics of images.[17] He analyzes how Ezekiel purposely heightens the complexity of the individual elements of the vision to create constructs which are extremely rich of details; e.g. by intensifying the number of heaven-bearers as well as the number of their wings and faces. He speaks of a nearly surrealistic potentiation of concrete visible details with the paradoxal effect that the visible becomes invisible, the concrete abstract. In that way, we can observe that the invisible penetrates the visible, which on its turn dissolves itself in the invisible at the point of its extreme complexity.

5) Commentators have often expressed their amazement at the fact that the prophet who so radically denounces the use of images (see Ezek 8) dares here to describe with such concrete details the appearance of the Divine Glory, especially in «the form like the appearance of a man» (v. 27). It has been rightly emphasized, that the author is very cautious and uses constantly expression of approximation such as בְּ, דְּמוּת, מַרְאֵה.[18] Moreover I have suggested that the

---

[16]For the Egyptian elements, which have been somehow neglected, see the article of M. Görg on רְקִיעַ in: *TWAT* VII, cols 668-675, spec. 671f.

[17]*Das Gefühl des Erhabenen und die Herrlichkeit Gottes. Studien zur Beziehung von philosophischer und theologischer Ästhetik*, Bonner dogmatische Studien 5, Würzburg 1989, pp. 134-149.

[18]L. C. Allen (1993) [note 12] rightly insists that the vision as such does not convey a message of hope. However his assertion that «the intention of the vision is to reveal Yahweh as judge» (p. 159) does not touch the salient point, for the vision prepares also the messages of chaps 37 and 43. The accent should be placed on the experience of the overwhelming presence of the living God, as it is also the case for ὤφθη in the

particular logic of the description and the complexity of the images which generates a surprising dialectic of visibility and unvisibility, of clarity and blinding, of revelation and hiding, far from making God tangible to human imagination, instead heightens and intensifies His distance and transcendance. The central and durable effect of the vision is the overwhelming confrontation with the Divine Reality which makes the prophet «embittered in the rage of his spirit» and «consternated» (3:14f; 1:28), as the women after the appearance of Jesus were filled with τρόμος καὶ ἔκστασις and at first had no language to communicate to others their experience (Mark 16:8).

The main point of contact between this long description of the appearance of the כְּבוֹד יהוה in Ezek 1 and the event expressed *in nuce* with ὤφθη in I Cor 15:5 is this experience of the overwhelming confrontation with the reality of the divine.[19] A confrontation which renders one at first speechless until this experience finds an adequate language to express the unspeakable. An experience which also makes the apostle - as it was the case for the prophet (e.g. Ezek 8-11) - a participant of God's perception of reality and a co-worker of God's action in the world. A spiritual bridge can certainly be imagined between the appearance of the Glory of Yahweh according to Ezek 1 and the appearance of the elevated Christ.

3. Trajectory

It is well known that Ezek 1 has had a decisive influence on early Jewish and Christian devotion, thought and literature. This can easily be explained by the dynamics of the vision narrative itself that created awe, praise, and reflection which, in the logic of the imagery language of the text, expresses itself through the -----combination and arrangement of other images, as can well be observed in Rev 4.

On the trajectory between Ezek 1 and Rev 4 or I Cor 15:5, we find some very interesting texts, which help us to understand how and why the event of the christophany could be expressed in terms of the throne-vision of Ezek 1. I survey briefly the most important ones.

[1] This survey on the *Wirkungsgeschichte* of Ezek 1, must start by recalling that the throne-vision plays an important role in other passages of the book of Ezekiel itself, mainly in 3:12-15; 3:23; 8:2-4; 9:3; 10; 11:22-24; 43. These passages are

christophany. This experience implies death and life, break and renewal.

[19]See e.g. K. Seybold, Art. כ, in: *TWAT* IV, cols 1-7, especially col. 7.

already partially interpretative expansions on the throne-vision of chap 1. Noteworthy is the fact that the expression כְּבוֹד יהוה, which signifies at first the throne-vision as a whole, tends to be more specially applied to the One sitting on the throne (9:3; 10:4-9; 11:22). A still more remarkable phenomenon is a kind of disjunction which appears in 8:2, where «the figure of the appearance of a man» is said to «stretch out the form of a hand» and to catch the prophet by a lock of his hair. «The figure of the appearance of a man» acts here «as a quasi-angelic mediator».[20]

[2] When later interpreters read Ezekiel, they did it in the context of the whole book and with the help of analogous texts such as Isa 6:1-3 and Exod 24:9-11. This is especially the case for Dan 7:9-13, a most influential text for the christological formulation of the early church. Amazingly, Dan 7 presents two divine beings whose descriptions originate from Ezek 1: first, «the Ancient of Days» (עַתִּיק יוֹמִין vv. 9-13), who takes his seat on the throne, whose «wheels are a burning fire», and, second, the «One like a Son of Man» (כְּבַר אֱנָשׁ v. 13), who comes «with the clouds of heaven» (עִם עֲנָנֵי שְׁמַיָּא v. 13), as did the כְּבוֹד יהוה according to Ezek 1,4, and to whom is given glory. M. Black infers that the « כְּבַר אֱנָשׁ symbolizes the theophanic *numen praesens* of Yahweh as a man».[21]

[3] Ezek 1 plays an essential role in the numerous texts which reflect on the *Merkabah*, an expression which, since Ben Sirach (49:8 ἐπὶ ἅρματος χερουβιν), has become a *terminus technicus* for the throne-vision of Ezek 1. Most of these texts belong to the apocalyptical-mystical tradition, such as represented in the *hekhalot* literature, and are younger than the Paulinian epistles. We find however in Qumran certain isolated fragmentary texts which might be the witnesses of a

---

[20]See C. Rowland, n: *The Open Heaven: A study of Apocalyptic in Judaim and Early Christianity*, London 1982, p. 96.

[21]The Throne Theophany. Prophetic Commission and the "Son of Man": A Study in Tradition-History, in: R. G. Hamerton-Kelly [ed], *Jews, Greeks and Christians: Religious Cultures in Late Antiquity. FS William D. Davies*, Leiden 1976, pp. 57-73, p. 62. The «One like a man» is then comparable to the so-called «Angel of YHWH» (מַלְאַךְ יהוה), whose distinction to Yahweh himself is often difficult to make. See G. von Rad, Art. ἄγγελος. O.T., in: *TDNT* I, pp. 76-80 (p. 77: «when the reference is to God apart from man, Yahweh is used, when God enters the apperception of man, the מַלְאַךְ יהוה is introduced»); and D. N. Freedman, B. E. Willoughby, H.-J. Fabry, Art. מַלְאַךְ in *TWAT* IV, cols 887-904. God appears as man-like to interfere in the history of mankind.

merkabah-exegetical-tradition at the turn of the Christian Era.[22] This is the case for 4 Q 385 4, a late Hasmonean or early Herodian fragment belonging to the so-called Pseudo-Ezekiel.[23] This text contains a rewritten version of Ezek 1, which follows the narrative sequence of Ezek 1, yet with remarkable omissions and alterations. In line 6, the term «radiance» (נגה), which is so characteristic of the description of the «Glory of Yahweh» in Ezek 1 (vv. 4,27,28), is associated directly and explicitly with the chariot: «the radiance of the chariot» (נגה מרכבה). Insofar the fragment 4 Q 385 4 represents «the oldest witness at our disposal to post-biblical exegesis of the biblical *Merkabah* vision».[24]

[4] Apart from the attention on the *Merkabah* as such, we find very early an interpretative interest in the praise of God's glory by the angelic beings surrounding the throne. This exegetical tradition takes its start in Ezek 3:12-13 itself. This passage interprets the «noise» (קול) provoked by the moving of the wings (1:24) indirectly as a «voice» of praise, in so far as it is associated with the following acclamation: «Blessed (בָּרוּךְ) be the glory of Yahweh from his place» (v. 12). Moreover v. 13 mentions also the קול of the אוֹפַנִּים («wheels») which are then easily identified as angelic beings. This angelic-liturgical line of interpretation, which can be observed as well in the massoretic text as in the Septuaginta version, is well attested in 4 Q 403, the Qumran Sabbath *Shiroth* or «Songs of the Sabbath Sacrifice».[25] Fragment 1 ii 1. 15 reads: «and the *merkaboth* of his *debir* praise him together. And their *cherubim* and the[ir] *ophanim* bless him». The interest is

---

[22]On the book of Ezekiel at Qumran, see: J. Lust, Ezekiel Manuscripts in Qumran: Preliminary Edition of 4QEz a and b, in: Idem (ed), op. cit. [note 9], pp. 90-100; G. J. Brooke, Ezekiel in Some Qumran and New Testament Texts, in: J. T. Barrera and L. V. Montaner (eds), *The Madrid Qumran Congress 1991*, STDJ XI,1, Leiden 1992, pp. 317-337. Fragments of the canonical text of Ezek 1 are found in 4 Q Ezek[b] (1:1-24*), which proves some interest at Qumran for the throne vision.

[23]D. Dimant and J. Strugnell, The Merkavah Vision in Second Ezekiel (4Q385 4), in: *RevQ* 14, 1990, pp. 331-348; D. Dimant, New Light from Qumran on the Jewish Pseudepigrapha - 4 Q 390, in: *The Madrid Qumran Congress 1991*, op. cit. [note 22], pp. 405-447.

[24]D. Dimant and J. Strugnell, op. cit. [note 23], p. 348.

[25]C. A. Newsom, *Songs of the Sabbath Sacrifice A Critical Edition*, HSS 27, Atlanta 1985; Idem, Merkabah Exegesis in the Qumran Sabbath Shirot, in: JJS 38, 1987, pp. 11-30; J. M. Baumgarten, The Qumran Sabbath Shirot and Rabbinic Merkabah Traditions, in: *RevQ* 13, 1988, pp. 199-213.

concentrated on the form and content of the heavenly liturgy: «... the Sabbath songs do not associate the *merkabah* with a scene of revelatory disclosure. Instead, the *merkabah* is presented as the central cult object of the heavenly temple».[26] Other texts which seem to clarify this subject (catchword קֹול e.g. 1 Kgs 19:12 and Ps 68) are associated with Ezek 1.

[5] Another well known text is the throne scene from the Book of Enoch[27], chap. 14 (and 71), a text directly dependent on Ezek 1 (associated with Dan 7): «And from underneath the throne came forth streams of blazing fire, and I was unable to look on it. And the Glory of the Great One sat thereon, and his raiment was brighter than the sun, and whiter than any snow...» (14, lines 19f).

[6] These few texts are not a sufficient basis on which could be built a coherent image of a «Jewish mystical-apocalyptic grid» based on Ezek 1 that would be useful as a new paradigm to understand the history of early Christianity, and more specifically to explain why christophany was so central in understanding Paul's theological utterances.[28] On the whole, we observe a relative paucity of Ezekiel texts at Qumran. Second-Ezekiel itself is rather atypical of Qumran Sect ideology. As for the apocalyptic material, 1 Enoch 14 and 71 stand rather isolate: apocalyptic literature is not saturated with *merkabah* speculation. The evidence for a mystical-apocalyptic tradition inspired by Ezek 1 in early rabbinic Judaism remains very controversial. C. Rowland is convinced, however, that «ecstatic mystical and esoteric exegetical traditions were being developed in circles associated with some rabbinic teachers during the first century CE».[29] We should evidently not forget that the mighty and protrusive text of Ezek 1 itself was heard

---

[26]C. A. Newsom, op. cit. (1987 [note 25]), p. 29.

[27]Translation of ch. 14 in M. Black, *The Book of Enoch. A New English Edition*, SVTPs 7, Leiden 1985, pp. 32-34 with commentary in pp. 145-152.

[28]This is the one-sided thesis of P. Segal, *Paul the Convert: The Apostolate and Apostasy of Saul the Pharisee*, New Haven 1990.

[29]C. Rowland, The Parting of the Ways: The Evidence of Jewish and Christian Apocalyptic and Mystical Material, in: J. D. G. Dunn (ed), *Jews and Christians. The Parting of the Ways. A.D. 70 to 135*, WUNT 66, Tübingen 1993, pp. 213-237, p. 225. He presumes a controversy concerning the status and legitimacy of the traditions «during the first century, probably because of the way in which such traditions were developed in the extra-rabbinic circle, not least Christianity». See however the more reserved presentation of rabbinic evidence in D. Halperin, *The Faces of the Chariot*, TSAJ 16, Tübingen 1988.

and read regularly in the synagogue.

Conclusion

We agree with C. C. Newman's emphasis on «Christophany as a "sign" with "signifying" potential».[30] This sign is understandable within the code which generate the Jewish Scriptures, in particular Ezek 1. The Christ event on its turn restructures the semantic system to elaborate the meaning of the sign in a new language (e.g. Rev 4).

In the Paulinian theology as already in the pre-Paulinian creed, the christophany is not an isolated sign. If Paul wants to summarize the Gospel, he does not express it in terms of christophany, but in terms of «the cross of our Lord Jesus Christ» (Gal 6:14). The paradoxal combination of σταυρός with κύριος[31] in the example given, however, and the association of this expression with καινὴ κρίσις in v. 15 which follows show that Paul's formulation necessarily includes what is expressed with ὤφθη: the «sign» of God's overwhelming eschatological presence through the Christ event. In the pre-Paulinian creed I Cor 15:3b-15 there is already an arch that leads from the first proposition (ὅτι Χριστὸς ἀπέθανεν) to the last (ὅτι ὤφθη). The bridge would fall if one pillar would be missing.

The christophanies we spoke of are part of the foundational story of God's revelation. Günther Wagner has taught us as students - based on a sound Paulinian theology - that Christ reveals himself today through the preaching of the gospel which He himself generated. May this very fragmentary contribution to his *Festschrift* be accepted as a token of gratitude for his teaching and companionship during our studies at Rüschlikon.

---

[30] Op. cit. [note 3], p. 184.

[31] Is really ἐν τῷ σταυρῷ τοῦ κυρίου «a formal statement», as states D. B. Cares in his *Old Testament Yahweh Texts in Paul's Christology*, WUNT 2/47, Tübingen 1992, p. 76, note 159. Does it not belong also to what he calls «Yahweh Texts»?

THE HOLY SPIRIT - SOURCE OF SANCTIFICATION[1]

REFLECTIONS ON BASIL THE GREAT'S TREATISE ON THE HOLY SPIRIT

Lukas Vischer

Introduction

During the decades of his teaching activity at the Seminary of Rüschlikon Günter Wagner was associated in many ways with the ecumenical movement. For many years he was a member of the Faith and Order Commission of the World Council of Churches and participated in meetings and consultations on a wide range of themes. He contributed significantly to the elaboration of the agreed statements on Baptism, the Eucharist, and the Ministry which captured the attention of the churches for several years. He was also the driving force in the dialogue between Baptists and Reformed theologians leading to conclusions which, in my view, have not yet sufficiently been explored. He pursued the ecumenical cause with impressive steadiness and quiet passion combining faithfulness to the convictions of his church with openness and understanding for other traditions.

As I think of him as a companion on the ecumenical journey above all memories of common adventures in Orthodox lands come to my mind - especially the memory of a consultation in Odessa in which we participated together. It is therefore fitting, I think, to contribute to his "Festschrift" a study which has its "Sitz im Leben" in the dialogue with the Orthodox - an attempt at showing the relevance of Basil the Great's Treatise on the Holy Spirit for a deeper mutual understanding between the Orthodox and all those who claim for themselves the heritage of Calvin's Reformation in Geneva.

The treatise on the Holy Spirit can be approached from various angles. Attention is usually focussed on the question as to how far this text led to the development of the dogma of the Trinity or even to its completion.[2] But the treatise is also important from other points of view. It shows us how a church father of the fourth century conceived and performed the task of theology. It is important not only in virtue of the theological insights it presents but also because the author's approach to theology is so clearly revealed in it.

---

[1] de spiritu sancto, ch. 9.

[2] Hermann Dörries, *de spiritu sanco, Der Beitrag des Basilius zum Abschluss des trinitarischen Dogmas*, Göttingen 1956.

In this paper I want to draw attention to this second aspect. Two questions in particular will be discussed. I want, on the one hand, to examine the question of Basil's view of the responsibility of theological talk about God. What is the significance of words? To what extent are theological utterances capable of effecting a genuine clarification? I want, on the other hand, to try to make clear the connection Basil sees between theological utterances and the calling of the Christian to salvation. To what extent, in Basil's view, are theological insights rooted in the spiritual experience of the Church?

As I see it, these two questions are important for the dialogue between the Orthodox and the Churches of the Reformed tradition. For I have the impression that to this aspect of Basil the Great's life and work there are surprising parallels to be found in the time of the Reformation.

1. Responsible Talk

Basil shares with many other church fathers the conviction that there are strict limits to theological utterances. He repeatedly urges caution. The traditional doctrine is not to be scoured and researched with a fine tooth comb but rather to be believed and acknowledged. To be sure, in doctrine are hidden all the treasures of knowledge and wisdom but from that it cannot be concluded that these treasures can also be brought into the open. "We, however, teach those who hope in Christ not to explore anything superfluous but to stick rather to the ancient faith; for as we believe, so also have we been baptized, and as we have been baptized so we should also bring honour ... In other words, our salvation is not based on the discovery of new names but rather on the sound confession of the Godhead in whom we believe."[3]

Karl Holl commented as follows on a similar passage: "How different from the spirit of his teacher Origen! Here we feel the senescence of Hellenism."[4] But this verdict is unwarranted. The caution here recommended by Basil is rooted rather in the knowledge that God's essence is unknowable and unsearchable. It would be presumptious of us to want to cross the frontiers established for us. "In short, how proud and arrogant we would be to think of searching the being and essence of God! With such big talk we would even almost outdistance the king of Babylon with his boast: 'I will set my throne high above the stars of God' (Isa 14:13). For

[3]Ep. 175; 32, 652D.

[4]Karl Holl, *Amphilochius von Ikonium*, Tübingen 1904, p. 130.

we would not merely be trespassing against the stars and the heavens but actually imagining that we could even invade the essence of the almighty God Himself!"[5]

Certainly Basil knows, too, that the doctrine as handed down in the church needs to be developed. In actual fact fuller theological utterances cannot be avoided. They become necessary from the moment that the fundamental truths of the Gospel are called in question. The attack must be countered so that the Church is not exposed to the danger of error. This defense, moreover, cannot be confined to the demonstration that the divergent view is heretical. The controversy also compels the positive development of the traditional teaching. It has to be made clear what the simple formulas of traditional faith really mean.

"In my view, to praise Him is simply to list the wonderful titles due to Him. Our opponents must either forbid us to remember His kindnesses or else grant that the glorification of His name is the most perfect form of praise. We cannot in fact praise God, the Father of our Lord Jesus Christ, His only begotten Son, otherwise than by relating to the best of our ability the mighty acts of the Holy Spirit."[6]

But how in fact can doctrine be developed? How do valid theological statements emerge? Basil stresses that every statement must result from Scripture. If a statement is to be made responsibly we must ensure that it is in accord with the witness of Scripture and is rooted in the traditional life of the Church. To claim validity in the Church a statement can never be a novel idea but must always be in the continuity of Scripture and Tradition. The theologian's first task, therefore, is to demonstrate this accord. Basil sees Scripture and Tradition as a single whole. The mystery of revelation is attested by Scripture and Tradition. Everything essential is expressed by Scripture. But there is nothing exclusive about this attestation. It lives in the Tradition of the church and is illuminated and enlarged by it. Even unwritten traditions are important; they are experienced and lived in the Church as the fellowship called into being by the Holy Spirit and they demand the attention of the theologians. Scripture and Tradition are not mutually contradictory; on the contrary, together they belong to the testimony given by the Holy Spirit to the Church.

This living Tradition comes most clearly to expression in the worship of the Church. The theological utterance, therefore, has a special and privileged relationship to worship. It must match the praise offered by the Church in

[5]Adversus Eunomium I, 12.

[6]de spiritu sancto, ch. 23.

worship. Doctrine cannot utter anything other than what the Church utters in prayer; conversely, the Church cannot praise God in prayer otherwise than in doctrine. It is certainly no accident, therefore, that, in his reflections on the nature of the Holy Spirit, Basil starts from a liturgical formula. He demonstrates that a definite form of praise can quite legitimately be used in the Church's liturgy: namely, "Praised be God the Father with (meta) the son and (syn) the Holy Spirit". This corresponds with the witness of Scripture and with the Tradition of the church. Having demonstrated the legitimacy of the use of the formula in worship, he has at the same time demonstrated also the theological legitimacy of the statement. Responsible theological utterances do not float free above the life of the Church but arise so to speak from the Church's liturgical praise.

One of the important features of the theological work of Basil the Great is its orientation on the life of the Church. His utterances are not the fruit of the need for intellectual achievement. What he is seeking to do in his utterances, on the contrary, is to serve the growth of the Church. This attitude finds expression first of all in the fact that almost all his theological writings - the meditations on the work of creation in six days are perhaps the only exception - were the fruit of specific external occasions. He accepts a partner and the description of his theology as a theology of dialogue is not inaccurate. When he writes, he has the situation of the Church in view. His most important work, the treatise on the Holy Spirit, is a good example of this. It is addressed to Amphilochius of Iconium, a bishop who cherishes friendly feelings towards him. In the preface he emphasizes how important the atmosphere of friendship is for him. It alone makes it possible for him to develop his thoughts about the Holy Spirit. The treatise, therefore, is not addressed primarily to the general public. But it is nevertheless not an "esoteric book".[7] On the contrary, Basil hopes to be able in this atmosphere of friendship to sow a seed which can later on flourish in the Church. In response to the treatise Amphilochius summoned a synod in Iconium which gave its support to Basil's ideas.

The orientation on the life of the Church in the work of Basil can also take the form of a self-imposed silence. He had a sharp antenna for when, where and how saying something was possible and necessary or not. The fact that a statement corresponds to the truth does not automatically mean that it must also be publicly announced. Basil never at any time in his life expressly declared that the Holy Spirit is God. While this affirmation was undoubtedly his belief, indeed, while to achieve for this affirmation universal acceptance in the Church was undoubtedly

[7]So Hermann Dörries, op. cit. sup., p. 46.

his dearest wish and his whole treatise **de spirito sancto** was meant to serve this goal, he nevertheless avoided bluntly making this statement even in this treatise.

How is this attitude to be explained? Already in his lifetime it was found puzzling. Many interpreted it as an unwillingness of Basil's part to confess his faith. Gregory of Nazianzus tells of a monk who publicly upbraided Basil with talking marvellously about the divinity of the Father and the Son but, like a torrent which goes round the difficult stone in its path and floods the sand, avoided speaking of the divinity of the Holy Spirit. "He gives a hazy picture of the faith, conceals it in shadow and does not gladly confess the truth." But Basil refused to let himself be diverted from his attitude by complaints of this kind. He avoided speaking explicitly of the Holy Spirit as God.

One explanation of this striking attitude is found in the last chapter of the treatise on the Holy Spirit. In view of the confused situation, Basil considers it better to deliberately avoid speaking openly. "The present situation of the Church is like a fierce naval battle which has in addition to be fought out in a cyclone and mountainous waves, so that the individual ships of the storm-tossed fleet harassed by the enemy, endanger one another even when they still remain united ... And even now, so close to disaster, a vain thirst for glory makes the sailors quarrel over precedence!" From this he concludes: "In face of this situation, I reached the conclusion that it was better to hold my peace than to speak; for amid such confusion a human voice cannot make itself heard. If the words of the Preacher (Eccl 9:17) are true and 'the words of the wise heard in quiet are better than the shouting of a ruler among fools' it becomes clear at once how little the necessary conditions for speaking on the theme of the Spirit exist at the present time."[8]

In order to be able to speak constructively, the ground needs to be prepared. If the right conditions do not exist, theological statements which go beyond what is strictly necessary, however true they may be, will only produce fresh misunderstanding. "How difficult it is to find a person who loves knowledge and seeks the truth in order to be healed from ignorance! The questions which are put to us by many are like the hunter's net or an ambush in war. Their purpose is not to derive benefit from the answer but rather to use it, when it fails to meet expectations, as a pretext for war."[9] Basil therefore holds himself back. Above all, he avoids provocative terms and slogans which could give yet another impetus to quarrels which are already in any case almost legion.

[8]de spiritu sancto, ch. 30.

[9]de spiritu sancto, ch. 1.

When Basil lauds the virtue of silence, it is probably also the monk in him who speaks. Silence is the signal virtue of the monk. Basil warns the monks against overhasty speech. Silence may be likened to the calm sea in which impurity is cleansed and clarified. Silence always seeks peace. But hasty words are an occasion of conflict; once uttered, they can no longer be retracted but proceed on their way and do their damage. In silence we are able to take upon ourselves the guilt of the world and thereby expel it from the world. To contradict, however, is only to make it all the greater. Silence helps to promote fellowship. In silence it is possible to become one, to be reconciled, where words only lead to strife.[10]

Obviously, silence alone cannot be the answer. When the truth is in danger, it is imperative to speak. "I believe I had to remain silent in face of the countless assaults of our enemies on us, calmly to accept their reproaches and not to answer back those who employ the lie as a weapon, this evil weapon which often pierces even the truth with its sharp end. But you were right in urging me not to betray the truth but rather to convince the false accuser lest many should be injured by the victory of the lie over the truth."[11]

The all important question, therefore, is what and how much must be said at a specific point in time. In his answer to this question, Basil obviously let himself be guided by the following criterion: What and how much is necessary in order that the fundamental truth should continue to be preserved in the Church? The important thing is that the faithful should stand firm in the truth. Once that can be counted on, Basil allows a certain flexibility in the formulations employed. He could declare himself in agreement with the term **homoiousios** as long as it was quite clear that this did not mean any difference in essence from the Father and the Son.[12] When the quarrel over the divinity of the Spirit broke out, the only condition he required for fellowship was the declaration that the Spirit is not a creature. He contented himself with the negative formulation and refused to project the line to the positive statement that "the Spirit is God". And when the conflict intensified he developed his reflections on the **homotimia** of the Spirit, but continued avoiding overstretching the bow by the explicit confession of the divinity of the Spirit. He was obviously upheld by the confidence that only the fundamental decisions really mattered; once the points were correctly set, the journey was bound to arrive at its goal.

[10]cf. for example, Ep. 2:1 in Is. comm 158; PG 30, 377B.

[11]Ep. 189:1.

[12]Ep. 9; 32, 272a.

The way in which Basil distinguishes between **kerygma** and **dogma** is interesting. He defines **kerygma** as the truth which must be proclaimed and attested by the Church and in the Church in all circumstances, as those fundamental statements which are the presupposition of every Christian life. **Dogmata**, on the other hand, are in his view deeper insights which follow from the **kerygma**. The **kerygma** stands at the beginning of the spiritual life; **dogmata** grow from it like fruits. In Hermann Dörries' view[13], this distinction between **kerygma** and **dogma** justifies Basil's caution; he was unwilling to come before the congregation with a doctrinal formula which could not yet be adopted by it. It was not right that "too heavy a demand should be laid on the congregation. So he allowed it its time and did not utter all that he knew."

Responsible talk always serves the end that the truth which brings salvation is proclaimed and heard in the Church.

2. Theological Statements and the Spiritual Life of Christians

Basil's thought and speech is deeply rooted in spiritual experience. Theological knowledge grows from experience and itself in turn aids spiritual experience. God can only be known from His works. "From the works comes knowledge and from knowledge worship."[14] Theological statements are necessary as a presupposition of spiritual experience.

As a young man Basil decided on an ascetic life and the spiritual experience which was connected with this decision became increasingly important for him as the years passed. He repeatedly stresses that what counts in God's sight are not knowledge and words but the practice of spiritual life. Looking back on his youth, his verdict is: "I spent much time on vain things, wasted almost my entire youth in futile endeavour, for I tried to acquire knowledge of the wisdom which has been turned by God into folly."[15] The goal of life is future blessedness. The way to this goal is virtue. But virtue consists in concern for the soul and detachment from the world. The Christian should therefore concentrate on this task. "My sheep hear my voice. Look, this is how God is known! We know Him by keeping His commandments and putting them into practice. Knowledge is keeping His commandments. What? Not endless seeking and studying God's nature? Not the

---

[13]Hermann Dörries, "Basilius und das Dogma vom Heiligen Geist", in: Wort und Stunde I, Göttingen 1966, pp. 127ff.

[14]Ep. 324,3.

[15]Ep. 223, 2; 32 824.

probing of the supernatural? Not reflection on what is invisible to humanity? My sheep know me and I know my sheep. It is enough for you to know that He is the good shepherd and that he has given His life for the sheep. The knowledge of God lies within these limits. But to ask how great God is and what His dimensions are and wherein His nature consists - these are dangerous questions and impossible to answer. The one who really respects these things is the one who keeps silent about them. My sheep hear My voice, God says."[16]

Theological statements are necessary only if they help to clarify and deepen our calling. Then, indeed, it is impossible to take seriously enough the need to be precise in what we assert. Every syllable counts and it would be irresponsible not to test every phrase right down to the very last detail. "Not to take lightly theological statements but on the contrary to try to discover the hidden meaning in each word, indeed in each syllable - this is the mark not of those who are lazy in their spiritual life but of those who have grasped the goal of our calling. For the promise made to us is that we are to become like God to the extent that human nature is capable of this. But likeness is not achieved without knowledge nor knowledge without instruction. The Word stands at the beginning of all instruction and the Word is composed of words and syllables. To enquire the meaning of syllables, therefore, is by no means a pointless exercise."[17]

But where does the Holy Spirit come in all this? Why is it so important to affirm that He is God and not a creature? Answer: in this affirmation the whole of our spiritual calling is at stake. The Spirit must be worshipped as God because only God has the power to transform the human being and to make him or her like unto Himself. The Spirit must be what through his activity He gives to the human being. If the Spirit were a creature, He would not be able to transform creatures and to make them like God. "When we hear the word 'Spirit' we do not think of a limited nature which is subject to changes and transformations, similar in every respect to created things. On the contrary, anyone who lifts up his or her thoughts to the Highest necessarily thinks of a spiritual being, unlimited in its power, infinite in its magnitude, exalted far above the measure of time and the centuries, of a spiritual being which distributes the blessings at its disposal. It is to Him that all who need sanctification turn. It is to Him that the longing turns of all those whose life is ruled by virtue and who are refreshed by His breath ... He has the power to make the rest perfect; He lacks nothing. He does not have a life which needs constantly to be renewed but on the contrary is Himself the master

[16]Hom. in Mam. mart. 4; pg 31 597 A.

[17]de spiritu sancto, ch. 1.

(**choregos**) of life ... The Spirit imparts Himself like a ray of the sun whose grace is present with the one who receives it as if this one were the only one to receive it, and which nevertheless lights up the earth and the ocean and mingles itself with the air. So too is the Spirit present with everyone who is capable of receiving Him, as if each alone received Him, and yet He radiates in remaining intact and undivided, a grace which is sufficient for all. Those who partake of the spirit receive Him according to the measure of their nature but not according to the measure in which he could impart Himself."[18] The theological affirmation that the Spirit is divine simply means the praise of that power which can deliver the life of humanity from its fallen state, transform it and make it like God.

The treatise on the Holy Spirit focusses on the question as to how the Holy Spirit can be rightly praised by the Church and in the church. Basil does not doubt that the formula "Glory to the Father through the Son in the Holy Spirit" has a sound basis. But he argues emphatically that the formula "Glory to the Father with the Son and with the Holy Spirit" also has its place in the liturgy. The first of these two formulas puts the emphasis on the gifts of God and is to be preferred when we are speaking of Christ as "the door or the way" of salvation.[19] In the Holy Spirit we know how God turns graciously towards us in Jesus Christ. The second formula, by contrast, emphasizes the objective ground of redemption: it makes it clear that Father, Son and Holy Spirit are entitled to the same honour and glory. Only when both formulas are taken together does the whole truth become visible.

The way of our calling begins with baptism. Basil pays special attention, therefore, to the moment of baptism. The Spirit operates in baptism. He takes possession of those who are open to His influence and are willing to let themselves be led by Him. "But why is water associated with the Spirit? Because baptism pursues a double goal: to destroy the body of sin so that it may no longer produce the fruits of death and to enable life out of the Spirit and bringing forth the fruits of holiness."[20] Because the Spirit acts in baptism it is important that at this moment we should confess Him in the right way. The confession of faith in which we joined in baptism must be preserved intact in order that the Spirit may complete His work. "How do we come to be Christians? Through faith, we say. In what way are we being saved? By being born again, which means through the grace of baptism. How could it be otherwise? Once we have achieved knowledge of grace as accomplished by the Father and the Son and the Holy Spirit, how could we ever

[18]de spiritu sancto, ch. 9.

[19]de spiritu sancto, ch. 8.

[20]de spiritu sancto, ch. 15.

again abandon this form of doctrine? What a disaster it would be if we were further away from salvation today than in the moment when we first came to believe!"[21] The grace of baptism can only be kept if we also keep without qualifications the faith which we confessed in the moment of baptism. Only on the basis of this confession of faith can the goal of our calling be reached.

It is in accordance with this heavy emphasis on the calling to eternal salvation that Basil describes the Holy Spirit as the power of sanctification and perfecting. It is the Spirit who leads to holiness and perfection those who prove themselves capable. Because the Spirit is God to the same degree as the Father and the Son He is the power of sanctification and perfection from all eternity. He was present as this power in the creation and in the revelation in Jesus Christ. "Understand that in the act of the creation of all things the Father is the original cause of everything created, the Son the executive cause and the Spirit the completing and perfecting cause. The invisible ministering spirits exist through the will of the Father, come into being through the act of the Son and receive their perfection through the presence of the Spirit."[22]

This does not signify that the work of the Father or of the Son would be incomplete without the Spirit. What it does signify, however, is that through the Spirit, Father and Son **purpose** to lead to holiness and perfection. The creation is called into existence through the Word and perfected by the Spirit. As basis for this dynamic view of the Spirit, Basil cites Psalm 33: "By the word of the Lord the heavens were made, and by the breath of His mouth all their power" (Ps 33:6).[23]

From all eternity, therefore, the Spirit is the source and power of sanctification. "You think then of the Three: the Lord who orders all things, the Word that creates all things, and the Breath which establishes all things. But what does "establish" mean but perfecting in holiness? For this word cannot relate to anything else than to the fact that the Spirit makes the created world constant, immovable and established in the good. Without the Spirit there is no sanctification. For the powers of heaven are not by nature holy. Otherwise they would in fact be indistinguishable from the Holy Spirit."[24]

---

[21] de spiritu sancto, ch. 10.

[22] de spiritu sancto, ch. 16.

[23] de spiritu sancto, ch. 16.

[24] de spiritu sancto, ch. 16.

The connection between the doctrine of the divinity of the Spirit and the spiritual life of the Christian could hardly be more clearly stated. The power which leads me to salvation is, at the same time, the power which maintains and perfects the whole of creation. And conversely: because I am permitted to know that the Spirit who upholds and perfects the whole of creation was at work in the moment of my baptism, I can have confidence that the way He points does in fact lead to the promised likeness to God.

3. How far are these reflections of importance for the Orthodox-Reformed dialogue?

The two aspects of the treatise **de spiritu sancto** are of importance for the dialogue between the Orthodox and the Churches of Reformed tradition because it is possible to find certain correspondance in the thought and attitude of the Reformers. There is an undeniable affinity across the intervening centuries. A comparison will, of course, also reveal at once the considerable differences separating the Reformers from the period of the fourth century. But it will also make clear which questions must engage the attention of future exchanges.

a) The Reformers adopted the doctrine of the Ancient Church and developed it in their writings. They certainly did not do so without examining it carefully. The critical controversy with the Church of their time also led them to pose the fundamental question as to whether the tradition of the Ancient Church could and should claim authority and if so to what extent. Are the doctrines of the Trinity and the two natures really a statement of the revealed truth? Is the terminology used by the church fathers really suitable for the mystery of God?

What is the explanation of this caution? It was undoubtedly due in part to the concern to keep the mystery of revelation intact. What is unsearchable should be recognized as unsearchable. Theology must not have any illusions as to its ability to unlock the mystery by definitions. To do so would actually mean bypassing the deepest purpose of the revelation in Christ: God's will is to be known and recognized as Saviour. When the Reformers stress the limits to knowledge, it is certainly not their intention to deny that definite and reliable statements can be made about God. It was the humanists rather than the Reformers who were characterized by a general scepticism. Erasmus of Rotterdam, for example, can differentiate between things it is necessary to know and things which are better-advised "to leave to God and to pray devoutly rather than to investigate the unsearchable". He included among these "unsearchable things" also the "distinction of persons and the union of the divine and human nature in Christ". These he regards as academic questions. To discuss them "in the presence of a

213

motley crowd seems to me not merely useless but even positively dangerous".[25]
The Reformers, on the contrary, were convinced that God reveals Himself and
makes Himself known to us in His Word. The mystery of His gracious work can be
grasped and expressed in words.

The reason for the Reformers' caution is to be found, rather, precisely in their
radical emphasis on God's Word. Through His Word, God speaks to the Church.
The aim of the Reformers was to make room in the Church for this divine
utterance. The Scriptures which bear witness to this Word of God are placed in the
centre, therefore. Nothing must be allowed to detract from this direct encounter of
the Word and the Church. No utterance of the Church can be permitted to come
between them. From this standpoint, a question mark was set even against the
Creed. God's Word and the Scripture which attests that Word are the touchstone
for the life of the Church. The Ancient Church doctrine can therefore claim no **a
priori** authority. It is binding on the Church to the extent that it is supported and
shown to be true by the testimony of Scripture.

The task confronting the Reformers, therefore, is to demonstrate the harmony
between the Scriptures and the Ancient Church doctrine. They must, so to speak,
once more repeat the process from the beginnings of the proclamation down to the
formulation of the Ancient Church doctrine in its time. Before they repeat the
Ancient Church formulas as binding doctrine, they must make certain that they
can be defended on the basis of the biblical testimony.

An incident from Calvin's early period illustrates this attitude. In 1537 Petrus
Caroli, a preacher in Lausanne, accused Pierre Viret, the Lausanne Reformer, and
with him Calvin of not accepting the creeds of the Ancient Church. He failed to
find in Calvin any clear statements about the Trinity and was disturbed, above all,
by the fact that Calvin seemed to avoid the term **persona**. He therefore demanded
that Calvin should substantiate his faith in the doctrine of the Ancient Church by
publicly signing the ancient creeds of the Church. Calvin refused. Part of the
explanation of the refusal is found in the situation at that time. Calvin was not
willing to submit to Caroli's inquisitorial pressure. But there was a deeper reason
for his refusal. Calvin was not prepared to acknowledge the formal authority of the
creeds independently of the witness of Scripture. For him, the decisive authority
was Scripture. Compared with Scripture, the creeds could only claim a derived
authority.

---

[25]Jan Koopmans, *Das altkirchliche Dogma in der Reformation,* Munich 1955, p. 22

Certainly these reflections remain somewhat theoretical to the extent that **de facto** the Refomers adopted the Ancient Church doctrine: "The Ancient Church's confession of faith was their confession of faith."[26] By the reception of the Ancient Church dogma, Reformation theology voluntarily subordinated itself so to speak "to the control of an unquestionably classic period of dogmatic thought. That period was not to be assigned the status of a formal authority. This was sharply expressed in the struggle against the Roman principle of tradition. The basic idea, rather, was that those dogma were intended to be a confession to the same revelation as that confessed in the Reformation doctrine of justification."[27]

Calvin reached this conclusion on the basis of independent biblical exegesis. He called in question the cogency of certain traditional **dicta probantia**. But this study of Scripture reinforced his conviction "that what was intended by the doctrine of the Trinity - the distinction of Father, Son and Holy Spirit and the attestation of their equal eternal divinity - was to be found everywhere in Scripture."[28]

Calvin dealt with the doctrine of the Trinity repeatedly. He made it the basis of the structure of his **Institutes**. The Ancient Church doctrine became important to him above all for its clear demarcations. In his controversies with theological opponents it became clear to him that the development of the doctrine of the Trinity was necessary in the interests of the clarity of the Christian message. The Ancient Church formulations were like a defensive wall around the pure truth of the Gospel. In itself, it would be better if the necessity of appealing to the formulas of the Ancient Church did not arise at all. "If only they (all these expressions) were buried, if only this faith were established among us, namely, the faith that Father, Son and Holy Spirit are **one** God and that the Son is not the Father nor the Holy Spirit the Son but that they are distinct from one another by a definite characteristic!"[29] But because the testimony of Scripture is liable to misinterpretation, additional explanations are necessary. "What is to prevent us from explaining in clearer words what is difficult and unclear to our comprehension in Scripture?"[30] Above all, the Ancient Church formulations are an indispensable aid in combatting heresies. "For if these expressions were not

[26]Koopmans, op. cit., p. 100

[27]W. Elert, Morphologie des Luthertums I, 1931, p. 183f.

[28]Werner Krusche, *Das Wirken des Heiligen Geistes nach Calvin*, Berlin 1957, p. 3.

[29]Quoted in: Koopmans, p. 55.

[30]Calvin, Institutes I, 13, 3.

developed without good reason, they are certainly rejected without good reason". Opposition to the Ancient Church doctrine is the sure sign of a heretical view. Since the Ancient Church doctrine is designed as a standard, the erroneous nature of heretical teachings becomes visible.

In principle, the Ancient Church doctrine remains subordinate to the testimony of Scripture. Even after it was shown to be valid on the basis of Scripture, it does not become a court of appeal which could be viewed and developed independently of Scripture. Nor, therefore, is the task of demonstrating the concordance between Scripture and Ancient Church doctrine ever finished. On the contrary, it is necessary to make this demonstration again and again from scratch. It is a living possession of the Church only when it constantly grows afresh from the witness of Scripture.

This is not the place for a detailed presentation of Calvin's doctrine of the Trinity. The important point in our present context is that Calvin was compelled by his Reformation approach to repeat in his own day the intellectual process which led in the Ancient Church to the formulation of the doctrine of the Trinity. It became increasingly clear to him that the God of the Bible can only be thought of in trinitarian terms. The doctrine of the Trinity is dealt with in Calvin's **Institutes** immediately after the initial chapters on the knowledge of God. He does not preface it with a general doctrine of God, His nature and His attributes. He regards the doctrine of the Trinity as so fundamental that he asserts that "without this dogma (sc. of the three persons) only the bare and empty name of God flits about in our brains to the exclusion of the true God".[31]

For Calvin, the most important biblical launching pad is Ephesians 4:4-6. He regards these passages as compelling; to be sure, only **one** argument but an argument which could stand in for a thousand others. Paul argues from the oneness of God, whereas we have nevertheless been baptised in the name of the Father and of the Son and of the Holy Spirit. This passage from Ephesians makes it clear why, on the basis of these biblical reflections, Calvin can say with Gregory of Nazianzus: "I cannot think on the one without immediately being encircled by the splendour of the three; nor can I discern the three without being straightaway carried back to the one."[32]

[31]Institutes I, 13, 2.

[32]Institutes I, 13, 17.

Calvin emphasizes the interrelationship of **essentia** and **persona** in the Trinity. The one true God is encountered in Father, Son and Holy Spirit. But the one God is not to be understood as something **abstractum** which could be thought of independently of Father, Son and Holy Spirit, and therefore, in a certain sense as some fourth being. Conversely, Father, Son and Holy Spirit are also not mere attributes of God like the wisdom of God or the power of God. To describe these modes of being, Calvin prefers the term **subsistentia** to the term **persona**. Apart from the fact that he regards **subsistentia** (a literal translation of **hypostasis**) as a biblical concept, this term in his view more effectively avoids suggesting the idea of three separate individualities within the one Godhead. Father, Son and Holy Spirit are modes of being of the whole being of God. By subsistentia he means an "independence in God's essence which, while related to the others, is distinguished by an incommunicable quality".[33] These formulations are inspired by a concern to express in an appropriate manner not only the unity of God but also the difference of persons.

b) The Reformers strongly emphasize the close connection between the doctrine of the Trinity and the salvation imparted to humanity in Christ. In their view, the Ancient Church doctrine is the precondition for being able to speak correctly of election, justification and sanctification. It therefore is binding in character because thereby confession is made of the same God who justifies and sanctifies the sinner. The doctrine of the Trinity is not a self-contained theme which could be dealt with separately from the proclamation of salvation in Christ. Theology does not enter a completely new field once it begins to deal with the appropriation of salvation. It is already basically concerned with this theme when it is developing the dogma of the Trinity. Conversely, the doctrine of justification and sanctification is unthinkable without the trinitarian foundation: it is its necessary realization and application.

Characteristic of Calvin is the special emphasis he places on the role of the Spirit in God's gracious turning to the world. He maintains the doctrine of the immanent Trinity. It is for him important that God's being and God's work should not fall apart. There must be the most precise correspondence between the interaction and coexistence of the three modes of being in the being of God, on the one hand, and their interaction and coexistence in His works, on the other. But Calvin's main interest is in God's work **ad extra**. Calvin differentiates between emphases in God's activity. **"Patri principium agendi, rerumque omnium fons et scaturigo attribuitur; Filio sapientia, consilium, ipsaque in rebus agendis dispensatio, at**

---

[33]Institutes I, 13, 6.

Spiritui virtus et efficacia assignatur actionis.[34] To the Holy Spirit, therefore, he attributes in a special way the strength (**virtus**) and the efficacity (**efficacia**) of the action of the Trinity. This emphasis remains characteristic of Calvin's theology as a whole. "Everything which God does - and He does everything and works always - is in its effect an operation of the Holy Spirit. There is no action of the Father and of the Son that takes effect without the activity of the Holy Spirit. All divine action is pneumatological in its thrust."[35]

The Spirit is the Creator, present in all things as the life-creating power but without being subsumed in them. The Spirit is the co-Creator of human life, imparting to it the gifts of the Spirit which make it possible for human beings to become the image of God. Above all he is the creative power calling fallen humanity to new life: justification and sanctification become possible only through his activity. In this he is never separated from the Father and the Son; whether he is at work in the cosmos or sustaining humanity or bringing about the new creation in the Church, he is the Spirit of the Father and the Son. He is the power **qua consilii sui decreta exequitur**.

In Calvin, the divinity of the Spirit is the presupposition of the new life in Christ. He emphasizes even more strongly than Basil does that humanity depends on the operation of the divine Spirit if its relationship to God is to be restored. For Calvin's starting point in fact is that humanity by the fall has lost all capacity to open itself up to God and to draw near to Him. Humanity has lost the gifts of the Spirit which made the first creature in God's likeness. Only by the intervention of the Spirit can humanity now be rescued. The dead humanity is in need of a second creation, a new nature, a rebirth. The blind humanity is in need of new eyes. The humanity deprived of the freedom of its will is in need of a new will. In fallen humanity, the Holy Spirit finds nothing to latch on to or to build upon. The aim of the operation of the Spirit is not to correct, to supplement or to set to rights. In making humanity anew in God's image and likeness, the Spirit is the creator of a new creation.

The difference between Calvin and Basil is obvious. Despite the prevailing agreement that the Spirit is God and that salvation can only become a reality by His divine operation, Basil and Calvin differ in their appraisal of the capabilities of fallen humanity. This difference of emphasis will necessarily have to be on the agenda of future encounters.

[34]Institutes I, 13, 18.

[35]Krusche, op. cit., p. 11.

4. Reformed Witness Today

One of the characteristics of the Churches indebted to the Reformation is that they never regard the Church's confession of faith as finally closed. It is their conviction that in new circumstances new insights can emerge from the Word of God, but, above all, that in new situations certain aspects deserve special emphasis. This does not mean that they do not take seriously the utterances of earlier centuries. The Ancient Church creeds in particular still are signposts and guides even for the present time. What they emphasize, however, is that the Church's confession of faith is in constant need of being related to life in the present time.

Many Reformed Churches have in recent times faced up to this task. A whole series of new confessions of faith has been the result. Each of these confessions of faith seeks to embody the essential core of the biblical message in relation to a specific historical context. It is especially significant that Churches in Asia, Africa and Latin America have had the courage to take this task in hand. Confessions of faith from Korea, Taiwan, Indonesia, South Africa and Cuba can be mentioned as examples.[36] A glance at these recent confessions of faith shows that faith in the Triune God is everywhere accepted and confessed. Some of these texts confine themselves simply to recalling the Ancient Church creeds. Others summarise faith in the Triune God in a short formula. Most of the texts depend for their structure on the pattern of the Ancient Church creeds.

There can be no doubt that the faith in the one God, Father, Son and Holy Spirit is firmly established among the Churches of the Reformation. In his treatise on the Holy Spirit, Basil points out that the formula "Glory to the Father and to the Son and to the Holy Spirit!" is spread abroad and used in all languages - whether in Mesopotamia, Cappadocia, Illyria or any other people right to the ends of the earth. "For already at the time of the confusion of tongues, the Spirit had foreseen the usefulness of this formula."[37] In contact with the Reformed Churches of today, this observation could be repeated. The fundamental confession of the Trinity is the common basis across the frontiers of nations and languages.

Certainly it may be asked whether this fundamental profession of faith is being adequately developed in the Churches of the Reformation. Certain individual texts

---

[36]*Reformed Witness Today. A Collection of Confessions and Statements of Faith Issued by Reformed Churches*, edited by Lukas Vischer, Berne 1982.

[37]de spiritu sancto, ch. 29.

attempt to do so. For example the confession of Faith of the Congregational Church in England and Wales (1967). In some texts there is some evidence of the struggle with the context in which the Church in question lives and bears witness. For example, the Confession of the Church of Toraja (Indonesia) reflects something of the controversy on the Trinity with Islam. The text tries to give special emphasis to demonstrating that the oneness of God is in no way cancelled out by the distinction between the three modes of being or "subsistences". But these examples are the exception rather than the rule.

The dialogue with the Orthodox Churches may provide the Churches of the Reformation with the welcome occasion of re-appropriating and developing anew their own understanding of the trinitarian dogma in our time.

Das geistliche Leitungsamt in den Mönchsgemeinschaften Benedikts von Nursia

Gerhard Voss

Viel von dem, was in diesem Beitrag zur Sprache kommt, war des öfteren schon Gegenstand eingehender Untersuchungen. Ich verzichte bewußt auf entsprechende Hinweise. Denn ich möchte keine neuen Forschungsergebnisse vorlegen, sondern durch meine Darstellung einer Baptisten zumeist fremden - und wohl auch befremdlichen - Form christlichen Gemeinschaftslebens zur ökumenischen Verständigung beitragen. Im Thema spiegelt sich meine eigene Lebenswelt wider: ein (mit Unterbrechungen seit 731 bestehendes) Kloster, für dessen Lebensordnung bis heute die "Regel" des abendländischen Mönchsvaters Benedikt von Nursia aus dem ersten Drittel des 6. Jahrhunderts maßgeblich ist: die *Regula Benedicti*, ein ursprünglich lateinisch geschriebenes Büchlein mit 73 kleinen Kapiteln (nachfolgend abgekürzt: RB mit Kapitel- und Verszahl). Von ihrem Verfasser hat Papst Gregor I. in seinen "Dialogen" ein anschauliches Lebensbild gezeichnet. Darin heißt es von diesem Benedictus, daß für ihn zutraf, was sein Name besagt: ein "Gesegneter" Gottes zu sein: ein *vir gratia Benedictus et nomine*. Wie sehr er in seiner "Regel" in wörtlichen Anspielungen und kleineren Zitaten oder sogar in der wörtlichen Übernahme ganzer Kapitel ältere Ordnungen und Zeugnisse klösterlichen Gemeinschaftslebens aufgreift, wie sehr er als nüchterner und zugleich sehr sensibler Römer aber auch eigene Akzente setzt, kann hier außer acht bleiben.

Für mein Leben blieb jedoch nicht nur von akademischem Interesse, daß das II. Vatikanische Konzil mit seinem Dekret über die zeitgemäße Erneuerung des Ordenslebens *"Perfectae Caritatis"* vom 28.10.1965 die katholischen Ordensgemeinschaften dazu aufgefordert hat, "zu den Quellen jedes christlichen Lebens und zum Geist des Ursprungs der einzelnen Institute" zurückzukehren und zugleich "die veränderten Zeitverhältnisse" zu berücksichtigen. Ich gehörte nach dem Konzil zu der Kommission, die mit der Umsetzung dieser Aufforderung in den Klöstern der Bayerischen Benediktiner-Kongregation beauftragt war. Damals hat sich für mich manches in den Anweisungen Benedikts neu mit Leben gefüllt gerade durch meine intensive Begegnung mit Günter Wagner und den anderen Mitherausgebern unserer Zeitschrift UNA SANCTA und mit vielen anderen Brüdern und Schwestern besonders aus kongregationalistisch orientierten Kirchen innerhalb der Arbeitsgemeinschaft christlicher Kirchen in Bayern, in deren Gremien ich von Anfang an mitgearbeitet habe und deren Vorsitzender ich z. Z. bin. Eine besondere Bedeutung gewann für mich durch diesen Erfahrungsaustausch der Begriff der "Einmütigkeit" zur Charakterisierung des Zieles der Entscheidungsfindungsprozesse in der christlichen Gemeinde.

In der römisch-katholischen Kirche, zu der ich gehöre, spielt für die konkrete Entscheidungsfindung die persongebundene Amtsautorität des Papstes, des Bischofs und - in einem benediktinischen Kloster - des Abtes eine große Rolle. Daß eine einbahnige Ausübung dieser Autorität zu großen Konflikten führen kann, ist in den letzten Jahren gerade in der Schweiz deutlich geworden. Die sechziger Jahre waren jedoch auch in der katholischen Kirche von einer Neubesinnung auf das gemeinsame Priestertum aller Gläubigen geprägt. Viele plädierten für eine "Demokratisierung" in der Kirche. Von seinem staatlichen Verstehenshintergrund her ist "Demokratie" jedoch ebensowenig wie "Monarchie" geeignet zur Charakterisierung der Struktur kirchlicher Gemeinschaft. In der Bindung an das Wort Gottes und im Ernstnehmen der vielfältigen Gaben des Geistes Gottes ist eine kirchliche Synode etwas anderes als ein weltliches Parlament. Jedenfalls darf in einer Synode die Stimmenmehrheit nicht allein ausschlaggebend sein, ebensowenig freilich ein Ansehen der Person. "Einmütig" ist eine Gemeinschaft in ihrer Entscheidung dann, wenn ihr Entscheidungsfindungsprozeß im Hören aller aufeinander so lange weitergegangen ist, bis auch die Minderheiten trotz weiterhin bestehender Gewissensbedenken das mittragen können, worauf man sich schließlich einigt, weil ihre Einwände mitberücksichtigt sind - modifizierend und/oder dadurch, daß die Entscheidung im Wissen um die vorgebrachten Einwände nun zu einem von allen gemeinsam verantworteten Wagnis geworden ist. In den damals von unserer Kommission erarbeiteten neuen Satzungen der Bayerischen Benediktiner-Kongregation heißt es: "Der Abt beteilige alle an der Entscheidungsfindung, lasse Minderheiten nicht kurzerhand niederstimmen und versuche, auch von der Mehrheit gefaßte Beschlüsse in versöhnte Einmütigkeit zu verwandeln."

Ausdrücklich ist von der Einmütigkeit der ganzen Gemeinschaft des Klosters nur einmal in der RB die Rede, nämlich im 64. Kapitel, das von der Einsetzung des Abtes handelt: "Es werde der bestellt, den die ganze Gemeinschaft einmütig (*omnis concors congregatio*) in Gottesfurcht gewählt hat oder ein noch so kleiner Teil in besserer Einsicht." Die Bestellung wird vom zuständigen Bischof vorgenommen (heute vom "Praeses", d.i. dem Vorsitzenden unter den Äbten einer "Kongregation", d.i. eines Verbandes mehrerer Klöster). Dieser ist an die einmütige Entscheidung der ganzen Gemeinschaft gebunden, soll gegebenenfalls jedoch der besseren Einsicht einer Minorität folgen. Benedikt sagt auch, worauf sich die bessere Einsicht beziehen muß, was also die für die Wahl und Bestellung eines Abtes entscheidenden Kriterien sind: "Bewährung im Leben und Weisheit in der Lehre". Möglich ist ja durchaus, daß sich die Mehrheit der Wähler von anderen Kriterien hat leiten lassen. Benedikt rechnet sogar damit, daß es vorkommen kann, daß eine klösterliche Gemeinschaft insgesamt ein lasterhaftes

Leben führt und übereinstimmend jemanden zum Abt wählt, "der mit ihrem sündhaften Leben einverstanden ist". Wenn der Bischof oder auch "die Äbte oder Christen der Nachbarschaft" davon erfahren, müssen sie zu verhindern suchen, daß ein solcher "Konsens" von Lasterhaften sich durchsetzt. Hier wird deutlich, daß eine einzelne klösterliche Gemeinschaft, daß eine einzelne christliche Gemeinde nicht die Garantie hat, in ihren Entscheidungen, selbst wenn sie einmütig sind, vom Geist Gottes inspiriert zu sein. Sie bedarf einer wachsamen Führung, wie sie im Neuen Testament im Bild des guten Hirten zum Ausdruck kommt.

Für die klösterliche Gemeinschaft die Sorge des guten Hirten zu übernehmen, ist die dem Abt anvertraute Aufgabe. Er hat vor allem für den Frieden der Gemeinschaft zu sorgen. "Friede" ist für Benedikt der umfassendere Begriff, der auch die "Einmütigkeit" einschließt. "Nach einem Streit noch vor Sonnenuntergang zum Frieden zurückkehren" (RB 4,73) ist ihm eines der wichtigen "Werkzeuge der geistlichen Kunst". Bevor auf die Aufgabe des Abtes näher eingegangen werden kann, ist zunächst das Selbstverständnis benediktinischer Mönchsgemeinschaften zu klären, in denen der Abt sein geistliches Leitungsamt ausübt.

1. Zum Selbstverständnis benediktinischer Mönchsgemeinschaften

Benediktinische Mönchsgemeinschaften sehen ihr besonderes Vorbild in der Urgemeinde, wie die Apostelgeschichte sie zeichnet (Apg 2:44-47; 4:32-35). Innerhalb der (Volks)-Kirche wollen sie mit besonderer Ernsthaftigkeit den Weg des Evangeliums gehen (vgl. RB, Prolog 21; 73,3) und so in besonderer Zeichenhaftigkeit leben, was die Kirche insgesamt ihrer ursprünglichen Bestimmung gemäß sein soll. Darin - und nicht in besonderen Aktivitäten - sehen sie ihre missionarische Bedeutung. Das Mönchtum entsteht als eine an der Urkirche orientierte Form der Heiligung in dem Augenblick der Kirchengeschichte, als die Kirche den Staat und die ganze Gesellschaft erfaßt hat und damit die Versuchung der "billigen Gnade" gegeben war. Benedikt bezeichnet das Kloster als "Haus Gottes", als "Werkstatt" geistlichen Lebens oder auch als eine "Schule für den Dienst des Herrn". Das Kloster ist eine "Kirche im kleinen": *ecclesiola in ecclesia*. Diese uns heute geläufige Vorstellung findet sich bei Benedikt zwar nicht mit diesen Worten, wohl aber der Sache nach, und sie hat auffällige Parallelen im protestantischen Pietismus (wie schon Karl Holl, Enthusiasmus und Bußgebet beim griechischen Mönchtum, 1898, S. 168 feststellte). Auch hier ging es den Gläubigen, die sich in den Hauskreisen und

Konventikeln oder in Gerhard Tersteegens "Pilgerhütte" auf der Otterbeck zusammenfanden, um eine Wiederbelebung des urkichlichen Enthusiasmus.

Gemäß der Benediktusregel bindet sich der einzelne Mönch an das Kloster durch ein Gelübde, in dem er *stabilitas, conversatio morum* und *oboedientia* verspricht: *Stabilitas* = Beständigkeit meint das "Bleiben" in der Liebe Christi, das denen, die zu Christus gehören, im Johannesevangelium als jetzt schon geschenkte Erfahrung und zugleich als das entscheidende "Gebot" vor Augen gestellt wird. *Conversatio* ist die Iterativform von *conversio* = Bekehrung, womit die Taufe gemeint ist, die es in einem entsprechenden Lebenswandel täglich neu zu verwirklichen gilt.

Oboedientia ist wie auch das althochdeutsche Äquivalent "gehorsami" ein weiblicher Begriff. Wir sollten ihn vielleicht besser mit "Gehorsamkeit" statt mit "Gehorsam" übersetzen. Gemeint ist eine Grundausrichtung, eine Empfänglichkeit für das Wort Gottes, nicht ein Funktionieren. "Höre, Israel!" Dieser zentralen biblischen Forderung entsprechend beginnt die Benediktusregel mit der Mahnung: "Höre, mein Sohn..., neige das Ohr deines Herzens!" Ziel des Hörens ist die Rückkehr zu Dem, Den wir durch unsere Eigenwilligkeit, "durch die Trägheit des Ungehorsams" verlassen haben. *Oboedientia* ist die Bereitschaft, "für Christus, den Herrn und wahren König" zu kämpfen. *Oboedientia* ist darum die Bereitschaft, für den geistlichen Kampf konkrete Weisungen zu empfangen - die "Weisung des Meisters", den "Zuspruch des gütigen Vaters" -, damit der Lebenswandel in Wahrheit zu einem gewandelten Leben führt: "zu jener vollendeten Gottesliebe, die alle Furcht vertreibt" (RB 7,67). Benedikt ist überzeugt, daß dies "der Herr... schon jetzt gütig durch den Heiligen Geist erweisen" wird an denen, die diesen Weg konsequent gehen (RB 7,70). So mahnt er im Prolog seiner Regel: "Öffnen wir unsere Augen dem göttlichen Licht, und hören wir mit aufgeschrecktem Ohr, wozu uns die Stimme Gottes täglich mahnt und aufruft: 'Heute, wenn ihr seine Stimme hört, verhärtet eure Herzen nicht!' (Ps 95:8). Und wiederum: 'Wer Ohren hat zu hören, der höre, was der Geist den Gemeinden sagt!' (Offb 2:7). ... Gürten wir uns also mit Glauben und Treue im Guten, und gehen wir unter der Führung des Evangeliums Seine Wege, damit wir Ihn schauen dürfen, Der uns in Sein Reich gerufen hat."

2. Der Abt als Stellvertreter Christi

Der Meister, auf dessen Weisung zu hören Benedikt dem Mönch ans Herz legt, ist primär und letztlich Christus, der als der auferstandene Herr in seiner Kirche gegenwärtig ist durch den Heiligen Geist. Gegenwärtig ist Er in seiner Kirche aber auch durch verschiedene sozusagen leibhaftige Bezeugungsgestalten, vor allem durch das Wort der Heiligen Schrift, dann aber auch durch die, die Er zu "Verwaltern" (vgl. Lk 12,42) seines Hauses bestellt hat. Verwalter Christi im Kloster ist der Abt. In diesem Sinne ist er "Oberer", lateinisch: *maior* (RB 2,1) - "Hausmeier". In der Sicht des Glaubens steht er an Christi Statt. Zweimal betont Benedikt in seinem Kapitel über den Gehorsam, daß ihm das Wort Christi gilt: "Wer euch hört, hört mich" (Lk 10:16; RB 5,6.15). Konkret ist darum der Abt der "Meister", auf dessen Weisung der Mönch hören soll. Freilich: "Deshalb darf der Abt nur lehren oder bestimmen und befehlen, was der Weisung des Herrn entspricht" (RB 2,4), und er wird vor Gott selbst Rechenschaft ablegen müssen über seine Verwaltung.

Der Abt muß der Lehrer seiner Mönche sein "mehr durch sein Leben als durch sein Lehren"; er muß die Weisungen Gottes "durch sein Beispiel veranschaulichen" (RB 2,12). Ja, er muß für Christus, den Herrn, den er im Kloster vertritt und bezeugt, vor allem dadurch transparent sein, daß er seinen Mönchen die Liebe Christi konkret erfahrbar macht. Die Bezeichnung "Abt" weist darauf hin, daß es vor allem seine Aufgabe ist, dafür zu sorgen, daß im Kloster die geistliche Atmosphäre herrscht, in der das Apostelwort Röm 8:15 zur lebendigen Erfahrung werden kann: "Ihr habt den Geist empfangen, der euch zu Söhnen macht, den Geist, in dem wir rufen: Abba, Vater!" (RB 2,2). Darum werde er "mit 'Herr' und 'Abt' angeredet, weil man im Glauben erkennt, daß er Christi Stelle vertritt" (RB 63,13).

"Abt", lateinisch: *abbas*, ist abgeleitet von dem aramäischen Wort, mit dem Jesus seinen himmlischen Vater anredete (Mk 14:36) und mit dem Röm 8:15 und Gal 4:6 das Zutrauen seinen Ausdruck findet, das wir als Kinder Gottes zu diesem himmlischen Vater haben dürfen und das der Geist Gottes selbst in uns wirkt. Es mag verwundern, daß man gerade mit diesem Wort die Christus-Stellvertretung des Abtes charakterisiert. Doch: "In der alten Kirche war man gewöhnt, Christus als Vater zu sehen, weil er neues Leben vermittelt" (G. Holzherr, Die Benediktusregel, 1980, S.59). Nach 1 Kor 4:15 versteht Paulus sich als Vater der von ihm gegründeten Gemeinde. Er hebt damit seine Bedeutung für seine Gemeinde ab von der der zahllosen "Pädagogen", die diese Gemeinde ebenfalls in der Lehre des Evangeliums unterweisen: "Doch habt ihr in Christus nicht viele Väter. Ich habe euch in Christus Jesus durch das Evangelium gezeugt." Wie Christus den Vater offenbart - "Wer mich gesehen hat, hat den Vater gesehen" (Joh 14:9) -, so soll auch der, der Ihn vertritt, die väterliche Liebe Gottes im Kloster bezeugen. Der Abt ist darum nicht nur Lehrer, sondern auch Hirt und Seelsorger.

In zwei längeren Kapiteln (RB 2 und RB 64) konkretisiert Benedikt das Bild des Abtes. Manches daraus habe ich schon zitiert. Ich möchte hier die wichtigsten Abschnitte über die Aufgaben des Abtes im Zusammenhang folgen lassen. Kapitel 2 hat Benedikt fast vollständig aus der Tradition übernommen. Es faßt vor allem das Meister-Jünger-Verhältnis ins Auge. Kapitel 64 ist wohl von Benedikt selbst verfaßt. Es faßt stärker die Gemeinschaft ins Auge, der der Abt vorsteht.

In Kapitel 2 heißt es: "Der Abt, der würdig ist, einem Kloster vorzustehen, muß immer bedenken, wie man ihn anredet, und er verwirkliche durch sein Tun, was diese Anrede für einen Oberen bedeutet. Der Glaube sagt ja: Er vertritt im Kloster die Stelle Christi; wird er doch mit dessen Namen angeredet nach dem Wort des Apostels: 'Ihr habt den Geist empfangen, der euch zu Söhnen macht, den Geist, in dem wir rufen: Abba, Vater!' (Röm 8:15). Deshalb darf der Abt nur lehren oder bestimmen und befehlen, was der Weisung des Herrn entspricht. Sein Befehl und seine Lehre sollen wie Sauerteig göttlicher Heilsgerechtigkeit die Herzen seiner Jünger durchdringen... Wer also den Namen 'Abt' annimmt, muß seinen Jüngern in zweifacher Weise als Lehrer vorstehen: Er mache alles Gute und Heilige mehr durch sein Leben als durch sein Reden sichtbar. Einsichtigen Jüngern wird er die Gebote des Herrn mit Worten darlegen, hartherzigen aber und einfältigen wird er die Weisungen Gottes durch sein Beispiel veranschaulichen. In seinem Handeln zeige er, was er seine Jünger lehrt, daß man nicht tun darf, was mit dem Gebot Gottes unvereinbar ist. Sonst würde er anderen predigen und dabei selbst verworfen werden. Gott könnte ihm eines Tages sein Versagen vorwerfen: 'Was zählst du meine Gebote auf und nimmst meinen Bund in deinen Mund? Dabei ist Zucht dir verhaßt, meine Worte wirfst du hinter dich' (Ps 50:16f.). Auch gilt: 'Du sahst im Auge deines Bruders den Splitter, in deinem hast du den Balken nicht bemerkt' (Mt 7:3). Der Abt bevorzuge im Kloster keinen wegen seines Ansehens. Den einen liebe er nicht mehr als den anderen, es sei denn, er finde einen, der eifriger ist in guten Werken und im Gehorsam. ... Der Abt soll also alle in gleicher Weise lieben, ein und dieselbe Ordnung lasse er für alle gelten - wie es jeder verdient. Wenn der Abt lehrt, halte er sich immer an das Beispiel des Apostels, der sagt: 'Tadle, ermutige, weise streng zurecht' (2 Tim 4:2). Das bedeutet für ihn: Er lasse sich vom Gespür für den rechten Augenblick leiten und verbinde Strenge mit gutem Zureden. Er zeige den entschlossenen Ernst des Meisters und die liebevolle Güte des Vaters... Er muß wissen, welch schwierige und mühevolle Aufgabe er auf sich nimmt: Menschen zu führen und der Eigenart vieler zu dienen. Muß er doch dem einen mit gewinnenden, dem anderen mit tadelnden, dem dritten mit überzeugenden Worten begegnen. Nach der Eigenart und Fassungskraft jedes einzelnen soll er sich auf alle einstellen und auf sie eingehen... Vor allem darf er über das Heil der ihm Anvertrauten nicht hinwegsehen oder es geringschätzen und sich größere Sorge machen um vergängliche, irdische und hinfällige Dinge. Stets denke er daran: Er hat die Aufgabe übernommen, Menschen zu führen, für die er einmal Rechenschaft ablegen muß... Immer in Furcht vor der bevorstehenden Untersuchung des Hirten über die ihm anvertrauten Schafe, sorgt er für seine eigene Rechenschaft, wenn er sich um die der anderen kümmert."

"Menschen führen" heißt "der Eigenart vieler dienen". Dem entspricht die Weisung von Kapitel 34, in dem deutlich wird, daß der Friede der Gemeinschaft nicht auf Uniformität beruht, sondern darauf, daß jeder der Brüder sich in seiner Eigenart und seinen Bedürfnissen geliebt weiß: "Man halte sich also an das Wort der Schrift: 'Jedem wurde so viel zugeteilt, wie er nötig hatte' (Apg 4:35). Damit sagen wir nicht, daß jemand wegen seines Ansehens bevorzugt werden soll, was ferne sei. Wohl aber nehme man Rücksicht auf Schwächen. Wer wenig braucht, danke Gott und sei nicht traurig. Wer mehr braucht, werde demütig wegen seiner Schwächen und nicht überheblich wegen der ihm erwiesenen Barmherzigkeit. So werden alle Glieder der Gemeinschaft in Frieden sein" (RB 34,1-5).

In Kapitel 64 heißt es: "Der eingesetzte Abt bedenke stets, welche Bürde er auf sich genommen hat und wem er Rechenschaft über seine Verwaltung ablegen muß. Er wisse, daß er mehr helfen als herrschen soll... Immer gehe ihm Barmherzigkeit über strenges Gericht (Jak 2:13), damit er selbst Gleiches erfahre. Er hasse die Fehler, er liebe die Brüder. Muß er aber zurechtweisen, handle er klug und gehe nicht zu weit; sonst könnte das Gefäß zerbrechen, wenn er den Rost allzu heftig auskratzen will. Stets rechne er mit seiner eigenen Gebrechlichkeit. Er denke daran, daß man das geknickte Rohr nicht zerbrechen darf (Jes 42:3). Damit wollen wir nicht sagen, er dürfe Fehler wuchern lassen, vielmehr schneide er sie klug und liebevoll weg, wie es seiner Ansicht nach jedem weiterhilft... Er suche, mehr geliebt als gefürchtet zu werden. Er sei nicht stürmisch und nicht ängstlich, nicht maßlos und nicht engstirnig, nicht eifersüchtig und allzu argwöhnisch, sonst kommt er nie zur Ruhe. In seinen Befehlen sei er vorausschauend und besonnen. Bei geistlichen wie weltlichen Aufträgen unterscheide er genau und halte Maß. Er denke an die maßvolle Unterscheidung des heiligen Jakob, der sprach: 'Wenn ich meine Herden unterwegs überanstrenge, werden alle an einem Tag zugrundegehen' (Gen 33:13). Diese und andere Zeugnisse maßvoller Unterscheidung, der Mutter aller Tugenden, beherzige er. So halte er in allem Maß, damit die Starken finden, wonach sie verlangen, und die Schwachen nicht davonlaufen."

3. Die Einbindung des Abtes in die klösterliche Gemeinschaft

Es dürfte deutlich geworden sein, daß Benedikt an das Amt des Abtes hohe Anforderungen stellt: Ihm ist aufgetragen, dafür zu sorgen, daß die Gemeinschaft der Brüder, die sich ihm anvertraut, auf dem Weg des Heiles bleibt. "Er wisse, daß er mehr helfen als herrschen soll" (RB 64,8). Darum muß er in der Liebe, die er allen gleichermaßen erweisen soll, "der Eigenart vieler dienen" (RB 2,31) und in weiser *discretio* maßvoll zu unterscheiden wissen, was jedem einzelnen zuzumuten ist. Das hierfür notwendige Gespür ist seine Weise der "Gehorsamkeit". Immer wieder weist Benedikt den Abt darauf hin, daß er vor Gott "Rechenschaft über seine Verwaltung ablegen muß" (RB 64,7). Entscheidend ist vor allem, daß er selber lebt, was er anderen predigt, daß er selber in überzeugender Weise ein eifriger Mönch ist.

Was dem Abt in besonderer Weise aufgetragen ist, daran sind schließlich alle beteiligt. Von allen Mönchen erwartet Benedikt, daß sie beseelt sind von einem guten Eifer - nicht von einem "bitteren und bösen Eifer, der von Gott trennt", sondern vom "guten Eifer, der von der Sünde trennt". In RB 72 heißt es: "Diesen Eifer sollen also die Mönche mit glühender Liebe in die Tat umsetzen, das bedeutet: Sie sollen einander in gegenseitiger Achtung zuvorkommen; ihre körperlichen und charakterlichen Schwächen sollen sie mit unerschöpflicher Geduld ertragen; im gegenseitigen Gehorsam sollen sie miteinader wetteifern; keiner achte auf das eigene Wohl, sondern mehr auf das des anderen; die Bruderliebe sollen sie einander selbstlos erweisen.... Christus sollen sie überhaupt nichts vorziehen. Er führe uns gemeinsam zum ewigen Leben." Hinter diesen Sätzen steht die Überzeugung, daß Christus selbst uns in jedem der Brüder - also nicht nur im Abt - begegnet.

Um bei sich selbst den guten Eifer vom bösen unterscheiden zu können, bedarf es einer sensiblen Kenntnis des eigenen Herzens. Gegen die Gefahr der Selbsttäuschung ist hier der Abt wie jeder andere Mönch auf die Hilfe eines persönlichen geistlichen Vaters angewiesen. Und wie der Abt so ist auch die ganze Gemeinschaft darauf angewiesen, daß die Mönche in den verschiedenen Bereichen des Klosters einander mit ihren Fähigkeiten, mit Liebe und Sachverstand dienen. Die verschiedenen Dienstämter im Kloster mit geeigneten Brüdern zu besetzen - sie notfalls auch wieder abzusetzen -, ist freilich wieder die besondere Aufgabe des Abtes. Benedikt hält das "für angebracht zur Wahrung des Friedens und der Liebe" (RB 65,11).

Gerade hier konzentriert sich nun aber die Kompetenz des Abtes, ist damit jedoch auch in besonderer Weise die Gefahr des Machtmißbrauchs oder zumindest des Mißgriffes gegeben. Darum fügt Benedikt dem Kapitel über den Abt (RB 2) ein eigenes Kapitel an über "die Einberufung der Brüder zum Rat" (RB 3). Darin heißt es: "Sooft etwas Wichtiges im Kloster zu behandeln ist, soll der Abt die ganze Gemeinschaft zusammenrufen und selbst darlegen, worum es geht. Er soll den Rat der Brüder anhören und dann mit sich selbst zu Rate gehen. Was er für zuträglich hält, das tue er. Daß aber alle zur Beratung zu rufen seien, haben wir deshalb gesagt, weil der Herr oft einem Jüngeren offenbart, was das Bessere ist. Die Brüder sollen ... nicht anmaßend und hartnäckig ihre eigenen Ansichten verteidigen. Vielmehr liegt die Entscheidung im Ermessen des Abtes: Was er für heilsamer hält, darin sollen ihm alle gehorchen. Wie es jedoch den Jüngeren zukommt, dem Meister zu gehorchen, muß er seinerseits alles vorausschauend und gerecht ordnen... Der Abt muß seine Entscheidungen immer in Gottesfurcht treffen und sich dabei an die Regel halten." Er muß wissen, daß er sich ohne Zweifel für all seine Entscheidungen vor Gott, dem gerechten Richter, zu verantworten hat. Wenn weniger wichtige Angelegenheiten des Klosters zu behandeln sind, soll er nur die Älteren um Rat fragen, lesen wir doch in der Schrift: 'Tue alles mit Rat, dann brauchst du nach der Tat nichts zu bereuen'" (Sir 32:24). (Mit den hier genannten "Älteren" sind nicht die Greise gemeint, sonderen der Ältestenrat als eine Einrichtung mit z.T. gewählten Vertretern der Mönchsgemeinschaft, die wir uns bei Benedikt nicht allzu klein vorzustellen haben.)

Der Rat der Brüder gehört zu jenen Elementen klösterlichen Lebens, die infolge des II. Vatikanischen Konzils wieder neu an Bedeutung gewonnen haben. Als Einrichtung hat es ihn immer gegeben. Doch da Benedikt die Entscheidung ins Ermessen des Abtes stellt, war es notwendig geworden, juristisch genau festzulegen, in welchen Angelegenheiten der Abt an eine Mehrheitsentscheidung gebunden ist. Darüberhinaus war die von Benedikt vorgesehene Beratungsfunktion im allgemeinen sehr verkümmert. Doch hat ein neues Verständnis dieses Kapitels wieder zu der Einsicht geführt, daß das Zusammenrufen der ganzen Gemeinschaft zur Beratung notwendige Voraussetzung für die Einmütigkeit der Gemeinschaft ist - für eine Einmütigkeit im Sinne der *con-cordia* (vgl. RB 64,1), des Eines-Herzens-Seins (Apg 4:32), nicht bloß des *con-sensus* (vgl. RB 64,3). Eine nicht nur quantitative, sondern auch qualitative Berücksichtigung der Stimmen, wie sie hierfür nötig ist, ist freilich juristisch schwer zu fassen. Daß der Abt nach eingehender Beratung "mit sich selbst zu Rate gehen soll", was er für "zuträglicher" und "heilsamer" hält, und es bei ihm liegt, entsprechend für alle verbindlich zu entscheiden, gibt ihm die

Möglichkeit, die Bedenken von Minderheiten zu berücksichtigen, ohne daß diese andererseits für die Gesamtheit ständig zu einer Blockade werden. (Ähnlich muß auch verstanden werden, wenn das I. Vatikanische Konzil dem Papst die Vollmacht zuschreibt, in Glaubensfragen "aus sich, nicht aber aufgrund der Zustimmung der Kirche" zu entscheiden.)

Freilich betont Benedikt gerade hier nochmals, daß der Abt sich "für all seine Entscheidungen vor Gott, dem gerechten Richter, zu verantworten hat" (RB 3,11). Benedikt rechnet jedoch auch mit der Möglichkeit, daß ein Abt verwerflich handelt, ungerecht oder herrschsüchtig wird oder daß er auf bestimmten Anordnungen besteht, obwohl der betroffene Mönch damit überfordert ist. Benedikt sagt, der Mönch solle trotzdem gehorchen: "überzeugt, daß es so für ihn gut ist; und im Vertrauen auf Gottes Hilfe gehorche er aus Liebe" (RB 68,4f.)."Im Kloster ausharren bis zum Tod", wozu sich der Mönch im Gelübde der "Beständigkeit" verpflichtet hat, bedeutet immer auch: "in Geduld an den Leiden Christi Anteil haben" (RB, Prolog 50). Wahre Liebe, die bemüht ist, die anderen in ihrem Sosein anzunehmen, ist immer auch ein Leiden-Können und Leiden-Mögen. Viele, die die katholische Kirche als Heilige verehrt, sind auf dem Weg ihrer Heiligung gereift in der Liebe durch Leiden, die ihnen in der Kirche zugefügt worden sind.

4. Der Dienst des Abtes und das Amt des Bischofs

Vieles von dem, was Benedikt über den Dienst des Abtes in seiner *ecclesiola* sagt, gilt auch für den Bischof in seinem kirchlichen Amtsbereich. Die Parallele ist immer wieder betont worden und kommt heute auch im äußeren Erscheinungsbild zum Ausdruck: Wie der Bischof so trägt auch der Abt bei feierlichen Gottesdiensten als Symbole der ihm übertragenen Stellvertretung Christi die Mitra (als priesterliche Kopfbedeckung), den Hirtenstab, ein Kreuz und einen Ring (als Zeichen einer Verbundenheit mit seiner Kirche, wie sie Eph 5:32 in Parallele zum Ehebund gesehen wird). Das äußerlich gleiche Erscheinungsbild täuscht jedoch insofern, als die Bestellung eines Abtes sich nach katholischem Verständnis sehr von der Bestellung eines Bischofs unterscheidet. Ein Bischof wird ordiniert und wird Bischof durch die Ordination. Er wird durch die Handauflegung zu einem Glied in der Traditionskette der Nachfolger der Apostel.

Ein Abt wird dadurch Abt, daß er seine Wahl annimmt. Die nachfolgende liturgische Einsetzung in sein Amt ist lediglich eine *benedictio*, eine Einsegnung, mit der z.B. nicht die Vollmacht übertragen wird - wie bei der Bischofsordination-

, Priester zu weihen. Will der Abt, daß jemand in seinem Kloster zum Priester geweiht wird, braucht er dazu den Bischof.

Das entspricht durchaus dem Abtsverständnis Benedikts. Aus der Mönchstradition vor ihm übernimmt er die Wendung, daß der *Glaube* im Abt denjenigen sieht, der im Kloster an Christi Stelle steht, Christus repräsentiert. Benedikt vermeidet das sehr institutionell klingende Wort "Stellvertreter". Und er läßt aus der gleichen Quelle (der sog. Magisterregel) alle Passagen weg, in denen der Abt in Parallele zum Bischof, zum Klerus gesehen wird (z.B. Magisterregel 11,9ff.). Benedikt war selbst wohl auch nicht Priester - geschweige denn Bischof - und sieht auch nicht vor, daß der Abt, wie das heute der Fall ist, zugleich Priester ist. Die Bedeutung der *ecclesiola* des Mönchsklosters liegt in der geistlichen Autorität. Im Maße der Qualität ihres geistlichen Zeugnisses hat sie in der Gesamtkirche und für die Gesamtkirche eine prophetische Aufgabe. Diesem klösterlichen Selbstverständnis entspricht das benediktinische Verständnis äbtlicher Autorität. Es ist eine geistliche Autorität, die Autorität dessen, den seine Brüder zu ihrem Abt gewählt haben, weil sie in ihm das Wirken des Heiligen Geistes erkannt haben.

Vielleicht ist gerade dieses Verständnis eine Hilfe in der heutigen Krise kirchlicher Autorität, einer Krise allgemeiner Verunsicherung, in der Autorität ja nicht einfach abgelehnt, in der vielmehr zugleich überzeugende Autorität gesucht wird. Neureligiöse Bewegungen mit autoritärer Struktur haben Hochkonjunktur. Wie es scheint, sind jedoch viele ihrer Autoritätspersonen weder besonders sensibel noch auf das Heil derer bedacht, die sich ihnen anvertrauen. Doch wo religiöse Autorität nicht transparent wird für die Offenbarung der Liebe Gottes, sondern die eigene Ehre sucht, führt sie unweigerlich zur Unfreiheit. Dagegen können benediktinische Mönche vieler Generationen bezeugen, was Benedikt am Ende des Prologs seiner Regel denen sagt, die auf seine Weisung hören: "Wer im klösterlichen Leben und im Glauben fortschreitet, dem wird das Herz weit, und er läuft in unsagbarem Glück der Liebe den Weg der Gebote Gottes."

Warum ich trotzdem Ökumeniker bin
Statement von Günter Wagner (Baptist)*

I.

Vor kurzem las ich einen Hinweis auf den Abschluß eines bilateralen ökumenischen Dialogs. Er war überschäumend enthusiastisch und explodierte vor Freude über "das wichtigste Ereignis in der Geschichte" seiner "Kirche in diesem Jahrhundert". Schön, daß es das gibt! - Ich denke auch an eine Tagung ostafrikanischer Theologen in Nairobi. Ein anglikanischer Theologe leitete uns in einem bewegenden Gebet und schrie mit den Worten des Psalmisten wie ein dürstender Hirsch nach frischem Wasser "in unserer ökumenischen Wüste". In der Erinnerung geht mir seine ergreifende Klage immer wieder ans Mark. Schön, daß einer noch so schreien kann!

In meinem ökumenischen Engagement bewege ich mich ständig - und vielleicht auch in schneller werdendem Rhythmus - zwischen enthusiastischer Freude und sich befreien wollender Klage. Zur Zeit wandere ich durch die Wüste.

Aber ich will mir sagen, daß das ein undankbarer Satz ist. In einem amerikanischen Kirchenlied heißt es: "Count your many blessings, name them one by one". Wenn ich über ökumenisch schon Erreichtes nachdenken würde und aufzählen sollte, wie viele tausend Fäden in diesem Jahrhundert zwischen den Kirchen und ihren Gliedern im gottesdienstlichen Leben, im gemeinsamen Zeugnis und in praktischer Zusammenarbeit geknüpft worden sind, dann brauchte ich Komputerunterstützung.

Die Erfahrung der Wüste ist aber nicht weniger wirklich: Rückschritte nach dem zweiten Vatikanischen Konzil; Gedächtnisschwund, was die Leuenberger Konkordie angeht; kirchenamtliche Domestizierung des durch die Lima-Texte ausgelösten Konvergenzprozesses (den Protestanten sind die Dokumente "zu katholisch und orthodox"; Katholiken und Orthodoxe meinen, Protestanten müßten noch ein wenig mehr nachdenken und sakramentalen Tiefgang gewinnen). Im Schatten der politischen Entspannung zwischen Ost und West werden in den Kirchen die Bogen neu gespannt: in Osteuropa brechen Konflikte zwischen Katholiken und Orthodoxen neu auf; russische Exil-Orthodoxe kommen zurück und trüben die Gewässer; einheimische Orthodoxe oder Katholiken suchen einen Status als Staatskirche und fangen an, sich staatlicher Machtmittel gegen andere Kirchen zu bedienen; Freikirchen meinen, unter dem kommunistischen Regime habe es größeren ökumenischen Frieden gegeben; alle beklagen sich über die rivalisierende Art, in der evangelikale Gruppen in Osteuropa missionarisch

* Mit Genehmigung des Verlages entnommen aus: UNA SANCTA 4/1991.

aktiv werden. Die katholische Kirche wappnet sich, Europa zu "re-missionieren": dem können die Protestanten nicht tatenlos zusehen und entwerfen ihre eigene Strategie. Weltweit geht das (nun wahrhaftig nicht furchterregende) "Gespenst" der Frauen-Ordination um und entzweit die Kirchen. Der weite Bereich der ökumenisch zu verantwortenden ethischen und politischen Entscheide ruft nach einem umsichtigen gemeinsamen Vorgehen, wollen wir als Kirchen uns nicht auch noch von dieser Seite her auseinanderdividieren lassen.

II.

Unsere ökumenischen Erfahrungen heute dürften je nach Situation verschieden aussehen. Meinem ökumenischen Wohlbefinden sind zur Zeit zwei Umstände besonders abträglich. Das eine ist die Situation in der Diözese Chur (Schweiz), in deren geographischem Raum ich lebe. Seit nun schon drei Jahren vergeht keine Woche, ohne daß nicht die Medien etwas über Bischof Wolfgang Haas zu berichten hätten. Es ist für mich unfaßbar, wie in heutiger Zeit ein Bischof seine Diözese so "regieren" kann, wie er es tut. Ich will die anklagenden Reizwörter nicht aufzählen, muß aber unterstreichen, daß protestantische Stimmen sehr verhalten sind, während die schärfsten Klagen vom katholischen Kirchenvolk und den Priestern selber kommen. Wie lange soll dieses der Kirche abträgliche Schauspiel mit einem ausgeflippten[1] Bischof als Hauptdarsteller noch weitergehen? Die katholische Diözese leidet (und wir mit ihr), und die ökumenischen Auswirkungen sind katastrophal. Ich will mich vor Verallgemeinerungen hüten; trotzdem melden sich die ganze Kirche betreffende Fragen an.

Als Baptist habe ich aber kein Recht, mich anmaßend über hierarchischen Machtmißbrauch in der katholischen Kirche (es gibt ihn nicht nur in der Diözese Chur!) zu beklagen. Machtmißbrauch, der zum Widerstand förmlich zwingt, gibt es auch im Bereich der baptistischen Weltgemeinschaft. In den letzten zwölf Jahren hat es in der "Southern Baptist Convention" (der Baptisten im Süden der USA) zwischen "Konservativen" und "Fundamentalisten" einen Kampf um die Macht über die Kontrolle der der Kirche gehörenden Institutionen gegeben, den die "Fundamentalisten" mit raffinierter Ausnützung der Befugnisse der jedes Jahr neu gewählten Präsidenten der Kirche gewonnen haben.[2] Dr. E. Glenn Hinson,

---

[1] Der jüngst verstorbene katholische Moraltheologe Professor Franz Boeckle bescheinigte dem Herrn Bischof einen "pathologischen Ausfall an Klugheit" (Religion & Gesellschaft 8/91, 25. April 1991, S. 11).

Professor der Kirchengeschichte am Southern Baptist Theological Seminary in Louisville/Kentucky und früheres Mitglied der Kommission für Glauben und Kirchenverfassung des Ökumenischen Rates, wird von ihnen besonders angegriffen, weil er Fundamentalisten eben Fundamentalisten nennt und ihre Vergötzung der Bibel nicht mitvollziehen kann, sondern sie als Irrlehre bezeichnet. Er ist zur Zeit für vier Monate Gastprofessor für Kirchengeschichte an der Baptistischen Theologischen Hochschule in Rüschlikon bei Zürich, an der ich seit 1958 Neues Testament lehre. Weil wir ihn für ein Semester als Gast eingeladen haben, wird uns nun durch Majoritätsentscheidung der Missionsgesellschaft der Southern Baptists ihre finanzielle Unterstützung (die etwa 40 % unseres Budgets ausmacht) gegen alle bestehenden Abmachungen innerhalb von 10 Wochen entzogen. Ich verrate hier keine internen Geheimnisse, sondern beziehe mich u. a. auf die Tageszeitungen, die manchmal präzisere Auskunft geben als kirchliche Pressedienste.[3]

Die Baptistische Theologische Hochschule in Rüschlikon wird die Attacke, so Gott will, überleben, genauso wie die katholischen Kirchgemeinden der Diözese Chur, so Gott will, aus ihrer Bedrängnis gestärkt hervorgehen werden - jedenfalls beten und wirken wir für beides. Aber was mir im Blick auf die "Southern Baptists" Kummer macht, ist der Einfluß ihrer Fehlentwicklung auf den Baptistischen Weltbund und auf ökumenische Entwicklungen in den USA. Sie sind mit ihren mehr als 15 Millionen Mitgliedern die größte einzelne protestantische Kirche der Vereinigten Staaten und machen etwa 42 % der Mitglieder des Baptistischen Weltbundes aus.

Beide Situationen - die in der Diözese Chur und die innerhalb meiner eigenen konfessionellen Weltgemeinschaft - haben, wie gesagt, eines gemeinsam: den Machtmißbrauch in der Kirche. Welche Schlußfolgerungen ziehen wir für die Frage nach der "Einheit, die wir suchen"? Der Zug der hierarchisch-sakramental orientierten monolithischen Einheit ist für mich genauso abgefahren wie der der selbsternannten fundamentalistischen Diktatoren. Wann werden wir dahin kommen, daß wir die geistliche Vergewaltigung in der Kirche "an allen Orten" überwinden, nachdem in unsern Tagen so viele weltliche Diktatoren von ihren Sesseln gehoben worden sind? In diesem Licht ist der "Paradigmenwechsel", von dem Konrad Raiser spricht[4], nicht nur zu bedenken, sondern zu fordern und zu

[2] Vgl. den Artikel von Glenn Hinson im nächsten Heft (1/92) von UNA SANCTA.

[3] Richmond Times-Dispatch, 10. Oktober 1991.

fördern. Wir müssen den Umgang miteinander als "Hausgenossen" im gemeinsamen Hause des Vaters - nicht des autoritären "Königs" - lernen. Das sind für mich keine theoretischen Fragen "ökumenischer Thologie", sondern Fragen der eigenen christlichen Identität - eben die Frage, wo man "zuhause" ist.

III.

Orientierung suche ich im Neuen Testament - das verwundert ja auch nicht. Aber vielleicht muß man es doch immer wieder sagen: das Neue Testament bezeugt *die Einheit* des Volkes Gottes, des Leibes Christi, der vom Geiste Gottes gewirkten Gemeinschaft der Glaubenden und entläßt uns unter keinen Umständen aus der Verantwortung, die von Gott geschenkte Einheit auch zur Geltung kommen zu lassen im Gottesdienst, in missionarischer Verkündigung und in allem "weltlichen" Tun. Das allein begründet zur Genüge, "warum ich trotzdem Ökumeniker bin". Ich bin "Ökumeniker", weil ich Neutestamentler bin. So einfach ist das - und selbstverständlich.

Aber man braucht keine wissenschaftlichen Kommentare zu konsultieren, um ein paar Anfragen an die heutige ökumenische Diskussion zu stellen. Kurz gesagt - und deshalb

auch nicht differenziert genug:
(1) Die neutestamentlichen Schriften implizieren verschieden akzentuierte Ekklesiologien (auch die "Lima-Texte" stellen das fest). Woher kommt eigentlich der Drang zur Uniformität bei der Frage nach der Gestalt der "einen" Kirche? Weshalb tut man sich so schwer bei der Anerkennung legitimer Vielfalt und stellt immer noch "Einheit" und "Vielfalt" gegenüber, statt mit der Vielfalt *in* der Einheit *ernstzumachen?*
(2) Paulus unterscheidet Apostel, Propheten, Lehrer ... (1 Kor 12,29; vgl. Eph 4,11). Weshalb wird der Dienst der Apostel (und ihrer "Nachfolger") allen anderen Ämtern *über*geordnet?
(3) Weshalb werden überhaupt die Gaben der "Ämter" - trotz der eindeutigen Äußerungen des Paulus zur Frage nach der "Hierarchie der Wahrheiten"[5] - *über*

[4] Ökumene im Übergang. Paradigmenwechsel in der ökumenischen Bewegung? München 1989.

[5] Ich "spiele" ernst mit diesem Ausdruck. Vgl. "Der Begriff der 'Hierarchie der Wahrheiten' - eine ökumenische Interpretation", Anhang zum Sechsten Bericht der Gemeinsamen Arbeitsgruppe des Ökumenischen Rates der Kirchen und der

die Gaben von "Glaube, Hoffnung, Liebe" gestellt (1 Kor 12,31; 13,13)? Ich bin nun - weiß Gott - mit Leib und Seele Theologe und habe auch über dreißig Jahre lang versucht, Theologie ökumenisch zu betreiben. Aber angesichts der Tatsache, daß der Apostel Paulus "Glaube, Hoffnung, Liebe" *definitiv höher* einschätzt als "Weisheit" und "Erkenntnis" (1 Kor 12,8; 13,2.8), frage ich mich doch, woher eigentlich die im ökumenischen Ringen immer wieder sichtbar werdende Überheblichkeit der *"Theologie"* gegenüber der *Praxis* christlicher Existenz kommt. Stehen Glaube, Hoffnung, Liebe (und zwar primär als *Praxis*, nicht als inhaltliche Beschreibung) oder Weisheit und Erkenntnis an der Spitze der Hierarchie? Steht hier paulinische "apostolische" Autorität in der ökumenischen Bewegung in Geltung oder nicht?

(4) Und weshalb denkt man, wenn von *sichtbarer* Einheit die Rede ist, offenkundig immer zuerst an die die Einheit symbolisieren sollenden Personen und Strukturen und nicht an die Sichtbarwerdung von Glaube (Röm 1,8), Hoffnung (1 Petr 3,15) und Liebe (Joh 13,34-35). Ich gehöre nicht zu denen, die immer gleich fragen: "Was würde Jesus tun/sagen, wenn" - obwohl das natürlich eine hilfreiche Frage ist. Jedenfalls kommt mir Matthäus 5,23-24 in den Sinn und damit die Lust zu "übersetzen": "Wenn dich deine Liebe zu Gott treibt, in die Geheimnisse der Trinität einzudringen und in das Geheimnis der Liebe zwischen Vater, Sohn und Heiligem Geist, und dir dabei einfällt, daß dein Bruder sich über deinen Mangel an Liebe beklagt, so unterbrich deine Meditation und tue, was die Liebe gebietet; dann fahre fort, die geheimnisvolle Liebe in der Trinität zu ergründen."

(5) Das Neue Testament bewahrt uns vor der Idealisierung von "Einheit". Die "Urgemeinde" war voller Konflikte. Die Erfahrung der "communio" schloß Spannungen nicht aus (1 Kor 11). Die Apostel blieben von Auseinandersetzungen nicht verschont (Gal 1-2; 2 Kor 10-12). Die Einheit der Gemeinde war vielfach bedroht (1 Kor 1ff.; 1.2.3 Joh). Vielleicht sollten wir uns für eine gebührende Zeit weniger mit der Ausarbeitung ökumeischer Einheitsmodelle am Reißbrett konzentrieren, als vielmehr auf das Verstehen und Bejahen der Einheit der Kirche als Prozeß[6] einlassen und uns begreifend in Konfliktbewältigung einüben. Das ist leichter gesagt als getan (s. oben). Und wenn uns das Wissen um die Schwierigkeiten zum Gebet treibt, so gehört das eben auch - und nicht als letztes! - zur Suche nach dem gemeinsamen Leben und Dienst.

römisch-katholischen Kirche, Genf/Rom 1990, in: UNA SANCTA 45 (1990), 262-270. Ich schätze den Bericht. Die oben gestellte Anfrage bleibt.

[6] Christian Link/ Ulrich Luz/ Lukas Vischer, Sie aber hielten fest an der Gemeinschaft ... Einheit der Kirche als Prozeß im Neuen Testament und heute. Zürich, Benziger Verlag 1988.

IV.

Impulse für ökumenisches Engagement kommen nicht nur aus dem Neuen Testament. Alles, was wir heute über die Themen "Gerechtigkeit, Frieden und Bewahrung der Schöpfung" wissen, reicht aus, um uns Christen buchstäblich zusammenzutreiben und unsere Verantwortung gemeinsam wahrzunehmen - anders geht es ja gar nicht. Ich meine, darüber kann es auch gar keine Diskussion geben. Ich schlage die heutige Tageszeitung auf und lese: "Mehr als 500 Millionen Menschen sind heute unterernährt, und Jahr für Jahr sterben schätzungsweise 15 Millionen Frauen, Männer oder Kinder, weil sie nicht genug zu essen bekommen."[7] Vielleicht hat es nie zuvor einen Kontext gegeben, in dem das Wort Jakobus 4,17 so gewichtig geworden ist wie in unseren Tagen: "Wer nun weiß, Gutes zu tun und tut's nicht, dem ist es Sünde." Ich muß hinzufügen: Dieses "Wissen" bedarf keiner theologischen Grundlagenforschung!

V.

Als dritten (und letzten) Impuls möchte ich die perönliche Erfahrung nennen. Sie beginnt mit meiner Taufe als 18-Jähriger. Mein Leben lang habe ich mich an die Taufpredigt erinnert: "Du wirst hineingetauft nicht nur in diese Ortsgemeinde, sondern in den universalen Leib Christi ..." Als Student suchte ich in kirchengeschichtlichen Seminaren nach Ökumenikern unter den Baptisten. Meine erste hauptamtliche Tätigkeit nach den Studienjahren war die des ersten freikirchlichen Assistenten in der Ökumenischen Centrale in Frankfurt (unter Martin Niemöller und Hanfried Krüger). Als Dolmetscher nahm ich an der Weltkonferenz für Glauben und Kirchenverfassung in Montreal teil (1963), wurde "consultant" und dann in Uppsala Mitglied (1968 bis 1991) der Kommission für Glauben und Kirchenverfassung. Ich habe den Baptistischen Weltbund im bilateralen Gespräch mit dem Reformierten Weltbund vertreten, die Kommission für Glauben und Kirchenverfassung im Dialog zwischen Katholiken und Reformierten und bin seit etwa 15 Jahren in der Kommission des Baptistischen Weltbundes, die sich mit Fragen der Lehre und ökumenischer Zusammenarbeit befaßt. Etwas vom Schönsten ist die jahrelange Mitarbeit im ökumenischen Arbeitskreis des Dorfes Rüschlikon, wo wir regelmäßig ökumenische Gottesdienste feiern und Bibelseminare durchführen. Die drei Ortsgemeinden der Reformierten, Katholiken und Baptisten schlagen abwechselnd "Dritte-Welt-

---

[7] Tages-Anzeiger (Zürich), 17. Oktober 1991, S. 3.

Projekte" vor, die wir gemeinsam (und mit Unterstützung der politischen Gemeinde) durchführen. Jedes Projekt hält uns gewöhnlich drei bis vier Jahre auf Trab.

Obwohl ich auch heute noch mit Freuden Baptist und mehr denn je von der guten Praxis der Taufe auf das Bekenntnis des Glaubens hin überzeugt bin (wenn ich auch in der Frage der "Anerkennung" der Taufe anderer Kirchen eine andere Meinung vertrete als die meisten meiner baptistischen Kollegen), so muß ich doch gestehen, daß mich die ökumenischen Begegnungen mit anderen Christen unglaublich bereichert haben und ich in diesen Begegnungen die "Gemeinschaft des Heiligen Geistes" spürbarer, ja geradezu "greifbarer" erfahren habe als in den bewegenden geistlichen Erfahrungen in meiner eigenen Kirche. Nie werde ich die Stunde vergessen, in der wir in Bangalore den x-ten und letzten Entwurf unserer "Rechenschaft von der Hoffnung, die in uns ist" angenommen und bekräftigt haben. Das war für mich ein "enthusiastischer" Augenblick (im Kontrast dazu hatte ich in Lima das Gefühl, mit hängender Zunge und total ausgepumpter Lunge über die Ziellinie zu stolpern - und das sage ich als einer, der mehr als ein Dutzend Jahre an den Lima-Texten mitgearbeitet hatte). Gott sei Dank, kann man auch heute noch Ökumeniker sein, wenn Gott einem solche oder ähnliche Erlebnisse wie in Bangalore schenkt - und man obendrein noch lesen kann, daß betrübliche Erfahrungen in der eigenen Kirchenfamilie gar nicht so ungewöhnlich sind.[8] Die Einheit der Kirche ist am Ende doch die Gemeinschaft derer, die einem *gekreuzigten* Herrn nachfolgen, und das ist nun wahrhaftig eine außergewöhnliche Gesellschaft mit einer außergewöhnlichen Gemeinschaft.

---

[8] Marianne Müssle (Hrsg.), Unsere Erfahrungen mit der Kirche. Freiburg, Herder ²1991.

BIBLIOGRAPHY

Günter Wagner

1957 - Reviews of: Walter Marshall Horton, Christian Theology. An Ecumenical Approach. London, Lutterworth Press 1956, in: *Ökumenische Rundschau* 6 (1957), 187.
Jean-Louis Leuba, Institution und Ereignis. Gemeinsamkeiten und Unterschiede der beiden Arten von Gottes Wirken nach dem Neuen Testament. Göttingen, Vandenhoeck & Ruprecht 1957, in: *Ökumenische Rundschau* 6 (1957), 187-188.

1958 - Co-translator of: Ruth Rouse und Stephen Charles Neill, Geschichte der Ökumenischen Bewegung 1517-1948. Zwei Bände. Göttingen, Vandenhoeck & Ruprecht 1958, XIX + 556 pages and XI + 525 pages.

1961- Reviews of: Hermann Mentz, Taufe und Kirche in ihrem ursprünglichen Zusammenhang. München, Chr. Kaiser Verlag 1960, in: *Ökumenische Rundschau* 10 (1961), 113-114.
Markus Barth, Solidarität mit den Sündern: Wesen und Auftrag der Gemeinde nach dem Epheserbrief. Kassel, J.G. Oncken Verlag 1961, in: *European Baptist Press Service* 1961, No. 74 (December 7, 1961), 30.

1962- Das religionsgeschichtliche Problem von Römer 6, 1-11 (Abhandlungen zur Theologie des Alten und Neuen Testaments, hrsg. von W. Eichrodt und O. Cullmann, 39). Zürich/ Stuttgart, Zwingli Verlag 1962. 351 pages.

"Das Werk des Heiligen Geistes", *Der Gemeindebote* 39, Nr. 11/12 (1.Juni 1962), 1-3.

Reviews of: G. R. Beasley-Murray, Baptism in the New Testament. London/New York, Macmillan & Co. 1962, in: *Die Gemeinde* 1962, Nr. 44 (4. November 1962), 18.
E. Klaar, Die Taufe nach paulinischem Verständnis (ThEx NF 93). München, Chr. Kaiser Verlag 1961, in: *Evangelische Theologie* 22 (1962), 669-671.
R.E.O. White, Dass Christus in euch Gestalt gewinne. Eine biblische Studie. Kassel, J.G. Oncken Verlag 1962, in: *Der Gemeindebote* 39, Nr. 21 (1. November 1962), 8.

1962/63- "Aus einer Verlegenheit befreit", *Semesterzeitschrift* (Kassel) WS 1962/63, 13-14.

"Die neue Kontroverse über die Kindertaufe", *Semesterzeitschrift* (Kassel) WS 1962/63, 11-12.

Review of: G.R. Beasley-Murray, Baptism in the New Testament. London/New York, Macmillan & Co. 1962, in: *Semesterzeitschrift* (Kassel) WS 1962/63, 30.

1964- "Die Entstehung der Bibel in heutiger Sicht", *Wort + Tat* 18 (1964), 189-197.

"Sterben und Danach", *Der Gemeindebote* 42, Nr.1 (1. Januar 1964), 4-6; Nr.2 (15. Januar 1964), 4-6; Nr.3 (1. Februar 1964), 5-7; Nr.4 (15. Februar 1964), 3-5; Nr. 5 (1. März 1964), 2-5; Nr. 6 (15. März 1964), 3-6; Nr. 7 (1. April 1964), 4-7; Nr.8 (15. April 1964), 2-5; Nr.9 (1. Mai 1964), 2-4.

1965-"Growing Strong in Faith" (Romans 4:16-25), *European Baptist Press Service* 65:55 (February 20, 1965), 29-30.

"New Life in Christ (I Peter 1:3-5)", *European Baptist Press Service* 65:322 (November 17, 1965), 28-30

Review of: Ehrhard Kamlah, Die Form der katalogischen Paränese im Neuen Testament (Wissenschaftliche Untersuchungen zum Neuen Testament, 7). Tübingen, J.C.B. Mohr 1964, in: *Wort + Tat* 19 (1965), 339-341.

1966- Att Dö Och Sedan...? (Krista Nutidsfragor I). Oversättning och redigering David Hellholm & Rolf Kristoffersson. Stockholm, Westerbergs 1966. 85 pages. (see under 1964).

"New Life in Christ", *The Australian Baptist,* January 12, 1966;
"New Life in Christ (I Peter 1:3)", *The Baptist World* 12, No.1 (January 1966), 2;
"Nowe Zycie W Chrystusie (I Piotr 1:3-5)", *Slowo Prawdy* Luty 1966 (Nr. 2), 1-3;
"New Life in Christ", *The Guardian* (India) March 10, 1966, 6-7; also in *Croire Et Servir* (France), May 1966, 3 (see under 1965).
"Easter Did Happen", *The Sunday School Times* 108, No. 13 (March 26, 1966), 221-222.
"Unanswered Prayer", *European Baptist Press Service* 66:68 (March 18, 1966), 28-30.

1966ff- Co-editor of: Die Kirchen der Welt. Stuttgart, Evangelisches Verlagswerk, Band III - Band XX, 1966-1988.

1967- "Die Bibel - ihre Entstehung in heutiger Sicht", in: Verlässliche Kunde. Beiträge zum Bibelgespräch der Gemeinde heute. Berlin, Evangelische Versandbuchhandlung O. Ekelmann Nachf. 1967, 30-47 (see under 1964).

"The Cleansing of the Temple" (Inaugural Lecture as Professor of New Testament delivered November 15, 1966), *Survey Bulletin 1966-1967*. Rüschlikon, Baptist Theological Seminary 1967, 18-29.

Pauline Baptism and the Pagan Mysteries. The Problem of the Pauline Doctrine of Baptism in Romans VI. 1-11, in the Light of its Religio-Historical "Parallels". Translated by J.P. Smith. Edinburgh and London, Oliver & Boyd 1967, 330 pages (revised dissertation, see under 1962).

"Unanswered Prayer", *World Outlook* No. 251 (October 1967), 4-6 (see under 1966).

"Youth in Germany", *Royal Service*, October 1967, 9-11.

1968- "Bibelarbeit über Eph. 4, 1-16: Die Einheit als Gabe und Aufgabe", *Der Gemeindebote* 46, Nr. 22-23 (1. Dezember 1968), 2-4.

"Niewzruszony Jak Opoka", *Slowo Prawdy* 1968, No. 2, 3-5.

"Unsere ökumenische Zusammenarbeit", *Der Gemeindebote* 46, Nr. 22-23 (1. Dezember 1968), 4-13.

Translator of: George R. Beasley-Murray, Die christliche Taufe. Eine Untersuchung über ihr Verständnis in Geschichte und Gegenwart. Kassel, J.G. Oncken Verlag 1968. 546 pages.

1969- "Guiding Principles for a New Testament Theology of Baptism", *Anvil: A Baptist Quarterly* (Melbourne) 1 (1969), 10-11.

"Die Taktlosigkeit Jesu", *Der Gemeindebote* 47 (1. April 1969), 1-2.

"Unsere ökumenische Zusammenarbeit", *Die Gemeinde* 1969, Nr.4 (19. Januar), 2-6.11 (see under 1968).

"Zur Methode des Herrn Pfarrer Albert Lüscher", *Der Gemeindebote* 47, Nr.3 (1. Februar 1969), 3-5.

1970- Leitsätze zur Tauftheologie im Neuen Testament", *Una Sancta* 25 (1970), 367-370 (see under 1969).

"Die Problematik der gegenwärtigen Taufpraxis der verschiedenen Kirchen und Gemeinschaften", *Ökumenische Rundschau* 19 (1970), 366-394.

"Zwischenkirchliche Zusammenarbeit - das Gebot der Stunde für uns", *Der Gemeindebote* 48, Nr. 13-15 (1. Juli, 15. Juli, 1. August 1970), 2-9.

Reviews of: Josef Blank, Schriftauslegung in Theorie und Praxis (Biblische Handbibliothek, Band V). München, Kösel Verlag 1969, in: *Wort + Tat* 24 (1970), 322.

Helmut Bintz, Das Skandalon als Grundlagenproblem der Dogmatik. Eine Auseinandersetzung mit Karl Barth. Berlin, de Gruyter 1969, in: *Wort + Tat* 24 (1970), 252.

Hans Conzelmann, Geschichte des Urchristentums (Grundrisse zum Neuen Testament. Das Neue Testament Deutsch, Ergänzungsreihe, Band 5). Göttingen, Vandenhoeck & Ruprecht 1969, in: *Wort + Tat 24* (1970), 252.

Günter Klein, Rekonstruktion und Interpretation. Gesammelte Aufsätze zum Neuen Testament (Beiträge zur evangelischen Theologie, Band 50). München, Chr. Kaiser Verlag 1969, in: *Wort + Tat* 24 (1970), 251.

Martin Künzi, Das Naherwartungslogion Matthäus 10,23. Geschichte seiner Auslegung. (Beiträge zur Geschichte der Biblischen Exegese, 9). Tübingen, J.C.B. Mohr 1970, in: *Wort + Tat* 24 (1970), 322

Edmund Schlink, Die Lehre von der Taufe. Kassel, Stauda Verlag 1969, in: *Ökumenische Rundschau* 19 (1970), 338-340.

Eduard Schweizer, Neues Testament und heutige Verkündigung. Neukirchen-Vluyn, Neukirchener Verlag 1969, in: *Wort + Tat* 24 (1970), 252.

1971- "Christian Unity in the New Testament", in: *Reconciliation Through Christ* (Official Report of the Twelfth Congress. Baptist World Alliance, Tokyo, Japan, July 12-18, 1970). Valley Forge, Pennsylvania, U.S.A., Judson Press 1971, 326-339.

"Current baptismal practice in various churches", *Theology Digest* 19 (1971), 235-241.

"Die Entdeckung der einen Kirche: Biblische Grundlagen", in: *Ökumene in Schule und Gemeinde. Ein Arbeitsbuch*, hrsg. von Friedrich Hasselhoff und Hanfried Krüger. Stuttgart. Evangelischer Missionsverlag 1971, 155-163.

"Die Entdeckung des einen Zeugnisses: Biblische Grundlagen", in: *ibid.* 212-220.

"Die Entdeckung des einen Dienstes: Biblische Grundlagen", in: *ibid.* 311-319.

"Die neutestamentliche Taufe", *Wort + Tat* 25 (1971), 147-160.

"Problematiken i nuvarande doppraxis i olika kyrkor", *tro och liv* 1971 Nr.2, 61-68.

Reviews of: Horst R. Balz, Christus in Korinth. Eine Einführung in den ersten Korintherbrief. (Kleine Kasseler Bibelhilfe). Kassel, J.G. Oncken Verlag 1970, in: *Wort + Tat* 25 (1971), 178.
Friedrich Cornelius, Die Glaubwürdigkeit der Evangelien. Philologische Untersuchungen. München/Basel, Ernst Reinhardt Verlag 1969, in: *Wort + Tat* 25 (1971), 144.
Niklaus Gäumann, Taufe und Ethik. Studien zu Römer 6 (Beiträge zur evangelischen Theologie, Band 47). München, Chr. Kaiser Verlag 1967, in: *Wort + Tat* 25 (1971), 286.
Herman Möllers, Kirche und Religion im Widerspruch. Dimensionen des Gottesdienstes von morgen. Berlin, Luther-Verlag 1970, in: *Wort + Tat* 25 (1971) 143-144.

1971ff-Co-editor of: *Una Sancta. Zeitschrift für ökumenische Begegnung* 26 (1971) -

1972- et al., "'Einheit der Kirche - Einheit der Menschheit'. Bericht über die Ergebnisse der Konferenz des ÖRK für Glauben und Kirchenverfassung in Löwen/Belgien, 2.-12. August 1971", *Ökumenische Rundschau* 21 (1972), 4-22.

"Gestalten des Gottesdienstes in neutestamentlicher Zeit", *Wort + Tat* 26 (1972), 291-297.

"Neutestamentliche Perspektiven zum Thema 'Gottesdienst'", *Wort + Tat* 26 (1972), 255-260.

"One Church: The Witness of the New Testament", in: *Christian Unity in India* (Report of the National Faith and Order Study Conference, Nasrapur, 9-16 August 1972. Published for the Continuation Committee by The Christian Literature Society). Madras, At the Diocesan Press 1972, 34-45.

1973- Editor: An Exegetical Bibliography on The Gospel of Mark (*Bibliographical Aids, First Series*, No.2) Rüschlikon, Baptist Theological Seminary 1973. 185 cards.

Editor: An Exegetical Bibliography on The Letter to the Romans (*Bibliographical Aids, First Series*, No. 3). Rüschlikon, Baptist Theological Seminary 1973. 177 cards.

"Wie 'eins' ist die 'eine Taufe'?", *Ökumenische Rundschau* 22 (1973), 395-400.

Review of: Eduard Schweizer, Beiträge zur Theologie des Neuen Testaments. Neutestamentliche Aufsätze (1955-1970). Zürich, Zwingli Verlag 1970, in: *Wort + Tat* 27 (1973), 72.

1974- "Katholische Stellungnahmen zu Karl Barths Tauflehre", *Ökumenische Rundschau* 23 (1974), 555-556.

"Sterben und Danach", *Wort + Tat* 28 (1974), 111-121. 147-160. 166 (see under 1964).

Co-Author: Draft Discussion Paper on the Ecumenical Roles of the World Confessional Families and The World Council of Churches. Geneva, Conference of General Secretaries of World Confessional Families 1974.

Co-author: "Konziliarität und Konzil. Bericht einer Studiengruppe des Deutschen Ökumenischen Studienausschusses 1970-1973", in: Richard Boeckler (Hrsg.), Interkommunion - Konziliarität (*Beiheft zur Ökumenischen Rundschau, Nr. 25*). Korntal bei Stuttgart, Evangelischer Missionsverlag GMBH 1974, 128-165.

English Translation: "Councils, Conciliarity and a Genuinely Universal Council", *Study Encounter* X/2 (1974) (=SE/57).

Editor: An Exegetical Bibliography on The Gospel of Matthew (*Bibliographical Aids, First Series*, No. 4a: Mt 1-12, 233 cards; No. 4b: Mt 13-28, 249 cards). Rüschlikon, Baptist Theological Seminary 1974.

Editor: An Exegetical Bibliography on The Gospel of Luke (*Bibliographical Aids, First Series*, No.5). Rüschlikon, Baptist Theological Seminary 1974. 319 cards.

1975- Editor: An Exegetical Bibliography on The First Letter to the Corinthians (*Bibliographical Aids, First Series*, No. 6). Rüschlikon, Baptist Theological Seminary 1975. 193 cards.

Editor: An Exegetical Bibliography on The Acts of the Apostles (*Bibliographical Aids, First Series*, No. 7). Rüschlikon, Baptist Theological Seminary 1975. 233 cards.

Editor: An Exegetical Bibliography on The Gospel of John (*Bibliographical Aids, First Series* No. 8). Rüschlikon, Baptist Theological Seminary 1975. 289 cards.

1976- "La Chiesa locale e le altre Chiese nel N.T.", *Il Testimonio* (Roma) 93, N.1 (Gennaio-Febbraio 1976), 20-27; 93, N.2 (Marzo-Aprile 1976), 72-77,; 93, N.4-5 (Luglio-Ottobre 1976), 202-210.

"Rechenschaft vom hoffenden Glauben (1. Petrus 3,15b)", *Der Gemeindebote* 54 (Juli-August 1976), 1-5.

Editor: An Exegetical Bibliography on The Second Letter to the Corinthians (*Bibliographical Aids, First Series*, No.9). Rüschlikon, Baptist Theololgical Seminary 1976. 136 cards.

1977- Co-author: Rechenschaft vom Glauben, Bund der Baptistengemeinden in der Schweiz 1977. 16 pages.

Co-author: Report of Theological Conversations, sponsored by the World Alliance of Reformed Churches and the Baptist World Alliance 1973-77. Geneva, W.A.R.C.; Washington, B.W.A. 1977. 21 pages.

Editor: An Exegetical Bibliography on The Letter to the Galatians and Philippians (*Bibliographical Aids, First Series,* No. 10). Rüschlikon, Baptist Theological Seminary 1977. 157 cards.

Editor: An Exegetical Bibliography on The Letters to the Ephesians, Colossians and Philemon (*Bibliographical Aids, First Series,* No.11). Rüschlikon, Baptist Theological Seminry 1977. 142 cards.

1979- Editor: An Exegetical Bibliography on The Letters to the Thessalonians and The Pastoral Epistles *(Bibliographical Aids, First Series,* No.12). Rüschlikon, Baptist Theological Seminary 1979. 130 cards.

Editor: An Exegetical Bibliography on The Catholic Epistles (*Bibliographical Aids, First Series,* No.13). Rüschlikon, Baptist Theological Seminary 1979. 243 cards.

Editor: An Exegetical Bibliography on The Letter to the Hebrews and the Revelation of John (*Bibliographical Aids, First Series,* No.14). Rüschlikon, Baptist Theological Seminary 1979). 213 cards.

1980- G.W. und Ilse Wieser, "Das Bild der Frau in der biblischen Tradition", *Theologisches Gespräch* 1980, Nr.3-6, 18-33. Also in: *Una Sancta* 35 (1980) 296-316.

"Taufe und offene Mitgliedschaft", *Blickpunkt Gemeinde* 1980, Nr.6, 2-6.

"Maria hat das Bessere gewählt", *Una Sancta* 35 (1980) 267-268.

1981- Editor: An Exegetical Bibliography on The Gospel of Matthew (*Bibliographical Aids, Second Series,* No.1). Rüschlikon, Baptist Theological Seminary 1981. 240 cards.

Editor: An Exegetical Bibliography on The Gospel of Mark (*Bibliographical Aids, Second Series,* No.2). Rüschlikon, Baptist Theological Seminay 1981. 277 cards.

"...leeres Gerede...", *Der Gemeindebote* 59/4 (April 1981) (= *Gemeinde unterwegs,* Arbeitsblatt B.2.2).

Co-author: "The Ecumenical Importance of the Nice-Constantinopolitan Creed. Odessa Report". Geneva, Faith and Order Secretariat 1981 (FO/81:17 November 1981). 16 pages.

1982- "Müssen wir noch erzogen werden? Gemeindezucht im Neuen Testament und Heute",
Teil I: *Der Gemeindebote* 59/8 (August 1982)= *Gemeinde unterwegs* B.4.1.
Teil II: "   59/9 (September 1982)=   "   B.4.2.
Teil III: "   59/10 (October 1982)=   "   B.4.3.
Teil IV: "   59/11 (November 1982)=   "   B.4.4.

1983- Co-editor: *New Testament Studies.* An International Journal published quarterly under the auspicies of STUDIORUM NOVI TESTAMENTI SOCIETAS. Cambridge and New York, Cambridge University Press. Vol. 29 (1983) - 32 (1986)

"Taufe", *Lexikon Kirchen und ökumenische Bewegung.* Frankfurt a.M., Verlag Otto Lembeck, 1983, 1140-1142

"Baptism from Accra to Lima", in: *Ecumenical Perspectives on Baptism, Eucharist, and Ministry,* ed. by Max Thurian. Geneva, World Council of Churches 1983, 12-32.

"Taufe", in: *Oekumenische Perspektiven zu Taufe, Eucharistie und Amt,* hrsg. von Max Thurian. Frankfurt a.M., Verlag Otto Lembeck 1983, 43-63.

Editor: An Exegetical Bibliography on The Gospel of Luke *(Bibliographical Aids, Second Series,* No.3). Rüschlikon, Baptist Theological Seminary 1983. 311 cards.

Editor: An Exegetical Bibliography on The Acts of the Apostles *(Bibliographical Aids, Second Series,* No. 4). Rüschlikon, Baptist Theological Seminary 1983, 228 cards.

"The Apostolic Faith According to the New Testament....", Geneva, World Council of Churches/Commisssion on Faith and Order, FO/83:4, September 1983, 29pp., mimeographed.

An Exegetical Bibliography of the New Testament, Volume 1: Matthew & Mark. Macon/Georgia, Mercer University Press 1983, 668pp.

1984- "The Apostolic Faith according to the New Testament. The Interpretation in the letters and later parts of the New Testament. The Pauline Homologoumena", in: Hans-Georg Link (ed.), The Roots of Our Common Faith. Faith in the Scriptures and in the Early Church (=*Faith and Order Paper* No.119). Geneva, World Council of Churches 1984, 55-71

(Contributor) Baptists and Reformed in Dialogue. Documents from the Conversations sponsored by the World Alliance of Reformed Churches and the Baptist World Alliance (Studies from the World Alliance of Reformed Churches, 4). Geneva, World Alliance of Reformed Churches 1984, 56pp.

"Paul and the Apostolic Faith", *Africa Journal of Theology* 13, 1984, 115-135.

1985- "Der apostolische Glaube nach dem Neuen Testament: seine Auslegung in den paulinischen Homologoumena", in: Wurzeln unseres Glaubens: Glaube in der Bibel und in der Alten Kirche, hrsg. von Hans-Georg Link. Frankfurt am Main, Verlag Otto Lembeck 1985, 66-84

An Exegetical Bibliography of the New Testament: Luke and Acts. Macon/Georgia, Mercer University Press 1985, 550pp.

1986- A Survey of Baptist Responses to "Baptism, Eucharist and Ministry" (*Faith and Order Paper* No.111. Geneva, WCC 1982). Rüschlikon, Baptist Theological Seminary - Institute for Baptist and Anabaptist Studies 1986. 57 pp.

1987- An Exegetical Bibliography of the New Testament: John and 1,2,3 John. Macon/Georgia, Mercer University Press 1987, 350pp.

1988- "The Future of Israel: Reflections on Romans 9-11", in: W. Hulitt Gloer (ed.), *Eschatology and the New Testament: Essays in Honor of George Raymond Beasley-Murray.* Peabody/Massachusetts, Hendrickson Publishers 1988, 77-112.

Contributor: "We Believe in One God. An Ecumenical Explication. Report of a Faith and Order Consultation held at Kinshasa, Zaire, 14-22 March 1986", in: One God, One Lord, One Spirit. On the Explication of the Apostolic Faith Today. Edited by Hans-Georg Link (*Faith and Order Paper* No. 139). Geneva, World Council of Churches 1988, 17-39.

1990- Contributor: BAPTISM, EUCHARIST & MINISTRY 1982-1990. Report on the Process and Responses (*Faith and Order Paper* No. 149). Geneva, WCC Publications 1990. 160pp.

Die Diskussion über Taufe, Eucharistie und Amt 1982-1990. Stellungnahmen, Auswirkungen, Weiterarbeit. Frankfurt am Main, Verlag Otto Lembeck; Paderborn, Bonifatius Verlag 1990. 158pp.

1991- "Warum ich trotzdem Oekumeniker bin. Statements der Herausgeber", *Una Sancta* 46 (1991) 331-336.

1992- "Was heisst 'Liberale Theologie'?", *Gemeindebote* 70/4 (April 1992) 5-9.

"Ist die Frage nach der Endzeit eine heute aktuelle Frage?", *Gemeindebote* 70/11 (November 1992) 4-6.

1993- Editor: An Exegetical Bibliography on The Letter to the Romans. (*Second Series, Bibliographical Aids* No. 11/6). Rüschlikon, Baptist Theological Seminary. xiii & 554 cards.